Micro Human Efforts in Disaster Rebuilding

This book unlocks the transformative potential of Micro Human Efforts (MHE) in the domain of disaster resilience through an interwoven narrative of human resilience, grounded in insights from the influential special issue of the *International Journal of Mass Emergencies and Disasters*.

This work delves into the critical, often-neglected, role of individual, intuitive initiatives in the wake of catastrophic events. By illuminating how these efforts can significantly reshape post-disaster recovery strategies, this book underscores the importance of local knowledge and community ingenuity. It posits that MHE has the capability to amplify grassroots movements into impactful agents of change. Readers will embark on a comprehensive exploration that redefines disaster management through a human-centred lens and highlights the essential contributions of individuals in fostering resilience.

The volume serves as an invaluable resource for academics, practitioners, and all stakeholders committed to advancing sustainable and adaptive responses in the face of climate-induced environmental challenges.

Chamila (Don) Subasinghe's interest in circumnavigating micro aspects of disasters focuses on building resilience within. A chartered architect by profession, his academic career began upon receiving a principal Fulbright scholarship to the USA in 2006 and his PhD in 2011, which he completed with Tau Sigma Delta honours awarded to academics with the highest scholastic standing in architecture and allied disciplines. An alumnus of Harvard Kennedy School's executive training in Public Leadership, Don currently leads the degree apprenticeship programme at Grenfell Bains Institute of Architecture at University of Lancashire, UK. This is his third book on micro-related concepts among many publications, awards, and grants, including the UNESCO-KNUH chair grant. He is also a senior fellow of Higher Education Academy UK and a fellow of the Higher Education Research and Development Society of Australasia.

Sanjoy Mazumdar's emic up-close and micro-ecological research is in cultures and their planned and designed environments, including attempts to apprehend the efforts by disaster victims to rebuild life in post-disaster temporary housing. These and research on culture, religion, ecology and sustainability have led to publications in 24 journals and many books. Academic training includes a B.Arch. (Hons), (IIT Kharagpur), M.Arch.A.S., M.C.P., PhD (MIT). He has been on the editorial boards of several journals and was awarded the Environmental Design Research Association's Career Award (2006), JSPS Invitation Fellowship, elected Fellow of the Design Research Society, Chair of EDRA (1999–2000), and Cultural Aspects of Design Network. He is a professor emeritus in the School of Social Ecology, Religious Studies, and Asian-American Studies at the University of California, Irvine.

Micro Human Efforts in Disaster Rebuilding

Cultural and Contextual Lessons for Resilience

Edited by
Chamila (Don) Subasinghe and
Sanjoy Mazumdar

Routledge
Taylor & Francis Group
LONDON AND NEW YORK

Designed cover image: Getty Images

First published 2026
by Routledge
4 Park Square, Milton Park, Abingdon, Oxon OX14 4RN

and by Routledge
605 Third Avenue, New York, NY 10158

Routledge is an imprint of the Taylor & Francis Group, an informa business

British Library Cataloguing-in-Publication Data
A catalogue record for this book is available from the British Library

ISBN: 978-1-032-20583-0 (hbk)
ISBN: 978-1-041-01672-4 (pbk)
ISBN: 978-1-003-61590-3 (ebk)

DOI: 10.4324/9781003615903

Typeset in Times New Roman
by Deanta Global Publishing Services, Chennai, India

To, silent supporters of "self"
and
the survivors of the 2004 Indian Ocean Tsunami,
exactly two decades ago, on this day of December 26th.

26 December 2024

Contents

Contributors

Winifred Asare-Doku leads a research program at the National Drug & Alcohol Research Centre, University of New South Wales, Australia, focused on understanding substance use, harms, and treatment for culturally and linguistically diverse (CALD) populations. Her research also explores the intersections of mental health, substance use, and suicide prevention, with a focus on vulnerable groups, including young people and individuals in the criminal justice system. Dr Asare-Doku holds a PhD in Psychiatry from the University of Newcastle, Australia, and an MPhil in Clinical Psychology from the University of Ghana, Ghana.

Barry Ballinger has over a decade of wide-ranging design experience on diverse building types including healthcare, hospitality, K-12, multifamily residential, and higher-ed. He has worked on all phases of project delivery in firms in California, Colorado, Oklahoma, Missouri, and Kansas. He earned a Bachelor of Architecture degree from Oklahoma State and a PhD from the University of Kansas, USA. His research focuses on the confluence of architecture, power structures, social movement, and contentious politics. As a PhD student, he earned a Fulbright Research Grant to do fieldwork in Ankara, Turkey's informal settlements. He has presented his research on informal settlements, politics of space, and knowledge management at international conferences in the USA, Turkey, Austria, and Portugal. Barry has six years of experience teaching architecture studio, freshman seminar, social movements and the city, and leading a study abroad.

Akihiko Hokugo is an emeritus professor in the Graduate School of Engineering, Research Center for Urban Safety and Security at Kobe University, Japan. He has conducted several studies and researched disaster recovery in some countries, including China, India, Iran, Turkey, Myanmar, and Japan, upon which many papers, research reports, and book chapters on various aspects of recovery comprising resilient recovery, community-based recovery, housing, tsunami evacuation, and land-use planning has been published by him.

Teruyuki Isagawa is an associate professor of the Department of Urban Life Studies at Tokyo City University, Japan, where he teaches Urban Disaster Mitigation and Environment Behaviour Studies. He graduated from the College of Policy and Planning Sciences, University of Tsukuba, Japan, and earned master's and doctoral degrees from the Department of Built Environment at Tokyo Institute of Technology. His research specialization covers urban and regional planning, architectural planning, and disaster management. It examines the interrelationships between humans and surrounding environments, especially evacuation behaviour and risk perception towards natural disasters. He is generally interested in human locomotion in daily life, such as way-finding or navigation. In 2016, he received the Encouragement Prize from Architectural Institute of Japan (AIJ).

Yamuna Kaluarachchi is a professor of Architecture and Urban Resilience at the Manchester School of Architecture, UK. She completed her BSc in Built Environment (First Class Honours) and MSc in Architecture at the University of Moratuwa, Sri Lanka; and the Bartlett School of Architecture, UCL; and PhD in Architecture at the University of Cambridge. Yamuna's research expertise includes Smart and Green Cities, Resilience of Cities and Communities, Biomimicry and Nature Solutions for Architecture and User Behaviour and Engagement in Sustainability. She has won EPSRC and GCRF research grants as Principal Investigator and worked as co-investigator in several UK, EU, and international projects. Her recent project, "Gender and disability inclusion in Build Back Better Programmes", was chosen as the LSBU, UKRI impact study. Her collaborative international research covering Global South (Brazil, Sri Lanka, Bangladesh, Mozambique) focuses on Societal Resilience, Inclusivity, Equality, and Sustainable Development Goals and has real-world implications and impact.

Kevin Kupietz is the chair of the Department of Aviation and Emergency Management and Associate Professor of Emergency Management at Elizabeth City State University in North Carolina, USA. He is a certified Firefighter/Paramedic with over 30 years of emergency response experience with local, state, and federal agencies. He comes with diverse emergency response, research, and educational expertise. His field of research interest is in how to build resilient communities, often looking at the individuals in the community who make a difference and technology that can supplement the workforce to do more while providing higher levels of safety.

Kalindu Mendis holds a PhD in Disaster Management and a Bachelor of Science Honours in Facilities Management from the Department of Building Economics at the University of Moratuwa, Sri Lanka. She has won the gold medal for the most outstanding doctoral researcher at the University of Moratuwa. She has been involved in several funded projects from the Global Challenge Research Fund, Senate Research Committee, and Northumbria University, United Kingdom. She has published several conference papers and journal papers. She won the Best Presenter Award at the International Postgraduate Research Conference (IPGRC) 2022, UK, for her PhD study. Her research interests include disaster management, waste management, policy studies, marginalised communities, and sustainable water management.

Mitoko Nakashima in the Faculty of Engineering and Design at Kagawa University, Japan, specialized in research on the living environment for social minorities such as the elderly and people with intellectual disabilities. Recently, she researched the living environment of disaster sufferers in disaster-affected areas, such as Ofunato City, Iwate Prefecture, one of the areas affected by the 2011 Great East Japan Earthquake and Tsunami, and Mabi-cho, Kurashiki City, Okayama Prefecture, one of the areas affected by the 2018 Western Japan flood. Her main field of study is architectural planning, and she is also closely linked with disaster studies and welfare studies.

Nilgün Okay is a professor of Disaster Risk Reduction and Resilience Studies at the Istanbul Technical University, Türkiye. She played a key role in the establishment and development of the World Bank Institute Turkey Natural Disaster Risk Reduction Distance Education Programme. As a founding member of the ITU Disaster Management Center, she teaches graduate-level courses in disaster risk reduction at the ITU Disaster Management Institute. She serves as the editor of *Resilience Journal* and plays a pivotal role in organizing the International Disaster Resilience Conferences on an annual basis. Nilgün Okay, who is engaged in district-level risk management planning and community disaster resilience project studies with local governments, is currently pursuing research on the social dimension of disasters and the status of women in disasters.

Richard Oloruntoba is currently the Discipline Lead Supply Chain Management and an associate professor of Supply Chain Management at Curtin University, Perth, Australia. Richard's university teaching and research career of 21 years has been recognized with several awards, such as the Faculty of Business and Law University of Newcastle Individual Teaching Excellence Award (2017) and the University of Newcastle Vice Chancellor's Teaching Excellence Award (2013). Richard has undertaken research and published over 60 refereed articles in leading international journals and flagship conference proceedings on supply chain management, logistics, operations management, disaster management, and public health.

Ebru Inal Önal is an associate professor in Emergency Aid and Disaster Management at Canakkale Onsekiz Mart University, Türkiye. Her research areas include disaster management and public health. She has many studies, including scale studies in general disaster preparedness, examination of formal education in terms of disaster education adequacy, determination of willingness to work in disasters, and the impact of disasters on the resilience process, including various groups. She especially carries out studies on the reflection and effects of gender dynamics in disasters.

Zhila Pooyan is an independent scholar of disaster recovery, specifically community disaster recovery and resilient recovery. She studied the role of community-based organizations in the recovery of Kobe City after the Southern Hyogo Earthquake (1995). Her other investigations include the recovery experiences of various earthquakes in Iran, including those of Manjil (1990) and Bam (2003), as well as the recovery experiences of the Great East Japan Earthquake and Tsunami (2011). She has published papers, research reports, and book chapters on related topics.

Kapila D. Silva is a professor of Architecture and Associate Dean in the School of Architecture and Design at the University of Kansas, USA. He has previously taught at the University of Wisconsin–Milwaukee, USA, from where he received his doctorate, and at the University of Moratuwa in Sri Lanka, from where he received professional architectural education. He is the lead editor of four volumes on cultural heritage management in the Asia-Pacific region (all published by Routledge), lead editor of *Theorizing Built Form and Culture: The Legacy of Amos Rapoport* (Routledge, 2024), and co-author of *The Ṭāmpiṭavihāras of Sri Lanka: Elevated Image-houses in Buddhist Architecture* (Anthem Press, 2021).

Andrew J. Strathern and **Pamela J. Stewart** (Strathern) are a husband-and-wife research team at the Department to Anthropology at the University of Pittsburgh, USA, as Andrew W. Mellon Professor and Senior Research Associate, respectively. They are the co-authors and co-editors of over 50 books, and hundreds of articles, essays, and book chapters. Their most recent co-authored books include: *The Palgrave Handbook of Anthropological Ritual Studies*; *Heritage: Ritual, Tradition, and Contestation*; *Scotland, Ireland and Wales: Identity and History*; *Sustainability, Conservation and Creativity: Ethnographic Learning from Small Scale Practices*; and *Language and Culture in Dialogue*. They are co-editors of *Dealing with Disasters: Perspectives from Eco-Cosmologies* (with Diana Riboli and Davide Torri).

Shiori Suzawa is a junior associate professor of the Department of Architecture at Tokai University, Japan, where she teaches architectural planning and design. She graduated from the Department of Civil Engineering and Architecture at Niigata University and completed a master's degree in Environmental Science and Technology at Niigata University, Japan. She received a doctorate from the Department of Architecture at the University of Tokyo, Japan. She specializes in architectural and city planning, and housing policy. Her research focuses on residential relocation, as well as housing and living supports and services during both disaster and regular times. She is currently conducting action research on the 2024 Noto Peninsula Earthquake, drawing from her experience with the Great East Japan Earthquake and Tsunami. In 2023, she received the Doctoral Dissertation Prize from JUSOKEN, a housing research foundation in Japan.

Menaha Thayaparan is a senior lecturer at the Department of Building Economics, Faculty of Architecture, University of Moratuwa, Sri Lanka. She is a fellow of the Higher Education Academy (FHEA, UK). She is the Director of Faculty of Architecture Research Unit (FARU) and also the Director of multidisciplinary research Centre for Disaster Risk Reduction (CDRR) at the University of Moratuwa. She is a principal/co-investigator on many local and international collaborative research projects. She has over 15 years of teaching and research experience and over 50 publications in book chapters, peer-reviewed journals, conference papers, and research reports. She is also a scientific committee member and coordinator of several conferences. Among her research interests are disaster resilience, marginalised communities, higher education, the built environment, the circular economy, and women in construction.

Ryosuke Tomiyasu is a first-class registered architect in Japan and an associate professor of the Department of Human Environment Design at Toyo University, Japan, where he teaches architectural planning and design. He is also a member of the Center for Sustainable Development Studies. He graduated from the Department of Architecture at the University of Tokyo, Japan, and received master's and doctoral degrees from the Department of Architecture. His research interest is the living environment for elderly and disabled people, focusing on post-disaster housing, particularly social systems and the physical environment. He has also designed temporary housing after the Great East Japan Earthquake and Tsunami. He received the University of Tokyo President's Award in 2011 and the Encouragement Prize from AIJ in 2016.

Ken Tsubouchi is an assistant professor at the Faculty of Engineering at Hokkaido University, Japan. He specializes in architectural planning research and environmental behaviour studies. He graduated from the Faculty of Socio-Environmental Engineering at Hokkaido University, Japan. He received his master's and doctoral degree from the Division of Architectural and Structural Design at Hokkaido University, Japan. His research focuses on human-centred planning methods for community relocation after disaster, combining interviews as social surveys and behaviour observations that reveal the actuality of the physical environment. In 2024, he received the Encouragement Prize from the Architectural Institute of Japan (AIJ).

Preface - Part 1

Chamila (Don) Subasinghe

I sat right in the middle of the road. The bus I was on couldn't continue, as it was too risky to drive next to the Indian Ocean while the 2004 Tsunami was raging.

I sat on the road in frustration; no one wanted to drive me to my fiancée. The hospital where she worked was just a few yards away from the Indian Ocean. The last message I received through a disembodied voice call mentioned seeing her car parked outside her workplace, lifted by ocean waves as tall as a coconut tree—a local expression for "a way higher than a wave could reach".

I sat on the road, waiting to be heard because there was no phone or network connection. My only option was to walk hundreds of miles or wait indefinitely to witness the unfolding of an unprecedented human catastrophe. I chose to stay seated and observe what other aimless people like me were doing when options were not really options.

Right there on that road, exactly two decades ago, I began my "micro-human" journey. Amid the chaotic human traffic, I witnessed people helping each other by first helping themselves. With no prior exposure akin to an in-flight safety demonstration, individuals took on the role of first responders, rescuing themselves and clearing the chaos consequently. When the first responders eventually arrived, all they had to deal with was organized chaos. While individuals' intuition made it quite challenging for the first responders, it made it easier for individuals to network a self-rescue system.

I witnessed individuals being reprimanded for their reckless crisis behaviours. Instead of fleeing from the sites of the disaster, out of curiosity, they ran towards it. As the second tsunami wave claimed more lives than the first, this behaviour later emerged as a significant statistic contributing to higher mortalities. Misguided curiosity, colloquially known as individual "idiocy", caused more harm than the tsunami itself. "Curiosity killed the cat" theories made rounds as they hinted at how people are drawn to disasters sadistically.

It needed more introspective views of life than the research to see traces of subtle micro matters humans spontaneously tackle under disaster stress. So, I saw an alternative explanation to the cat theory: People seek experiential exposure to disaster grounds and related instantaneous reactions that make or break their survival. They created stories to best describe rescue and survival without waiting for formal information to be formulated. People's sensorial self-reporting via kinesthetic experience of life under extenuating circumstances is what I now see as a probable impetus for resilience. This idea became obsessively authentic when I saw people's laid-back attitude, even when given full credit for their small yet transformative efforts in overcoming disasters. They called it "life as it comes".

Chamila (Don) Subasinghe
26/12/2024
Preston, Lancashire, UK

Preface - Part 2

Sanjoy Mazumdar

The Great East Japan Earthquake and Tsunami (GEJET) was a rather unusual event that occurred on 11th of March 2011. The prefectures the most affected by it were Miyagi, Iwate, and Fukushima.

The Japan Society for the Promotion of Science (JSPS) awarded me their Invitational Fellowship in 2015 to conduct research in Japan (I was unable to travel in 2013 when they offered it the first time). During that trip Professor Shunsuke Itoh very kindly became my guide and interpreter and provided crucial help in conducting research and observations to study GEJET's effects in Ichinoseki, Iwaizumi, Kamaishi (location of Tono Temporary Housing), Ofunato, Rikuzen-takata, Iwaizumi, Kitakami (in Iwate Prefecture), Minami-sanriku and Sendai (in Miyagi Prefecture).

The magnitude 9.0 GEJE was so powerful that it caused a huge tsunami, which inundated and destroyed many areas. Reports indicate that the tsunami height reached up to 39.7m (130 feet 2.64 inches) (NCEI NOAA 2025, Spencer 2025, Mazumdar, Itoh, & Iwasa 2021). Both the earthquake and the tsunami caused fires in many places. The relative power, suddenness and swiftness of the disasters contributed to chaos and lack of ability to carry out disaster plans (Isagawa & Ohno 2018). Sometimes these effects are so powerful and swift that the places quickly become unrecognizable making it hard to believe that a settlement existed there just a little earlier.

During my visit in 2015, four years after GEJET, much of its impacts were still perceivable. Several of the places we visited seemed underpopulated with few people visible. This was in part because of loss of lives to these twin disasters. In Miyagi prefecture there were 10,483 deaths; in Iwate 5,642, and in Fukushima 1,757[1], totaling 17,882 in the three prefectures (Source: Ministry of Health, Labour and Welfare "Status of Death in the Great East Japan Earthquake in view of the Vital Statistics", n.d.). Across Japan 18,703 people died (https://www.pref.miyagi.jp/documents/3687/2digest.pdf). Some of these counts were later revised upward, for example Fukushima Prefecture's count was increased to 2,335 deaths (Asahi Shimbun, 2023). Moreover, many people moved to relatives' houses in unaffected prefectures, which also led to depopulation in the disaster affected prefectures.

In the disaster affected areas the bustle of activities was much reduced and the sound level was low as some of the industrial and commercial activities were not being conducted. Shinkansen (Bullet) and some other trains were not operating due to damage to tracks and stations. Many highways, bridges, and roads were moderately to severely damaged. On operable roads and highways there were few vehicles.

Visiting research sites in disaster affected areas was complicated. Because many hotels were destroyed, finding one with available rooms, especially without prior reservation, was difficult. For an overnight stay, all we could find was a construction workers' "hotel", a hastily constituted contraption of ill-ventilated temporary metal structures, wherein breathing was made arduous by the cigarette smoke that replaced breathable air, with no human employees, only automated checkin, checkout, and vending machines selling packaged food, snacks, cigarettes, etc.

In Japan in total 126,574 buildings were completely and 272,302 were partially destroyed and perhaps unlivable (https://www.pref.miyagi.jp/documents/3687/2digest.pdf). In Iwate 19,508, Miyagi 83,005, and in Fukushima 15435 buildings were destroyed for a total of 117,948. In these three prefectures nearly 244,484 buildings were partially damaged and in total, 362,432 buildings were damaged or destroyed. Most houses were constructed of wood. Besides houses, destructed buildings included many offices, industrial buildings/factories, commercial buildings, governmental buildings, and hospitals. These numbers provide an idea of the devastation, much of which was visible.

In Rikuzen-takata we visited an area where almost every building, except perhaps two, was destroyed (Figure 1). The scattered debris prevented obtaining a closer look; but views from roads and accessible paths were quite revealing (for e.g. see https://www.cbsnews.com/pictures/devastation-in-japan/6/). The devastation was astounding. Vast areas were completely altered but work was proceeding on removing the debris (Figure 2).

Figure 1 GEJET caused devastation as seen from high ground (Photo: Sanjoy Mazumdar)

I saw a 5-story concrete-and-brick building still standing (Figure 3). However, everything on its lower four floors, including window and door fixtures, were gone (i.e. the tsunami at that particular place had reached a height of 40 to 45 feet). From a distance, the fifth floor appeared undamaged. I could sense that the tsunami was extremely powerful and high.

Figure 2 Work done to remove GEJET debris and level the ground (Photo: Sanjoy Mazumdar)

Figure 3 Five storied building of which the tsunami destroyed the four lower floors (Photo: Sanjoy Mazumdar)

Faint evidence of major streets provided a ghostly picture of neighborhoods that had been there. This made me strangely aware of the township that had previously flourished there.

The character and texture of the earlier town containing the internal neighborhood street pattern with oku that Maki (1979a:53, 1979b) described were gone leaving only scant material remains and very little evidence of earlier presence. Entire neighborhoods and almost all residential buildings, mostly made of wood, were transformed into rubble, with only small portions of roofs and piles of wood strewn around or in heaps, in many cases at large distances from their original sites. Almost everything else was washed away. The surroundings appeared gray, with hardly any brightness. The air smelled of wet wood and the sea. There seemed to be an eerie dullness of suppressed low audible sounds punctuated by the sounds of heavy construction equipment. Scant material remains can signal the unexpectedness and unusual magnitude of this earthquake and tsunami disaster, which took nearly everything that was not well anchored.

Besides humans and human occupied land disasters also affect animal and plant life. No birds or untamed animals were visible. Nearly all trees in the area had fallen to the tsunami except one lone pine tree that survived the onslaught (Figure 4).

Figure 4 Miracle Pine - the original lone tree that survived the tsunami (Photo: Sanjoy Mazumdar)

It became a symbol of hope for the community. Unfortunately, later it too suc-cumbed to the tsunami's salt water. An almost identical artificial pine tree was made to replace it. The trees in the nearby forest were a contrast to the gray of the affected areas.

To prevent recurrence of similar loss, the authorities in Rikuzen-Takata and several more municipalities decided to raise the ground level by as much as 33 feet (10m), by cut-and-fill from nearby mountains; this decision changed the landscape drastically (Figure 5). Many of Japan's earlier construction materials —wood, paper, clay tiles— were reusable, bio-degradable, left scant material remains, and were not expected to leave long-lasting traces or problems. However, many modern materials, e.g. concrete, steel, plastics, and others although stronger and longer lasting, could be polluting while being made, afterward, and may not be bio-degradable.

Many temples were not destroyed. These sacred structures seemed to have been overlooked. It is possible that somehow the earthquake and tsunami did not affect these (much like a fire might consume several building but spare one in the mid-dle). But it could also be because temples were likely located in less prone areas, with greater attention given to constructing out of heavy non-flammable materials (like stone), or because special care was taken with their siting (using geomantic principles), atop hills.

Disasters and their effects are not confined by political boundaries. With a tinge of surprise and unhappiness several writings stated that some of Japan's GEJET debris later came ashore in Washington and Oregon in the USA (e.g. https://response.restoration.noaa.gov/about/media/how-japan-tsunami-marine-debris-cleaned-west-coast.html (dated 02July2012)).

Figure 5 Pipeline transporting soil cut from mountain to raise ground level of Rikuzen-takata (Photo: Sanjoy Mazumdar)

I was left wondering how these flooded places affected the psyche of the residents, how they adjusted to the raising of the land, and importantly what efforts they made to regain their lives, environments, and occupations. Governmental and other help, though useful, may not be adequate for restarting life. Nor could they wait for these to arrive. Mostly, disaster affected people take action on their own. These micro human efforts (MHE) are of primary interest here.

~ *Sanjoy Mazumdar*

Note

1 Other death numbers are also presented: 931 in Miyagi Prefecture and 470 in Iwate Prefecture and (Asahi Shimbun 2023 Mar 12; https://www.asahi.com/ajw/articles/14859669).

References cited

Asahi Shimbun, (2023/03/12). Fukushima prefecture posts 2,335 deaths tied to 3/11 disaster. https://www.asahi.com/ajw/articles/14859669.

Global Centre for Disaster Statistics, IRIDeS, Tohoku University (n.d.) Statistical Database on the Great East Japan Earthquake, (2015). http://www.geje-gcds.jp/pdf/01-155-0203_e.pdf and http://www.geje-gcds.jp/en-contents/ - statistics and pie chart on GEJET deaths.

Isagawa, Teriyuki & Ohno, Ryuzo (2018) Influence of residents' cognition of their local environment on evacuation behavior from tsunamis: A case study of Onjuku, Chiba prefecture, *Japan architecture; Review*, vol 1(4): 486–503. https://doi.org/10.1002/2475-8876.12045.

Maki, Fumihiko (1979a) Japanese city spaces and the concept of *oku, Japan Architect*, 265 (May) 7905:51–62.

Maki, Fumihiko (1979b) The city and inner space, *Ekistics*, 46(278) (Sep/Oct): 328-334.

Mazumdar, Sanjoy; Itoh, Shunsuke; & Iwasa, Akihiko (2021). Post-disaster temporary housing: An *emic* study of lived experiences of victims of the Great East Japan earthquake and tsunami, *International Journal of Mass Emergencies and Disasters*. 39(1)(Mar):87–119.

National Centers for Environmental Information (NCEI) (2011/2025). How tall was the 2011 Japan tsunami? https://www.ncei.noaa.gov/news/day-2011-japan-earthquake-and-tsunami.

Spencer, Molly (2025). The Forest of Symbols: Aspects of Ndembu Ritual. *Geographic FAQ*, NCESC.com, https://www.ncesc.com/geographic-faq/how-tall-was-the-2011-japan-tsunami/ visited 04/03/25.

Foreword

Amy Donovan

This new book is an exciting contribution to the emerging field of critical disaster studies, focusing on micro-scale interventions that enhance disaster resilience. It draws on intersectional feminist scholarship to focus specifically on the ad hoc, individual actions that enhance resilience in disaster contexts. The editors explain the definition and relevance of "micro-human efforts" in the introduction; here, I want to emphasize five ideas that stood out to me as important contributions.

The first is the significance of tacit knowledge in disasters. As the editors state in the introduction, there is a tendency for disaster research to focus too greatly on those things that are readily quantified and therefore to miss the values, personality traits and cultural factors that motivate individuals to take small-scale actions (Birkmann and Wisner, 2006). This reductivism can lead to misrepresentations and a lack of awareness of the significant impact that individuals may have on the emergence of particular characteristics of a disaster – and in the building of resilience. This includes both individuals within communities on the ground, and the role of individuals and their personalities when they occupy powerful or central administrative positions. Indeed, paying attention to human nature, desires, and frailties can provide important insights that mainstream approaches may ignore.

The second point is that a potential explanation for the lack of attention paid to individual action is the focus on the collective in disaster research and a failure to pay sufficient attention to concepts of scale. The geographical concept of "scale" remains inherent to this volume. Indeed, it may be read as an exercise in the flattening of scale, which is so often focused at national or global level (Marston, Jones III and Woodward, 2005). Individual actions are often driven by social values and concern for the collective. This is enhanced by the term "micro" itself, holding within it a tension between tiny and impactful, and a sense also of something hidden (perhaps too small to see). The focus here on the "micro" also leads to reflections on the challenges of making certain things visible – or, rather, the importance of paying attention to the immaterial and expressive elements of disasters-in-the-making (McGowran and Donovan, 2021). Understanding individual actions can enable analysis of the socio-cultural fabric that underlies whether or not people are resilient to disaster: how can resilience be deepened through the cultivation of such efforts?

Thirdly, feminist theory has long had a deep interest in "the everyday": the ways in which large-scale narratives impinge upon the everyday lives of citizens, and how everyday activities respond (Rigg, 2007). Micro-human efforts further emphasize the ways in which this individualized scale may respond in exceptional ways to extreme situations. They thus introduce an element of hope into the critical discourse, alongside critiques of power and calls for empowerment (Castree et al., 2010; Hazlewood, Middleton Manning and Casolo, 2023). Hope is an important motivator, both for those affected by disasters and those who study them!

Fourthly, it is striking to read, in a volume about disasters, that we should focus on positioning people to "react": much of disaster risk reduction focuses on the reduction of vulnerability prior to disasters. Yet the capability to react is built prior to the disaster, and vulnerability approaches can sometimes infer insufficient agency on the part of those affected. The book suggests therefore that enhancing the societal values that produce significant micro-human efforts would increase societal resilience, and resonates with research on disasters that seeks to build an ethic of care (Puig de La Bellacasa, 2017; Donovan et al., 2024). While the focus is apparently on the recovery phase, it reads the recovery phase through the conditions prior to disaster that either enhance or reduce the capacities of individuals to respond effectively.

Finally, and relatedly, it is important to emphasize that a focus on micro-human effort does not remove the responsibility of powerful actors to take decisions for the common good. It does, however, draw attention to the power of the collective and the importance of community. This is in stark contrast to the libertarian narratives pervading the West at present, and a powerful challenge to them. Indeed, the experiences documented in this volume demonstrate the importance of social cohesion and ways in which disasters may serve as catalysts for change in unequal societies even as their impacts are unjustly distributed. There is an inherent tension in that celebrating individual resourcefulness and seeking to enhance it appears to draw emphasis away from the social contract: the rights and protections from disaster that citizens should be able to expect from the state. However, another reading flips that premise around and suggests, instead, that governments should work to create societies in which the agency of individuals within the collective is maximized, not to deflect attention from the role of government, but to work with it.

There is already a lot of literature on volunteerism in disasters (Michel, 2007; Carlile et al., 2014; Whittaker, McLennan and Handmer, 2015; Rivera and Wood, 2016); work on MHE, however, further considers processes of memorialization, repurposing, retraining, and recommitting. It also frames the actions slightly differently, focusing attention on the emotions, sacrifices and cultures that underlie such activities. As noted above, it explicitly emphasizes the significance of scale in disaster contexts – specifically, the "micro" – and the effect is to re-empower citizens in disaster contexts, demonstrating often-unseen agencies that vulnerable groups can hold and that can be catalysed and nurtured. This in turn leads to potential options to reduce vulnerability through the development of such agencies. As such, this collection is a welcome addition to the evidence base for disaster risk reduction and disaster research.

Amy Donovan is a professor of Environmental Geography at the University of Cambridge and a Fellow of Girton College. As co-chair of the steering committee for the UK Alliance for Disaster Research (UKADR), she helps to convene discussions on the future of disaster research in the UK. An interdisciplinary geographer with a deep understanding of intersectional feminism, Professor Donovan investigates the complex geographies of risk and knowledge related to disaster risk reduction.

Her research bridges the gap between scientific inquiry and policy formulation while examining the cultural and political dimensions of geology and volcanology. Professor Donovan's collaborative work includes a wide range of international partnerships with researchers studying active volcanic activity in regions such as Chile, Argentina, Iceland, Mexico, Japan, North Korea, China, Ethiopia, Eritrea, and the United States, among others. In addition to her emphasis on volcanology, her expertise also covers other high-risk environments susceptible to landslides and earthquakes. Professor Donovan's contributions extend beyond academic discourse; they reflect her commitment to understanding and mitigating the challenges faced by communities in vulnerable situations.

References

Birkmann, J. and Wisner, B. (2006) *Measuring the unmeasurable: the challenge of vulnerability*. UNU-EHS.

Carlile, J.A. *et al.* (2014) 'Local volunteerism and resilience following large-scale disaster: Outcomes for health support team volunteers in Haiti', *International Journal of Disaster Risk Science*, 5, pp. 206–213.

Castree, N. *et al.* (2010) *The Point is to Change it: Geographies of Hope and Survival in an Age of Crisis*. John Wiley & Sons.

Donovan, A. *et al.* (2024) 'Critical geographies of disaster, and the geographical imagination', *Progress in Environmental Geography*, 3(3), pp. 212–230.

Hazlewood, J.A., Middleton Manning, B.R. and Casolo, J.J. (2023) 'Geographies of Hope-in-Praxis: Collaboratively decolonizing relations and regenerating relational spaces', *Environment and Planning E: Nature and Space*, 6(3), pp. 1417–1446.

de La Bellacasa, M.P. (2017) *Matters of care: Speculative ethics in more than human worlds*. U of Minnesota Press.

Marston, S.A., Jones III, J.P. and Woodward, K. (2005) 'Human geography without scale', *Transactions of the Institute of British Geographers*, 30(4), pp. 416–432.

McGowran, P. and Donovan, A. (2021) 'Assemblage theory and disaster risk management', *Progress in Human Geography*, 45(6), pp. 1601–1624. Available at: https://doi.org/10.1177/03091325211003328.

Michel, L.M. (2007) 'Personal responsibility and volunteering after a natural disaster: The case of Hurricane Katrina', *Sociological Spectrum*, 27(6), pp. 633–652.

Rigg, J. (2007) *An everyday geography of the global south*. Routledge.

Rivera, J.D. and Wood, Z.D. (2016) 'Disaster relief volunteerism: Evaluating cities' planning for the usage and management of spontaneous volunteers', *Journal of Emergency Management*, 14(2), pp. 127–138.

Whittaker, J., McLennan, B. and Handmer, J. (2015) 'A review of informal volunteerism in emergencies and disasters: Definition, opportunities and challenges', *International journal of disaster risk reduction*, 13, pp. 358–368.

Acknowledgement

Originally conceived as a framework for post-tsunami rehabilitation efforts, "micro-human efforts" embody the enduring spirit of grassroots activism and its relentless drive. Evolving from mere infrastructure rebuilding, it now fosters a culture that recognizes, harnesses, and actively engages the immense power of unseen individual interventions in overcoming disasters.

Our chapter contributors collaborated under challenging conditions, bridging continents to unveil alternative pathways to resilience. Their stories reflect personal projects born from necessity, demonstrating unwavering commitment even amid personal tragedies like the loss of loved ones and displacement during climate calamities, such as the devastating 2023 Turkey–Syria earthquake. Your resilience and journey inspire us all.

We are profoundly grateful to Amy Donovan, professor of Environmental Geography and Fellow of Girton College at the University of Cambridge, for recognizing micro-human efforts and offering her insights for its future. Her foreword stands as a beacon for the evolution of Micro Human Efforts through critical geographies, serving as a disaster manifesto that refuses to be relegated to the margins of discourse.

The Grenfell Baines Institute of Architecture (GBIA) at the University of Lancashire and Asian American Studies at the University of California, Irvine, provided essential institutional support, helping us navigate the challenges of this book's publication journey. Despite occasional setbacks, the team at Routledge partnered closely with the editors to realize our vision: slow local actions with a global impact.

Chamila (Don) Subasinghe
University of Lancashire
Preston, UK

Professor Sanjoy Mazumdar
University of California Irvine
Irvine, USA

Abbreviations

ACHA	American College Health Association
AICPA	Association of International Certified Professional Accountants,
AIDR	Australian Institute for Disaster Resilience
APA	American Planning Association
BBB	Build Back Better
CBO	Community-based Organizations
CDP	Center for Domestic Preparedness
CERT	Community Emergency Response Teams
CPR	Cardiopulmonary Resuscitation
DAP	Disaster-Affected Persons
DART	Damage Assessment Response Team
DIY	Do-It-Yourself
DPH	Disaster Public Housing
DRPO	Disaster relief processes and operations
DRR	Disaster Risk Reduction
DV	Disaster Victims
EBS	Environmental-behaviour Studies
ECSU	Elizabeth City State University
EM	Emergency Management
ETH	Emergency temporary housing
EU	European Union
FDMA	Fire and Disaster Management Agency
FEMA	Federal Emergency Management Agency
FGD	Focus Group Discussion
GEJET	The 2011 Great East Japan Earthquake and Tsunami
GFDRR	Global Facility for Disaster Risk Reduction
GRB	Glocal Resilience Building
GSDF	Ground Self-Defense Force
HBCU	Historically Black Colleges and Universities
HOPE	Hope, efficacy, resilience, and optimism
HUD	Housing and Uban Development
IJMED	International Journal of Mass Emergencies and Disasters
IK	Indigenous Knowledge
IPCC	The Paris Climate Agreement

IRP	International Recovery Platform
ISA	International Sociological Association
IV	Intravenous
JRCS	Japanese Red Cross Society
LWM	Leisure and Wellbeing Model
MHE	Micro Human Efforts
NAACP	National Associations of Colored People
NFPA	National Fire Protection Agency
NGO	Non-governmental organizations
NIBS	National Institute of Building Sciences
NOAA	National Oceanic and Atmospheric Administration
NUA	The New Urban Agenda
PDR	Post Disaster Rebuilding
PI	Pacific Island
PNG	Papua New Guinea
PRISMA	Preferred Reporting Items for Systematic Reviews and Meta-Analyses
PSDMA	Public sector disaster management agencies
PsyCap	Psychological capital
SAR	Search and Rescue
SCI	Science Citation Index
SDGs	Sustainable Development Goals
SFDRR	Sendai Framework for Disaster Risk Reduction
SSCI	Social Science Citation Index
TEK	Traditional Ecological Knowledge
TS	Temporary shelters
UN	United Nations
UNC	University of North Carolina System
UNCRD	United Nations Center for Regional Development
UNDP	United Nations Development Programme
UNDRR	United Nations Office for Disaster Risk Reduction
US	United States

1 Micro Human Efforts in Disaster Resiliency

An Introduction

*Chamila (Don) Subasinghe and
Sanjoy Mazumdar*

In 2021, a thought-provoking special issue of the *International Journal of Mass Emergencies and Disasters* (IJMED) ignited an important conversation about Micro Human Efforts (MHE). Titled "Multidisciplinary Perspectives of Micro Human Efforts in Post-Disaster Recovery", this issue opened the door to exploring the vital, yet often overlooked, role of small-scale human efforts during extreme climatic events. Recognizing the emerging significance of MHE, the special issue's editors teamed up with IJMED to establish some preliminary definitions. As the official dissemination platform of the International Sociological Association's (ISA) Research Committee on Sociology of Disasters (RC39), IJMED stood out as a credible platform for addressing these multifaceted themes tied to climate-induced disasters.

RC39's mission is clear: "to provide a forum where academics and practitioners can share insights on all aspects of disasters". The editors embraced this vision, believing it fostered dynamic interactions across diverse fields that intersect with MHE literature. They identified key operational areas, particularly in rebuilding resilience, where MHE plays an indispensable role in the disaster management narrative. However, they also highlighted the challenges of integrating MHE into traditional disaster management practices – despite its humane appeal and potential effectiveness. To clarify the context, the editors thoughtfully segmented disasters into categories dominated by climatic and environmental factors, setting aside the complexities of human-led events. The decision to spotlight the post-disaster phase stemmed from a realization: MHE is most visible and impactful in the moments following a disaster rather than in the liminal spaces before and during such events.

"Multidisciplinary Perspectives of Micro Human Efforts" aimed to illuminate often-ignored human traits that could transform ambitious post-disaster recovery plans. As self-quarantine became a standard safety protocol due to the COVID-19 pandemic, MHE concepts surged in relevance. Self-quarantine itself emerged as a prominent example of MHE, becoming a household term as the pandemic unfolded in early 2020. Using this context as a launching pad, the editors sought to reframe rebuilding strategies from a human-centred perspective. This shift allowed individuals, community groups, NGOs, and institutions to learn from the rich tapestry of cultural and contextual conditions. By emphasizing the value of human capital, we aimed to equip organized groups with a clearer understanding of MHEs, enabling

DOI: 10.4324/9781003615903-1

stakeholders to evaluate their impact and resourcefulness in designing practical, human-centred objectives for complex rebuilding initiatives.

One of our key objectives was to explore how MHE could serve as a transformative force in shaping our collective future in a world frequently beset by disasters. By engaging disaster evacuees in meaningful and therapeutic ways, we sought to cut socio-environmental costs while amplifying the voices of those most affected. In the face of adversity, the potential for MHE to drive positive change has never been more critical. In an intriguing revelation, the editors discovered that the widespread influence of MHE could be harnessed to elevate slow, local actions into movements with global significance. This concept of slow local actions was later recognized as a vital strategy for Glocal Resilience Building (GRB). It is important, however, to differentiate GRB from the global resilience approaches championed by various global networks, particularly the 100 Resilient Cities initiative, which is implemented at the local level (Marom & Shlomo, 2022).

MHE-inspired GRB is rooted in the belief that the wisdom passed down through generations can shape effective local survival strategies that meet global sustainability goals. By focusing on converting local challenges into opportunities rather than seeking solutions from afar, MHE places a premium on the value of time-tested tacit knowledge. This shift in perspective not only celebrates community ingenuity but also empowers local efforts to drive meaningful change on a larger scale.

1.1   Why MHE?

Build Back Better, a trending movement for bouncing back after major devastation, including disasters, marks a moment for MHE.

The MHE discourse emerged to signpost the remarkable resourcefulness and resilience that individuals display in the face of disasters. Its goal is to inspire responsible agents and agencies to recognize and prioritize the small yet significant contributions that people make within broader social frameworks. Unfortunately, there is a risk that these individual efforts go unnoticed or are overshadowed by grand narratives, especially in the complex arena of post-disaster rebuilding. While the idea of microhuman actions is not new and has been discussed across various disciplines, applying these concepts effectively to manage disaster situations through spontaneous individual actions remains largely overlooked in rebuilding strategies. This gap is echoed in the longitudinal studies of researchers like Han (2023), who highlighted the challenges faced by personal efforts within Work, Labour, and Action theory. Han poignantly observes that, in a world often beset by disasters, simply choosing to do nothing – being inactive – actually takes effort. This nuanced form of existence, where inactivity can define humanity, encourages us to rethink our understanding of action. The editors propose that MHEs – micro-human Efforts – do not merely add another dimension to human involvement but rather integrate the concepts of Work, Labour, and Action, particularly in post-disaster contexts. When calamity strikes, individuals often create their own timelines for recovery, engaging in processes like intuitive "self-therapy" and "self-reliance" to regain a sense of normalcy.

The ground-shifting MHE discourse introduced by IJMED challenges rebuilding trends like "Build Back Better", emphasizing evacuees' potential to develop new competencies beyond their existing knowledge. This shift not only aids them in navigating a new normal but also opens opportunities to rethink interactions between humans and the environment. Through this discourse, the editors laid the groundwork for understanding how individual contributions can reshape power dynamics, technology, education, and behaviours towards fostering a culture of risk reduction and recovery. This book seeks to unravel the intricate interplay between reduction and recovery cultures, offering rich cultural and contextual perspectives illuminating the diverse expressions of MHEs and their subtle yet powerful role within collective action. In this introductory chapter, the editors set the stage with a series of sequential objectives (A to E) designed to explore the nuanced micro-human concepts found across various disciplines. These objectives are articulated through theories of the human condition, specifically focusing on the fourth objective (F), where the editors aspire to trace the steps from A to E and uncover potential MHE silos (Burr & Dick, 2021; Han, 2023). With these foundations, the editors deep dive into established individual action concepts within these silos, aiming to pinpoint a core for post-disaster rebuilding grounded in MHE. This structured approach not only organizes the chapter sequence but also allows for a thorough examination of each objective from the perspectives of concept development and theory validation. The four main objectives (A to D) form a solid framework for the chapter layout, while the sub-objectives (E) and (F) help us draw meaningful conclusions.

By building on the foundational discussions from IJMED, the editors aim to merge and clarify what has often been a fragmented body of knowledge. This book seeks to affirm the unique insights emerging from innate human improvizations – elements that have traditionally been overlooked due to their inability to yield easily quantifiable results akin to the familiar behaviours recognized in scientific studies. The findings could reshape how donors and decision-makers assess the success of rebuilding efforts, prompting a reevaluation of inclusive redevelopment as a dynamic rebuilding process. Moreover, the editors aim to synthesize self-based ideologies by interlinking often unrecognized human responses that become visible through specific academic lenses. This fusion allows experts from various disciplines to launch their research efforts focused on developing ethical and empathetic rebuilding models – ones that could help mitigate the pitfalls of strictly technocratic recovery processes. At the grassroots level, stakeholders can leverage MHE as a vital tool to navigate the complexities of donor-driven rebuilding initiatives. It would further allow the gravity of the latent coping concepts related to self-Work, Labour, and Action present in disaster discussions to surface. These concepts can act as social levellers that foster healing, drawing parallels to the rise of DIY (Do-It-Yourself) practices that have gained traction in diverse socio-economic environments. This exploration could unravel the contrasting dynamics of self-labour practices: where affluent groups turn to DIY when professional labour is unavailable or too costly, while rural communities often perceive inexpensive hired labour as undesirable. By intertwining these distinct yet connected self-work concepts, we aspire to reveal broader socio-economic implications.

While current literature on post-disaster rebuilding tends to focus on enhancing individual capacities, strengthening communities, and fostering resilient environments, the studies presented in this book invite a deeper reflection on resilience as a process of reimagining the human condition. Recognizing the significance of each individual's intuitive actions and casual contributions within the ever-changing landscape is as crucial as nurturing the collective. As the book moves forward with the sub-objectives, it emphasizes the importance of cultural and contextual insights in helping disaster-specific MHEs carve out their place in resilience building. Hence, it aims to evaluate the applicability of these concepts, delving into the challenges they may face in adapting to an evolving disaster environment. Ultimately, the book explores how notions of victimization shape individuals' capacity to take charge of their recovery processes. Examining "self-reliant" practices such as self-labour will uncover how MHEs offer the flexibility needed for rapid resource mobilization in the fast-paced landscape of post-disaster rebuilding. Additionally, the book will offer an overview of how agents and agencies can effectively harness these humble yet powerful human capacities through innovative methodologies, paving the way for a more autonomous rebuilding process. Unlike most social inquiries, this book's cultural and contextual lessons are re-learned. The editors resisted concluding solutions but curated an evidence-based set of resilience scenarios. Although most scenarios curated here have perpetually roamed in the resiliency repertoire, they have yet to be specifically obtained for their MHE potential. Hence, based on evolving observations and emerging theories, the insights in this book feature a road map instead of a concrete set of recommendations (Strandh & Eklund, 2018).

1.2   Multiple Meanings of MHE

The world of disaster resilience operates on multiple levels, and understanding these layers is crucial for effective management. At the macro level, we see large-scale organizational efforts engaging entire communities. Meso brings us to more minor, formal or informal groups while micro zeroes in on individual experiences (Riebschleger, 2018). In the context of disaster resilience, the core principles of MHE are emerging as pivotal in shaping sustainable disaster management strategies and fostering growth in vulnerable communities. While advancements in disaster science are improving prediction and early warning systems, the reality is that vulnerabilities and the frequency of disasters are escalating at an alarming rate. This creates a troubling dynamic, intertwining resilience with what is known as "dependency syndrome" (Subasinghe & Miranda, 2007). This duality can stifle a community's ability to regain control and rebuild after a disaster, often leaving them reliant on external aid instead of empowering them to forge their own path to recovery and resilience. The discourse surrounding MHE emphasizes the complex relationship between recovery and resilience. On one side, long-term recovery is heralded as an essential part of building resilience. On the other hand, true resilience aims to bridge the gap between recovery and a return to normalcy (Subasinghe, Sutrisna, & Olatunji, 2021). What becomes the driving force in this process? Should it be a robust recovery-embedded rebuilding methodology that acknowledges the often-overlooked psychophysiological efforts of individuals we refer to as MHE?

This approach may seem minor or insignificant at first glance, mainly because its impact is not always immediately visible within the broader collective recovery processes. However, these individual efforts are indispensable, acting as the quiet catalysts for transformation in the aftermath of disaster. In a world where the stakes are high, recognizing and nurturing these vital components can lead to meaningful change and sustainable recovery for communities striving to rebuild and thrive. One of the barriers to MHE manifesting itself in its original form may be its status as a self-focused and self-benefit-driven endeavour in a process known for its collective community contribution. Hence, the spontaneous rebuilding responses of evacuees are largely overlooked, although an indispensable benchmark towards resilience. This book unpacks MHE by analyzing residues of well-defined tacit knowledge based on self-reliance, self-sufficiency, self-provision, and self-dependence that tend to sweep away from the knowledge core to the peripheries; this often occurs as a result of their vulnerability to data-centric, methodological research that typically leads to quasi-empirical inquiry (Subasinghe, 2021). Thus, the cultural and contextual lessons in this book delve into the advantages of MHE and its potential to address critical clinical errors while reducing socio-environmental costs, which also play a significant role in social inquiry. This could be done by systematically mapping MHE on a broader framework of vulnerability alleviation – an area that offers a tangible process to decipher residues of tacit knowledge in sustainable recovery. Hence, we targeted identifying many socio-cultural facets of resiliency for policy recommendations, protocol formulations, statutory strategies, and the development of technical tools via humanistic (naturalistic) rigour that typically is inaccessible through scientific inquiry (Lincoln & Guba, 1985).

1.3 MHE-Disaster Nexus

Disasters often strike with little warning, challenging our ability to predict their impact even with advanced meteorological tools. This unpredictability captures our interest in human resilience during such crises. It is essential to scrutinize how individuals summon various active and passive forces against disaster recurrence, not just on the scientific and technical aspects. Imagine people navigating a landscape of familiarity and unfamiliarity – where the expected suddenly turns unexpectedly chaotic. Vulnerable individuals in these communities often find themselves constrained by their surroundings – both geographically, in disaster-prone areas, and socio-economically, through challenging human-environment interactions. This is where the fascinating concept of "disaster instincts" comes into play. These innate human responses to extreme conditions can illuminate the critical connections often overlooked in mainstream disaster discussions.

To better understand this relationship, this book distilled six distinct traits of "disaster instincts" and crafted a few authentic questions to further explore the MHE nexus. One compelling question stands out: How do individuals confront the unexpected and manage their fears when faced with the overwhelming scale and magnitude of disasters while striving to reclaim a sense of normality? This inquiry invites us to delve deeper into the human spirit's resilience in times of crisis.

a. *Coping*: How do people carry culturally and contextually cultivated mechanisms to contain and recalibrate psychophysiological damage and humanize do-gooder rebuilding approaches that typically provide marginal allowances for numerous diversities that characterize a robust recovery system?
b. *Adjusting*: How do people take charge of disaster recovery as an organic process on a timeline of its own, where actors can find their respective roles without directors?
c. *Rebuilding*: What other alternative altruism beyond Build Back Better is out there to engineer latent human capacities into rebuilding engines?
d. *Resilience*: Where does a collective of MHE fit into the grand scheme of things, such as Build Back Better (BBB) (Clinton, 2006)?

While this book explores these vital disaster instincts that deeply resonate with MHE, it does not claim that resilience stands as the pinnacle of MHE – rather, that judgement rests with you, the reader. In essence, micro-human efforts in disaster recovery represent the self-driven decisions that empower individuals to cope, adapt, rebuild, and find resilience amid extreme changes – often without external aid. MHE easily resonates with rigorous capacity building across diverse social layers, but it is crucial to highlight that certain concepts within MHE serve as indispensable recovery tools for marginalized communities. These same concepts can complement the efforts of more affluent communities facing disaster risks. Take self-labour, for instance: it emerges as a crucial recovery strategy, particularly for low-income groups who may lack formal skills or stable employment opportunities.

The concept of self-work is an essential component of being "active" during a crisis. This framework highlights how human actions can powerfully interact with environmental responses, creating a dynamic interplay that forms the basis of our understanding of disaster recovery uncovered through small human acts. Moreover, it is vital to have a broader lens on the socio-economic benefits generated by these efforts, especially in how they foster inclusive entrepreneurship. By doing so, one can re-examine cultural and contextual adaptations that are vital for bridging the gaps in existing recovery and resilience practices. Through a set of curious queries, this book offers a fresh perspective that fills a crucial void in disaster recovery research and practice, organizing a multitude of ideas and their unique applications across various disciplines.

1.4   Micro in Disaster Discourse: A Shape?

The MHE container and its components serve as fascinating self-activism, reflecting a rich tapestry of cultural and contextual characteristics. To explore the emerging concepts tied to microhuman interactions and the intricate connections among individual efforts, it is essential to know how the notion of "micro" influences instincts of individuals and how, in turn, the condition of "self" shapes the concept of micro. Etymologically, "micro" originates from the Greek word "mickros", which signifies the smallest measurable part of a whole. Yet, it carries more than just a numerical connotation; it also embodies ideas of visibility and significance. When we think of it in terms of impact, "micro" suggests something slight, minor, or even marginal – yet its effects can be profound, making it impossible to ignore or dismiss. When paired with terms like "very", "extremely", "ultra", and "hyper", "micro" takes on a dynamic quality, emphasizing size and impact in relation to the bigger picture. Like many hybrid concepts, it spans a spectrum of meanings across various fields and discussions. For instance, as noted by Ritzer (1991), interpretations of "micro" can range widely – from individual psychological experiences to patterns of interpersonal interactions, depending on the background and perspective of the person defining it. Today, "micro" is often contextualized in terms of both measurement and magnitude, revealing its layered complexity and importance in our understanding of the world around us. While "micro" typically signifies something small or miniature, in the context of disaster recovery, this book proposes an alternative view: it represents the "unseen" elements – those that may appear peripheral, insignificant, or even overlooked. When paired with "human", the term takes on an intriguing angle, suggesting a space devoid of the biases that often arise from sociodemographic or political contexts. This approach moves beyond mere quantification; it prompts us to explore the intricate, often intangible nature of human behaviours and interactions, particularly within identifiable situations.

In the realm of micro-human discourse, this book uncovers subtle yet deterministic dynamics that shape group interactions. It highlights how micro-level actions influence the collective functioning of a group and their relationship to broader operational behaviours. The processes examined here relate not just to the "how" of achieving objectives but intricately tie into the "when" of individual contributions, ultimately giving rise to what we call micro-social orders (Choudhary, Memon & Mishra, 2020). These micro-human elements are deeply embedded in our intuitive structures, often vanishing within the complexities of daily interactions, whether they are between individuals or groups. Despite their latent presence, these transactions significantly impact society and are, in turn, shaped by individual actions, organizational processes, and environmental factors (Chia and MacKay, 2007). In studies of organizational behaviour, there is a frequent emphasis on optimizing these micro-level activities to enhance the management of more extensive operations. While calls for a deeper investigation into the micro-dynamics that underlie macro-level processes are plentiful, there remains a glaring gap in robust, evidence-based research within the MHE field.

While it does not directly decipher the concepts of Work, Labour, and Action, the various domains explored in this book augment a microhuman microcosm rich with traces of individual effort. As readers delve into this introduction, they will discover pivotal connections that reveal the presence of these concepts. Each connection highlights unique psychophysiological activities: Work anchors us to the world, Labour embodies the essence of life itself, and Action reflects the conditions life imposes and the inherent dependencies we navigate. This perspective, known as "vita activa", intricately encapsulates the power of human capabilities as expressed through these three activities (Zdravković, 2021). Even though this framework has limitations and complexities, referencing Labour, Work, and Action opens up a dialogue about their distinctions, fundamentally through the lens of microhuman traits in specific contexts (see Table 1.1). However, it is important to note that these distinctions can be liminal, often overlapping, and influenced by disciplinary inertia. For instance, the differentiation between Work and Labour is blurred considerably, a point that even the authors of these frameworks question. In fact, they argue that modernity has caused the silo of Work to envelop nearly all human activities, complicating the separation of these concepts.

What makes "vita activa" so captivating is its recognition of Work as the cornerstone of human activity, providing a profound sense of fulfilment in our essence. The notions (a) acknowledgement of one's active engagement in the affairs of the world in which one lives in, (b) the condition to which one is subject, and (c) one's own activities in it are partial to MHE (Parekh, 1981). These relate to human emancipation through self-labour under extreme challenges, akin to post-disaster recovery (Subasinghe, 2013). Deactivating dependency syndrome after disasters, another core concept of MHE, is also closely tied to the *vita activa*: regaining the freedom of movement and choosing one's own activities. In reality, however, the multitude of such activities is too complex to track, especially among the complexities of other attributing activities. Hence, the micro-human concepts in the wheel are in a constant state of shifting silos. We propose a series of latent yet pertinent cultural variations possible in inter-contextual situations for MHE (Figure 1.1).

Although collated, thematized, and categorized micro-human notions in Figure 1.1 and Table 1.1 are rudimentary, they assist in describing the emerging presence and distribution of individual efforts in microhuman literature. For example, in Figure 1.1, understanding the distribution of micro-human research through a fivefold field of research distils potential MHE concepts. We see a higher distribution of ideas in Systems and Management and relatively limited work and variety in the Trial and Clinical Processes area. Although inconclusive, Table 1.1 shows a shift in micro-human discourse from work (belongingness) to action (social and political life) through labour ("self" or life itself). As conceptualized through active and inactive, "self" or labour was at the very core of micro-human efforts that make the pivot between work and action (Burr & Dick, 2021; Han, 2023). Perhaps, this may assist in tracing the directionality of multidisciplinary MHE notions, making it an established field of research.

a.   cascades, radiates or ripples from Work to Action through Labour and/or
b.   Action as the point of departure towards Work as the destination through Labour.

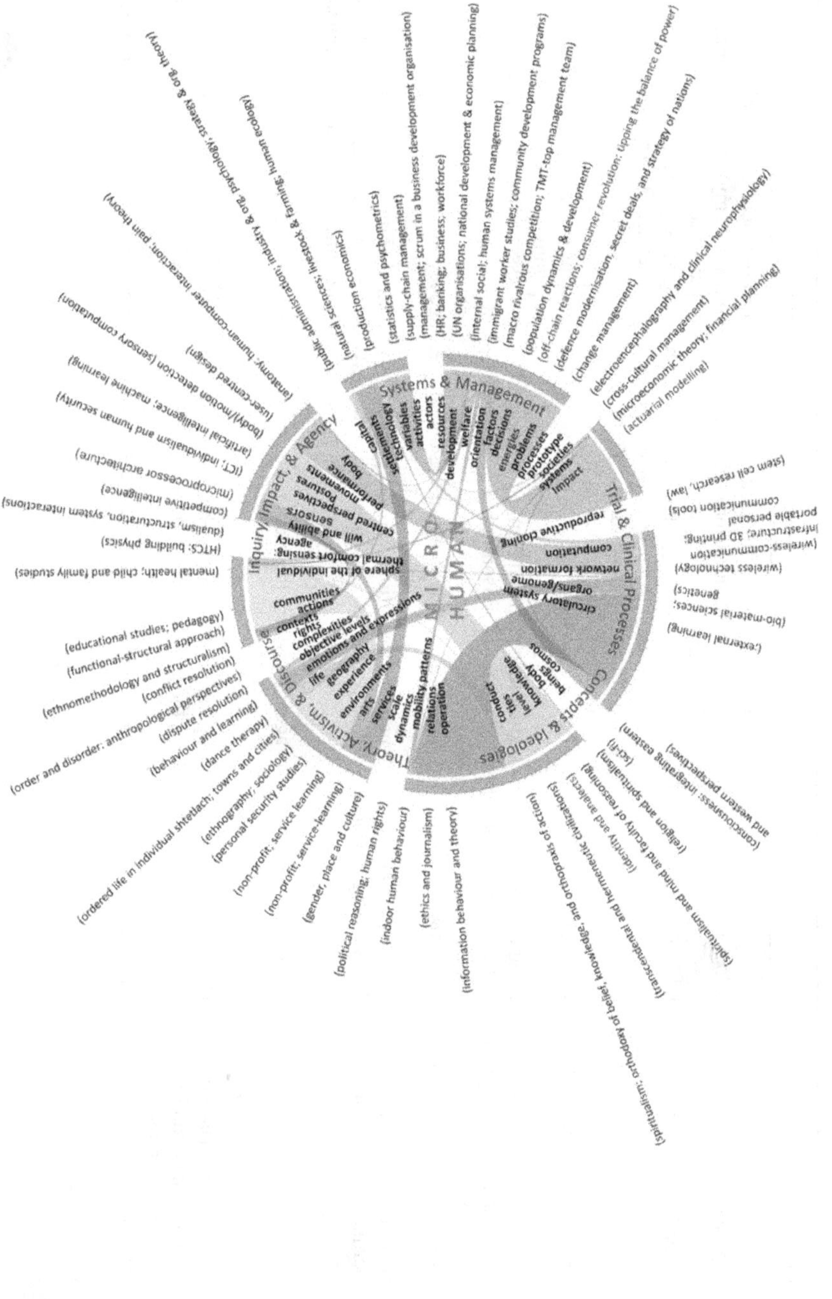

Figure 1.1 Micro-human Concepts in Diverse Fields of Research.

Table 1.1 Multidisciplinary Micro-human Notions in Work, Labour, and Action

Micro	Human	Silos
Work (belongingness)	**Labour** ("self" or life itself)	**Action** (social and political life)
experience (ethnography; sociology)	emotions and expressions (behaviour and learning)	body (anatomy): human-computer interaction; pain theory
sphere of the individual (mental health; child and family studies)	body (religion and spiritualism): the term micro human has been used for man, and macro human for the world as a human is part of the world	geography (Ordered Life in Individual Shtetlach, Towns and Cities)
centred perspectives (ICT; individualism and human security)	beings (Sci-fi)	systems (microeconomic theory; financial planning)
capital (Public Administration, Industry & Organizational psychology; strategy & organization theory)	knowledge (spiritualism and mind and faculty of reasoning)	processes (change management)
movements (body/motion detection (sensory computation)	activities (supply-chain management)	agency (dualism, Theory of Structuration)
mobility patterns (indoor human behaviour)	network formation (wireless technology)	actions (Functional-Structural approach)
thermal comfort sensing: HTCS (Building Physics)	environments (personal security studies)	settlements (natural sciences, livestock & farming, human ecology, human settlement science)
performance (user-centred design)	agency (system interactions)	communities (educational studies; micro human communities are built by teachers with the special interests of learners in mind?)
interactive interface design (3D printing: wireless-communication infrastructure and portable personal communication tools)	operation (information behaviour and theory)	resources and resource management and development (HR/banking/business/workforce)
variables (statistics and psychometrics)	reproductive cloning (stem cell research, law)	technology (production Economics)
organs/genome (bio-material sciences; genetics)	circulatory system (extreme learning)	relations (ethics and journalism)

(Continued)

Table 1.1 (Continued)

Micro	Human	Silos
orientation (immigrant worker studies; advocates for power and control to each individual so that they can overcome problems which occur in the implementation of community development programs)	postures (artificial intelligence; machine learning)	relationships (foreign policy)
life (dance therapy)	will and ability (competitive intelligence)	services (Non-profit/service-learning)
impact (actuarial modelling)	conduct (spiritualism; orthodoxy of belief, knowledge, and orthopraxis of Action)	attributes (social networking: activity and social ability)
	level (vs macro cosmic)	rights (conflict resolution)
Prototype (Electroencephalography and clinical Neurophysiology)	sensors (microprocessor architecture)	societies (cross-cultural management)
	complexities (Order and Disorder: Anthropological Perspectives)	contexts (ethnomethodology and structuralism)
	cosmos (Consciousness: Integrating Eastern and Western Perspectives)	development (UN organizations; national development and economic planning)
		welfare (internal social; Human Systems Management)
		decisions (Population dynamics & development)
		scale (gender, place and culture)
		dynamics (political reasoning; human rights)
		factors (macro rivalrous competition; TMT-Top Management Team)
		ties (transcendental and hermeneutic civilizations)
		energies (off-chain reactions; Consumer Revolution: Tipping the Balance of Power)
		actors (Management; Scrum in a business development organization)
		objective levels (dispute resolution)
		problems (Defence Modernization, Secret Deals, and Strategy of Nations)

Independent of the discoveries the editors made through the various theoretical and field explorations in the chapters, this is a formative milestone of the MHE journey, which tagged Labour as the pivotal or transitional actor between Work and Action. This enabled the editors to use the micro-human fields of research thematized in Figure 1.1 and multidisciplinary micro-human notions listed in Table 1.1 to divide sections (A to D objectives) and establish chapter sequence as follows.

1.4.1 Section

a. Emerging insights from innate human improvizations
b. Rethinking inclusive redevelopments as a rebuilding process
c. Understanding "self-work/labour/action" coping concepts
d. Synthesizing isolated/interrelated "self-work/labour/action" for socio-economic outcomes

1.4.2 Emerging Insights from Innate Human Improvizations

Micro-responses to Disasters: The Roles of Ritual draws insights from longitudinal ethnographical work by Pamela J. Stewart (Strathern) and Andrew J. Strathern. This chapter's critical insights stem from the explosive yet emotive engagement with people and their reactive production of memorials. Extrapolating on Strathern and Strathern's previous studies, this chapter discusses the expansion of evolving innovative ritual practices that express individual feelings triggered by disasters. The narrative establishes disasters as events that are eventually marked by some forms of memorials via "structured time". According to the authors, the "lest we forget" spiritualization process through mass media sensationalization is another phenomenon that triggers micro-variations of self-expression of grief. Also, the monumentalization of such grief-associated memory through object spiritualization and the psychophysiological process of that spiritualization of objects and disaster memories reveals a series of micro-human healing and reconciliation efforts. Micro-acts imbued in Traditional Ecological Knowledge (TEK) revealed through discursive ethnographical and anthropological cases make this chapter different from numerous similar reviews on tacit knowledge under disaster conditions. Drawn on senses of community cohesion came together as a memory recitation of a tragic individual event, the authors conclude discernible "ritual density" or "condensed ritual activity". How disaster responses evolve from spontaneous individual elements into event clusters and operate within cultural parameters discussed in this chapter demonstrates material manifestations of MHE.

Silva, Subasinghe, and Ballinger also scrutinize self-responses through material manifestations in the aftermath of a disaster. However, they add another dimension: people and professionals conflict in producing the post-disaster place. Methodologically, this chapter takes a different route. Unlike Strathern's prolonged engagement with people and their self-made monuments, this chapter relies on time-specific data on user-initiated changes to rehousing. Here, the material manifestation is the individual abode: home in the socio-physical environment.

Closing on user-initiated changes to rehousing designs, authors draw on insights from misalignments between architectural outcomes and user expectations. Their critical insights come from a detailed decoding of mishaps in architectural designs for underserved groups who have already been caught between cultural and contextual polarities. The Indian Ocean tsunami in 2004 rehousing projects in coastal Sri Lanka reveals a few mismatched expectations manifested in changes inhabitants made. People's efforts to survive their lives and livelihoods in houses designed by professionals denote dissonance in the designs. The authors' interest in finding meaningful user-initiated home extensions reveals a distinct divide between human efforts and professional agency. Some of these user-initiated extensions are rather deliberate, suggesting a rally of reactions against the inflexibility of architectural designs. It signals an ongoing process of user reactions to rehousing designs. The authors reveal a connection between the degree of practical and symbolic improvements by inhabitants and the degree of freedom offered for such improvements in rehousing designs. The case studies in this chapter examine user-initiated incremental improvements and decode cultural and contextual insights for architectural decision-making. This chapter concludes with a missing human effort criterion overlooked in the rehousing real estate approach: rehousing residents as "thought providers" in an "incremental" route to post-disaster redevelopment.

Holistic recovery is a reduction of future risks. What is critical to reduction is positioning people to do what they do best: reaction. Reaction management is a self-empowered process that offers valuable insights into micro-human inputs. Pooyan and Hokugo's chapter discusses MHEs distilled from the Great East Japan Earthquake and Tsunami in 2011. They ask how local communities act to save lives, self-help, and protect themselves against future hazards. What factors motivate or prevent them from taking post-event actions and initiatives? The authors identify microhuman initiatives as an influential variable in risk reduction and disaster preparedness as they influence the overall disaster management process outcomes. The looming question here is how to coordinate a multitude of complex administrative, social, and economic factors to enable MHEs' effectiveness. Hence, the evaluation of disincentives is as crucial as incentives at the micro level and is equally critical to streamlining MHEs to deliver rapid recovery at a sustainable cost. There, the authors ascertain micro-human roles in rebuilding programmes like Build Back Better through a global agenda such as the UN's Sendai Framework for Disaster Risk Reduction. In order to situate the reader in the context and culture, the authors let the readers immerse themselves in the harsh realities of unforeseen circumstances people faced: population loss, structural and infrastructural demolition, economic decline, and environmental degradation. Utilizing specific dimensions and components of Build Back Better makes it easier for readers to assess the impact of micro-human efforts. The MHE improvizations, heard in the voices of local authorities, community organizations' leaders, and volunteer groups, demonstrate micro-level-made, self-formed procedures. According to Pooyan and Hokugo, post-event could trigger self-recovery with or without grand schemes like BBB in other words, the affected are not recipients waiting to be rescued.

1.4.3   Rethinking Inclusive Redevelopments as a Rebuilding Process

Community Disaster Resilience and Elderly Women is a revisit to ageism in post-disaster conditions that has not been obtained for resilience. Nilgün Okay and Ebru Inal Önal interrogate an emerging gap in the role of older women in building community disaster capacity. Although there is no shortage of research on the general vulnerability of women and children, the authors direct the readers' attention to younger seniors aged between 65 and 75 who were more visible and independent due to their health and financial security. The authors enable rethinking this particular vulnerability from an alternative paradigm of resilience: their ability to build resilience via this group's experience, endurance and self-emancipation. Through small-scale, individual efforts unique to this age group, this study shows how self-help, self-preparedness, and self-resilience mechanisms can impact building resilience. Okay and Önal obtained these coping abilities to demonstrate how they can bolster individual and community resilience. In this chapter, post-disaster recovery is not a particular phase of disaster management but rather an integrated process of building up the community's readiness, enhancing social connections and assets, and engaging them in disaster risk reduction efforts towards resilience. Essentializing capacity building of the vulnerable, this chapter further emphasizes the changing demographic composition of the populations that could potentially shape disaster recovery policies. As this demographic group is an indispensable part of human instrumentation, it suggests rethinking rebuilding policies to accommodate the ageing population. Hence, this chapter highlights the essentiality of advancing inclusive emergency services to support this gender and age group. The authors suggest a dual approach to rebuilding communities by integrating this productive population through optimizing existing resources and a comprehensive disaster risk reduction and adaptation plan.

1.4.4   Understanding "Self-work/Labour/Action" Coping Concepts

Focusing on the location, *Micro Human Efforts in the post-disaster rebuilding of communities in Japan* discusses a three-step coping process from the occurrence of a disaster to recovery. According to Tomiyasu, Isagawa, Suzawa and Tsubouchi, this three-step geospatial process unpacks a transitional nature of displacement. In a country where major natural disasters are frequent, familiar, and perhaps welcomed, this transitional setting leverages a unique point of view for MHE. Hence, the chapter is a sense-making of associated self-efforts, making recovery a singular reality channelled through the government. The chapter narrates ways in which coping concepts materialize through MHE-related transitions from one phase to the other and within each phase. According to the authors, while step one signals a micro (selective) communication process, a yearning to extend self-related mechanisms to the meso level, step two signals people's behaviour during the evacuation from the disaster to evacuation shelters. Through a case study analysis, this step is an attempt to understand people's refusal to respond to early warning. The authors note people's refusal to evacuate even after hearing the tsunami warning and the call for evacuation by the local government. The authors direct the readers' attention to the number of people who evacuated immediately after being urged to do so by neighbours or family members. Noticed among neighbour behaviours, this adds another layer to micro-communication where timely evacuation was responsive and collective. While in emergency shelters where close neighbours meet for a neighbourhood talk over a cup of green tea, sharing one's life brings a culturally understood communal communication system. This chapter asserts a location-based distinction on rebuilding, which requires communication as a means of sharing time, place, and experiences based on customs and culture. The third step decodes the reconstruction of life in public disaster housing or rebuilt homes. This step involves community-based relocation from temporary to public housing in a neighbouring area. It decolonizes community-based relocation practised in Japanese culture, which reduces relocation effects as a result of friends from the temporary shelters talking to each other. The sustained relationships at the temporary shelter extended beyond the physical boundaries towards a more mobile communication system. This chapter highlights a lesser-known mode of micro-communication that even local participants may be unaware of.

Focusing on female activism, Nakashima's chapter, *Building a New Community in the Emergency Temporary Housing,* uncovers another aspect of displacement. Through women-led efforts highlighted in this chapter, the author asserts gender-based leadership, which adds and extends the discourse of the three-stepped, location-based transitional displacement discoursed in Tomiyasu, Isagawa, Suzawa, and Tsubouchi chapter. It deepens the understanding of women taking charge of establishing a support network while living in tight, temporary and transitional conditions. Based on a study of transitional housing, this chapter narrates a process of women stepping into enabling group activities. Although this appears purely for pragmatic purposes of distributing support supplies, organizing volunteers, and running events in the community hall, it had deeper desires. Beyond the urgent necessities, the deeper desires included women exploiting women's specific coping strategies to help families. This coping mechanism established a system of self-help that had a positive influence on gender, child-rearing, and unemployment issues. According to the author, women taking different roles in support systems filled specific assistance needed at various stages of displacement. This chapter demonstrates women's resilience in adapting to the changes in each role after establishing formal connections with designated officials.

1.4.5 Synthesizing Isolated/Interrelated "Self-work/Labour/Action" for Socio-economic Outcomes

If people making efforts to do what is necessary as a response to disasters are not acknowledged, they might not keep doing it. Under relief providers' watchful eyes, they might either wait for instructions or isolate their efforts from the recovery process; thus, there is a need to synthesize at least visible MHE with the process. Kaluarachchi, Thayaparan, and Mendis identified a knowledge gap in how women navigate post-disaster challenges in South Asia. They highlight livelihood catalysts when they are largely overlooked. Their chapter Enhancing Micro-Human Efforts through Livelihood Assistance for Women in Post-Disaster Recovery in Sri Lanka synthesizes livelihood empowerment with meaningful inclusivity. It reports on a missing piece of the recovery repertoire of a vulnerable group: livelihood-related microhuman efforts of women. Given that post-disaster settings provide a rather productive podium to redefine development, the well-founded premise here is that inclusive livelihood assistance is not enough. Although it can even be grounds for women to negotiate fair opportunities, inclusivity without responsivity is perhaps unhelpful. The type of livelihood assistance authors discuss here is not women as passive recipients but active participants who know the process that prevents them from using the scarce assistance. Thus, the active participation via microhuman efforts impacts the economic resilience of family and familial networks. This chapter is narrated through the post-disaster gender inclusion studies and theories on grand schemes like Build Back Better. Then, the stories of the Sri Lankan women are used to obtain the cultural and contextual nuances and variations. This is where the chapter reveals a dissonance between external assistance and system resistance to receive women's responses. The practicalities of using the assistance to achieve their intended objectives were muddled within the assistance system itself; there needed to be an internal mechanism to receive and respond to constraints faced by these recipients. Unless carefully curated, micro-human efforts of vulnerable groups could easily be discouraged and disappear into the unknown.

Kevin Kupietz's chapter "The Creation of Self-resiliency through Neighbours Helping Neighbours: An Example of Micro-Human Efforts in Disasters", is rethinking human skills and time in hours of desperation. It synthesizes MHEs associated with disaster recovery volunteerism on self-enrolled training of first responders. This chapter is built on volunteerism in the absence of enough professional responders to rescue masses of victims. Through the lens of volunteerism, the author projects the increasing frequency and severity of disasters onto self-enrolment in first-responder training programmes. It flags a range of "individuals" through their usefulness as volunteers. Kupietz sees self-driven motives in individuals, families, and communities as "individual" because of their self-goodness or what is generally identified in literature as personal goodness. The dual perspective is that (a) more people threatened by disasters receive heightened attention to people's involvement, and (b) local efforts increase as disasters are geospatially local. The self-initiated aspect of human efforts is through individuals in a communal system to examine and embrace the available resources that are locally available. The core to Kupietz's rethinking of volunteerism is unaddressed challenges in volunteerism because it can worsen the disaster for the affected. As volunteers come with their unique set of challenges, through training and recognition, making average citizens rise to the occasion is the reframed volunteerism portrayed in this chapter. Unaddressed, these challenges from volunteer efforts can make the situation worse. Through a detailed study, this chapter rethinks volunteerism as a streamlined system and a plan in place. Another dimension of volunteerism in this chapter narrates trained individuals teaching preparedness to individuals along with mitigation, response, and recovery. Using Federal emergency Management Agency, USA (FEMA) as an example of a trained group, Kupietz discusses enabling a group like Community Emergency Response Teams (CERT) to take charge (streamlining) of immediate emergency response. According to the author, such streamlining can effectively embed the MHE, prevent it from driving in different directions, and focus on defined tasks. The realistic expectation is here to help communities to take a step towards resilience rather than achieve resilience. Thus, the chapter makes a compelling case for individuals to invest their MHE efforts in a coordinated way to ensure safer lives and environments against future disasters. This chapter teaches us how to utilize microhuman efforts in volunteerism as they represent safe and efficient ways.

Beyond "Vita Activa", self-governance has been recognized as a coping mechanism capable of absorbing the impact of complex challenges such as disaster stress. A higher degree of self-governance in individual capacities has been noticed in community resilience under disaster stress (Ostram, 1999; Jacob, 1961). In *Self-Governance as Agency in Post-Disaster Recovery,* Oloruntoba and Asare-Doku assert that the institutional disaster recovery process often overlooks the vital role of self-governance despite its readiness to serve. The authors sort self-governance into several decipherable traits such as self-reorientation, self-reorganization, and utilization of peoples' resources and abilities to rebuild their lives and communities. According to the authors, having or not having these characteristics could potentially decide the winners and victims under disaster stress. Via an evidence-based approach, this chapter systematically establishes self-governance among victims as positive psychology. The authors interrogate how individuals in a community acquire positive psychology and deploy it as a proper coping strategy. They argue that faith-induced hope and optimism in religious communities have an edge in enabling MHE. However, MHE should leverage individuals' pre-existing motivational and psychological bearings and resources to ensure timely recovery and influence resilience. The criticality of understanding challenges surrounding cultural and contextual modifiers of MHE is that they can make or break MHE's resourcefulness. This chapter's contribution to MHE is that it substantiates self-governance as one of many internal resources that individuals possess that they themselves need to be fully aware of.

The concluding comments by Mazumdar and Subasinghe synthesize resonating themes from the chapters demonstrating the poverty of impact case studies on micro-human aspects in disaster discourse. Based on the cultural and contextual variations in the chapters, the comments conclude an MHE manifesto, a mandatory step towards building resilience. This manifesto will pave the way to more focused studies to identify specific MHEs strategic to each step of the resilience-building process – MHE more as a pulse check rather than a remedial reaction after each disaster. The conclusion further offers a set of recommendations to mainstream disaster resilience and the MHE nexus for both theory and practice. The six traits of "disaster instinct" proposed earlier have been reformulated into the following sequence of resilience building.

a. *Dealing*: Beyond returning to normality, people use MHE to face fears, tackle the unexpected, and deal with the increasing intensity of disasters.
b. *Coping*: While dealing with the unexpected, people conduct culturally and contextually cultivated surveillance systems to contain and recalibrate psychophysiological damage. They further humanize do-gooder rebuilding

approaches that typically provide marginal allowances for numerous diversities, which is critical to human recovery systems.

c. *Adjusting*: When mastering coping, people spontaneously adjust to changed conditions through response and reaction on a timeline of their own, even without external assistance.

d. *Rebuilding*: In addition to top-down grand schemes like Build Back Better, people develop alternative altruism, such as MHE, by adjusting to the newly formed status quo.

e. *Resilience*: MHE is the missing piece that can tailor both culturally and contextually the grand scheme, such as Build Back Better, to target long-term sustainability-resilience.

References

Burr, V., & Dick, P. (2021). A social constructionist critique of positive psychology. In T. Teo (Ed.), The Routledge international handbook of theoretical and philosophical psychology: Critiques, problems, and alternatives to psychological ideas (pp. 151–169). Routledge.

Chia, R. and McKay, B. (2007) 'Post-Processual Challenges for the Emerging Strategy-as-Practice Perspective: Discovering Strategy in the Logic of Practice', Human Relations 60(1): 217–42.

Choudhary, S., Memon, N. Z., & Mishra, K. (2020). Examining the influence of human capital on employees' innovative work behaviour: A moderated serial mediation model. *South Asian Journal of Human Resources Management, 7*(2), 189–213.

Clinton, W.J. (2006), Lessons Learned from Tsunami Recovery: Key Propositions for Building Back Better, United Nations Secretary-General's Special Envoy for Tsunami Recovery, United Nations, New York.

Guba, E. G., & Lincoln, Y. S. (1985). Naturalistic Inquiry. Thousand Oaks, Calif, Sage.

Han, B. C. (2023). *Vita contemplativa: In praise of inactivity*. John Wiley & Sons.

Jacobs, J. (1961). *The death and life of Great American Cities*. Random House.

Marom, N., & Shlomo, O. (2022). Green, gray, glocal: Governing urban resilience in the Tel Aviv metropolitan region. *Urban Geography, 43*, 1–24.

Ostrom, E. (1999). Social capital: A fad or a fundamental concept? In D. G. Partha & S. Ismail (Eds.), *Social capital: A multifaceted perspective* (pp. 172–214). The International Bank for Reconstruction and Development/THE WORLD BANK.

Parekh, B. (1981). The vita activa and the vita contemplativa. In Hannah Arendt (Eds.),*and the search for a new political philosophy* (pp. 103–130). Palgrave Macmillan UK.

Riebschleger, J., & Pierce, B. J. (2018). Rural child welfare practice: Stories from the field. Oxford University Press.

Ritzer, G. (1991). *Metatheorizing in sociology*. D.C. Heath.

Strandh, V., & Eklund, N. (2018). Emergent groups in disaster research: Varieties of scientific observation over time and across studies of nine natural disasters. *Journal of Contingencies and Crisis Management, 26*(3), 329–337.

Subasinghe, C. (2013). Spatial confrontations: Abandonment of self-labor in transitional sheltering after a natural disaster. *International Journal of Disaster Risk Reduction, 6*, 78–86.

Subasinghe, C. T., and Miranda, V. (2007). *Dependency syndrome revisited: Post-tsunami recovery in transitional shelters*. Paper presented at the International Conference on Sustainable Urbanism, Texas A & M University, College Station, TX.

Subasinghe, C., Sutrisna, M., & Olatunji, O. (2021). Multidisciplinary perspectives of micro human efforts in post-disaster recovery. *International Journal of Mass Emergencies & Disasters, 39*(1), 1–10. https://doi.org/10.1177/028072702103900101

Zdravković, L. (2021). The concept of emancipation as political action (marx, arendt, rancière). Filozofski vestnik, 42(1).

Section I

Emerging Insights from Innate Human Improvizations

2 Micro-responses to Disasters

The Roles of Ritual

Pamela J. Stewart and Andrew J. Strathern

Disasters elicit a range of emergency responses as methods of short-term or longer-term coping and recovery from their effects. Among these responses, ritual plays a part, and it is on this theme that we concentrate in the present paper (see, for example, Riboli et al, 2021). We have discussed ritual in many of our prior publications (Stewart and Strathern 2014a, 2014b, 2015, 2016a, 2016b, 2021a; Strathern and Stewart 1999, 2007). Here, we take up the significance of ritual practices in processes of response to and recovery from stressful results of disasters that impact human interrelationships and test capacities related to resilience. We give examples of spontaneous and often small-scale ritualized actions, both individual and communal, that aid people in their attempts to cope with difficulties arising from the physical and emotional outcomes of disasters, involving the sudden emergence of disorder, perhaps unprecedented, and the problems of recreating order in people's lives. We ask here, what is the role of ritual in moving sufferers from one stage to another in disasters? Ritual in general functions as a way of bringing people together, and this function is enhanced in situations of stress and danger.

We draw here on extensive work on Disaster Ritual in a pivotal volume co-authored by Professor Paul Post and collaborators at the University of Tilburg in the Netherlands (Post et al, 2003), focusing primarily on disasters in the Netherlands between 1990 and 2001. The authors define a special arena of interest to them in terms of "ritual density" or "condensed ritual activity" based on senses of community identity and cohesion (loc. cit., p 54). Interest here centres on emerging ritual repertoires based on cultural forms of expectations, such as "floral tributes, candles, stuffed toys, notes of condolence, and drawings" (p. 56). Another, related category is the whole ritual repertoire that grows up around the death of people in disasters centred on grief and mourning, particularly "the large context of innovation and self-chosen ritual surrounding dying and death" (p 55). Taken together, these remarks indicate that deaths caused by disasters trigger an expansion of ritual innovative practices that give vent to individual feelings. The drive in these practices, however, is to establish memorials in which innovations become sedimented into repeated performances at ritualized times marking the disasters themselves as events. Memorials take the form of "lest we forget" iterations, and so the unique event is placed back into "structured time", the calendrical marking of happenings and the stirring of emotions that preserve a sense of the event and its ritual transformation into a perennial memorialization. Reviewing the very detailed and

DOI: 10.4324/9781003615903-3

careful descriptions of disaster events in the volume edited by Paul Post and his colleagues, one can see that responses to disasters make up chains of activity. The assemblage of such chains of cultural items constitutes a kind of semantic brico- lage creatively selected by participants. From the point of view of understand- ing how responses to disaster build up from spontaneous individual elements into event clusters, it is important to see choice operating within cultural parameters. The outcome of a number of spontaneous expressions of grief and memory is often the translation of feelings into a material form such as a plaque or a monument. A spontaneous lighting of a candle may morph into a formal number of candles, one for each victim of a disaster. A monument may take various forms. In one case we ourselves know from Glen Isla in Angus County in Scotland, the mother of a youth who had died from a drug overdose planted a sapling on his grave site, and in sub- sequent years it grew to be a medium-sized tree. Although the mother did not con- tinue to visit the site so often, the tree itself came to be the objectified witness of the relationship, being visible across a church cemetery wall from the roadside where people regularly passed by. A comparable example indicates how ritual responses can be multiplied, thus being made formal and longer lasting. In this case, fol- lowing an outbreak of Legionnaires' disease resulting in deaths, mourners for the dead planted 28 trees with bushes marking persons still ill. These plants were then transformed into a park, and finally a "basalt monument" (2003, p 61), in the shape of a book "with a memorial text" and a poem directed to the dead, was set in place.

These kinds of features show similarities among numbers of kinds of disasters, whether arising from lethal disasters caused by environmental events or from one- time accidents, such as airline crashes, or more broadly travel accidents. Because all disasters, of whatever kind, usually involve deaths and the sense of grief that goes with these, mourning processes are an integral part of disaster responses. Moreover, accidents may result from environmental events and produce further environmental consequences, so the commonalities are shown here, but there are different timescales of responses and suffering that are at work. Also, memories may work differently in different kinds of disasters and how they affect people's sensibilities.

Common features in many cases of disasters include flowers, processions, visit- ing dignitaries, flags lowered to half mast, and moments of silence, all these ele- ments contributing to an overall process of ritualization. Another feature is the making of contacts with groups that have suffered comparable catastrophes (Post et al., p 63). And a further point of note is how media outlets amplify the impacts of a disaster, ensuring that expressions of grief can be broadcast widely and at the same time individual micro-variations of expression can be accommodated. These then are transmuted into formal memorials. Individuals who have suffered and died in support of some heroic cause are transformed into sacred characters by a gradual process of building them up, ritual piece by piece, in an escalating flow of apprecia- tion. Silent marches express immediate grief. Flower tributes express continuing grief and respect, reminding viewers of the role of flowers as tributes at funerals and gravesites. Ringing church bells inform parishioners of the role of the Christian church. Linkages are made among the symbols deployed, as when candles from a disaster memorial church service are carried to a café at the actual site of the disaster (p 69). A particular symbol may be re-deployed over various categories of disastrous events. Post et al. also cite in this context silent marches or processions (p.71). They also note the symbolism attached to the use of the colour white as a marker of mourning and/or of the innocence of the victim in cases of death by violence. Processions usually start from a public square and go on to the site of the disaster, where those who have died in the disaster receive their commemoration (p. 76). The act of procession heightens the sense of solidarity in the face of trouble, with people coming together after a grievous loss (p. 77). Post et al. comment at the end of their survey of Dutch disaster rituals (p. 77) that collective acts expressing compassion are ritual efforts to create or restore communal spirit. Each ritual item, starting as an individual choice, becomes followed into a broader collective panorama, finally leaving some historical markers of the death in focus (Post et al, 2003, p 86), on the construction of a monument at the site of an air crash in which many people of different ethnicities died. Symbols are gradually created, piece by piece, around a disaster itself. In one case (the Bijlmer air crash) it was decided that a tree which stood at the site and had escaped destruction should be given ritual centrality, and a whole memorial park grew up around this decision (Nugteren in Post et al, 2003, p 86). We are not told what type of tree this was, but we learn why it was accorded ritual centrality, having become a focus of spontaneous interest. It was named "the tree that witnessed everything", for it "remained standing at the scene of the disaster" (p. 86). We see in this way how a material entity is appropriated as ritually significant, undoubtedly because in Mary Douglas' terms, it is seen as a "natural symbol" (Douglas 1970) and in Victor Turner's terms, it is "multivocal", resonating with experience in multiple ways (Turner 1967). We highlight this example of the bricolage of symbol-making, because it shows that micro-decisions can over time build up to macro-results, in this case the development of a whole ceremonial park around a disaster site. This kind of ritual build-up may also be triggered by reactions of particular groups or individuals, depending on their experience of suffering and closeness to the event of the disaster, notably when people are reacting to environmental disasters. Also, many specific ritual elements can be brought to bear, and among these there is an overall message, that "love is stronger than death. Love never passes away" (from a poem read by a humanist at a disaster memorial, p 104). Each small ritual act leads up to projecting a synthetic image of a particular ethos that pervades the whole ritual assemblage. In this way micro-acts are combined into a sense of an overall purpose or theme that provides a macro-framework for action. Environmental disasters tend to produce the longest lasting and intense responses because of the challenges of reconstruction that they generate. Rituals in general provide a means of solace for the sufferers during this process, helping people to calibrate progress in recovery from the events of the disaster. This issue of recovery operates at many levels from individuals up to national contexts. Both innovative and newly fashioned rituals may be called into play as a part of overall responses here. Initial ritual actions are often followed by repeated commemorations keeping alive memories and sacralizing the roles of victims. Again, this process is likely to be intensified when deaths have occurred, especially if persons have died as a result of the events. Post-disaster commemorative events not only constitute ways of ensuring that events are memorized, but also they are a significant part of the recovery from the trauma of disruption of living patterns.

We venture to suggest that this ritual pattern is widespread and extends to pragmatic sequences of action not explicitly linked to rituals but trending in the direction of instilling hope and endurance among those most affected by disasters. Ritual and other practices form an ensemble in which spontaneous individual acts are built into formal ritual assemblages of factions. We will take some examples from our own areas of fieldwork to explore this point further.

Our basic interpretive standing here is that many indigenous rituals are at heart influenced by ecological circumstances and can be seen as adaptive responses to ecological crises. Initial responses are spontaneous, building up into major efforts once resources are mobilized. It is in the spontaneous arena that micro-efforts can be discerned, leading to macro-policies and actions aimed at recapturing positive community spirit. Spontaneous actions are the source and product of resilience in responses to the difficult circumstances of lives. The ritual character of such responses is especially clear in the cases examined by Paul Post and his many colleagues, because the disasters they studied were in the main travel accidents resulting in deaths and the expressions of mourning that followed these (Post et al, 2003). The same patterns of response, by and large, would occur after acts of violence/terror challenging senses of order in society and also providing a violent "other" against whom emotional stances of blaming can be generated. With environmental disasters, blame can be laid on human agents as implicated in causing the disaster, either directly by material actions or indirectly by provoking tutelary spirits of the landscape with taboo forms of behaviour.

Regardless of differences between these cases, a single pattern of response is found on the front of ritual, beginning with small, individual spontaneous actions and ending with larger-scale collective actions aimed at re-establishing harmony in communal and cosmological terms. Micro-contexts point towards macro ones, whether or not this point of completeness is eventually met or not.

We will now illustrate this argument by adding some materials from Papua New Guinea (PNG) and also Japan and Taiwan, all places where we have carried out fieldwork. We choose first two major ritual complexes from the PNG Highlands, the Melpa speakers of Mount Hagen and the Duna of Hela Province (see, for example, Stewart and Strathern 2002; Strathern and Stewart 1999). We have studied these ritual complexes in some detail over periods of years.

Among Melpa speakers, there was a prestigious circulating ceremonial practice known as the Female Spirit festival (*Amb Kor* or *Kor Ngenap*). The festival was elaborate and the required preparations for it were very detailed. An essential starting point for the whole complex was an act of discovery. The Spirit revealed herself to a group leader in the form of a special stone, elongated or round in shape. The event of finding the stone was referred to by assigning agency to the Spirit in the stone. "My stone/spirit comes to me" is the expression in the Melpa language (*nanga kor e na-kin onom*). The Spirit announces herself to the leader, thereby pointing the way to a whole complex of activities. It is a tiny beginning, a micro-effort between stone and leader, triggering the whole process. After a climactic dance embodying the Spirit and her powers, a number of sacred stones held to be homes of the Spirit are collected for the ritually built houses in seclusion away from uninitiated males, and these are buried secretly in the earth, awaiting a time when the practice is renewed in response to a perceived ecological need. The most significant point to note here is that failure of crops, damaging storms, and sickness in the group of the leader may all be invoked as a catalyst for the renewal of the Spirit's power to confer fertility and well-being on her worshippers. The finding of a spirit stone is like a micro-effort at renewal, leading up to the macro-level of a celebratory ritual marked by special ritual houses and a striking ritual dance by pairs of male celebrants wearing the white head-net that is appropriate for the honouring of the Spirit. All the sequences of preparation for the final festival begin with small actions like finding the spirit stones that are considered necessary for the larger enterprises. A river eel has to be captured from a distant place; a tall sapling must be set up at the entrance to the secret ritual site, and pieces of cooked pig meat have to be put in post holes of the fence at the edge of the site. All these small actions are to be performed at the proper time.

The closest parallel to the Female Spirit complex is found among the Duna speakers of Hela Province, out of the Lake Kopiago government station in the Aluni Valley. These Duna groups had a practice known as *rindi kiniya*, healing the ground, entered into when there were environmental difficulties: flooding, drought, crop failure, sickness, or death of children; all these could trigger plans to perform the main healing ritual. The starting point would always be some small action seen as a trigger or signal for a bigger sequence. Fundamentally, these actions were signs of an ecological disturbance that had to be rectified by ritual means. Practical actions in response to environmental conditions would be pursued, but always in conjunction with what we may call meta-practical efforts cast in the form of rituals. The marking of a pig for use in the healing ritual would be followed by more such markings and eventually lead to a large-scale sacrifice.

The full *rindi kiniya* cycle was no longer performed after conversion to Christianity in the 1960s onward, but one striking ritual occasion demonstrated the spontaneous, creative beginnings of a new phase of collaboration between traditional and introduced ways of responding to an environmental problem. On one occasion among the Duna of the Aluni Valley, a forest fire, started inadvertently by youths, destroyed large stands of trees, spoiling areas important for hunting and also for traditional places of secondary burial with associated ritually important stones considered to be the abode of ancestral spirits. Over time, the forest would naturally regenerate, but in the short and medium terms, a response was needed. To this end people brought pigs and vegetables to a forest clearing. There they ceremonially killed the pigs and prepared earth ovens for cooking the food, laying out the sides of pork before cutting them into smaller pieces ready for complete sharing. Before the act of consumption, they brought together traditional leaders to make speeches to the ancestors, apologizing for the destruction of forest life caused by the fire, and prayers were made by Christian pastors of the same group asking for God's blessing and favourable attention to their needs as they dealt with this environmental issue. The agreement to have traditional and Christian speakers combine together for the occasion was innovative and spontaneous, a small change in practices that represented a big change in overall cosmology and adaptation to historical events. Processes and events of this kind tend to be undertaken by people whenever they encounter problems in subsistence practices or unfavourable signs of spirit disturbance. Indeed, there is a seamless set of practices that may be set in hand involving ritual and other practical procedures whenever ecological well-being is at stake. In Pangia in the Southern Highlands Province of Papua New Guinea, as observed in the early 1970s, elaborate ritual performances were set in hand involving pig sacrifices and dancing in finery. Seasonal shortages of food crops, however, also happened, and gave rise to emergency pig-killings as efforts both to regain support from the spirits and to supplement nutrition in the face of shortages of valued forms of meat.

In our studies of responses to disasters in parts of Japan and Taiwan, we have observed comparable patterns of response to stressful change. In Japan, a major environmental disaster was experienced in a combined earthquake and tsunami flood that severely damaged a whole seaboard area, destroying buildings and homes and taking many lives, notably in the Sendai area (Stewart and Strathern 2016b, 2018). Among other effects of the disaster was the loss of workshops of artists in the area. After returning to their workshops some artists began making a new version of a special kind of sculpture, wooden statues of a type of female doll known as *kokeshi*, with heads that can be swivelled around to look in different directions. The *kokeshi* dolls carried a special resonance after the disaster, imagined as young females adrift in the floodwater. One artist decided to make an innovation by depicting the *kokeshi* with a face looking upward to the sky as a symbol of hope for the future [we purchased one of these dolls and have it in our collection]. The craftsperson's decision was a micro-effort for recovery from the disaster, and the new type of *kokeshi* enhanced the popularity of these dolls. The dolls became imbued with a form of spirituality by this means. Here, we see the importance of ritual in creating and strengthening of hope in people who are suffering or have suffered from the effects of environmental disasters. Ritual is not just symbolic here, it in fact is a vital part of practical means of coping with challenges posed by disasters.

In Taiwan, there is a historical division between the indigenous groups of people and incomers from China. Environmental disasters affect all categories of people but can disproportionally impact indigenous groups, living in rural environments where storms and floods can destroy their habitats [We have conducted research in Taiwan for many years, (Stewart and Strathern 2014b)]. Such was the case when a typhoon named Typhoon Morakot caused severe damage to local communities and their gardens in mountainous riverine locations in 2009. In at least one case, a landslide buried a whole village of people. In other cases, parts of village land were swept away. Ritual responses were to the fore in dealing with these events. Kinsfolk of villagers buried in the landslides set up arrangements with local ritual experts to act as interlocutors with the spirits of the dead and to help them find their way to an afterlife. This was an innovative act, generated out of a unique need. At a later phase, a formal memorial site was set up with stone pillars for each sub-group in the village and names of individuals marked on surfaces in a memorial area, and finally, a museum was built, financed by the government, to record and honour the cultural legacy of those lost in the disaster. The formal rituals were undertaken after impromptu expressions of grief by kinsfolk seeking relief from the fact that no bodies could be recovered from the landslide area.

In cases where village territory was lost but families and individuals survived, these survivors were moved into complexes of resettlement areas, and international charitable institutions built houses for them in introduced styles, with standard designs for each house. Cultural innovation came into play after this fact because local artists made paintings adorning the walls of the houses, and each group or sub-group drew on its own traditions to create these often colourful, designs. One person or family would do this, and others followed. A traditional chief's residence was often particularly adorned in this way. Thus, the indigenous people recreated a sense of themselves in the face of alienation and enforced resettlement.

Taken broadly, all these examples illuminate the capacities for resilience that people exhibit in the face of difficulties, and these capacities are shown clearly in ritual contexts; not only ritual contexts, of course, in multitudes of very pragmatic ways also, as when a group of Taiwanese indigenous families banded together under their female chief after being forced from their native domain and gathered logs propelled by flood from the hills into their yards and used these to create art forms sold to tourists. The government claimed these logs, but the people said the logs had washed up on their land, so they could use them. Resilience indeed! And all derived from one innovative idea of the female chief.

Overall, it is clear that the responses of indigenous people to environmental disasters are deeply influenced by cosmological ideas about the earth and the stewardship or abuse of its resources. This basic attitude of respect and consideration for the earth has two consequences. One is that in the face of disasters, numerous small efforts are made aimed at recovery. The other is that such efforts are all framed in terms of moral ideas of causation and human responsibility. Indeed, we can go further and say that the wider cosmological perceptions and interpretations of disasters influence and guide the small-scale and improvised practical efforts at recovery. In this way, new influences from outside may be facilitated. Disaster threatens the community as a whole, and recovery, or healing, requires the shared efforts of those affected by it. Involving environmental spirits as putative actors in the unfolding of events is a way of bonding together the practical and the ritual dimensions of the ways people engage in "Dealing with Disasters" (the title of the volume edited by Diana Riboli, ourselves, and Davide Torri (2021). Many of the cases described in the volume address very challenging situations faced by people, and consequently, we do not find in the volume many instances like the "success story" of the Paiwan female chief in Taitung, Taiwan. We do find that cosmology may be instrumental generally in making possible an arena of resilience in the face of difficult situations. This is made feasible because the participants in responses to disaster are political players as well as victims. We can refer back here to the Paiwan female chief. She could have traditionally held potential land rights in her own clan area, but she and her people were refugees from their interior territory, thrown up like flotsam in a new environmental context. In any case, it is most likely there could be an internal fight between groups over the rights to resources and for their disruption caused by new conflict.

One response to such situations of hardship is documented by Diana Riboli on the Batek, a small group of around 1500 individuals settled by the Malaysian government in a national park, squeezed in between large oil-palm plantations. Some 500 Batek still lead a nomadic life within the park and are vulnerable to the effects of pesticides, disease, logging of forests, and mining (Riboli 2021, p 23). The Malaysian government seeks to convert these Batek to Islam and the adoption of Malaysian culture in general. As a result, the Batek have chosen to migrate as labourers to Arab countries. The Batek, as a threatened minority enclave, understandably attribute misfortunes to the actions of outsiders (*gob*), and the effects of heavy thunderstorms and floods are traced to a supernatural being, the Lord of Thunder (*Gobar*), dwelling on high mountains or in the sky. *Gobar* is said to become angry and afflict the Batek with disasters. In 2004, following a 9.3 level earthquake in Sumatra, a huge tsunami ensued, killing over 230,000 people in a number of countries. Although this tsunami did not directly harm the Batek, a shaman among them reported a dream in which it was revealed to him that this disaster was brought about by a wrongful pollution of water by the menstrual fluids of a young Indonesian female labourer who had been ill-treated by her employer and had, in revenge, made a concoction of spells and her menstrual blood, intending it to kill the employer, an Arab in Dubai. The magical mixture tried to return to the young woman's home place in Sumatra, and when Gobar smelled it, he angrily sent the tsunami, it was said. The explanation links global and local forces together. A comparable story links the nuclear power accident at Fukushima in Japan to efforts by a Batek shaman to heal the cosmos against the effects of the accident (Riboli, loc. cit.).

Another chapter in the book, by Taj Khan Kalash, details a parallel cosmology story among the Kalasha, another minority group in Pakistan, following pre-Islamic religious notions and numbering some 4,000 people, ethnically distinct from the majority groups in Pakistan. The author refers to serious floods in 2010 and 2015 that devastated the area of the Kalasha. (As an update, this has later been followed by extensive flooding in 2022.) The Kalasha responded to the flood by interpreting it in terms of their own eco-cosmological ideas of purity and pollution (impurity). Purity is associated with males and their social domains, impurity with the female world of being, marked by a concern on the part of the males with menstruation and its powers. Ritual rules enjoin the need to separate the pure and the impure. The author comments that "maintaining this separation is important in preventing disaster" (Kalash 2021, p 105). In earlier times, such a breach of taboos was cited as the cause of small local disasters such as landslides or floods. Sacred goats were sacrificed in expiation of such infractions. Floods were likened to the flow of menstrual blood. This notion still informs Kalasha interpretations of why disastrous floods happen, attributing them to the breaking of spatial taboos connected with flows of menstrual blood (exactly parallel to the Batek idea).

In a separate way, the Kalasha also say the people should exhibit compassion towards living things, and if they do not, these beings may curse them. Such curses may also bring down floods (Kalash, p. 109). "Kalasha culture intrinsically defines naturel sites and areas as embedded with spiritual meanings and beings" (Kalash, p. 111). Such notions parallel those of many peoples around the world, including Pacific Islanders. Winter Solstice celebrations in Europe also parallel traditional ideas elsewhere, as we have discussed in the same volume where Kalash's paper is found (Stewart and Strathern 2021b). All of our examples reinforce the point of understanding the significance of Traditional Ecological Knowledge in responses to disasters, leading us to focus on adaptive cultural practices that often put together indigenous practice and government policy inputs.

Cosmological schemes do not mean that people simply accept catastrophes as inevitable. They make efforts to deal with them through sacrifices and observance of rules. The wider framework provides them with meanings for adverse events and gives them scope for handling disasters with attempts to heal the earth, as with Duna, PNG, *rindi kiniya*) discussed above in this chapter (see also Stewart and Strathern 2002).

The examples given here so far have emphasized cosmological ideas embedded in the responses of people to disasters. At a more mundane level, practical efforts based on pragmatic issues and economic needs, such as food, shelter, and hygiene, are invariably made to "cope" with the immediacies of stressful events (Stewart and Strathern 2018). Deeper cosmologies have to do with longer-term "hoping" for the future, e.g. ritually repairing transgressions and re-establishing order. In the domain of coping, we find small adaptations that provide stepping-stones to recovery and resilience. The significance of such actions is that they are generated by the people themselves without their having to rely on external agencies for help, or else they are linked to such external sources but provide their own impetus and creativity. Micro-acts of this kind also gain great significance when they are founded on established or innovative adaptive practices of a cultural kind linked to indigenous perceptions and experiences. We note that such practices emerge as Indigenous knowledge (IK) and, in particular, Traditional Ecological Knowledge (TEK), the sources out of which local adaptations to climate events can emerge. Such adaptations may be well-established; for example, methods of earth-mounding as a way of protecting plants against frost or adding plant materials to help warm and fertilize the mounds are salient techniques in horticultural practices in altitudes at 6,000 feet or more a.s.l. in Highlands New Guinea. Kinsfolk are characteristically called upon to assist with this work and also to help with emergency accommodation when needed. Sources of adaptation also belong with micro-observations of the surroundings. We came across a striking illustration of this point in the Cook Islands in the Pacific when an indigenous government officer gave an address to a cohort of students enrolled in our Study Abroad Programme at the University of Pittsburgh, in which we taught students in New Zealand, Samoa, and the Cook Islands over a number of months. The officer (Mr Charles Carlson) explained to our students that he was in charge of Emergency Management in the Prime Minister's Department, and he outlined the governmental structures that had been set up for this purpose. He went on to point out that what this hierarchical top-down model does not include is the potential input of traditional knowledge. For example, observation of the behaviour of plants may carry clues of impending changes or disasters. The double fruiting of mango trees was a case in point, where local people see this phenomenon as the tree's attempts to provide an abundance of fruit to help people stave off an impending disastrous loss of food supplies. As a general point of prime importance, Mr Carlson remarked that the government's hierarchical top-down model of disaster responses should be turned the other way round, emphasizing instead local capacities and knowledge as a prime source of resilience and coping with disasters (see Stewart and Strathern 2018, p 36–37).

Mr Carlson went on to point out that IK was better preserved in the more remote islands with less urbanization and outside influences, so that it was to these remote locations one should look for guidance on how to reincorporate IK (and TEK) into disaster planning. Northern Cook Islands such as Penrhyn / Tongareva could be easily devastated by typhoons, while to the south islands like Mangaia experienced depopulation as young males sought employment through migration elsewhere and elders continued to work through existing traditional group structures based on kinship to maintain an orderly social life.

It is evident that Pacific Island communities, especially on smaller islands, are vulnerable to flooding, drought, and salinization of water supplies. It is also evident that they can draw on traditions of coping with disasters, through TEK, from before their incorporation into colonial structures and also in contemporary times. A part of Pacific Island (PI) response to erosion of land space has been the development of various methods of building up land by the construction of islets and protective stone walls. A case in point is the island Kapingamerangi in Pohnpei, where people enhance sandy reefs to make new land (Bryant-Tokalau 2018, p 39).

In the Solomon Islands, the Langalanga people of Malaita built offshore islands used for residence and protection against disease and enemy attacks. These all represented small-scale or micro-efforts of adaptation built on IK/TEK for their success (Bryant-Tokalau 2018, p 49, citing Guo 2001). In other instances, special methods of crop storage in the wake of environmental damage have been adopted. Another response has been to flee to other places where kinship ties are maintained. In Aotearoa/New Zealand, the Polynesian Maori immigrants developed storage pits for sweet potatoes (*kumara*) as a response to the cool climate there.

Lyn Carter has made a detailed study of Maori adaptation to contemporary climate change (Carter 2019), including ways of combating erosion of land and the strengthening of maritime dunes and waterways. These efforts involve the planting of *pikao* grass, a strong sedge grass, spoken of as the eyelids of a deity of the land, Tane, in combat with the god of the sea, Takaroa. This grass strengthens the edges of the land against the sea. Another project aims to protect the habitat of an important freshwater fish, the whitebait *(Inaka)*. Events of flooding threaten the habitat of the whitebait, but the fish have adapted by spawning safely in an area of strong grasses growing in the upper reaches of rivers and planted by Maori. Small acts of planting like this by individuals contribute to larger projects of revival of community life and prevention of disasters.

To summarize what we have been pursuing in this chapter, the study of the genesis and importance of responses to disasters, from micro to macro contexts, has acquired a large salience in anthropological work in recent years. In our own fieldwork and writing, we have sought to apply theories of ritual in order to help in assessing the efficacy of responses to various kinds of disasters, especially among indigenous peoples for whom their own cultural knowledge is vital for their future, as well as for all groups faced with challenges emergent from threats to their environmental and social well-being.

References

Bryant-Tokalau, Jenny (2018). *Indigenous Pacific Approaches to Climate Change*. Palgrave Macmillan.

Carter, Lyn (2019). *Indigenous Approaches to Climate Change*. Palgrave Macmillan.

Douglas, Mary (1970). *Natural Symbols: Explorations in Cosmology*. Cresset Press.

Guo, Pei-yi (2001). *Landscape, Migration and History Among the Langalanga, Solomon Islands*. Ph.D, Dept. of Anthropology, University of Pittsburgh.

Kalash, Taj Khan (2021). Jinn Dance in the Floods: Perceptions of Flood Disaster Among the Kalasha of Pakistan. In *Dealing with Disasters -- Perspectives from Eco-Cosmologies*, edited by D. Riboli, P. J. Stewart, A. Strathern, & D. Torri, 101–128. Palgrave Macmillan.

Nugteren, A. (2003). Case Studies 1: Dutch Cases and Themes. In *Disaster Ritual Explorations of an Emerging Ritual Repertoire*, edited by P. Post, R. L. Grimes, A. Nugteren, P. Pettersson, and H. Zondag, 79–186. Liturgia Condenda 15. Peeters.

Post P., R. L. Grimes, A. Nugteren, P. Pettersson, and H. Zondag (2003). *Disaster Ritual Explorations of an Emerging Ritual Repertoire*. Liturgia Condenda 15. Peeters.

Riboli, Diana (2021). The War Has Just Begun: Nature's Fury Against Neocolonial 'Spirit/s': Shamanic Perceptions of Natural Disaster in Comparative Perspective. In Dealing with Disasters: Perspectives from Eco-Cosmologies, edited by Diana Riboli, Pamela J. Stewart, Andrew Strathern, and Davide Torri, 19–42. Palgrave Macmillan.

Riboli, Diana, Pamela J. Stewart, Andrew Strathern, and Davide Torri (eds.) (2021). *Dealing with Disasters -- Perspectives from Eco-Cosmologies*. Palgrave Macmillan.

Stewart, Pamela J. and Andrew Strathern (2002). *Remaking the World: Myth, Mining and Ritual Change among the Duna of Papua New Guinea*. For, Smithsonian Series in Ethnographic Inquiry, Washington, D.C.: Smithsonian Institution Press.

Stewart, Pamela J. and Andrew Strathern (2014a). *Ritual: Key Concepts in Religion*. Bloomsbury.

Stewart, Pamela J. and Andrew Strathern (2014b). *Working in the Field: Anthropological Experiences across the World*. Left Coast Press.

Stewart, Pamela J. and Andrew Strathern (2015). Disaster Anthropology. In *Research Companion to Anthropology*, edited by Pamela J. Stewart and Andrew Strathern, 411–422. Ashgate Publishing.

Stewart, Pamela J. and Andrew Strathern (eds.). (2016a, originally published 2010). *Ritual* (The International Library of Essays in Anthropology). Routledge Publishing.

Stewart, Pamela J and Andrew Strathern (eds.). (2016b, originally published 2015). *Research Companion to Anthropology*. Routledge Publishing.

Stewart, Pamela J. and Andrew Strathern (2018). *Diaspora, Disasters, and the Cosmos: Rituals and Images*. Carolina Academic Press.

Stewart, Pamela J. and Andrew Strathern (eds.). (2021a). *The Palgrave Handbook of Anthropological Ritual Studies*. Palgrave Macmillan.

Stewart, Pamela J. and Andrew Strathern (2021b). Eco-Cosmologies: Renewable Energy. In *Dealing with Disasters -- Perspectives from Eco-Cosmologies*, edited by Diana Riboli, Pamela J. Stewart, Andrew Strathern, and Davide Torri, 129–140. Palgrave Macmillan.

Strathern, A. and Pamela J. Stewart (1999). *The Spirit is Coming! A Photographic-Textual Exposition of the Female Spirit Cult Performance in Mt. Hagen.* Ritual Studies Monograph Series, Monograph No. 1. Pittsburgh.

Strathern, Andrew and Pamela J. Stewart (2007). Ritual from Five Angles: A Tool for Teaching. In *Teaching Ritual*, edited by Catherine Bell, 133–146. For, Teaching Religious Studies Series, Oxford and New York: Oxford University Press.

Turner, Victor (1967). *The Forest of Symbols: Aspects of Ndembu Ritual.* Cornell University Press.

3   Mismatched Manifestations

Lessons from User-Initiated Changes to Architect-Designed Post-tsunami Rehousing in Coastal Sri Lanka

Kapila D. Silva, Chamila D. Subasinghe, and Barry T. Ballinger

3.1   Introduction

Although inhabitants are at the core of architecture and associated practices, there seem to be misalignments between architectural outcomes and user expectations, as seen in user-initiated changes to resettlement projects. This phenomenon is quite pronounced in rehousing provided to the displaced people in the aftermath of disasters, particularly among the underserved groups who have already been denied equitable access to decision-making. As found in the 2004 Indian Ocean tsunami rehousing projects in coastal Sri Lanka, this study explores a few mismatched expectations manifested in the rehousing realities by examining user-initiated changes made in housing provided to them.

We investigated spatial elements specific to the syntax of rehousing designs that allowed or hindered meaningful user-initiated changes and extensions. We used fourfold criteria to analyse the improvements to housing carried out by the residents: their utilitarian spatial needs, their cultural and contextual needs, expandability embedded in housing designs, and the need for sustained communal character in rehousing designs. In the process, the study uncovered that the inhabitants interacted with their architect-designed homes physically and programmatically in ways that signalled latent yet pertinent patterns of user-initiated changes (UiC). Carried out by the end-users on replacement houses for their lost homes, these patterns signal an ongoing process of user reactions to rehousing designs. We found a connection between the degree of practical and symbolic improvements by inhabitants and the degree of freedom offered for such improvements in rehousing designs.

The user-initiated progressive changes to rehousing also reveal a process of architectural decision-making that shows a need for better manifestation of end-user needs. Here, the residents become "thought providers" on an "incremental" route to post-disaster redevelopment. What they indicated through UiC reflects their need-based reading of the housing, thus allowing architects and stakeholders to rethink rehousing criteria from the end-user perspective. The outcome demonstrates the need to evaluate the options available for UiC as an integral part of rehousing designs. Here, we identify UiCs as innovative interventions made by people at a micro (household) scale. Therefore, involving UiC criteria to

DOI: 10.4324/9781003615903-4

negotiate the rehousing designs with the end-users and integrate the outcome as guided options for changes could potentially diminish the mismatch. Evaluating the usability of existing rehousing schemes based on self-improvement criteria also adds to the rigour of user satisfaction measures, such as post-occupancy evaluations, that would help improve architectural designs for the future. Envisioning progressive rebuilding by users themselves over time at the initial resettlement planning and design stage may extend the discourse on designing for less-affluent communities across contexts and cultures. This study offers useful insights into how UiC could advance into self-improvement implemented by users, a critical micro-human effort when rehousing was designed in a manner that enables people to make positive interventions to architectural designs.

3.2   Post-tsunami Rehousing Efforts in Sri Lanka

The 2004 Tsunami in the Indian Ocean devastated two-third of Sri Lanka's 1,340 km long coastline and added a new dimension to the post-disaster rebuilding dynamics among stakeholders (Ratnasooriya, Samarawickrama, and Imamura 2007; Seneviratne 2011; Somasundaram 2014). Staggering numbers of human and property damage occurred, including over 35,000 mortalities, more than a million internally displaced people, and nearly 100,000 damaged or destroyed houses (Government of Sri Lanka and Development Partners 2005). The difference between property damage and estimated resettlement costs alone was more than $ one billion (Athukorala and Resosudarmo 2005; Pathiraja and Tombesi 2009). Its sheer magnitude and the misery of the human condition attracted unprecedented philanthropy from both local and international donors in support of fast-track resettlement and rehabilitation programmes (Boano 2009; Muggah 2008). Along with the aid for fast recovery also came the necessity for future disaster resilience. The central government of Sri Lanka took this upon itself. It came up with specific regulations to control further or new developments on the Western, Southern, and Eastern coastal belts. The initial decision to curtail any construction within the shoreline of 100 metres for some areas and 200 metres for the rest was further reduced as an outcome of contested realities between people and policymakers (Connolly 2007; Ratnasooriya et al. 2007). The central government used this buffer zone with local governments to set the resettlement agenda. Hence, all the houses destroyed within the buffer zones were rebuilt on identified land parcels available through government acquisition systems or public-private partnerships (Manatunge and Abeysinghe 2017). While cash grants and bank loans were provided to some, most of the low-income displaced people were rehoused through donor-driven settlement programmes. This donor-driven programme, the focus of this chapter, accounted for 32,000 permanent houses built across nearly 200 relocation projects in 13 districts (Government of Sri Lanka and Development Partners 2005). Another aspect of the resettlement agenda was setting certain habitation standards to ensure the evacuees' improved lives and livelihoods. This included guidelines for settlement design, limits on plot sizes, minimum dimensions for rooms in dwelling units, and construction and infrastructure provision (Emmanuel 2005).

Adding a new real estate model to the regional redevelopment landscape of Sri Lanka, this programme resulted in 110,000 houses by the end of 2009 (Silva and Ballinger 2021). It garnered particular attention from redevelopment stakeholders and scholars to date as it continues to question the comparison of the spatial logic of the "lost home" and the "new house" or mismatched expectations (Kamalrathne and Senanayake 2023). While dealing with the losses and residues of the damage, resettled communities strived to come to terms with their new houses, some more than others (Andrew et al. 2013). Despite improved design standards, construction, building services, and public infrastructure provided, a general hesitation over resettlement rehousing has been reported since the first post-occupancy data were posted (Dikmen and Elias-Ozkan 2016). Considering the "poor" condition of most informal housing destroyed versus the "higher" quality rehousing provided, this data questioned the role of the professionals involved, particularly architects, in materializing different ideals (Silva and Ballinger 2021).

3.3 Dissonance in the Designs: Case Studies from Coastal Sri Lanka

Even though the resettlement phase has been seen as a scale of success to secure future funding, very few studies have culturally and contextually looked at the versatility of planning and designs encouraging improvements initiated by end-users. While architects play a major role in planning new communities and designing most rehousing projects in the wake of disasters worldwide, it is doubtful whether they have fully understood the scope of UiC in the resettlement efforts. It is also unclear whether they have integrated UiCs into the design criteria to accommodate evacuees' efforts for inevitable future needs and wants. While many studies focus on residents' and donor organizations' assessment of the relocation experience, limited literature demonstrates architects' ability to integrate self-improvement in rehousing as a qualification for them to secure rehousing projects.

Therefore, this study on post-tsunami resettlements in Sri Lanka looked into (a) the planning and architectural intentions of professionals in their rehousing designs, (b) the evacuees' degree of satisfaction with spatial qualities of their new environments, including the opportunity for self-improvement, and (c) dissonance between the architectural intentions and the evacuees' expectations as reflected in improvements. We reviewed five post-tsunami resettlement projects in Sri Lanka, interviewing housing providers (the architects and representatives of donor agencies) and rehousing residents on the settlement and dwelling designs. A coded comparison was carried out to unbundle the nature of dissonance between architectural interpretations and end-user expectations. The findings demonstrate the limited scope for UiC considered in the resettlement effort. The lessons learned from this study would assist prequalification of professionals, such as architects, for future post-disaster rehousing projects. A comprehensive report on the research design, including the findings, is available in Silva and Ballinger (2021).

Three out of four cases chosen for the study were in the Southern province (*Kalamatiya, Kirinda, Samadhigama,* and *Yayawatte*) of Sri Lanka. The fifth (*Logoswatte*) was in the Western province. The resettlements took place in 2007 and 2008. *Kirinda* was the only exception in terms of ethnicity and relocation. At *Kirinda*, people were not relocated; damaged houses were repaired, and new ones were built in the same places instead. It was a minority Muslim community where the pre-tsunami settlement was consolidated, and new houses were built on their original properties as the settlement was just outside of the newly introduced buffer zone, which the Sri Lankan government arbitrarily established to mitigate future tsunami threats on settlements along the coast (Connolly, 2007; Ratnasooriya et al. 2007). The rest were relocated settlements, predominantly composed of the Sinhalese majority group. The project scale greatly varied from 30 units in *Kalamatiya* to 362 units in *Samadhigama*. Attempts at some forms of sustainable construction and site management practices were visible in all cases.

The rationale for case study selection was based on accessibility to the sites, residents' and architects' willingness to participate in the study, the type of settlement (consolidated or relocation), the settlement size, demographic characteristics of residents, and the use of sustainable building practices in rehousing. Three sets of interviews were conducted among residents, project architects, responsible local authorities, and non-profit organizations that sponsored the rehousing. The resident interviews were focused on eliciting feedback on their views on the design of the settlement form and house, the degree of their involvement in the resettlement process, the impact of dislocation and resettlement on their lives, the amenities and place management systems available at the settlements, and the types of architectural changes they made to the houses and premises after moving in. The sampling was convenience-based, chain-referral (snowball) grounded on inhabitants' willingness to comment on rehousing designs within the overall resettlement experience. The interviews with the architects focused on their role and experience in the resettlement process, the factors behind their initial design decisions, and the lessons they may have learned from the project. The interviews with the local authorities and non-profit organizations provided their perspectives on the stakeholder participation process. The manually coded interviews were further exhausted to uncover seven-fold UiC objectives: (a) symbolic and instrumental functionality of housing units, (b) expandability of house units, (c) climatic/sustainability response of house units, (d) cultural and contextual compatibility of house units, (e) place character/imagery response, (f) constructional aspects, (g) displacement impact, and (h) resettlement management. Five new codes also emerged, along with thematic variations within several codes: issues of site selection, designing for community cohesion, designing to evoke familiarity, recognizing the residents' lack of design understanding, and issues of architectural training.

Through structured observations on settlements, recorded via photography, field sketches, and notes, we examined settlements' and housing units' planning and design against their current condition. This was done by analysing plot sizes, street layout patterns, clustering of housing units, the location of communal facilities and open spaces, the infrastructure provided, and the connection of settlements to the

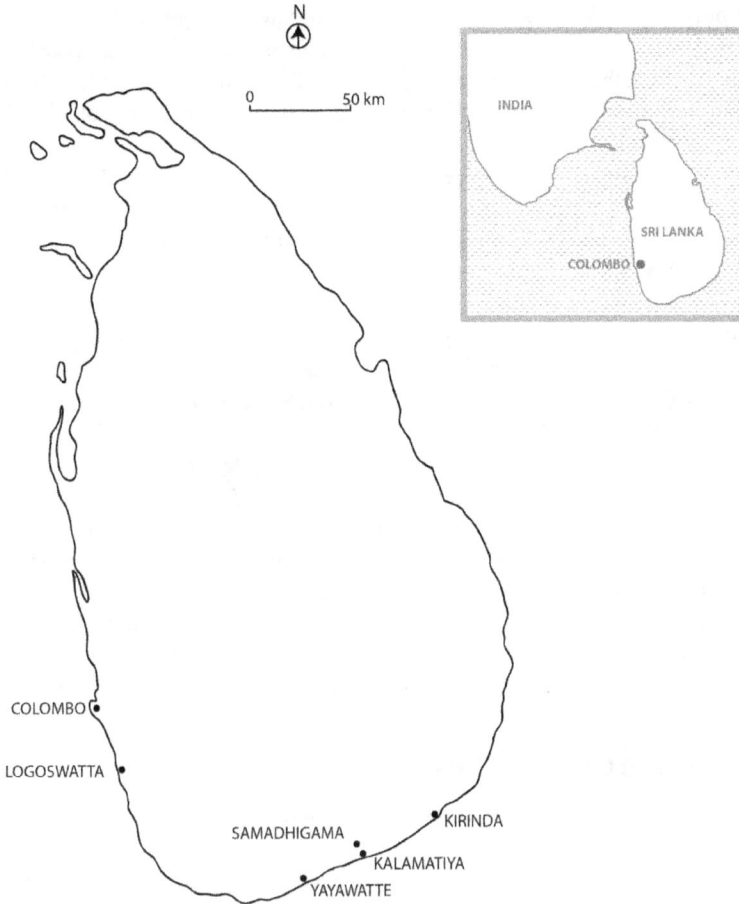

Figure 3.1 Map of Sri Lanka Showing the Locations of Resettlement Sites Studied.
Source: Kapila D. Silva

surrounding area and neighbourhoods. These observations were compared with the drawings architects provided of their original designs. The intention was to identify the design aspects that potentially caused liveability issues in the settlement plans and architectural forms. The analysis of these drawings and field sketches, using photographs as supplementary visual aids, was done in the form of a "design review". It resembled a typical architectural design assessment in a professional architectural studio setting. In reviewing both settlement plans and house designs, the study focused on their design attributes such as settlement layouts, plot sizes, clustering houses, roof design, and the like that intended to fulfil the seven-fold UiC objectives. These design objectives, borrowed from the coding framework for interview analysis, were the same criteria used to analyse architectural designs. One of the aspects of design reviews was to speculate on potential embedded in the design attributes of houses for eventual user-initiated changes. This was to gauge whether the design had reached its optimum in meeting the established design objectives or whether the opportunity for UiC had been made available to the users.

Using the feedback from residents as a guide and focusing on the design attributes, we examined the compatibility of the house plans in terms of functionality, expandability, climatic responsiveness, and cultural and contextual compatibility. In reviewing the expandability of each house design, we first considered the economic and technical feasibility of additions that could be carried out on the original designs without requiring major alterations. It was possible to identify the degree of flexibility embedded in the house designs and what design features would help or hinder UiC. A set of hypothetical ideas on expansion possibilities was used to compare with what architects envisioned as likely additions to identify the practicality of the latter. Next, the different house alterations the interviewees had carried out were mapped for each settlement by drawing over the original plan and comparing the resident-initiated changes with the architect-designed plans. We also considered the design features speculatively identified as perceived obstacles for essential expansions. Hence, this comparison furnished insight into the functional difficulties of original designs by responsible architects. Additionally, we used the published research and news articles on similar post-tsunami rehousing projects in Sri Lanka to obtain a wider sample of reported obstacles to UiC in the post-tsunami rehousing projects in the country. The outcome backed the notion that those residents also had concerns and experiences similar to those of the interviewees.

3.4   Analysis of Cases and Causes of Dissonance

In addition to the review of the latest literature and interviews with residents, architects, and representatives of donor organizations and government agencies, our database had comprehensive information collected through site visits, structured observations, and archives, including photographs and architectural drawings. Distilled from the latest research and substantiated through the field studies, we found four categories of UiCs: extended usable footprint, added spatial-functionality, reconfigured architectural layout, and altered external appearance. We called them affordances as they are relational concepts applied to understand and theorize social and technical relationships (Lanamäki, Thapa, and Stendal 2016).

Based on these affordances, we coded and assessed UiCs as displayed in Table 3.1 (A, B, C, D & E) for settlements in Kalamatiya, Kirinda, Logoswatte, Samadhigama, and Yayawatte. The tables display the design of house units originally provided for the displaced and a selection of UiCs carried out by residents on those house units in each settlement. The UiC index is based on parametric data of the UiC levels (minor, moderate and major) reported under the criteria. Although we do not intend to run a statistical analysis to show the significance, the index will indicate the distribution of UiCs across the criteria. Statistical analysis through future research could potentially argue our conclusions better. However, we attempted triangulation of results to conclude a set of practical recommendations, as shown in Tables 3.2 (A, B, C, D, E)

Table 3.1A Self-improvements coded and assessed (matrix template).

Self-improvement	Extended Usable Footprint			Added Spatial-functionality			Reconfigured Architectural Layout			Altered External Appearance		
	Minor	Moderate	Major	Minor	Moderate	Major	Minor	Moderate	Major	Minor	Moderate	Major

Architect's Plan

ARCHITECT'S PLAN

PLAN

(*Continued*)

Table 3.1A (Continued)

Self-improvement	Extended Usable Footprint	Added Spatial-functionality	Reconfigured Architectural Layout	Altered External Appearance
Extension – A	XX	XX	XX	XX

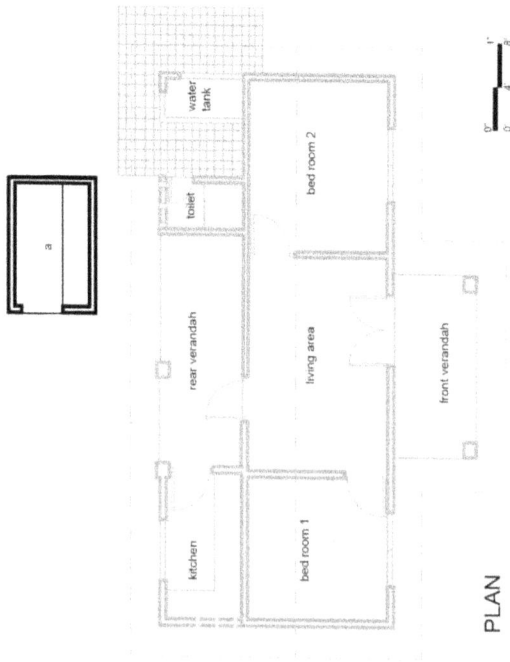

PLAN

(Continued)

Table 3.1A (Continued)

Self-improvement	Extended Usable Footprint	Added Spatial-functionality	Reconfigured Architectural Layout	Altered External Appearance
Extension – B	xx	xx	xx	XX

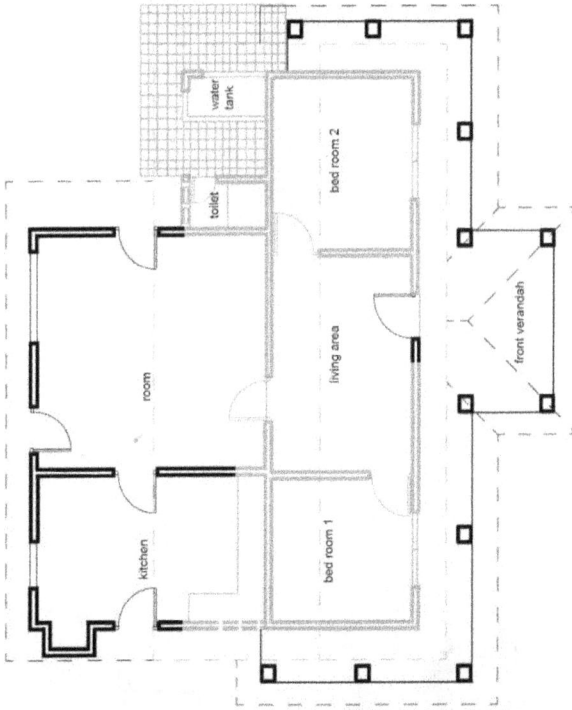

(Continued)

Table 3.1A (Continued)

Self-improvement	Extended Usable Footprint	Added Spatial-functionality	Reconfigured Architectural Layout	Altered External Appearance
Extension – C	XX	XX	XX	XX

PLAN

(Continued)

Table 3.1A (Continued)

Self-improvement	Extended Usable Footprint	Added Spatial-functionality	Reconfigured Architectural Layout	Altered External Appearance
Extension – D	XX	XX	XX	XX

PLAN

Table 3.1B

Self-improvement	*Extended Usable Footprint*			*Added Spatial-functionality*			*Reconfigured Architectural Layout*			*Altered External Appearance*		
	Minor	Moderate	Major	Minor	Moderate	Major	Minor	Moderate	Major	Minor	Moderate	Major

Architect's Plan

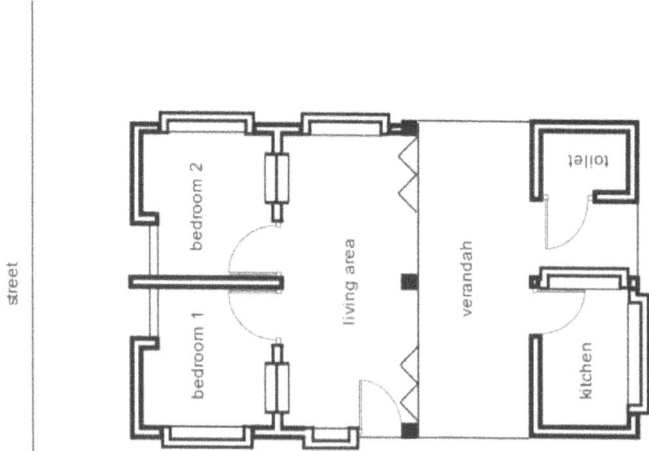

(*Continued*)

Table 3.1B (Continued)

Self-improvement	Extended Usable Footprint	Added Spatial-functionality	Reconfigured Architectural Layout	Altered External Appearance
Extension – A	√	√	√	√

(Continued)

Table 3.1B (Continued)

Self-improvement	Extended Usable Footprint	Added Spatial-functionality	Reconfigured Architectural Layout	Altered External Appearance
Extension – B	XX	XX	XX	XX XX

(Continued)

Table 3.1B (Continued)

Self-improvement	Extended Usable Footprint	Added Spatial-functionality	Reconfigured Architectural Layout	Altered External Appearance
Extension – C	xx	XX	XX	XX

Table 3.1C

Self-improvement	*Extended Usable Footprint*			*Added Spatial-functionality*			*Reconfigured Architectural Layout*			*Altered External Appearance*		
	Minor	Moderate	Major	Minor	Moderate	Major	Minor	Moderate	Major	Minor	Moderate	Major
Architect's Plan												

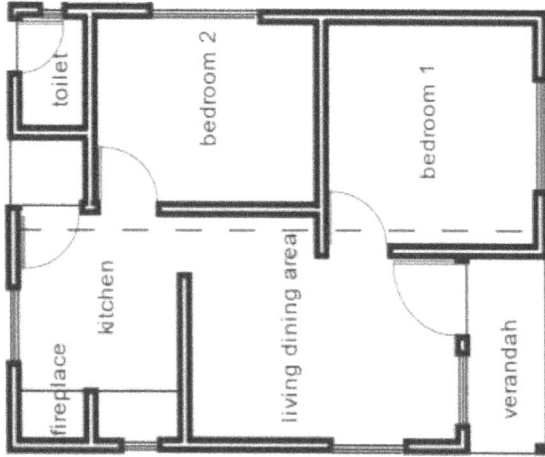

Architect's floor plan showing: fireplace, kitchen, toilet, bedroom 2, living dining area, bedroom 1, verandah

(*Continued*)

Table 3.1C (Continued)

Self-improvement	Extended Usable Footprint	Added Spatial-functionality	Reconfigured Architectural Layout	Altered External Appearance
Extension – A	√	√	√	√

(Continued)

Table 3.1C (Continued)

Self-improvement	Extended Usable Footprint	Added Spatial-functionality	Reconfigured Architectural Layout	Altered External Appearance
Extension – B	xx	xx	xx	xx

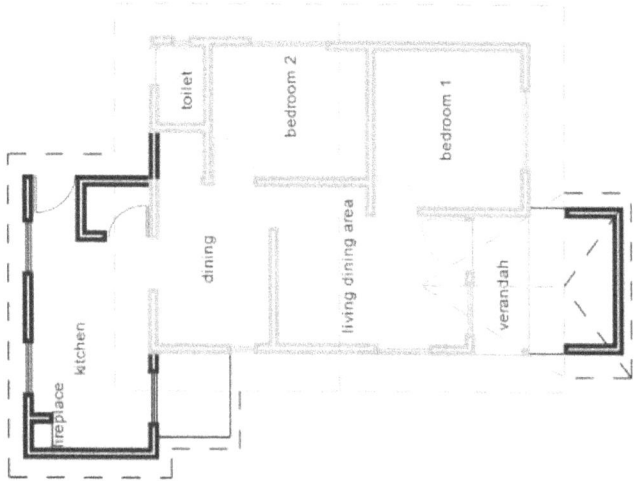

(Continued)

Table 3.1C (Continued)

Self-improvement	Extended Usable Footprint	Added Spatial-functionality	Reconfigured Architectural Layout	Altered External Appearance
Extension – C	XX	XX	XX	XX

(Continued)

Table 3.1C (Continued)

Self-improvement	Extended Usable Footprint	Added Spatial-functionality	Reconfigured Architectural Layout	Altered External Appearance
Extension – D	XX	XX	XX	XX

(Continued)

Table 3.1C (Continued)

Self-improvement	Extended Usable Footprint	Added Spatial-functionality	Reconfigured Architectural Layout	Altered External Appearance
Extension – E	XX	XX	XX	XX

Table 3.1D

Self-improvement	Extended Usable Footprint	Added Spatial-functionality	Reconfigured Architectural Layout	Altered External Appearance
	Minor	Minor	Minor	Minor
	Moderate	Moderate	Moderate	Moderate
	Major	Major	Major	Major

Architect's Plan

(*Continued*)

Table 3.1D (Continued)

Self-improvement	Extended Usable Footprint	Added Spatial-functionality	Reconfigured Architectural Layout	Altered External Appearance
Extension – A	XX	XX	XX	XX

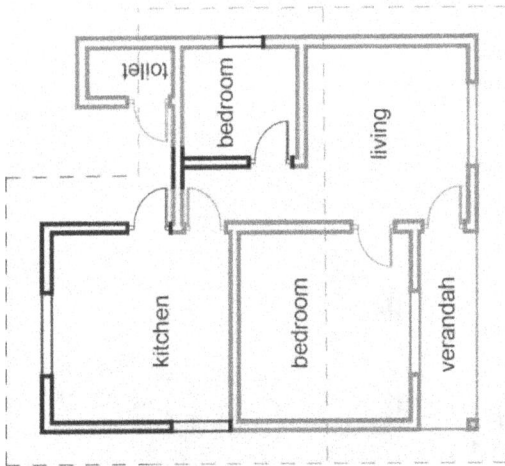

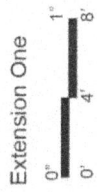

Extension One

0"   1"
0'   4'   8'

(Continued)

Table 3.1D (Continued)

Self-improvement	Extended Usable Footprint	Added Spatial-functionality	Reconfigured Architectural Layout	Altered External Appearance
Extension – B	XX	XX	XX	XX

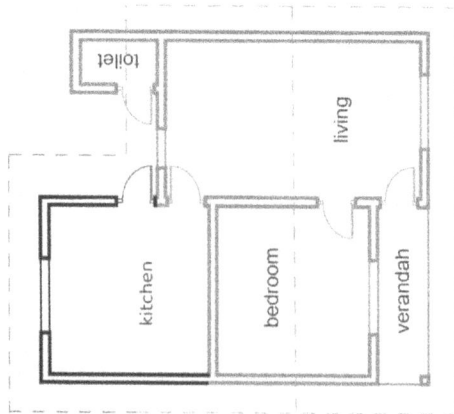

Extension Two

(Continued)

Table 3.1D (Continued)

Self-improvement	Extended Usable Footprint	Added Spatial-functionality	Reconfigured Architectural Layout	Altered External Appearance
Extension – C	XX	XX	XX	XX

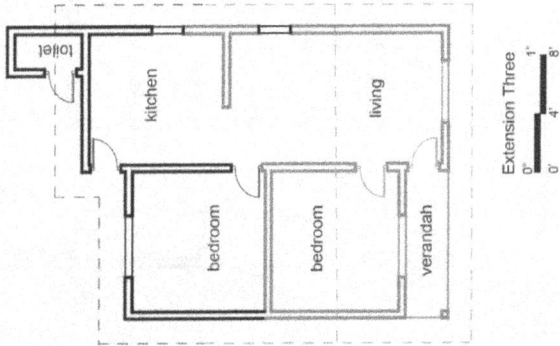

Extension Three

0' 4' 8'

0" 1"

Table 3.1E

Self-improvement	Extended Usable Footprint			Added Spatial-functionality			Reconfigured Architectural Layout			Altered External Appearance		
	Minor	Moderate	Major	Minor	Moderate	Major	Minor	Moderate	Major	Minor	Moderate	Major

Architect's Plan – Type 1

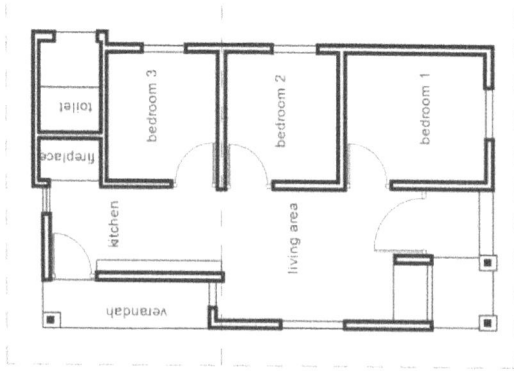

(Continued)

Table 3.1E (Continued)

Self-improvement	Extended Usable Footprint	Added Spatial-functionality	Reconfigured Architectural Layout	Altered External Appearance
Extension – A	xx	xx	xx	xx

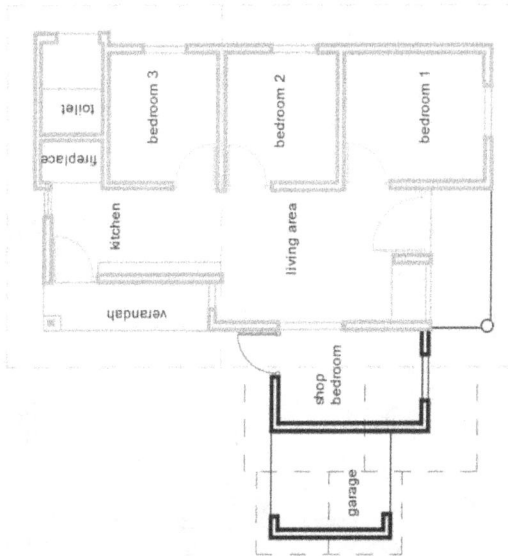

(*Continued*)

Table 3.1E (Continued)

Self-improvement	Extended Usable Footprint	Added Spatial-functionality	Reconfigured Architectural Layout	Altered External Appearance
Extension – B	xx	xx	xx	xx

(Continued)

Table 3.1E (Continued)

Self-improvement	Extended Usable Footprint	Added Spatial-functionality	Reconfigured Architectural Layout	Altered External Appearance
Extension – C	xx	xx	xx	xx

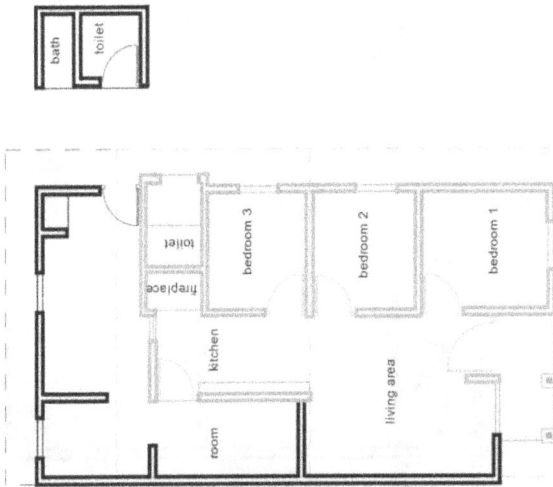

(Continued)

Table 3.1E (Continued)

Self-improvement	Extended Usable Footprint	Added Spatial-functionality	Reconfigured Architectural Layout	Altered External Appearance
Extention – D		xx	xx	xx

(Continued)

Table 3.1E (Continued)

Self-improvement	*Extended Usable Footprint*	*Added Spatial-functionality*	*Reconfigured Architectural Layout*	*Altered External Appearance*

Architect's Plan – Type 2

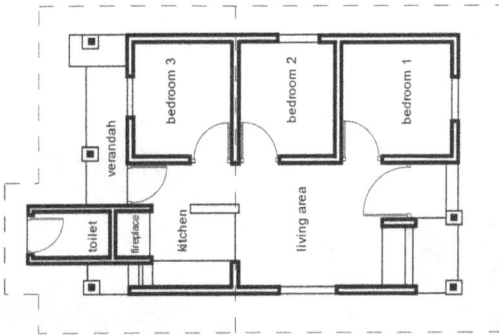

(Continued)

Table 3.1E (Continued)

Self-improvement	Extended Usable Footprint	Added Spatial-functionality	Reconfigured Architectural Layout	Altered External Appearance
Extention – A	xx	xx	xx	xx

toilet fireplace kitchen verandah bedroom 3 bedroom 2 bedroom 1 living area verandah and 3.3. Table 3.2A through E demonstrates the distribution of cultural and contextual affordances across the themes that emerged from the discourse analysis of data. These Pareto charts prioritize UiCs and then indicate UiCs with the most significant user reactions to architectural designs. Dalgleish (2004) mentions that in analyses like these, Pareto charts indicate the participants satisfaction on a personal level. Thus, the order of frequency shows the vital causes of the majority of reactions. For example, the Pareto Line shown in graph 3.2A indicates that 80% of the affordance relies on combined reactions of Functionality, Displacement Management, Issues of Resettlement Management and Lifestyle Needs Compatibility. While the first three UiCs stand out at 90%, lifestyle needs compatibility and place character sit partially for "Kalamatiya", accounting for 70% of UiCs or user reactions. As shown in the aggregate tabulation (Table 3.2F), while the first three factors remain constant for all cases with varying percentages on or above the 80% marker, the partial factor for Samadhigama is expandability, place character, and lifestyle needs, accounting for 70% of reactions. Although place character consistently stays at 70% or above for all cases, there is no partial factor for the rest of the case studies. The aggregate tabulation, Table 3.2F, established a hybrid of functionality, displacement management, and issues of resettlement management, resulting in 20% of UiCs responsible for 80% of the outcomes. Table 3.3 is based on the themes generated from interview data. This discourse analysis shows how discrete themes were distilled from the literature review and from the original research.

3.4.1 Findings: Where and Why Does Dissonance Occur?

While housing providers generally believed they effectively responded to the disaster, residents experienced a more nuanced process. Nearly ten years post-resettlement, residents revealed overall dissatisfaction with the resettlement efforts. Despite the providers', including the architects', well-meaning intentions to offer suitable housing, their lack of understanding regarding community design processes, the housing needs of an economically disadvantaged population, and strategies to mitigate displacement's effects became evident. Residents' discontent is linked to issues in the settlement functionality, expandability of the settlement and houses, climate-responsive design and sustainability, lifestyle compatibility, place character and imagery, displacement impact, and resettlement management issues (Figures 3.8–3.12).

First, the resettlements had significant functionality issues. Architects faced different challenges in each rehousing project. Some projects had underdeveloped physical and civic infrastructure and unmaintained public spaces, negatively impacting residents' perception of their settlements. Overall, the residents believe settlement design should have had larger plot sizes, well-managed public spaces, and adequate physical infrastructure.

Second, there was discontent with house design regarding expandability, which prompted numerous residents to undertake substantial alterations depending on their financial capacity, functional requirements, changing social status,

Table 3.2A Kalamatiya

	Functionality (of Settlement, House Designs, and Physical and Civic Infrastructure)	Expandability (of Settlement and House)	Climatic Design and Sustainability Response	Lifestyle Needs Compatibility (Privacy and Safety needs, Storage Needs, Choice of House Types, Ways of Cooking, etc.)	Place Character/ Imagery Response (Rural or Rustic Dwelling/ Settlement)	Displacement Impact (Loss of Livelihood and Social Networks, etc.)	Issues of Resettlement Management (Community Engagement, Settlement Upkeep, etc.)
Socio-cultural	X	X	X	X	X	X	X
Socio-economic	X	X	X	X		X	X
Spatial Function	X			X	X	X	X
Environmental-sustainability	X				X	X	X
	4	2	2	3	3	4	4

Table 3.2B Kirinda

	Functionality (of Settlement, House Designs, and Physical and Civic Infrastructure)	Expandability (of Settlement and House)	Climatic Design and Sustainability Response	Lifestyle Needs Compatibility (Privacy and Safety Needs, Storage Needs, Choice of House Types, Ways of Cooking, etc.)	Place Character/Imagery Response (Rural or Rustic Dwelling/Settlement)	Displacement Impact (Loss of Livelihood and Social Networks, etc.)	Issues of Resettlement Management (Community Engagement, Settlement Upkeep, etc.)
Socio-cultural	X	X	X	X	X		X
Socio-economic		X	X	X	X		X
Spatial Function		X	X	X		X	X
Environmental-sustainability		X	X	X	X		X
	1	4	4	4	3	1	4

Table 3.2C Logoswatte

	Functionality (of Settlement, House Designs, and Physical and Civic Infrastructure)	Expandability (of Settlement and house)	Climatic Design and Sustainability Response	Lifestyle Needs Compatibility (Privacy and Safety Needs, Storage Needs, Choice of House Types, Ways of Cooking, etc.)	Place Character/ Imagery Response (Rural or Rustic Dwelling/ Settlement)	Displacement Impact (Loss of Livelihood and Social Networks, etc.)	Issues of Resettlement Management (Community Engagement, Settlement Upkeep, etc.)
Socio-cultural	X	X	X	X	X	X	X
Socio-economic	X	X	X	X	X	X	X
Spatial Function	X	X			X	X	X
Environmental-sustainability	X	X	X		X	X	X
	4	4	3	2	4	4	4

Table 3.2D Samadhigama

	Functionality (of Settlement, House Designs, and Physical and Civic Infrastructure)	Expandability (of Settlement and House)	Climatic Design and Sustainability Response	Lifestyle Needs Compatibility (Privacy and Safety Needs, Storage Needs, Choice of House Types, Ways of Cooking, etc.)	Place Character/ Imagery Response (Rural or Rustic Dwelling/ Settlement)	Displacement Impact (Loss of Livelihood and Social Networks, etc.)	Issues of Resettlement Management (Community Engagement, Settlement Upkeep, etc.)
Socio-cultural	X	X	X	X		X	X
Socio-economic	X	X		X	X	X	X
Spatial Function	X	X	X	X	X	X	X
Environmental-sustainability	X				X	X	X
	4	3	2	3	3	4	4

Table 3.2E Yayawatte

	Functionality (of Settlement, House Designs, and Physical and Civic Infrastructure)	Expandability (of Settlement and House)	Climatic Design and Sustainability Response	Lifestyle Needs Compatibility (Privacy and Safety Needs, Storage Needs, Choice of House Types, Ways of Cooking, etc.)	Place Character/ Imagery Response (Rural or Rustic Dwelling/ Settlement)	Displacement Impact (Loss of Livelihood and Social Networks, etc.)	Issues of Resettlement Management (Community Engagement, Settlement Upkeep, etc.)
Socio-cultural	X	X	X	X	X	X	X
Socio-economic	X	X		X	X	X	X
Spatial Function	X	X	X	X	X	X	X
Environmental-sustainability	X	X	X	X	X	X	X
	4	4	3	4	4	4	4

Table 3.2F Aggregate Tabulation

	Functionality (of Settlement, House Designs, and Physical and Civic Infrastructure)	Expandability (of Settlement and House)	Climatic Design and Sustainability Response	Lifestyle Needs Compatibility (Privacy and Safety Needs, Storage Needs, Choice of House Types, Ways of Cooking, etc.)	Place Character/ Imagery Response (Rural or Rustic Dwelling/ Settlement)	Displacement Impact (Loss of Livelihood and Social Networks, etc.)	Issues of Resettlement Management (Community Engagement, Settlement Upkeep, etc.)
Kalamatiya	4	2	2	3	3	4	4
Kirinda	1	4	4	4	3	1	4
Logoswatte	4	4	3	2	4	4	4
Samadhigama	4	4	3	4	4	4	4
Yayawatte	4	2	2	3	3	4	4
	20	14	12	15	17	20	20

Table 3.3 A Discursive Tabulation to Distil a Summary from Literature Review and Original Research.

	Settlement Functionality (of Settlement and Physical and Civic Infrastructure)	Expandability (of Settlement and House)	Climatic Design, Sustainability Response, and Disaster Preparedness of Dwellings	Lifestyle Compatibility of Dwellings (Privacy and Safety Needs, Storage Needs, Choice of House Types, Ways of Cooking, etc.)	Place Character/ Imagery Response (Rural or Rustic Dwelling or Settlement)	Displacement Impact (Loss of Livelihood and Social Networks, etc.)	Issues of Resettlement Management (Community Engagement, Settlement Upkeep, etc.)
Socio-cultural	Surveillance/ safety needs; lack of civic infrastructure and amenities (schools, daycare centres, streetlights; shops, etc); any civic infrastructure provided either not enough or incompatible with community needs; Only civic amenity provided is Community Centre, which does not have any use without community organizing.	Lack of design cues to guide expansion; lack of education of settlers of the expandability possibilities of dwellings; Lack of awareness of proper ways of alteration and expansion of dwellings; some expansions/ alterations to housing units are mostly symbolic (express of social status, taste of design, and higher income) than utilitarian (useable space via expansion)	Lack of awareness of climate change impact; lack of awareness in sustainable design and technology; provision of verandah as a social space for tropical living; architects' lack of understanding of local climate and weather patterns;	Surveillance/safety needs; lack of privacy; dwelling design incompatible with belief systems; small kitchens; kitchens attached to houses; lack of storage; inappropriate storage; lack of garages; small house/room size does not accommodate the furniture needed or already possess; no "back yard" space for such "back yard" functions (storage, private functions, etc.); provision of verandah	Architects' decision on Rustic or Rural character as a suitable imagery for settlements; Locating houses away from main roads to maintain rural character; "unplanned" patterns of housing clusters to create a rural character; Lack of personal identity in dwellings;	Loss of sense of community and social networks; Loss of place attachment; loneliness; loss of social status, income, and lifestyle.	Lack of community engagement in the settlement process; Lack of community organizing for settlement management; lack of use of civic infrastructure provided; delay in providing legal ownership of properties leading to myriad of issues; lack of management leads to negative perception of settlements; Only civic amenity provided is Community Centre,

(Continued)

Table 3.3 (Continued)

Settlement Functionality (of Settlement and Physical and Civic Infrastructure)	Expandability (of Settlement and House)	Climatic Design, Sustainability Response, and Disaster Preparedness of Dwellings	Lifestyle Compatibility of Dwellings (Privacy and Safety Needs, Storage Needs, Choice of House Types, Ways of Cooking, etc.)	Place Character/ Imagery Response (Rural or Rustic Dwelling or Settlement)	Displacement Impact (Loss of Livelihood and Social Networks, etc.)	Issues of Resettlement Management (Community Engagement, Settlement Upkeep, etc.)
			as a social space for tropical living; Designers' and donors' lack of understanding of people's lifestyles and needs; architect's lack of understanding of people's preferences for spaces, material, colour, finishes, and expressive need of social status through dwellings; variations of the same house unit design are constructed assuming that these variations would fit different lifestyles;	patterns of clustering of housing units and number of house units in each cluster based on intended social interaction and place character; winding paths to generate a sense of mystery as an aspect of rural character; provision of verandah as a social space with columns to emulate rural and vernacular housing of the country;		which does not have any use without community organizing; architects not familiar with the lifestyle of people designing for the people; no studies conducted for understanding people's needs and lifestyles; fast-paced resettlement housing development and relocating people without much time to relearn from failures and mistakes; lack of careful study of *(Continued)*

Table 3.3 (Continued)

Settlement Functionality (of Settlement and Physical and Civic Infrastructure)	Expandability (of Settlement and House)	Climatic Design, Sustainability Response, and Disaster Preparedness of Dwellings	Lifestyle Compatibility (Privacy and Safety Needs, Storage Needs, Choice of House Types, Ways of Cooking, etc.)	Place Character/ Imagery Response (Rural or Rustic Dwelling or Settlement)	Displacement Impact (Loss of Livelihood and Social Networks, etc.)	Issues of Resettlement Management (Community Engagement, Settlement Upkeep, etc.)
						people's lifestyles and socio-cultural aspects and values; no opportunity for people to provide feedback on housing prototypes;
Socio-economic live-work symbiosis in terms of proximity; lack of work-related infrastructure;	Lack of income to make expansions; lack of technology, materials, and labour for expansions	No income to repair and sustain the solar panels/ rainwater harvesting devices/ technology; No training on these repairs and maintenance.	No income to make changes to dwellings to fit lifestyle needs;	Inclusion of a large number housing units and small housing units to save construction cost and maximize funding available;	Lack of Job training/ livelihood skills; small-scale livelihood means not enough; loss of livelihood; sporadic meagre earning; Live-livelihood autonomy.	Lack of work-related infrastructure; corruption in construction and project implementation resulting in low-quality construction;

(Continued)

Table 3.3 (Continued)

Settlement Functionality (of Settlement and Physical and Civic Infrastructure)	*Expandability (of Settlement and House)*	*Climatic Design, Sustainability Response, and Disaster Preparedness of Dwellings*	*Lifestyle Compatibility of Dwellings (Privacy and Safety Needs, Storage Needs, Choice of House Types, Ways of Cooking, etc.)*	*Place Character/ Imagery Response (Rural or Rustic Dwelling or Settlement)*	*Displacement Impact (Loss of Livelihood and Social Networks, etc.)*	*Issues of Resettlement Management (Community Engagement, Settlement Upkeep, etc.)*
Spatial-functional Proximity of housing to means of livelihood; safety of work equipment; no provision of work-related spatial needs;	Small land plots making expansions difficult; house designs that do not allow easy expansions; low roofs make it difficult to expand dwellings; land allocated for future settlement expansion, which has not realized yet; expansions/ alterations are very small in scale leading to not much functional space due to lack of space for appropriate expansions;	Lack of wide roof canopy for sun protection and rain protection; provisions for natural ventilation; architects' lack of attention to material performance in local climatic conditions; lack of pilot testing new sustainable material in constructability and performance under local climatic conditions;	Safety and security concerns; small size of plots lead to small houses with small rooms and kitchens; some natural ventilation options such as open rooms or large windows lead to privacy and safety issues; lack of chimneys or smoke stacks in kitchens;	Inclusion of a large number housing units in small lands leading to small plots and dwellings units; unpaved paths for rural character creates problems during rain and transportation and lead to road erosion;	Loss of lifestyle compatible spaces;	Land allocated for future settlement expansion has not realized yet due to lack of planning, management, lack of need, and funding. Such land is now waste land without use, upkeep, or ownership

(Continued)

Table 3.3 (Continued)

Settlement Functionality (of Settlement and Physical and Civic Infrastructure)	Expandability (of Settlement and House)	Climatic Design, Sustainability Response, and Disaster Preparedness of Dwellings	Lifestyle Compatibility of Dwellings (Privacy and Safety Needs, Storage Needs, Choice of House Types, Ways of Cooking, etc.)	Place Character/ Imagery Response (Rural or Rustic Dwelling or Settlement)	Displacement Impact (Loss of Livelihood and Social Networks, etc.)	Issues of Resettlement Management (Community Engagement, Settlement Upkeep, etc.)
Environmental- Lack of mass transit leads to more energy consumption at individual level; lack of reliable public transits; unused or underused of civic infrastructure provided in settlements;	The sustainable materials used in dwellings cannot be replicated/ reproduced due to lack of materials, skills, and technology;	Sustainable solutions incompatible with social status; sustainable solutions incompatible with belief systems; complete clearance of settlement lands leading to loss of tree cover; climatically inappropriate sustainable design elements integrated with dwellings (e.g. rainwater harvesting systems in areas that receive tropical monsoon rain year around);	Sustainable solutions incompatible with social status; sustainable solutions incompatible with belief systems;	Lack of settlement upkeep; wasted land areas without purpose or ownership; complete clearance of land leading to loss tree cover and sense of place; exposed mud brick as a sustainable building material generating a rustic and rural character.	Relocation takes people away from attending to the mitigation of environmental damage due to disaster;	Lack of settlement upkeep; lack of maintenance of sustainability systems provided; lack of mass transit options; land areas without ownership; lack of disaster preparedness and mitigation approaches; lack of regional authorities'' support to maintain sustainable waste management;

Sustainable

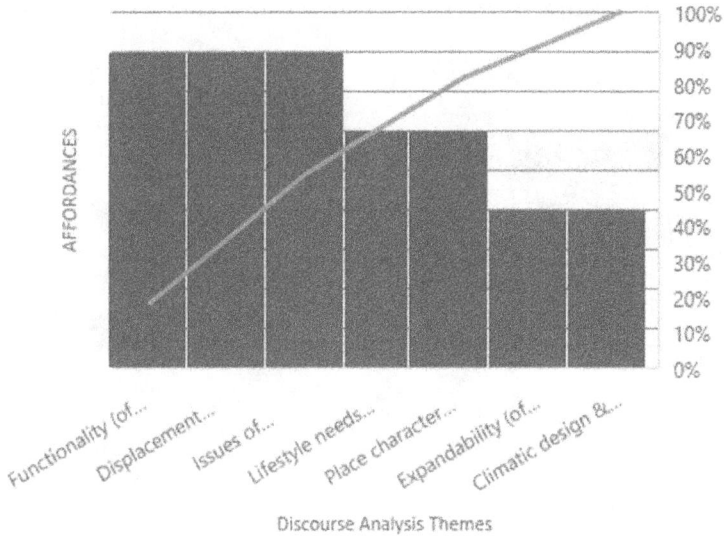

Figure 3.2 Pareto Line for Kalamatiya.

Source: Chamila Subasinghe

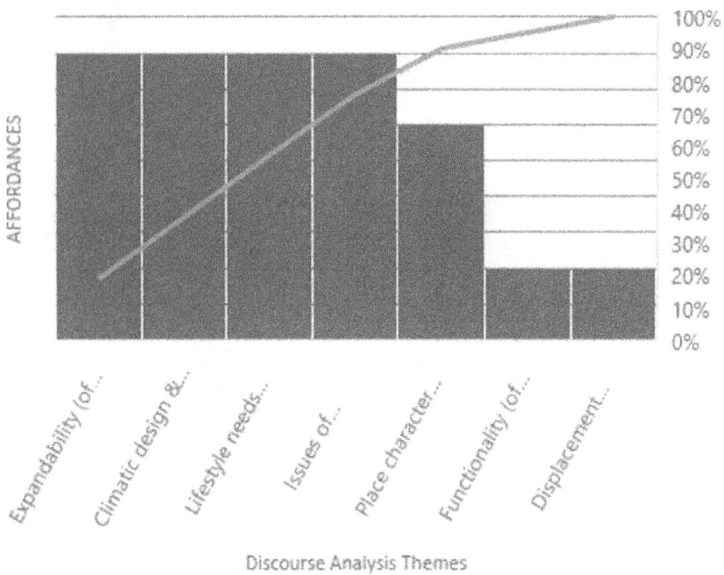

Figure 3.3 Pareto Line for Kirinda.

Source: Chamila Subasinghe

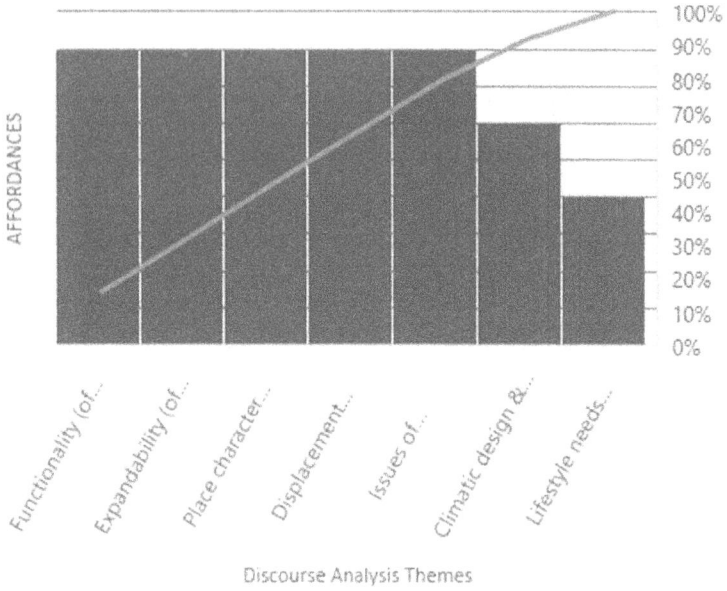

Figure 3.4 Pareto Line for Logoswatte.

Source: Chamila Subasinghe

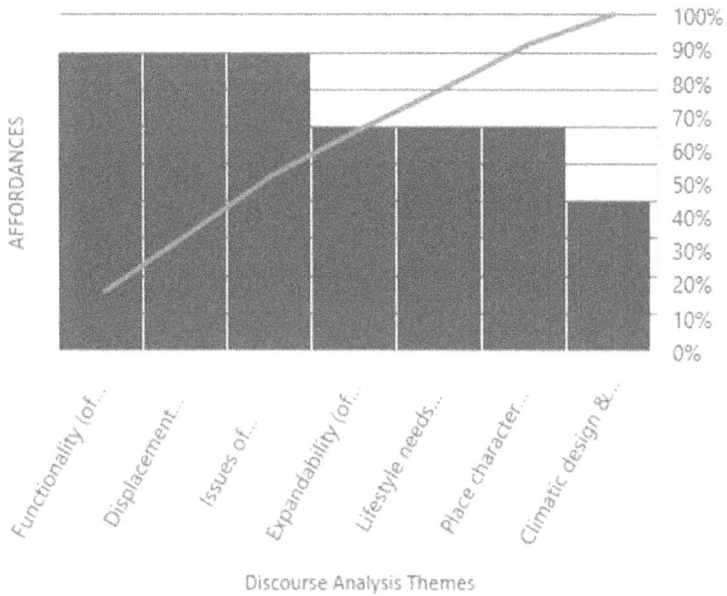

Figure 3.5 Pareto Line for Samadhigama.

Source: Chamila Subasinghe

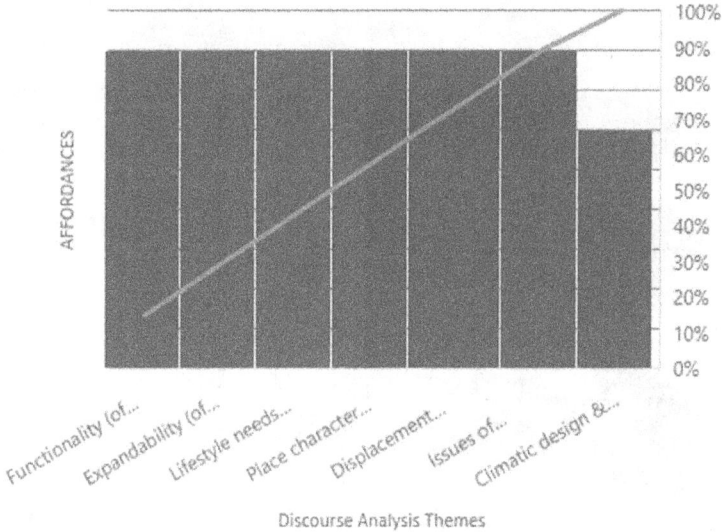

Figure 3.6 Pareto Line for Yayawatte

Source: Chamila Subasinghe

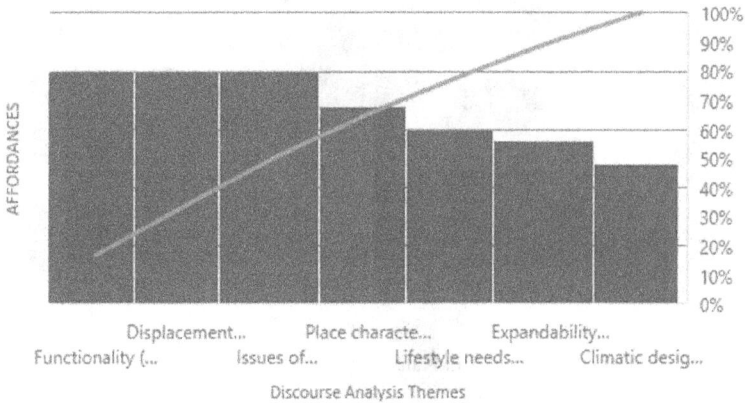

Figure 3.7 Pareto Line for aggregate analysis of all cases.

Source: Chamila Subasinghe

and aesthetic preferences. In some cases, original houses were demolished and reconstructed with new designs. Such situations indicate the designs' inability to adapt as residents tailored the houses to their needs, with some even opting for complete reconstruction. The design of housing units should consider the eventual need for residents to modify, expand, and easily personalize their initial homes. An incremental growth strategy, similar to vernacular settlements, involves utilizing adaptable models and variations. These models are usually simple and contain a

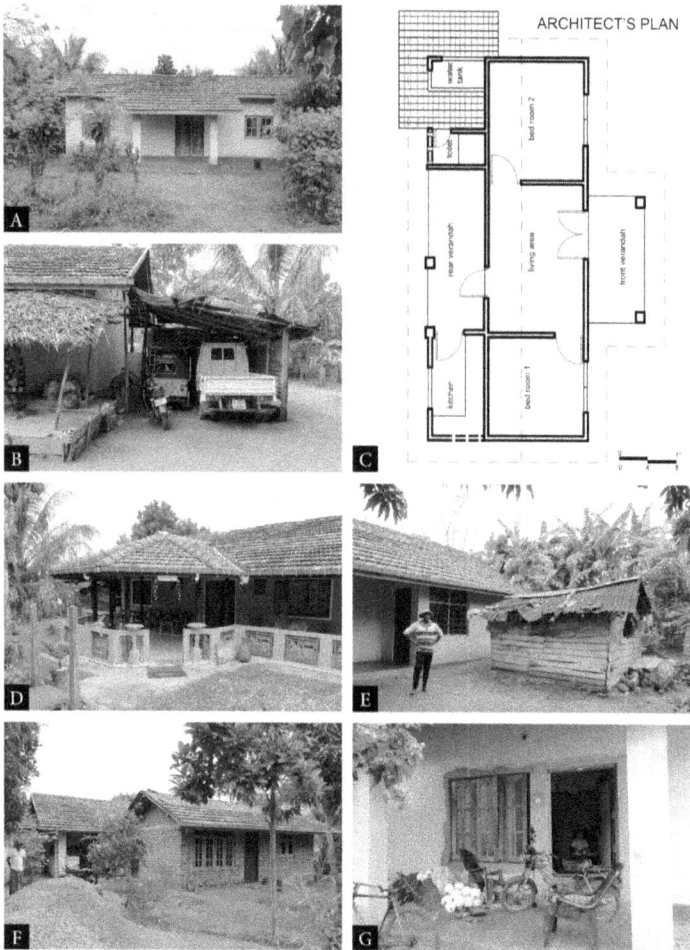

Figure 3.8 User-Initiated Changes in Kalamatiya

small kit of parts, which are reused and adjusted for different purposes like homes, institutions, and religious structures. Designers can implement a "model and variation" approach by collaborating with the community to establish a few house types and variations, indicating how expansions and adaptations can occur (Rapoport 1988). The findings support and add to research by Tipple (2000) on UiCs. This includes providing ample space for future expansions, easily extendable roofs, covering non-living areas, offering multiple design options, incorporating large rooms, accommodating symbolic extensions (to display users' aesthetic preferences and social status) and practical extensions (to address real spatial needs), and incorporating visual cues to suggest potential ways and zones of expansion. Our findings

Figure 3.9 User-Initiated Changes in Kirinda

support that settlements that directly address the requirements and lifestyles of the community were more successful in generating higher user satisfaction. For example, allocating larger plots allows residents to make independent home additions and changes. Aligned with Dikmen (2010) work, such plot dimensions can differ based on each household's needs, which are determined through consultations with each family. Similar to the findings of Lizarralde et al. (2017), we also found that when there's a chance for planned incremental improvements, residents might initially accept lower housing standards, making the rehousing process cost-effective. However, challenges arise when dwellings involve technologies and materials

Figure 3.10 User-Initiated Changes in Logoswatte

unfamiliar or unavailable to the residents, making expansion and adaptation more difficult.

Third, architects incorporated sustainable design and construction methods into house designs at the request of donors and governments. These practices include designing the building envelope with features like sun-baked bricks and clay roof tiles, fenestrations to maximize ventilation and natural light, creating roofs with extended eaves for sun protection, using locally sourced materials, installing solar panels for energy generation, rainwater harvesting systems for water collection, and creating green spaces for cooler microclimates within the settlement. However,

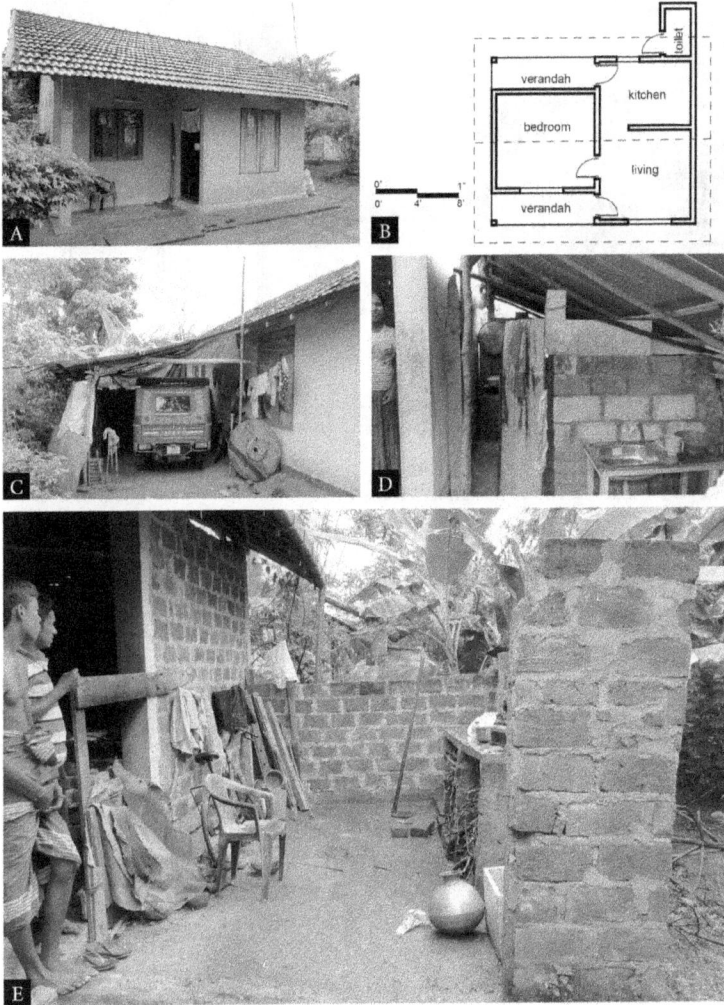

Figure 3.11 User-Initiated Changes in Samadhigama

residents' perceptions of these sustainable ideas have revealed architects' limited understanding of users' socio-cultural and economic contexts. Users saw sun-baked bricks as low-quality and low-status building materials. Fenestration design created security and safety threats and privacy concerns. In certain areas, annual rainfall was more than enough for users' water needs, and rainwater storage systems were unnecessary. Low-level extended roof eaves hindered the expansion of houses. Solar panels, rainwater harvesting systems, and green spaces were never maintained. Sustainable design often aligns with vernacular building traditions, suggesting designers rethink costly and culturally inappropriate contemporary practices

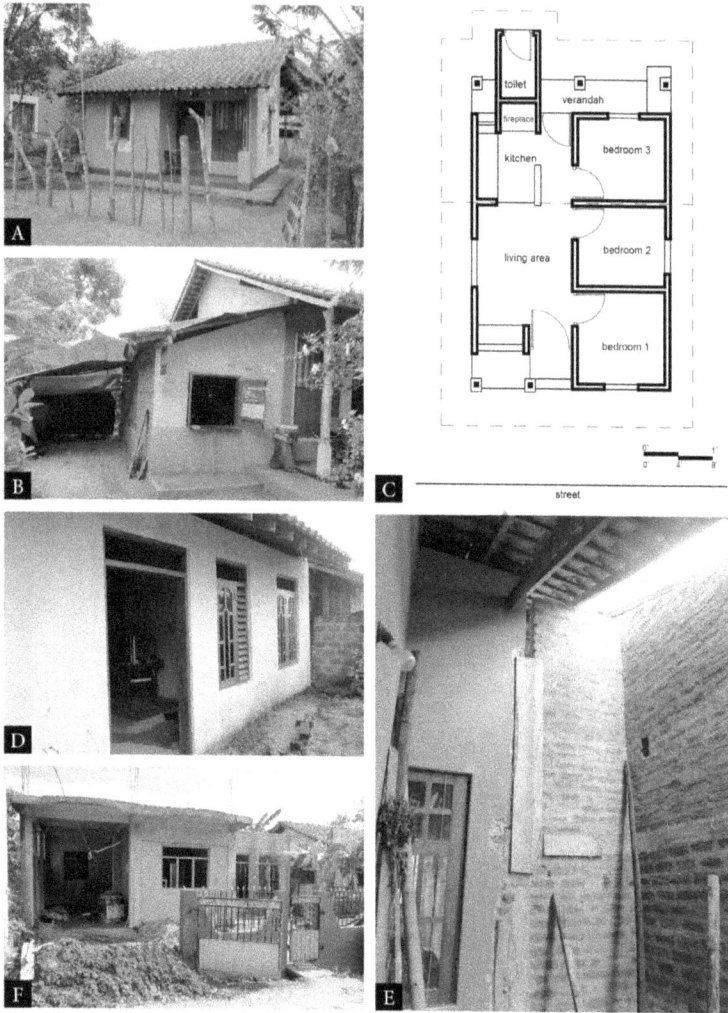

Figure 3.12 User-Initiated Changes in Yayawatte

and pay more attention to what people locally do for sustainability. Designers can assist in building local capacities in technology usage and maintenance. New construction materials and techniques should be introduced through ongoing dialogues between residents and designers, focusing on local capacity building related to new materials and technology. Evaluating sustainable design concepts against cultural and contextual suitability before implementation in resettlement housing is crucial, which is ideally carried out through community engagement. In summary, designers can introduce new technologies into local building methods, but it should be done sensitively, considering local technology and economy, and through community participation.

Fourth, there was a gap between what architects conceived the people would need and what was compatible with their lifestyle. Contrary to the architects' intentions, interviews with residents revealed that house designs were not practical and failed to align with the socio-cultural dimensions of their life routines. For example, the designs were too small, programmatically inadequate, and did not account for communal beliefs about privacy and security. Making no allowance for astrological/religious beliefs was another mismatch. Every interviewee commented on the houses being too small for their requirements. The integrated kitchenettes in the houses were too small or did not match the way they cooked. Statistically, around 90% of the study participants needed to modify house designs significantly to match their lifestyle, beliefs, privacy, and security requirements. Furthermore, architects' interviews indicated a lack of comprehension of users' socio-cultural lives. It may have resulted from the unavailability of comprehensive user studies, which eventually led to architectural elements based on assumptions of user needs, which proved inadequate.

Fifth, the character and imagery of the houses either neglected pre-disaster vernacular imagery or gave superficial reverence to it. Donor organizations desired architects to provide a maximum number of houses within a limited budget, leading to repeated, compact "cookie-cutter" houses in each settlement. In *Logoswatte* and *Yayawatte*, a few house types were developed with slight variations to the original design, aiming to introduce some formal and functional diversity while giving users a limited choice and enhancing visual appeal in the settlements. Architects believed incorporating imagery of vernacular peasant houses with tiled gable roofs and small front and/or back verandas would establish an idealized rural ambience. For example, architects designed the roofs in *Logoswatte* to mimic fishing boat sails to create a recognizable and familiar association for the fishing communities, despite not all residents being involved in fishing before the disaster.

Sixth, in four out of five resettlement areas, people were displaced up to eight kilometres inland from their original locations after the tsunami. For residents in these settlements, the government's buffer zone policy disrupted their livelihoods, social connections, land ownership, and attachment to their homes. Fisher communities, who depended on the shoreline to store their fishing equipment and boats, were the most affected. There was no public transportation provided from the resettlement to the coastline. Even though bicycles were supplied to every family in one of the resettlements, they were insufficient for livelihood and other transportation needs, and fishermen had to change professions. Unfortunately, no social support systems, such as job training, commercial facilities, or daycare services, were available. Relocating residents to safer zones should only be considered after consultation with the community and only if unavoidable (Silva 2011; Wu and Lindell 2004). Social support systems, including physical spaces such as houses of worship, parks, schools, and markets, are critical to creating a sense of community and protecting livelihood (I. Davis 2006; Kennedy et al. 2008; Subasinghe 2012; Winchester 2000). Additionally, socially sustainable management of settlement systems and mobilizing structures for political engagement can also aid in recovery, as McAdam, McCarthy, and Zald (1996) suggest.

Finally, the poor management of resettlements and the lack of community engagement created sustained issues. The Sri Lankan government established two programmes for rebuilding housing: owner-driven and donor-driven. The donor-driven reconstruction programme was responsible for relocating disaster-affected families inland. The government set standards for these relocation projects, including a minimum floor area per dwelling unit and a minimum cost. Donor agencies followed these minimum standards to build the maximum number of units on relocation sites with minimum expenditure. Architects followed the government's minimum building standards and the desires of donor agencies in the planning and design of settlements. This resulted in smaller plots, compact dwellings, and poor construction quality, which the study participants had to deal with eventually. The country's official institution of architects intervened to maintain an equitable distribution of reconstruction projects among its membership and to engage them in humanitarian work. Some donors recruited local architects and foreign consultants on their own. The lack of meaningful user participation in the resettlement process resulted in designers assuming rather than studying people's housing needs. This disengagement led to the eventual discontent of residents with the design of their dwellings and the absence of any sense of ownership and emotional connection with their new home environments. People felt disempowered and dependent on aid agencies and the government. Residents also questioned the competency of relief agencies in construction management and their ability to provide physical and social infrastructure and long-term maintenance/management plans for the settlements while fostering potent community agency throughout the settlement process.

The most critical lesson from past recovery and rehousing efforts is the need to actively engage residents in making their homes. The owner-driven approach to rehousing has proven to be faster, more cost-effective, and less problematic, leading to higher quality housing and greater resident satisfaction (Arlikatti and Andrew 2017; Ophiyandri 2011; Sapat and Esnard 2017). Effective stakeholder engagement is complex and requires a partnership among designers, funders, local organizations, and residents (Arnstein 1969;Sliwinski 2010). Sustainable recovery should be based on local knowledge and capabilities rather than on purely external input. Therefore, it is essential to understand the importance of studying the residents' patterns of settings and activities in the local cultural context. To achieve this, rigorous research that accounts for the connection between residents' daily lives and their built environment is required. Housing needs are seldom explicitly defined, making it more imperative for designers and donors to investigate rather than assume the community's needs for resettlement. Unless aid organizations and governments include residents more meaningfully, sheltering efforts will continue to miss their goals (Davis et al. 2015). The study also suggests that apart from limited user involvement in rehousing designs, physical and social support shortages, technology mismatch, and confined incremental growth, an overarching presence of professional dominance does exist in rehousing efforts.

3.5   Discussion

Failing to account for the people's core needs and giving little room for their involvement while focusing solely on physical needs and universal standards in housing provision suggests professional elitism (H. Davis 2006; Petal et al. 2008; Muggah 2008). This elitism causes disaster management efforts to repeat past mistakes and "perpetuate[s] oppression and vulnerability" by privileging "expert" knowledge over people's vernacular knowledge gained by experience (Petal et al. 2008; Schilderman, 2004). It also exposes the affected people to exploitation, marginalization, loss of agency, cultural imperialism, violence, and knowledge denial (Petal et al. 2008). To overcome some aspects of professional elitism, the notion of "shelter" as mere protection against the elements should be rethought by "sheltering"; this includes the political, humanitarian, economic, and physical processes of rebuilding communities impacted by disasters (Davis, I. P 2006). Sheltering is akin to the vernacular construction process in which users build their homes. It has become rare in the developed world due to professional elites who consolidate the production of space. In fact, according to Davis (2006), the affected communities in the developing world view professionals as unhelpful.

fessional education in architecture, engineering, and planning that are key to redevelopment efforts carries much of the blame because the discipline-specific education is mostly focused on developing technical skills or continuing stylistic tastes instead of gaining interdisciplinary knowledge (Capps 2011;Coleman 2010). Thus, it fails to address issues of social inequality associated with the designed environments (Anderson 2012; Davis 2006). "[T]he most important contribution of architects and other specialists does not come from where it is commonly believed to (design and construction) but instead from a proper understanding of the roles and capacities of the multiple actors involved" (Lizarralde et al. 2010:1). The existing body of research indicates potential domains of dominance related to professional elitism that put users at a disadvantage:

a.   Lack of early involvement of users in the resettlement processes and procedures.
b.   Lack of options for continuing or adapting users' lifestyles and livelihoods in new locations.
c.   Lack of scope for self-improvement within the rehousing infrastructure provision framework.

3.5.1   *Lack of Early Involvement of Users in Resettlement Processes and Procedures*

As substantiated in extensive research, disaster management is a complex process laden with many latent layers that command collaboration with communities (Conan 1987; I. Davis 1978, 2006; Davis et al. 2015; Hettige and Haigh 2016; Oliver 1986, 2006). The literature on post-disaster resettlement reveals problems with its process and resulting products in the preparation, response, recovery, and mitigation phases. Most efforts have failed because displaced people are not involved enough and early enough in the process and are often relocated away from their familiar environments. Although the question of "how early is early enough" to engage the users largely remains unanswered, the general belief from the social capital point of view is that at least at the early preparedness stage (Berke and Campanella 2006; Sadeka, Mohamad, Sarkar and Al-Amin 2020). Any national or regional disaster planning strategies need periodic local consultations and checkpoints, particularly with the vulnerable communities in disaster-prone areas (Hayles 2008). The argument is that access to such communities is more complex or even counterproductive during and after a disaster. Thus, the data drawn are not as reliable as one wanted them to be.

Why has collaboration with communities been an underserved area in recovery despite its *de facto* status in the disaster discourse? Because the focus is on the efficient procurement and coordination of finite resources such as land, infrastructure, building materials and equipment, construction workforce, and finances instead of community involvement (Hettige and Haigh 2016; Lizarralde, Johnson, and Davidson 2010; Petal et al. 2008; Rahmayati 2016). Sometimes, marginalized groups do not have the financial capital to bear even the lowest costs of recovery (Nakagawa and Shaw 2004). Thus, most of the rehousing for the marginalized are low-cost rapid resolutions to respond to an impending housing crisis. These projects are mostly centrally controlled, turning the community into passive recipients of external aids rather than active participants in charge of their recovery (Andrew et al. 2013; Berke, Kartez, and Wenger 1993; Lizarralde et al. 2017; Subasinghe 2012; Schilderman 2010). What is overlooked in such projects is the rich social capital of low socio-economic groups across the world. Such social capital leads communities to build resilience through pragmatic ways they manage, adapt, learn, and grow by facing the disaster challenges themselves (Kenney and Phibbs 2015:48).

Community involvement should be spontaneous. If post-disaster resettlements are coerced and exacerbate pre-existing disparities, end-user engagement potentially becomes a political issue (Hayles 2008). Institutional errors such as incompetencies of donor agencies and lack of coordination among managers could cause inequities in the rehousing distribution. The other significant consequences may include contested cultural identities, lack of sense of ownership, and challenged social status (Ranaweera 2007; Relief Web 2007; Weerakoon et al. 2007; Kennedy et al. 2008; Muggah 2008; Ahmed and McEvoy 2014; Boano 2009; Frerks 2010; Zetter and Boano 2010; de Silva 2017; Dias, Keraminiyage, and de Silva 2016; Fernando, Fernando, and Kumarasiri 2009; Gamburd 2014; Vithanagama et al. 2015; Hettige and Haigh 2016). The other reasons for failed efforts include settlement planning with limited scope for sustainable growth and the shelters in such settlements not adequately addressing people's changed needs (Oliver-Smith 1991, 1996; Sapat and Esnard 2017). In addition to limited access to decision-making, some communities are unaware of their rights and the disaster management agencies' responsibility to involve them in the process (Karanci and Aksit 1999).

Involvement needs to achieve equilibrium. When the use of available resources is in balance, community involvement in disaster mitigation and response has shown positive outcomes. It enables community members to help each other (Becker et al. 2014). Moreover, aligning resettlement efforts with communal socio-cultural norms aids a better understanding of mitigation and response procedures for stakeholders (Oliver 1986; Karanci and Aksit 1999; Gaillard 2015; Parkash 2008; Smith and Birkland 2012; Vithanagama et al. 2015). Although aid agencies acknowledge the capacity of social capital to reduce resettlement costs, they tend to focus more on physical and technical gains such as cheap labour and materials that are disconnected from the socio-economic realities of the affected (Esnard and Sapat 2014; Nakagawa and Shaw 2004; Sapat and Esnard 2017; Schilderman 2004). This may be due to donors', developers', designers', and governments' limited understanding of what is at stake when evacuees are not directly dealing with their resettlement process (I. Davis 2006). As a result, inhabitants receive little or no access to many facets of participatory planning, including resettlement and rehousing design (Andrew et al. 2013; Vithanagama et al. 2015). This does not imply intentional ignorance. In most cases, there could be a "token acknowledgement" of community participation in a very limited sense at an initial stage of resettlement. Another common "token" acknowledgement of cultural and climatic necessities occurs when rehousing designs are based on borrowed vernacular imagery by professionals, particularly architects, to create an illusion of responding to the place and culture of the displaced and of providing a sense of psychological comfort of a familiar place to the displaced via rehousing. These references are often manifest in forms of formal and visual appearance (Heath 2009; Oliver 1986; Rapoport 1983). Instead of sustained engagement via cultural compatibility, spatial adequacy, infrastructure availability, and livelihood support, these "token" acknowledgements of the displaced operate within a narrow world of transient stability. Hence, they only provide short-lived psychological comfort through familiarity and continuity (Gaillard 2015; Kennedy et al. 2008; Lizarralde et al. 2017; Oliver 1986; Oliver-Smith and de Sherbinin 2014; Rahmayati 2016).

What does communal involvement entail? As post-disaster recovery literature highlights, "lessons learned" or experiences gained from past sheltering efforts may have the power to decode involvement. This is possible through knowledge management that includes insights from knowledge creation, storage, transfer, and application (Chua, Kaynak and Foo 2007;Pathirage 2011). Such knowledge management extends beyond simply gathering data for storage and reuse. It systematically integrates existing tacit and explicit experiences reproduced by an agency through its transactions with its environment (Nonaka, Toyama, and Konno, 2000). Specific to disaster recovery, *knowledge creation* is a reciprocal relationship between internalized, tacit knowledge and codified, explicit knowledge that oscillates between state and non-governmental agencies (Alavi and Leidner 2001; Ballinger and Silva 2017). *Knowledge storage* maintains retrievable knowledge in its original form, perhaps in multiple formats depending on what to store (Alavi and Leidner 2001; Ballinger and Silva 2017). Equally important is how and who uses it. If the problem is communities being unaware of disaster response procedures and their purpose, the solution is to keep communities involved; then the integrated knowledge storage format works (Becker et al. 2014). K*nowledge transfer* refers to a trackable release of knowledge by codified experts to capable receivers (Alavi and Leidner, 2001). In the disaster mitigation and preparedness context, knowledge transfer focuses on building local capacities through community integration to generate culturally appropriate disaster response (Kenney and Phibbs 2015; Smith and Birkland 2012). *Knowledge application* facilitates an operational model through specific tools (Alavi and Leidner 2001). However, there seem to be inevitable limitations in applying knowledge across different contexts due to the varied economic, socio-cultural, and political conditions of affected communities in contexts (Esnard and Sapat 2014; Gaillard 2015). Even the few opportunities available for inhabitants to partake in rehousing designs are limited to aesthetic judgements (Rahmayati 2016). On the contrary, user-driven rehousing approaches with proper community engagement tend to deliver mutually beneficial outcomes. While optimizing resourcefulness and increasing individual and collective agency in the overall recovery process, such approaches ensure user satisfaction towards rapid recovery (Lizarralde et al. 2017; Sapat and Esnard 2017).

3.5.2 *Lack of Options for Continuing or Adapting Lifestyles and Livelihoods in New Locations*

The availability of options on where and how people live is considered a characteristic of an advanced society. It offers many perks, including participative spatial democracy (Roulleau-Berger 2015). However, options hardly come by when deciding on new locations for resettlement (Siriwardhana, Kulatunga, Samaraweera, and Shanika 2021). Such resettlements, either in a transitional setting temporarily and/ or in a new site permanently, are likely the outstanding outcome of many recovery processes (Muggah 2008). Fothergill and Peek (2012) describe a state of "permanent temporariness" – being perpetually in flux, unsettled, and uncertain – that survivors endure due to displacement. Muggah (2008) argues that displacement and resettlement should be considered together and could be understood in terms of voluntary or involuntary displacement/resettlement, geographic or socio-economic, and temporary or permanent. The dislocation dimension of the relocation further complicates the issue as it impedes the establishment of community solidarity among the newly resettled (Fu, Lin, and Shieh 2013). Difficulties in developing a sense of ownership and attachment to a particular place are at the core of the relocation issue that may cause interrupted income, habits and rituals, support networks, and access to affordable amenities (Arlikatti et.al, 2015; Esnard and Sapat 2014; Ingram et al. 2006; Jha et al. 2010; Lizarralde et al. 2017; Muggah 2008; Oliver-Smith 1991, 1996; Quarantelli 1982). A sense of ownership of the new location is vital to feeling secure or defensible, continuing with pre-disaster livelihoods or exploring new opportunities and, most importantly, securing systemic support.

Living and livelihoods together inextricably determine adaptability and continuity. Many rehousing projects reveal a disconnected relationship in terms of physical distance between pre-disaster homes and post-disaster housing (uprootment), as well as people's livelihoods and their replacement housing (livelihood disruption). It is also a decisive divide between "survivor" and "supporter" expectations. For example, survivors prefer to stay close to their destroyed homes or move in with relatives. However, supporters – aid agencies and governments – try to disaster-proof new settlements with buffer zones that displace survivors for the second time (Davis et al. 2015; Davis 2006; Oliver-Smith 1991; 1996). Although residents must bear the difficulties, the degree of displacement is often not based solely on safety precautions, but governments use them to consolidate power in profiting political programmes (Bristol 2010;Davis 2006; Korf 2005; Rice 2005). Hence, relocation becomes one of the critical causes of user discontent with post-disaster rehousing (Lizarralde et al. 2017). Consequently, donors, designers, and governments make weak assessments of the cultural needs of the evacuees (I. Davis 2006; Rahmayati 2016; Vithanagam et al. 2015). Decision-makers (i.e. governments, aid agencies, donors) often underestimate the degree of people's self-reliance and, thus, fail to assess the scale of the needs to allocate external aid proportionately (Davis et al. 2015). As a result, making a new home becomes an added challenge when evacuees encounter escalating construction costs, lack of skilled labour, building material shortages, and incompetencies of donor agencies along with poor coordination among relevant authorities (Boano 2009; Frerks 2010; Kennedy et al. 2008; Muggah 2008; Weerakoon et al. 2007; Subasinghe, 2018). Poor coordination among agencies could result from not being able to define suitable roles to scope the work ahead. While aid agencies overlook social organizations and miss opportunities to strengthen community-based organizations, displaced people deal with the dire consequences of livelihood losses (Hettige and Haigh 2016; Kennedy et.al. 2008).

Continuity, as in durability, is another vital factor for the sustainability of building methods and materials. In housing design, a lack of regard for choosing contextually and culturally appropriate materials and construction processes to maintain resettlement housing up to liveable standards is also problematic. Several studies reveal that when new houses are built with low-quality materials and technologies, it makes repair and maintenance difficult (Ahmed and Charlesworth 2015; Hettige and Haigh 2016). Unfortunately, the emphasis is placed on the image of settlements and dwellings rather than the quality of materials and durability (Rahmayati 2016). Although standard ready-made approaches to reconstruction aim for damage-proofing using new disaster-resistant construction materials and technologies, they tend to discriminate local, traditional, economic, and more familiar technologies and materials. Hence, some top-down approaches disregard the local construction sector, limit the transfer of knowledge and skills of new methods to local workers, and make eventual repairs and modifications expensive, difficult, and unsafe (Jigyasu 2010; Lizarralde et al. 2017). Sometimes the donor-built projects produce higher quality homes built quicker but indicate less user satisfaction rates than home-owner-driven reconstruction (Andrew et al. 2013). Apparently, houses provided without resident involvement do not meet cultural needs and, therefore, residents "naturally adopt a fatalistic view of the product (Bosher, 2008:91)". Consequently, inhabitants struggle to retrofit their homes using traditional construction methods to accommodate changes in family structure, livelihood, or safety needs (Mackay 1978; Maskrey 1995;Petal et al. 2008:192).

3.5.3   Lack of Scope for UiC within Rehousing Infrastructure Provision Framework

UiCs have often been referred to as self-improvement (Oxman and Carmon 1986). It is also considered an important trait of human settlement evolution (Song and Li 2023). However, the degree of freedom for UiC in rehousing design is a crucial matter yet to be investigated. As individual capacities have their own thresholds, defining a scope for UiC can be done by better understanding how social and physical infrastructure work harmoniously. While physical infrastructure ensures water, sanitation, energy, transportation, waste management, and other community amenities, social infrastructure enables access to local organizations, social networks, and support groups (Ahmed and McEvoy 2014; Karunasena 2011; Kennedy et al. 2008; Keraminiyage 2011; Berke et al. 1993; Hettige and Haigh 2016; Keraminiyage 2011). Aligning physical infrastructure with social support in resettlements enables communities to recover effectively, build organizational capacities, and prepare for future disasters (Berke et al. 1993; Esnard and Sapat 2014; Kenney and Phibbs 2015; Smith and Birkland 2012). Sustainable scale for such can be small, low-tech solutions that are easy for community members to construct and maintain (Twigg 2000; 2004). However, the reality is that most resettlement efforts fail to facilitate physical and social infrastructure that allows people to maintain their livelihoods, social networks, and day-to-day needs, in addition to the dislocation issues they deal with (Lizarralde et al. 2017; Lyons, Schilderman, and Boano 2010). Any successful and sustainable infrastructure solution balances close community consultation and local know-how innovation (Hettige and Haigh 2016; Haris, Cheema, Subasinghe, 2019; Jann and Platt 2009). According to Petal et al. (2008:191), "large-scale, top-down, technologically-driven reconstruction projects that typify post-disaster reconstruction engage outside engineers and builders, introduce new and expensive construction technologies, supplant both local knowledge and local labour and do not necessarily reduce vulnerability". While a lack of guidance and support on upkeeping civic infrastructure leads to poor quality or lack of communal spaces, poor livelihood options substantially increase vulnerabilities (Ahmed and McEvoy 2014; Zetter and Boano 2010; Rice 2005). Restrictive rehousing at the planning scale characterizes a lack of infrastructure, overly constrained sizes of houses and plots, and limits to housing flexibility. At the design scale, it shows a lack of provisions for rising construction costs, lack of skilled labour, substandard construction, and building material shortages (Ahmed and McEvoy 2014; Boano 2009; de Silva 2017; Dias, Keraminiyage, and de Silva 2016; Fernando, Fernando, and Kumarasiri 2009; Gamburd 2014; Hettige and Haigh 2016; Muggah 2008; Ranaweera 2007; Relief Web 2007; Vithanagama et al. 2015; Weerakoon et al. 2007; Zetter and Boano 2010).

Houses often require modifications, extensions, or additional structures to accommodate occupants' changing needs. Inhabitants intimately feel the flaws of the lack of scope for improvements in the housing provided for them. Some rehousing solutions are too small to support extended families and are not configured to meet cultural needs such as gender separation, privacy concerns, and compliance with belief systems (Arlikatti and Andrew 2017; Dikmen 2010; Oliver 2006; Silva and Ballinger 2021). Residents often struggle with required alterations as plots are too small, boundaries are ill-defined, houses are too close to each other or to the streets, spaces are too small, and roof forms prevent expansion (Silva and Ballinger 2021). On top of this, restrictive finances and building regulations further curtail inhabitants' scope for improvements (Silva, 2011; Zetter and Boano 2010).

3.6   Conclusion

The above principles are intuitive and supported by a wealth of existing knowledge. They emphasize a fundamental aspect of post-disaster housing and resettlement: housing goes beyond providing shelter to enabling displaced individuals to establish homes. This entails a quantitative provision of physical spaces and a qualitative emphasis on fostering emotional connections and a sense of ownership while promoting recovery across social, economic, and psychological dimensions. Achieving this requires architects and planners to base their designs on thoroughly researched user needs and contextual factors rather than assumptions. Design professionals often do not effectively transfer or apply this knowledge. Post-disaster resettlement necessitates multidisciplinary and integrated knowledge, both in architectural education and the profession itself. This, coupled with models encouraging socially engaged professional practice, would better equip designers to meet the growing demand for effective rehousing solutions. Effective professional engagement in humanitarian efforts hinges on a clear understanding of roles and capacities, transitioning from providers to facilitators and enablers of local capacity development. Moreover, donor agencies must enhance their competencies in recovery management to ensure successful outcomes.

Designers must transcend technical and aesthetic aspects to lead the use of a knowledge management system that evaluates citizen participation, support systems creation, incremental growth, and appropriate technologies. Such a model should be adaptable to different contexts and contribute to socially engaged architecture. However, further research is needed in various settings before transferring these models due to the complexity of factors influencing recovery processes. While strategies may have commonalities, their applicability depends on specific locations' cultural, social, economic, and political nuances.

To embed these models in professional practice, they should be integrated into the discourse of architecture and evaluated alongside new criteria prioritizing community development over aesthetics. Indeed, civic-minded design requires collaboration across disciplines like sociology, economics, and public policy, fostering holistic solutions that address beneficiaries' genuine needs rather than focusing solely on visual appeal. If we continue to leave UiCs on the sidelines, it could not only further divisive hierarchies between people and professionals but also diminish the potential for self-innovation – the efforts that make people fashion fast and efficient ways to manage challenges: our definition of resilience.

Acknowledgements

We would like to thank all the participants in the study for sharing their valuable experiences and views. This study was supported by the General Research Fund Award from the School of Architecture and Design at the University of Kansas, USA.

References

Ahmed, Iftekhar and Darryn McEvoy. 2014. "Post-Tsunami Resettlement in Sri Lanka and India: Site Planning, Infrastructure, and Services." *International Journal of Disaster Resilience in the Built Environment* 5(1):53–65.

Ahmed, Iftekhar and Esther Charlesworth. 2015. "Housing and Resilience: Case Studies from Sri Lanka." Pp. 417–34 in *Recovery from the Indian Ocean Tsunami*, edited by R. Shaw. Tokyo, JPN: Springer.

Alavi, Maryam and Dorothy E. Leidner. 2001. "Review: Knowledge Management and Knowledge Management Systems: Conceptual Foundations and Research Issues." *MIS Quarterly* 25(1):107–36.

Anderson, Nadia M. 2012. "Public Interest Design: A Vehicle for Change in Architectural Education and Practice." Pp. 268–74 in the *Proceedings of the 2012 ACSA International Conference on CHANGE, Architecture, Education, Practices*, edited by X. Costa and M. Thorne. Barcelona, ESP: ACSA.

Andrew, Simon A., Sudha Arlikatti, Laurie C. Long, and James M. Kendra. 2013. "The Effect of Housing Assistance Arrangements on Household Recovery: An Empirical Test of Donor-Assisted and Owner-Driven Approaches." *Journal of Housing and the Built Environment* 28(1):17–34.

Arlikatti, Sudha and Simon A. Andrew 2017. "Disaster Housing Recovery in Rural India: Lessons from 12 Years of Post-tsunami Housing Efforts." Pp. 175–90 in *Coming Home after Disaster: Multiple Dimensions of Housing Recovery*, edited by A. Sapat and A. Esnard. Boca Raton, FL: CRC Press.

Arlikatti, Sudha, Simon A. Andrew, James M. Kendra, and Carla S. Prater. 2015. "Temporary Sheltering, Psychological Stress Symptoms, and Perceptions of Recovery." *Natural Hazards Review* 16(3). https://doi.org/10.1061/(ASCE)NH.1527-6996.0000166.

Arnstein, Sherry R. 1969. "A Ladder of Citizen Participation." *Journal of the American Institute of Planners* 35(4):216–24.

Athukorala, Prema-chandra and Budy P. Resosudarmo. 2005. "The Indian Ocean Tsunami: Economic Impact, Disaster Management, and Lessons." *Asian Economic Papers* 4(1):1–39.

Ballinger, Barry and Kapila D. Silva. 2017. "Knowledge Management in Post-Disaster Resettlement Housing." Pp. 413–23 in *Architectural Research Addressing Societal Challenges: Proceedings of the EAAE/ARCC 10th International Conference*, edited by M. C. da Costa, F. Roseta, J. P. Lages, and S. C. da Costa. London, GBR: CRC Press.

Becker, Julia, Douglas Paton, David Johnston, and Kevin Ronan. 2014. "Societal Influences on Earthquake Information Meaning - Making and Household Preparedness." *International Journal of Mass Emergencies and Disasters* 32(2):317–52.

Berke, Philip R. and Thomas J. Campanella. 2006. "Planning for Post-disaster Resiliency." *The ANNALS of American Academy of Political and Social Science* 604(1):192–207.

Berke, Philip R., Jack Kartez, and Dennis Wenger. 1993. "Recovery after Disaster: Achieving Sustainable Development, Mitigation and Equity." *Disasters* 17(2):93–109.

Boano, Camillo. 2009. "Housing Anxiety and Multiple Geographies in Post-tsunami Sri Lanka." *Disasters* 33(4):762–85.

Bosher, L. 2008. *Hazards and the Built Environment: Attaining a Built-in Resilience.* London: Taylor and Francis.

Bristol, Graeme. 2010. "Surviving the Second Tsunami: Land Rights in the Face of Buffer Zones, Land Grabs and Development." Pp. 133–48 in *Rebuilding after Disasters: From Emergency to Sustainability,* edited by G. Lizarralde, C. Johnson, and C. Davidson. London, GBR: Spon Press.

Capps, Kriston. 2011. "Can Architecture Save Humanity?" *Architect: The Magazine of the American Institute of Architects* (September): 157–63.

Chua, Alton, Selcan Kaynak, and Schubert Foo. 2007. "An Analysis of the Delayed Response to Hurricane Katrina through the Lens of Knowledge Management." *Journal of the American Society for Information Science and Technology* 58(3):391–403.

Coleman, Nathaniel. 2010. "The Limits of Professional Architectural Education." *International Journal of Art and Design Education* 29(2):200–12.

Conan, Michel. 1987. "Dwellers' Involvement in Housing Design: A Developmental Perspective." *Journal of Architectural and Planning Research* 4(4):301–9.

Connolly, Patrick. 2007. "Complications of Land Reform in Posttsunami Sri Lanka." *Chazen Web Journal of International Business.* Retrieved May 10, 2020 (https://www0.gsb.columbia.edu/mygsb/faculty/research/pubfiles/2525/Land%20Reform%20in%20Posttsunami%20Sri%20Lanka_v02.pdf).

Dalgleish, S. 2004. "It's All About Quality: The Pursuit of Quality is Key to a Happy Life." *Quality* 43(6):18.

Davis, Howard. 2006. "Architectural Education and Vernacular Building." Pp. 231–44 in *Vernacular Architecture in the Twenty-First Century: Theory, Education and Practice,* edited by L. Asquith and M. Vellinga. London, GBR: Taylor and Francis.

Davis, Ian P. 1978. *Shelter after Disaster.* Oxford, GBR: Oxford Polytechnic Press.

Davis, Ian, Paul Thompson, and Frederick Krimgold, eds. 2015. *Sheltering after Disaster.* 2nd ed. Lyons, FRA: International Federation of the Red Cross and Red Crescent.

de Silva, Vasantha. 2017. "Kamburugamuva Samudratira Tsunami Nivasa Labadi Vasra 10, Oppu Neha (Even After a Decade, Residents Have Not Received Deeds for Their Tsunami Resettlement Houses at Kamburugamuva)." *Divaina,* August 27. Retrieved August 27, 2017. (http://www.divaina.com/2017/08/27/jana04.html).

Dias, Nuwan T., Kaushal Keraminiyage, and Kushani de Silva. 2016. "Long-term Satisfaction of Post Disaster Resettled Communities: The Case of Post Tsunami - Sri Lanka." *Disaster Prevention and Management* 25(5):581–94.

Dikmen, N. and S. T. Elias-Ozkan. 2016. "Housing after Disaster: A Post Occupancy Evaluation of a Reconstruction Project." *International Journal of Disaster Risk Reduction* 19:167–78.

Dikmen, Nese. 2010. "User Requirements and Responsible Reconstruction." Pp. 193–205 in *Rebuilding after Disasters: From Emergency to Sustainability,* edited by G. Lizarralde, C. Johnson, and C. Davidson. London, GBR: Spon Press.

Emmanuel, Rohinton, ed. 2005. *Guidelines for Housing Development in Coastal Sri Lanka: Statutory Requirements and Best-Practice Guide to Settlement Planning, Housing Design and Service Provision with Special Emphasis on Disaster Preparedness.* Colombo, LKA: National Housing Development Authority.

Esnard, Ann-Margaret and Alka Sapat. 2014. *Displaced by Disaster: Recovery and Resilience in a Globalizing World.* New York, NY: Routledge.

Fernando, Priyanthi, Karin Fernando, and Mansi Kumarasiri, eds. 2009. *Forced to Move: Involuntary Displacement and Resettlement – Policy and Practice.* Colombo, LKA: Centre for Poverty Analysis.

Fothergill, Alice and Lori Peek. 2012. "Permanent Temporariness: Displaced Children in Louisiana." Pp. 119–43 in *Displaced: Life in the Katrina Diaspora*, edited by L. Weber and L. Peek. Austin, TX: The University of Texas Press.

Frerks, Georg. 2010. "Principles Ignored and Lessons Unlearned: A Disaster Studies Perspective on the Tsunami Experience in Sri Lanka." Pp. 143–62 in *Tsunami Recovery in Sri Lanka: Ethnic and Regional Dimensions*, edited by D. B. McGilvray and M. R. Gamburd. London, GBR: Routledge.

Fu, Tsung-Hsi, Wan-I Lin, and Jyh-Cherng Shieh. 2013. "The Impact of Post-disaster Relocation on Community Solidarity: The Case of Post-Disaster Reconstruction after Typhoon Morakot in Taiwan." *World Academy of Science, Engineering and Technology* 78(1):1964–67.

Gaillard, J. C. 2015. *People's Response to Disasters in the Philippines: Vulnerability, Capacities, and Resilience*. New York, NY: Palgrave Macmillan.

Gamburd, Michele R. 2014. *The Golden Wave: Culture and Politics after Sri Lanka's Tsunami Disaster*. Bloomington, IN: The Indiana University Press.

Government of Sri Lanka and Development Partners. 2005. *Sri Lanka: Post Tsunami Recovery and Reconstruction: Progress, Challenges, Way Forward*. Joint Report of the Government of Sri Lanka and Development Partners, Colombo, LKA. Retrieved May 10, 2020 (https://reliefweb.int/sites/reliefweb.int/files/resources/AAE71FDFCCB2306 FC12570E400452DD5-govsri-sri-27dec.pdf).

Haris, M., Cheema, A. and Subasinghe, C. 2019, "Why lessons learnt are lost: Understanding the complexity of barriers to Build Back Better in Pakistan," Disaster Prevention and Management, 28 (5), pp. 677-690

Hayles, C. 2008. "An Exploration of Current Planning, Design and Building Issues in Post-disaster Housing Reconstruction." Women's career advancement and training & development in the, 983.

Heath, Kingston W. M., ed. 2009. "Finding Patterns within Local Building Culture and Preserving the Continuity of Tradition through Participatory Housing and Community Development." Pp 52–60 in *Vernacular Architecture and Regional Design: Cultural Process and Environmental Response*. Oxford, GBR: The Architectural Press.

Hettige, Siri and Richard Haigh. 2016. "An Integrated Social Response to Disasters: The Case of the Indian Ocean Tsunami in Sri Lanka." *Disaster Prevention and Management* 25(5):595–610.

Ingram, Jane C., Guillermo Franco, Christina R. Rio, and Bjian Khazai. 2006. "Post-disaster Recovery Dilemmas: Challenges in Balancing Short-term and Long-term Needs for Vulnerability Reduction." *Environmental Science and Policy* 9(7–8):607–13.

Jann, Marga and Stephen Platt. 2009. "Philanthropic Architecture: Non-governmental Development Projects in Latin America." *Journal of Architectural Education* 62(4): 82–91.

Jha, Abhas K., Jennifer D. Barenstein, Pricilla M. Phelps, Daniel Pittet, and Steven Sena. 2010. *Safer Homes, Stronger Communities: A Handbook for Reconstructing after Natural Disasters*. Washington DC: The World Bank.

Jigyasu, Rohit. 2010. "Appropriate Technology for Post-disaster Reconstruction." Pp. 49–69 in *Rebuilding after Disasters: From Emergency to Sustainability*, edited by G. Lizarralde, C. Johnson, and C. Davidson. London, GBR: Spon Press.

Kamalrathne, T., & Senanayake, A. (2023). Relocated or displaced? A social inquiry of tsunami-induced relocation programme in southern Sri Lanka. In Rebuilding Communities After Displacement: Sustainable and Resilience Approaches (pp. 459-477). Cham: Springer International Publishing.

Karanci, Nuray A. and Bahattin Aksit. 1999. "Strengthening Community Participation in Disaster Management by Strengthening Governmental and Non-governmental Organizations and Networks: A Case Study from Dinar and Bursa (Turkey)." *The Australian Journal of Emergency Management* 13(4):35–9.

Karunasena, Gayani. 2011. "Sustainable Post-Disaster Waste Management: Construction and Demolition Debris." Pp. 251–67 in *Post-Disaster Reconstruction of the Built Environment: Rebuilding for Resilience*, edited by D. Amaratunga and R. Haigh. West Sussex, GBR: Wiley-Blackwell.

Kennedy, Jim, Joseph Ashmore, Elizabeth Babister, and Ilan Kelman. 2008. "The Meaning of 'Build Back Better': Evidence from Post-Tsunami Aceh and Sri Lanka." *Journal of Contingencies and Crisis Management* 16(1):24–36.

Kenney, Christine M. and Suzanne Phibbs. 2015. "A Māori Love Story: Community-Led Disaster Management in Response to the Ōtautahi (Christchurch) Earthquakes as a Framework for Action." *International Journal of Disaster Risk Reduction* 14(1):46–55.

Keraminiyage, Kaushal. 2011. "Restoration of Major Infrastructure and Rehabilitation of Communities." Pp. 236–50 in *Post-Disaster Reconstruction of the Built Environment: Rebuilding for Resilience*, edited by D. Amaratunga and R. Haigh. West Sussex, GBR: Wiley-Blackwell.

Korf, Benedikt. 2005. "Sri Lanka: The Tsunami after the Tsunami." *International Development Planning Review* 27(3):I–VII.

Lanamäki, A., D. Thapa, and K. Stendal. 2016. When is an affordance? Outlining four stances. In Beyond Interpretivism? New Encounters with Technology and Organization: IFIP WG 8.2 Working Conference on Information Systems and Organizations, IS&O 2016, Dublin, Ireland, December 9–10, 2016, Proceedings (pp. 125–139). Springer International Publishing.

Lizarralde, Gonzalo, Mahmood Fayazi, Faten Kikano, and Isabelle Thomas-Maret. 2017. "Meta-Patterns in Post-Disaster Housing Reconstruction and Recovery." Pp. 229–62 in *Coming Home after Disaster: Multiple Dimensions of Housing Recovery*, edited by A. Sapat and A. Esnard. Boca Raton, FL: CRC Press.

Lizarralde, Gonzalo, Cassidy Johnson, and Colin Davidson, eds. 2010. *Rebuilding after Disasters: From Emergency to Sustainability*. London, GBR: Spon Press.

Lyons, Michal, Theo Schilderman, and Camillo Boano, eds. 2010. *Building Back Better: Delivering People-centred Housing Reconstruction at Scale*. London, GBR: Practical Action.

Manatunge, J. M. A., & Abeysinghe, U. (2017). Factors affecting the satisfaction of post-disaster resettlers in the long term: A case study on the resettlement sites of tsunami-affected communities in Sri Lanka. J. Asian Dev, 3(1), 94-124.

McAdam, Doug, John D. McCarthy, and Mayer N. Zald. 1996. *Comparative Perspectives on Social Movements: Political Opportunities, Mobilizing Structures, and Cultural Framings*. Cambridge, GBR: Cambridge University Press.

Muggah, Robert. 2008. *Relocation Failures in Sri Lanka: A Short History of Internal Displacement and Resettlement*. London, GBR: Zed Books.

Nakagawa, Yuko and Rajib Shaw. 2004. "Social Capital: A Missing Link to Disaster Recovery." *International Journal of Mass Emergencies and Disasters* 22(1):5–34.

Nonaka, Ikujiro, Ryoko Toyama, and Noboru Konno. 2000. "SECI, Ba and Leadership: A Unified Model of Dynamic Knowledge Creation." *Long Range Planning* 33(1):5–34.

Oliver, Paul. 1986. "Cultural Factors in the Acceptability of Resettlement Housing." Pp. 117–27 in *Architecture in Cultural Change: Essays in Built Form and Culture Research*, edited by D. Saile. Lawrence, KS: The University of Kansas Press.

Oliver, Paul. 2006. *Built to Meet Needs: Cultural Issues in Vernacular Architecture*. Oxford, GBR: The Architectural Press.

Oliver-Smith, Anthony. 1991. "Successes and Failures in Post-Disaster Resettlement." *Disasters* 15(1):12–23.

Oliver-Smith, Anthony. 1996. "Anthropological Research on Hazards and Disasters." *Annual Review of Anthropology* 25:303–28.

Oliver-Smith, Anthony and Alex de Sherbinin. 2014. "Resettlement in the Twenty-first Century." *Forced Migration Review, Crisis* 45:23–5.

Ophiyandri, Taufika. 2011. "Community-Based Post-Disaster Housing Reconstruction: Examples from Indonesia." Pp. 91–116 in *Post-Disaster Reconstruction of the Built Environment: Rebuilding for Resilience*, edited by D. Amaratunga and R. Haigh. West Sussex, GBR: Wiley-Blackwell.

Oxman, R., and N. Carmon. 1986. "Responsive Public Housing: An Alternative for Low-income Families." *Environment and Behavior* 18(2):258–84.

Pathirage, Chaminda. 2011. "Knowledge Management Practices and Systems Integration." Pp. 208–35 in *Post-Disaster Reconstruction of the Built Environment: Rebuilding for Resilience*, edited by D. Amaratunga and R. Haigh. West Sussex, GBR: Wiley-Blackwell.

Pathiraja, Milinda and Paolo Tombesi. 2009. "Towards a More "Robust" Technology? Capacity Building in Post-tsunami Sri Lanka." *Disaster Prevention and Management* 18(1):55–65.

Prakash, Surya. 2008. "A Methodology for Community Based Disaster Risk Management." Pp. 473–6 in *Proceedings of The First World Landslide Forum*, edited by K. Sassa. Kyoto, JPN: International Consortium on Landslides (ICL).

Petal, Marla, Rebekah Green, Ilan Kelman, and Rajib Shaw. 2008. "Community-based Construction for Disaster Risk Reduction." Pp. 191–217 in *Hazards and the Built Environment: Attaining Built-in Resilience*, edited by L. Bosher. London, GBR: Routledge.

Quarantelli, Enrico L. 1982. *Sheltering and Housing after Major Community Disasters: Case Studies and General Conclusions*. Final Project Report #29. Washington, DC: FEMA. Retrieved April 27, 2010 (https://udspace.udel.edu/handle/19716/1132).

Rahmayati, Yenny. 2016. "Reframing 'Building Back Better' for Post-Disaster Housing Design: A Community Perspective." *International Journal of Disaster Resilience in the Built Environment* 7(4):344–60.

Ranaweera, Dhammika. 2007. "Nihanda Novunu Andona. (Incessant Cries)." *Divaina*, December 26. Retrieved December 26, 2007 (http://www.divaina.com/2007/12/26/feature03.html).

Rapoport, Amos. 1983. "Development, Culture Change, and Supportive Design." *Habitat International* 7(5–6):249–68.

Rapoport, Amos. 1988. "Spontaneous Settlements as Vernacular Design." Pp. 51–77 in *Spontaneous Shelter: International Perspectives and Prospects*, edited by C. V. Patton. Philadelphia, PA: Temple University Press.

Ratnasooriya, Harsha A. R., Saman P. Samarawickrama, and Fumihiko Imamura. 2007. "Post Tsunami Recovery Process in Sri Lanka." *Journal of Natural Disaster Science* 29(1):21–8.

Relief Web. 2007. "Sri Lanka: Post-tsunami Recovery a Success for Most But Not All." *Relief Web*, December 24. Retrieved May 10, 2020 (https://reliefweb.int/report/sri-lanka/sri-lanka-post-tsunami-recovery-success-most-not-all).

Rice, Allison. 2005. *Post-tsunami Reconstruction and Tourism: A Second Disaster?* London, GBR: Tourism Concern. Retrieved May 10 2020 (https://mekongtourism.org/wp-content/uploads/Post-tsunami-Reconstruction-and-tourism-a-second-disaster.pdf).

Roulleau-Berger, L. 2015. "Life Exposed, Inequalities and Moral Economies in Post-disaster Societies: China, Japan and Indonesia." Pp. 163–182 in *Ecological Risks and Disasters-New Experiences in China and Europe*, edited by Michaela Krause, Weidong Liu, and Peter Haslinger. London: Routledge.

Sadeka, S., M. S. Mohamad, M. S. K. Sarkar, and A. Q. Al-Amin. 2020. "Conceptual Framework and Linkage Between Social Capital and Disaster Preparedness: A Case of Orang Asli Families in Malaysia." *Social Indicators Research* 150:479–99.

Sapat, Alka and Ann-Margaret Esnard, eds. 2017. *Coming Home after Disaster: Multiple Dimensions of Housing Recovery*. Boca Raton, FL: CRC Press.

Schilderman, Theo. 2004. "Adapting Traditional Shelter for Disaster Mitigation and Reconstruction: Experiences with Community-based Approaches." *Building Research and Information* 32(5):414–26.

Schilderman, Theo. 2010. "Putting People at the Centre of Reconstruction." Pp. 7–37 in *Building Back Better: Delivering People-centred Housing Reconstruction at Scale*, edited by M. Lyons, T. Schilderman, and C. Boano. London, GBR: Practical Action Publishing.

Seneviratne, Krisanthi. 2011. "Capacity of the Construction Industry for Post-Disaster Reconstruction: Post-Tsunami Sri Lanka." Pp. 30–50 in *Post-Disaster Reconstruction of the Built Environment: Rebuilding for Resilience*, edited by D. Amaratunga and R. Haigh. Chichester, GBR: Wiley-Blackwell.

Silva, Kapila D. 2011. "Resettlement Housing Design: Moving beyond Vernacular Imagery." *South Asia Journal of Culture* 5/6:117–35.

Silva, Kapila D. and Barry T. Ballinger. 2021. "Sustainable Re-housing after Disasters: Learning from Post-tsunami Resettlements in Sri Lanka." International Journal on Mass Emergencies and Disasters 39(1): 120-172.

Siriwardhana, S. D., U. Kulatunga, A. Samaraweera, and V. G. Shanika. 2021. "Cultural Issues of Community Resettlement in Post-Disaster Reconstruction Projects in Sri Lanka." *International Journal of Disaster Risk Reduction* 53:102017.

Sliwinski, Alicia. 2010. "The Politics of Participation: Involving Communities in Post-Disaster Construction." Pp. 177–92 in *Rebuilding after Disasters: From Emergency to Sustainability*, edited by G. Lizarralde, C. Johnson, and C. Davidson. London, GBR: Spon Press.

Smith, Gavin and Thomas Birkland. 2012. "Building a Theory of Recovery: Institutional Dimensions." *International Journal of Mass Emergencies and Disasters* 30(2):147–70.

Somasundaram, Daya. 2014. *Scarred Communities: Psychosocial Impact of Man-made and Natural Disasters on Sri Lankan Society*. New Delhi, IND: SAGE Publications.

Song, R. and X. Li. 2023. "Urban Human Settlement Vulnerability Evolution and Mechanisms: The Case of Anhui Province, China." *Land* 12(5):994.

Subasinghe, Chamila T. 2012. "Shelters of Sustainability: Reconfiguring Post-tsunami Recover via Self-labor Practices." *International Journal of Architecture, Engineering and Construction* 1(3):155–62.

Subasinghe, C. 2018. Is My House My Home? An Analysis of "Nowhereness" Among "Noknowers" in Transitional Settings. Space and Culture, 120633121876706. doi:10.1177/1206331218767063

Tipple, Graham. 2000. *Extending Themselves: User-initiated Transformations of Government-Built Housing in Developing Countries*. Liverpool, GBR: Liverpool University Press.

Twigg, John. 2000. "The Age of Accountability? Future Community Involvement in Disaster Reduction." *The Australian Journal of Emergency Management* 14(4):51–8.

Twigg, John. 2004. *Disaster Risk Reduction: Mitigation and Preparedness in Development and Emergency Programming*. Good Practice Review No. 9, London, GBR: Overseas Development Institute (ODI).

Vithanagama, Ranmini, Alikhan Mohideen, Danesh Jayatilaka, and Rajith Lakshman. 2015. *Planned Relocations in the Context of Natural Disasters: The Case of Sri Lanka*. Colombo, LKA: Centre for Migration Research and Development and Brookings Institute.

Weerakoon, Dushini, Sisira Jayasuriya, Nisha Arunatilake, and Paul Steele. 2007. "Economic Challenges of Post-tsunami Reconstruction in Sri Lanka." Discussion Paper No. 75. Asian Development Bank Institute, Tokyo, JPN. Retrieved November 3, 2019 (https://www.adb.org/sites/default/files/publication/156714/adbi-dp75.pdf).

Winchester, Peter. 2000. "Cyclone Mitigation, Resource Allocation and Post-disaster Reconstruction in South Asia: Lessons from Two Decades of Research." *Disasters* 24(1):18–37.

Wu, Jie-Ying and Michael K. Lindell. 2004. "Housing Reconstruction after Two Major Earthquakes: The 1994 Northridge Earthquake in the United States and the 1999 Chi-Chi Earthquake in Taiwan." *Disasters* 28(1):68–81.

Zetter, Roger and Camillo Boano. 2010. "Space and Place after Natural Disasters and Force Displacement." Pp. 206–30 in *Rebuilding after Disasters: From Emergency to Sustainability*, edited by G. Lizarralde, C. Johnson, and C. Davidson. London, GBR: Spon Press.

4 Micro Human Efforts in Disaster Resilience

Incentives and Disincentives

Zhila Pooyan and Akihiko Hokugo

4.1 Introduction

This chapter holds the crucial role of micro-human efforts (MHE) in disaster resilience, a topic that is often overlooked yet has a profound impact. Micro-human efforts refer to individual-level actions and initiatives in disaster management. These efforts, often carried out by local communities and individuals, play a significant role in risk reduction and disaster preparedness, and various administrative, social, and economic factors influence their effectiveness. Identifying incentives and disincentives for these micro-level efforts is helpful and essential in harmonizing the physical and social aspects of recovery. This harmonization results in compatibility and effectiveness of outcomes considering the duration and expenses of recovery. The Sendai Framework for Disaster Risk Reduction (SFDRR, 2015–2030), an international agreement adopted by the United Nations member states at the Third World Conference on Disaster Risk Reduction (2015), serves as a crucial reference point in this research. It emphasizes disaster risk reduction through building resilience. It promotes the concept of Build Back Better (BBB) to increase the resilience of nations and communities in the post-event phase. Therefore, we delve into the micro-human roles in disasters, focusing on resilience and BBB to underscore their importance and the potential to significantly impact disaster resilience, highlighting the urgency and importance of this research.

The primary research question is how MHE in the post-event phase contributes to resilience during recovery. This question is of paramount importance as it guides our understanding of the role of individual-level efforts in disaster resilience. The secondary research questions are as follows: How did local communities respond to save lives, provide self-help, and protect themselves against future hazards? What factors obstruct and motivate them in taking post-event acts and initiatives? These questions are crucial and urgent in understanding the dynamics of post-disaster community actions and the factors influencing them. Immediate action is needed to address these issues.

The chapter is based on studies and investigations conducted in the Tohoku region in Miyagi Prefecture in Ishinomaki City and its subordinate districts, as well as the Iwate prefecture in Kamaishi City and its subordinate towns and districts. All studied areas have suffered massive damage from the GEJET, leading to population loss, structural and infrastructural demolition, economic decline,

DOI: 10.4324/9781003615903-5

and environmental devastation. Thereupon, affected communities had to deal with harsh circumstances and unexpected challenges.

The chapter consists of a review of micro-human roles in times of disaster, considering resilience and BBB dimensions and components; then, impactful factors in micro-human efforts are derived. Second, the methodology is explained, the GEJET disaster is described, its characteristics, and consequences are outlined, and the areas of study are introduced. Third, local-level efforts in investigated areas based on field studies in explored areas, interviews with local authorities, community organizations' leaders, and volunteer groups are presented. Fourth, micro-human level efforts are discussed to identify the incentive and disincentive factors, and finally, conclusions are drawn.

4.2   Micro Human Roles in Disasters Considering Resilience and Building Back Better

The micro-human level includes the affected people who are the first responders in times of disaster; they are the first ones to rescue their family, neighbours, and anyone else even if they might be injured themselves. In various disasters around the world, affected people start to rescue, save lives, and assist one another. For example, in the Southern Hyogo Prefecture earthquake in Kobe City, Japan (1995), about 75% of those trapped under the rubble were rescued by ordinary citizens (UNCRD, 1995). In Manjil (1990) and Varzaghan (2012), earthquakes in Iran affected people started rescue and relief activities by themselves since the affected areas were inaccessible due to damages (Pooyan, 2016).

Self-motivated activities done by disaster victims are a leading factor in establishing order and peace post-event.

> Self-help done by disaster-affected people is uncontrollable as they are physically and psychologically dependent. One of the highest disaster costs of disasters ... is the effective undermining of any sense people have of their ability to control and manage their environments or lives.
>
> (Mazumdar et al., 2021)

Understanding micro-humans' views and ideas on recovery is indispensable for the optimum use of time and resources.

> Taking an emic perspective to obtain an in-depth and detailed understanding of affected people, including the situated context of their lives, what they value as important, how they prefer to live, what they view as problems, and even their fundamental views of humans, animals, nature, possessions, and space, as well as local cultural-ecological wisdom is essential.
>
> (Mazumdar et al., 2021)

MHEs play a crucial role as the primary source for promoting public awareness and stockpiling necessary materials. This is essential for implementing rescue and relief activities. We can ensure better emergency response by forming community volunteers and strengthening technical and logistical capacities. Additionally, communities can offer essential services in the post-event phase. Therefore, promoting regular disaster preparedness, response, and recovery exercises, such as evacuation drills, training, as well as establishing area-based support systems, is vital. These measures ensure a rapid and effective response to disasters and related displacement, including access to safe shelter, essential food, and non-food relief supplies tailored to the local community's needs. This strengthens the response capacity and efficiency in the post-event phase.

According to the SFDRR, resilience is the ability of a system, community, or society exposed to hazards to resist, absorb, accommodate, adapt to, transform, and recover from the effects of a hazard in a timely and efficient manner (SFDRR, 2015). This includes preserving and restoring its essential basic structures and functions through risk management. Resilience is a critical aspect of disaster management and has been characterized as having four dimensions (Tierney, 2014) (Figure 4.1).

Resilience and dimensions	Characteristics
1. Robustness:	like resistance or strength, robustness is a critical element of resilience, which is the ability to withstand stresses and demands without losing function.
2. Redundancy:	the degree to which other units of analysis or elements can be substituted for those lost or disrupted when disaster strikes while maintaining functionality. Redundancy encompasses diversity, substitutability, and heterogeneity and is an essential element of resilience because it increases options for adaptation and enhances overall system stability.
3. Resourcefulness:	the ability to identify problems and subsequently mobilize material, informational, monetary, and other resources to address disaster-related problems. It encompasses various capacities, and processes, including mobilizing resources in response to disasters, restoring resources lost due to disasters, and learning and applying knowledge across the hazard cycle. Resourcefulness also includes the ability to use creativity and to improvise in the face of disaster or disruption.
4. Rapidity:	a dimension of resilience that measures the time it takes to restore the system's functionality to its level before the disruption. This is a crucial aspect of resilience, as time is a critical factor in disaster-related activities. They exhibited before they experienced disruption. It is essential because time is a vital element in disaster-relevant activities. In addition to being a dimension of resilience, rapidity can be conceptualized as an outcome of the other three resilience aspects. Highly robust, redundant, and resourceful systems can be expected to experience less disaster-induced disruption and restore themselves more rapidly than less resilient ones. However, rapidity does not signify that the timeliness of recovery potentially undermines longer-term adaptability and sustainability.

Figure 4.1 Dimensions and Characteristics of Resilience

Resilient characteristics such as redundancy, resourcefulness, and rapidity depend on individuals' preparedness and capability, upon which such a system is robust.

Building back better involves utilizing the recovery, rehabilitation, and reconstruction phases after a disaster to increase the resilience of nations and communities by integrating disaster risk reduction measures into the restoration of physical infrastructure and societal systems, thereby revitalizing livelihoods, economies, and the environment (UNDRR, 2023). BBB ensures that the repaired or replaced assets are more resilient, that the recovery process is shorter and more efficient, and that the recovery process does not leave anyone behind. However, BBB is not only to "build back" as quickly as possible after disasters but to "build better" to improve the quality of life and reduce losses from future disasters. BBB has three dimensions that could be independent or together:

a. Building back stronger reduces losses to well-being by ensuring that reconstructed infrastructure can resist more intense events in the future.
b. Building back faster reduces disaster impacts by accelerating reconstruction through contingent reconstruction plans, pre-approved contracts, and financial arrangements.
c. Building back more inclusively ensures that post-disaster support reaches all affected population groups (GFDRR, 2018).

MHEs in resilience and BBB are observable as communities know the most about their local environment, culture, vulnerabilities, requirements, and building techniques. This knowledge empowers residents to work together to rebuild their lives, housing, and livelihoods. They should plan the reconstruction or, at the very least, oversee it. The affected community is not a monolith but a complex organism with many alliances and subgroups. The community's role in identifying concerns, goals, and abilities is crucial and should be respected. At the same time, there may not be concurrence on these matters (GFDRR, 2010). Still, the local level is the pioneer in post-event recovery, whether in immediate response or later in longer-term recovery. Resilience and BBB comprise the concept of sustainability through applying risk reduction measures to maintain the functionality of systems in times of disaster. Sustainability is the goal of resilient community recovery and, in this context, is not just a matter of maintaining and increasing numbers of people and facilities. While maintaining certain levels of quantity is important and efforts in this regard are necessary, even more important, in the end, is keeping the quality of life and, thus, the livelihoods (IRP, 2013).

Achieving a level of safety in formulating a recovery plan is essential and ensures that similar levels of damage will not recur in future disasters; however, if attempts are made to ensure safety using uniform methods of dealing with large-scale disasters at the national level, the rebuilt community may be changed entirely, such that livelihoods in that area will not be re-established. Community residents will not progress in their recovery, which contrasts with sustainability. Thus, community development efforts comprised of social elements must be undertaken through a bottom-up approach in collaboration with residents. To ensure a resilient recovery, such a community can better anticipate threats, limit their impacts, and recover more rapidly through adaptation and growth in the face of turbulent change. Thereupon, it is sufficiently able to resist or recover rapidly from disasters (APA, 2016).

4.2.1 Impactful Factors in Micro-human Efforts

The micro-human level is the main target of any damage reduction activity and the beneficiary of recovery-related efforts; however, it influences the direction and potential outcomes of recovery through self-initiated endeavors. However, the local level is influenced by some factors that impact the direction and procedure of their actions (Figure 4.2).

As Cutter stated, the socio-economic capacities of communities impact their ability to absorb losses and enhance their resilience to hazard impacts, as higher capacities enable communities to absorb and recover from losses more quickly due to social safety nets and entitlement programmes (Cutter et al., 2003).

In building resilience through collaborative action and shared capacity building, developing solid relationships built on mutual trust and respect (AIDR, 2020) is essential for upper and lower levels of relationships and community engagement. Burby mentioned that a sustainable community is derived from an open and participative process in which citizens and groups contemplate and coalesce around a desirable view of the future of their community (Burby, 1998).

March considered that a community's resilience depends on various inter-related elements, such as the physical characteristics of places and how human

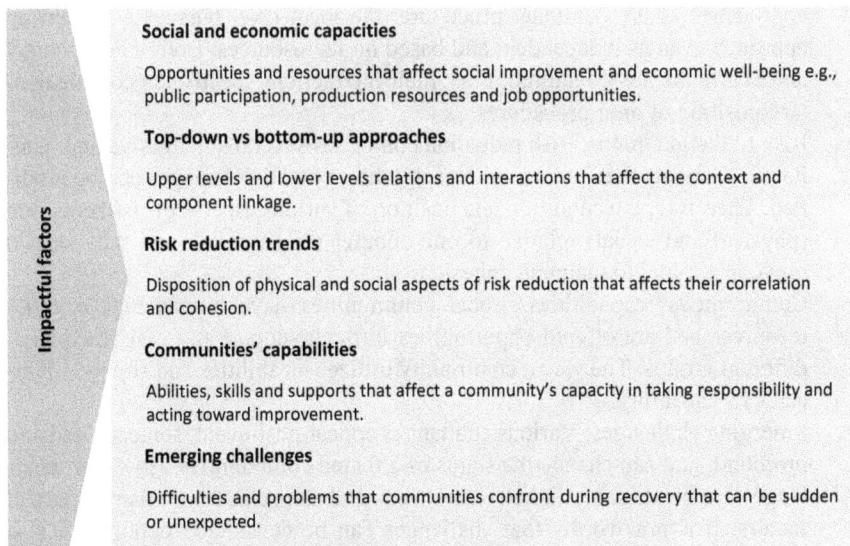

Social and economic capacities

Opportunities and resources that affect social improvement and economic well-being e.g., public participation, production resources and job opportunities.

Top-down vs bottom-up approaches

Upper levels and lower levels relations and interactions that affect the context and component linkage.

Risk reduction trends

Disposition of physical and social aspects of risk reduction that affects their correlation and cohesion.

Communities' capabilities

Abilities, skills and supports that affect a community's capacity in taking responsibility and acting toward improvement.

Emerging challenges

Difficulties and problems that communities confront during recovery that can be sudden or unexpected.

Figure 4.2 Impactful Factors in Micro-level Efforts

systems, including governance, economics, and social relations, interact with one another. Risk reduction trends can significantly contribute to a resilient recovery by enhancing the capacity of these elements, improving their resilience, ensuring ongoing maintenance, and improving overall performance (March et al., 2017). Mileti believed that a community's capabilities in integrating the micro-human level into regional and national networks require solid local governmental capacity and a cohesive system of public, private, and volunteer groups integrated within the community that influences the recovery process and the expected outcomes (Mileti, 1999).

It is worth noting that emerging challenges during recovery, whether stemming from pre-event trends or post-event situations, impact MHE. High damage to various subsystems can lead to immigration, relocations, or economic decline resulting in resource depletion, that affects recovery duration and outcomes (Pooyan et al., 2017).

Impactful factors can be the continuation of pre-event situations or consequences of disasters; however, their outcome depends on the status of the affected community. This indicates that impactful factors and their interactions in a community are variable. Considering our presentation so far, we define the meaning of impactful factors in MHEs that are used in our research.

- Social and economic capacities: Refer to all opportunities and resources in a given area that result in social improvements and economic well-being, such as public participation, production resources, and job opportunities. Such capacities can maintain the population, attract facilities, and financial sources that influence potential growth and progress.
- Top-down vs. bottom-up approaches: The national level adopts top-down approaches as the dominant procedure; the local level pursues a bottom-up approach even as independent and based on its resources. Both levels contact and communicate if required; thus, their interactions specify the complementary position of their procedures.
- Risk reduction trends: Risk reduction comprises several quantitative and qualitative elements that interact with each other; potential damages can be modified. Therefore, the condition and position of various aspects of risk reduction (physical and social) relative to one another are essential, and they should move in parallel to maintain cohesion.
- Communities' capabilities: Local communities have human and material resources and are offered opportunities through support and assistance from different groups. The way a community utilizes its abilities and supports indicates its capability.
- Emerging challenges: Various challenges appear post-event, some sudden and profound, and can change the status of affected communities. However, challenges are inextricably linked to recovery and can stem from other impactful factors. It is noteworthy that challenges can be considered opportunities to reduce potential damages.

4.3   Methodology, the GEJET Characteristics, and Introducing Studied Areas

As mentioned, the primary research question is how MHE in post-event smooths the path towards resilience during recovery, and the secondary questions are:

- How did local communities act to save lives, provide self-help, and protect themselves against future hazards?
- What factors encourage and discourage the human level from taking post-event acts and initiatives?

Following the research questions, we investigated local communities' actions on self-help, rescue and relief, disaster preparedness and driving recovery plans, as well as community-based recovery plans, volunteers' and supporters' roles, and existing challenges. We visited the studied areas between November 2016 and April 2018 and interviewed community-based organizations, regional authorities, social welfare organizations, and local associations in the studied regions.

The investigated topics included:

- What actions have local communities taken to improve local capacities, self-help, disaster drills, or any other activity to integrate disaster preparedness into their daily life?
- Have community-based recovery plans been formulated? If so, have these plans been considered by the national/prefectural government?
- How have local communities been effective in driving recovery plans in their domains?
- How did volunteers, supporters, and specialists help in micro-human efforts?
- What were the challenges for micro-human efforts in the GEJET recovery?

After collecting the inquired information, we analyzed it to determine the incentives and disincentives for MHEs.

The GEJET happened on 11 March 2011 at 02:46 PM, with an earthquake of magnitude 9.0 that generated a gigantic tsunami that hit a 700 km stretch of its Pacific coastlines. The tsunami devastated the Tohoku region of Japan, with Iwate, Miyagi, and Fukushima Prefectures being the worst affected (JRCS, 2021). Nineteen thousand seven hundred forty-seven people lost their lives (5,145 in Iwate prefecture, 10,567 in Miyagi prefecture), and 2,556 people are missing (1,111 in Iwate and 1,217 in Miyagi) (Reconstruction Agency, 2022). A 535 km^2 area of land was inundated, and nearly 400,000 houses were destroyed or damaged. Transport systems were extensively disrupted, and water and electricity shutdowns affected an extensive area beyond the Tohoku region (JRCS, 2021). The GEJET was not a single disaster event but a succession of interrelated events: earthquakes, tsunamis, power shortage nationwide, the disruption of supply chains, and its ripple effects on other countries, often referred to as "sequential crises", which hazards trigger cascading disasters in a range of interlocking systems that exponentially magnify the entire impact. The GEJET devastated numerous small fishing towns and villages on the Pacific coast, most of which faced particular difficulties as the tsunami devastated their communities and destroyed their economic base. These communities faced various issues related to population ageing even before the GEJET. For instance, the highly advanced tsunami early warning system was effective to a great extent but was insufficient to help many people escape smoothly and in time. The highly regarded breakwaters and seawalls were unable to withstand the tsunami waves (Koresawa, 2012).

National government responses to the earthquake and tsunami were immediate and have since resulted in some organizational changes as, for the first time, national-level field offices were also established in Iwate and Miyagi Prefectures and staffed with representatives from prefectural and national agencies; these offices have served a coordination and information-reporting role between the national, prefectural, and local governments (Luchi et al., 2013). In April 2011, Japan's Prime Minister established the National Reconstruction Design Council, which was charged with developing general concepts and strategies for recovery and rebuilding. Its 16 members came from academia, business, and religious groups, along with the governors of Iwate, Miyagi, and Fukushima Prefectures. This is the first national-level planning committee established following a disaster since the Great Kanto earthquake of 1923. In June 2011, the Council released its national recovery vision, "Toward Reconstruction: Hope beyond the Disaster". The vision outlines general concepts and strategies for physical recovery, ideas for job creation and regional economic recovery, repositioning Japan in the global economy, and advocates for long-term research on recovery. The vision also highlights the crucial role of local governments in driving the recovery. It is also the first document to introduce the concept of "disaster reduction" into reconstruction planning, calling for a two-level approach to future tsunami risk management. At the first level, "hard" measures, primarily structural such as levee construction, were recommended to address more likely future tsunami heights. At the second level, "softer", mostly non-structural measures, such as controlling land uses in the rebuilding and enhancing evacuation planning and drills, are recommended to deal with extraordinary and less likely tsunamis. This concept represents a fundamental shift in disaster policymaking in Japan, which has traditionally focused on "disaster prevention" – seeking to avoid damage altogether (Luchi et al., 2013).

The Iwate and Miyagi prefectural governments also established their own reconstruction bureaus to lead prefectural-level planning and implementation, and support the reconstruction work; committees were also established in each prefecture. Similar to the National Reconstruction Design Council, these committees have been composed of representatives from local government, industry, community leaders, and academics, who advise on the recovery processes.

In April 2011, Iwate Prefecture established its reconstruction bureau, with a 45-member staff drawn from other prefectural agencies. Charged with managing the entire reconstruction process, the bureau's priority task was to prepare the prefecture's reconstruction plan and accompanying implementation plan. Iwate Prefecture completed its draft reconstruction plan in June 2011, which sets goals to protect lives, coexist with the sea and earth, and enhance community well-being in Iwate. Its principles include promoting safety, resilient cities, tsunami mitigation, coastal protection facilities, and city facilities. It also has a set of recommended reconstruction patterns that are generally consistent with the national reconstruction vision (Visit Miyagi, 2023).

Miyagi Prefecture developed planning concepts by June 2011, referred to as a reconstruction "proposal", which was shared with cities and residents. Twelve cities in the prefecture were simultaneously developing their plans, utilizing the prefecture's concepts and formulating more specific policies and implementation approaches. Miyagi Prefecture incorporated this local feedback into its reconstruction plan, which was formally adopted in October 2011; two patterns of reconstruction are featured in the plan for urban and rural areas, respectively: (1) moving housing towards the hillsides and moving industry closer to the water but behind tsunami levee protection structures; and (2) adding tsunami protections, like elevated highways or rail lines, to protect agricultural areas. The plan also encompasses a variety of infrastructure and economic development initiatives (Luchi et al., 2013).

The studied areas include the Ogatsu district of Ishinomaki City in Miyagi Prefecture, the Otsuchi district of Otsuchi Town, and Unosumai district of Kamaishi City, as well as Yamada Town and Miyako City in Iwate Prefecture. Both studied prefectures have rich natural features, including mountains and lakes, which are popular scenic places in Japan. Miyagi prefecture has been a leading food-producing region for over four hundred years. Its agricultural products include rice, vegetables, and cattle. The fishing sector has been prosperous, with industries include lumber, foodstuffs, pulp, electrical machinery, and transport equipment (Visit Miyagi, 2023). Iwate prefecture's economy has been based on agriculture, forestry, fisheries, mining, manufacturing, and construction (Iwate Prefecture website, 2023). Both prefectures experienced population and economic decline before the GEJET, and these trends intensified after the GEJET.

Ishinomaki City, Kamaishi City, Otsuchi Town, and Yamada Town were the areas with the highest number of deaths (Tohoku earthquake-Wikipedia, 2023). Ishinomaki City suffered the most significant losses of life and property as the tsunami inundated much of the city's low-lying waterfront districts and neighbourhoods. A 14-metre-high tsunami hit Kamaishi City. The water swept over the city's recently completed tsunami breakwater and low-lying industrial districts, destroying the local fishing industry and leaving several huge ships on dry land. Also, in Kamaishi City, Otsuchi Town, and Miyako City, designated evacuation sites and schools were inundated (Kamaishi-Wikipedia, 2023; Otsuchi-Wikipedia, 2023; and Miyako-Wikipedia, 2023). The rising waters swept across many of the city's coastal districts, destroying homes, businesses, port facilities, and a large part of the local fishing fleet. The tsunami overtook the seawall protecting the town and sweeping boats, cars, and everything in its path (Japan guide, 2023). In the Ogatsu district, the tsunami destroyed buildings in the central area, including the town office, elementary and junior high schools, fishery union buildings, stores, and numerous other structures (Government of Japan, 2013). The GEJET damages led to population loss (human loss and, later on, immigration), destroying businesses and residential areas, and environmental devastation that caused sudden challenges for affected areas.

4.4   Micro-human Efforts in Affected Areas

The affected communities united in their shared adversity, engaged in self-help activities, sharing information, developing recovery plans, conducting disaster drills and workshops, and making concerted efforts to revive their communities. They received help and support, and together, they faced and overcame various challenges, demonstrating the power of unity and community spirit.

4.4.1   Self-help Activities

In Iwate prefecture, local communities tried to protect themselves. Because there was no shelter in some places, they had to make shelters, even in the mountains, to escape the tsunami. In some areas, they had to stay in such shelters for about one week.

> Ms. Iwasaki, the landlady of the Hamabeno Ryoriyado Horaikain, which is a hotel on Nebama Beach, Kamaishi-Iwate, mentioned that when the GEJET happened, guests, neighbor residents, employees, and everyone at the hotel fled to the mountains around and made fire. A carpenter made a hut and brought all the vending machines of the neighborhood association to be used. She obtained a generator from a fishing boat and gasoline from a car; when she returned to the hotel, there was a mini bulb so they could turn on the light; she had a drum and burned it to make a fire. Since water did not enter the refrigerator and the freezer, there was something to eat for three days. Some people made a restroom in a nearby forest. When the Kamaishi city staff brought food to that area, she rationed it for everyone; they had to live in such a situation while without a shelter.
>
> (Iwasaki, 2016)

In Miyagi prefecture, disaster countermeasure instructions had been issued from superordinate cities before the event, and local communities revised the city's model plan due to differences in the size and features of settlements. Thus, street-type fire extinguishers were installed, residential firefighters' groups were formed, and alarm devices for evacuation were also set up. While on the day of the disaster, the alarms sounded, but still, many people died (Aoki, 2017).

> Mr. Aoki, the community leader of the Namiita Lab in Ishinomaki city-Miyagi, mentioned that while evacuation considerations had been taken before the GEJET and voluntary disaster prevention activities were done and it had been decided on who to check on single elders' evacuation and who to close floodgates. However, on March 11, 2011, while an evacuation alarm was issued, some people died at home since they had not noticed the call. Also,

those who had escaped but returned to pick up their forgotten articles were inundated, and some people even reached the shelter, but the entrance was locked, and they could not enter the shelters.

(Aoki, 2017)

4.4.2 Informing Each Other

Communities had various communication methods to convey disaster-related information in affected areas.

Ms. Iwasaki contacted a cable television company to announce relief items, which affected areas received necessary items; the television company interviewed residents of every village and photographed from affected areas and also brought them souvenirs like soy sauce, paper, tatami[1] (initially, there was no tatami in temporary houses), rice cakes, etc., during the new year. She obtained information from the brigade radio about helicopters that rescue people relatively fast. Later, some residents and their relatives provided information on safety issues such as making culverts or soil types helpful in locating shelters.

(Iwasaki, 2016)

4.4.3 Working on Recovery Plans

Despite the initial setback of their community centres being destroyed, local communities have shown remarkable resilience. They have repurposed alternative locations as community centres, demonstrating their resourcefulness and inspiring hope for the future.

Ms. Iwasaki mentioned that after the GEJET, it was impossible to hold community meetings, but the hotel manager in Nebama district helped by breaking the mountain and setting up a house as a temporary community center where they started monthly meetings.

(Iwasaki, 2016)

Communities that suffered less damage have taken a proactive approach by holding regular monthly meetings. This commitment to communication and planning is a beacon of hope and a crucial part of their recovery strategy.

"Mr. Sasaki, the secretariat of Hashino district community center in Iwate, mentioned that they hold monthly meetings to discuss recovery plans, and he submitted the community-formulated plan to related municipalities" (Sasaki, 2016).

The local level mentioned that its activities in the pre-event were helpful in the post-event.

"Ms. Iwasaki mentioned the inland road completed just before the GEJET. Thereupon, relief supplies from nearby areas were delivered early" (Iwasaki, 2016).

To integrate recovery issues into current trends and daily affairs, local communities must strategically prioritize the more urgent ones, considering their financial sources and unique characteristics.

Community leaders of River Meeting in Kamaishi City have voiced their concerns about limited budgets and the rarity of events like the GEJET. Despite these challenges, they continue to work tirelessly. Their efforts are appreciated, and they need the support of national and prefectural governments to listen to residents' opinions.

(River Meeting, 2016)

Mr. Miura, the former branch manager of Ogatsu General Branch, said that they collected residents' opinions on the recovery plan and reflected them to the responsible organizations, but where the number of households was very few, there was no community center since managing and maintaining such centers was unaffordable so, the residents' opinions were not reflected to upper levels. The disaster prevention group of local communities of fishery settlements in Ogatsu, considering the proximity of jobs and fishing areas, helped arrange housing relocations to protect the vested interests of fishermen as their occupation is the indigenous identity of such settlements.

(Miura, 2017)

4.4.4   Holding Drills and Workshops

The local level holds drills and workshops to enhance residents' disaster awareness and preparedness capabilities by targeting various topics.

Certified specified non-profit organization Caritas Kamaishi mentioned they held workshops to improve local disaster prevention power of residents' study groups. Most participants were in their 60s or older, but people in their 30s and 40s also participated. Due to such events, a summary of opinions regarding the revision of the evacuation shelter management manual was submitted to the mayor. So far, tsunami disaster prevention, evacuation, housing reconstruction, and urban planning projects have been considered and discussed, with participation from people of various age groups. In these workshops, residents share their experiences with other prefecture volunteers.

(Caritas Kamaishi, 2017)

At the local level in Miyagi prefecture, evacuation training is conducted.

Mr. Miura believed that public risk consciousness is very influential since those residents who had experienced the Chile Valdivia earthquake and tsunami,[2] (1960) evacuated along with the tsunami warning upon which human loss was reduced. While, in relatively high-altitude places whose residents lacked risk consciousness, more human loss was mainly due to evacuation delays.

(Miura, 2017)

Mr. Tokumizu, the founder of Rose Garden Factory in Ishinomaki city-Miyagi, said that evacuation drills are held up to three times per year, and announcements are broadcast through administrative radio toll receivers installed in temporary and public housing sites[3] locations.

(Tokumizu, 2017)

Mr. Abe, the Representative of the Community Reconstruction Working Group in Ogatsu, mentioned that evacuation routes and manuals in the tsunami-inundated areas have been prepared as well as drills; even evacuation routes for areas located out of the tsunami inundation areas have been designated and been displayed in disaster prevention maps of evacuation manuals.

(Abe, 2017)

"Ms. Sato, a shop owner in Ogatsu, mentioned that temporary shopping centers hold evacuation drills and shops' employees practice evacuation by following specified escape routes" (Sato, 2017).

4.4.5 Reviving Communities

After the GEJET, local communities decided to attract people from outside to visit their areas, meet and interact with residents by establishing community centres and preserving the memory of the victims. Some communities made efforts such as planting flowers in memory of those who lost their liveslives. With the help of volunteers, a large site has been transformed into a diverse landscape featuring various types of flowers, fruit trees, and herbs used in drinks and sold. Community facilities host a variety of activities, including disaster preparedness seminars, concerts, workshops, and field trips (Tokumizu, 2017).

Mr. Tokumizu said that the tsunami swept away his mother-in-law's house, and she passed away; he thought it was an opportunity to plant flowers as a memorial for people who were deceased in the GEJET and opened the Rose Garden Factory. According to the recovery plan, a road would pass through the middle of the Rose Garden, which was deemed unreasonable. However, he attempted to collaborate with Ishinomaki City, and the mayor proposed that he plant olive trees. The city office told him, 'It is impossible to attract people to this area, so please do your best and create a tourism plantation'.

(Tokumizu, 2017)

4.4.6   *Volunteers and Supporters*

Volunteers, local autonomous associations, social welfare organizations, specialists, and academics have supported the local level in various phases of recovery.

Supporters, specialists, and government officers contributed to recovery activities in Iwate prefecture. Television broadcasting corporations have interviewed residents of affected areas, and through such programmes, local communities can continue to work and investigate reconstruction plans to ensure their suitability (Iwasaki, 2016).

> Ms. Iwasaki held monthly meetings, and residents participated; thereupon, they worked on their community's recovery and investigated the recovery plan through the perspective of a third party, so they refused construction of the seawall and protected the environmental attraction of their community.
>
> (Iwasaki, 2016)

The volunteer fire brigade, or "Shobodan",[4] helped rescue, set up field clinics in safe places, and transferred injured and older adults to such clinics.

"Mr. Suzuki, a Shobodan member of the Fire Brigade Office of Otsuchi town, said that Shobodan cooperated with Japan Ground Self-Defense Force[5] (JGSDF) in rescue operations, food and goods distribution, and debris cleaning" (Otsuchi Shobodan, 2018).

> Mr. Nihonmatsu, a Shobodan member in the Unosumai district of Kamaishi city-Iwate, went to the elementary school where his daughter was and was surprised to see that the school teachers did nothing, so he forced them to move after he closed the water gate. When students reached the first evacuation spot, he checked about everyone and reported to the higher level. While everyone was initially satisfied, he thought this place was not safe because some rocks in the mountains could fall easily, so he forced everyone to evacuate to the next location. When they reached the second place, he saw that the tsunami water was already very close to the second evacuation spot, so he noticed that this place was not safe enough. Again, he forced everyone to go farther to higher areas.

Residents trust Shobodan, so their instructions and advice are considered by residents, upon which Shobodan's ideas save students' and teachers' lives (Unosumai Shobodan, 2018).

In Kamaishi City, local autonomous associations effectively managed evacuation and emergency shelters, and residents evacuated and entered temporary houses within the predicted time frame (Kamaishi Local Autonomous Association Members, 2018).

The Social Welfare Association of Miyako City supported affected people by distributing goods dispatched from all over Japan, providing counselling services within the association, and, if necessary, referring them to relevant specialists. This association continued to host various entertainment activities and special events to foster a friendly living environment (Miyako Association, 2018).

Supporters and volunteers organized parties and festivals in affected areas, and younger residents participated because they wanted to contribute to the vitality of their communities. (Caritas Kamaishi, 2017).

In Miyagi prefecture, experts and researchers from different parts of Japan visited affected areas to assist the residents with a range of post-event issues. Thus, affected communities could learn from the recovery experiences of other parts of Japan, such as the lessons from the Southern Hyogo Prefecture earthquake. Additionally, connections with different universities were established and advice from academicians was acquired at different stages of recovery, including tourism improvement, business expansion, starting new businesses, and using regional resources to achieve a sustainable economic structure (Aoki, 2017 and Tokumizu, 2017). Besides, volunteer students from various universities in Japan visited affected areas to assist at the local level with resuming daily activities (Figure 4.3), holding festivals, and social events that were beneficial in helping residents recover their mental well-being. (Tokumizu, 2017 and Sato, 2017). Such support has been critical considering the majority of older residents in affected areas. Various social activities were organized in the public halls of temporary housing camps by social welfare councils to support the mental well-being of the residents (Miura, 2017).

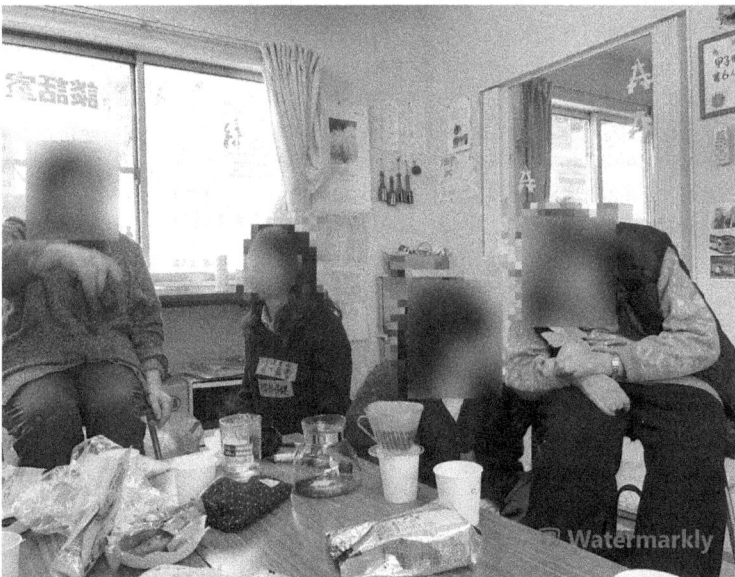

Figure 4.3 Volunteer Students Helped Residents in Temporary Houses in Iwate Prefecture
– Photograph by Authors

4.4.7 Challenges

Affected communities faced challenges due to the GEJET consequences and local and executive conditions. Challenges are inevitable, but identifying them presents opportunities to address vulnerabilities and make necessary modifications.

In Iwate prefecture, local communities mentioned that municipalities and prefectural governments do not consider residents' opinions on recovery; thus, communities had to do work such as river dredging on their own, which was challenging yet necessary.

> The river meeting said that government officers change frequently, so they doubt whether the upper administrations know what information must be issued for disaster prevention. They formed a residents' community organization and had to dredge rivers, which was necessary. The national-level budget allocation is roughly determined annually. Iwate prefecture's budget was minimal, and it needed substantial financial resources to create an annual plan. They expect that the national government will listen to the residents' opinions.
>
> (River Meeting, 2016)

The micro level suggests that the GEJET has proven that both structural and non-structural aspects should be improved simultaneously, and realities and countermeasures must be considered together. Local disaster prevention capabilities are critical, so communities' problems must be addressed at a small-scale within the region. Since younger people in affected areas have dispersed or immigrated to other places for employment, community members are generally older. At the same time, they hold meetings to discuss problems and issues; they cannot do everything alone, and their requests must be considered at the national and prefectural levels (River Meeting, 2016).

Some Shobodan members lost their lives in rescuing vulnerable, disabled, and older people. Due to an electricity cut, tsunami alarms did not work in some places; thus, Shobodan had to go to inform residents and rescue them, upon which some of them lost their lives (Otsuchi Shobodan, 2018).

"River meeting members mentioned that although the local fire department has an allowance in the event of a disaster, it is dangerous for an organization with residents to do all activities alone" (River Meeting, 2016).

> The Bureau of Coastal Broader Area, Promotion of Kamaishi city, mentioned that they surveyed in 2017, upon which main problems in resuming businesses were: 1. problem of business counterparts' loss; 2. lack of workforce because of population loss and immigration; 3. increased price of materials that has led to an increase the price of business productions.
>
> (Kamiashi Local Autonomous Association Members, 2018)

Ms. Sato, a resident, shared that the most daunting challenge in the recovery process is the loss of her fellow community members. This loss has particularly affected older individuals, such as peddlers, who find it increasingly difficult to sustain their sales jobs. Despite these challenges, the sharp decline in the number of households has made it challenging to maintain small businesses. For instance, in the disaster prevention group of the relocation complex where she now resides, there are only 30 households. Still, she believes that around 150 households are needed to sustain the business (Sato, 2017).

Business-related problems and population migration from smaller areas to more prominent places, in search of jobs and better living conditions influence the inner development of emigrated locations and hinder their improvement due to the loss of the factors that attract investment and human capital. This trend poses a greater challenge for smaller communities (Miura, 2017 and Tokumi, 2016).

Another pressing issue is the prolonged recovery period, as the stay in temporary housing has extended beyond the initially anticipated duration. This prolonged recovery not only adds to the psychological stress of the affected residents but also hampers the overall recovery process, underscoring the urgent need for immediate and substantial support and resources.

According to Mazmudar et al., temporary houses were required by law to last approximately two years and were subject to specific regulations. However, residents had to adjust to living in tiny and unsuitably designed houses, the non-permanence of hastily constructed homes, and the low-quality of the construction materials, which, among other consequences, affected family privacy. Due to the lack of space, residents faced impediments in preparing culturally important foods due to inadequate designs of kitchens, pantry, and dining space, limited capacity to be clean due to the proximity of the open kitchen to the toilet and bath, which also lacked ventilation as well as provisions for performing laundry, hindrances in properly memorializing ancestors, honoring gods, and worshipping due to the lack of appropriate religious space, and loss of the ability to feel calmness and peacefulness due to insufficient space and inadequate storage for household artefacts. These challenges have significantly impacted the recovery process.

The recovery plan has not progressed according to plan, which is problematic because it hinders the area and town's development, as residents have not settled down (Caritas Kamaishi, 2017).

"Caritas Kamaishi mentioned that in various damaged areas, many people still live in temporary houses, and they want to settle down in permanent housing quickly; until then, they cannot think about town development, and only evacuating shelters can be done" (Caritas Kamaishi, 2017).

Low financial resources and extended recovery periods have also affected most older residents. While subsidies have been provided to those in need and the elderly, some individuals still cannot afford housing reconstruction, and older adults have additional challenges due to their health conditions (Kamaishi city, 2018).

In Miyagi prefecture, temporary houses were in short supply. Thus, housing assignments were made through a lottery drawing, so some residents relocated to other areas, while others chose to rebuild on their own.

"Mr. Abe believed that "it was not a good idea for people to do housing reconstruction, but the residents of six districts of Miyagi prefecture gathered and tried to make a reconstruction plan by themselves. Self-housing reconstruction requires technical information on ground conditions, proper construction methods, and financial sources, and residents often lack access to these essential resources" (Abe, 2017).

In general, land acquisition for group transfer, provision of temporary storage, and reconstruction delays have been considerable challenges in Miyagi prefecture (Miura, 2017).

Another issue at the local level was increasing the height of seawalls and embankments. Based on Luchi et al., Iwate Prefecture conducted a series of simulations in collaboration with national agencies; the proposed heights range from 9.7 m to 15.5 m and are generally higher than the levees constructed before March 2011. Similarly, Miyagi Prefecture performed a series of joint simulations with national agencies. The proposed heights are usually highest in the north, with the highest recommendation of 11.8 m, and lower in the south, with the lowest height of 4.3 m. Some of these recommendations are up to three times higher than the levees previously constructed (Luchi et al., 2013).

Some affected communities opposed seawall construction.

"Mr. Tokumizu mentioned that seawall construction causes cultural loss in their towns, villages, and communities because such a trend influences the environmental beauty" (Tokumizu, 2017). Such projects have been implemented to prevent similar events from occurring (Figure 4.4 and Figure 5.5).

4.5   Discussion

Our investigations reveal similarities among the studied areas in both prefectures; in other words, the explored areas exhibit similar trends in both pre- and post-event periods, indicating that both prefectures share the same conditions regarding the impactful factors in their domains. There has been a decline in population and economic growth in affected areas, especially in smaller communities top-down and bottom-up trends did not align with each other; the physical and social aspects of damage reduction were separated; affected communities lacked significant power, and they had to deal with various challenges like business decline and reconstruction delays (Table 4.1).

National-level field offices in both prefectures opened, and a national recovery vision entitled "Toward Reconstruction: Hope beyond the Disaster" was released. Both prefectures established their reconstruction bureaus to do prefectural-level planning and implementation, and their recovery plans were consistent with the national reconstruction vision, but the micro level was the first responder to the event's consequences; upper levels mainly concentrated on structural aspects while affected communities applied self-made procedures like re-establishing community centres to resume their activities, revive communities, and maintain their residents (Iwate prefecture) or some other communities took advantage of their environmental opportunities to save damaged settlements from vanishing and protect the indigenous identity (Miyagi prefecture). Affected communities in both prefectures worked hard despite a lack of coordination and collaboration with upper levels, as well as financial constraints.

Figure 4.4 Seawall Construction in Iwate Prefecture. Photograph by Authors

Figure 4.5 Embankment Construction in Miyagi Prefecture. Photograph by Authors

Table 4.1 Impactful Factors Status in Studied Prefectures

Impactful Factors	Iwate Prefecture	Miyagi Prefecture
Social and economic capacities	Poor resources due to extensive social and economic damages: • Many killed; • Industries, fisheries, houses, ports, schools, and shelters were destroyed; • Affected production and jobs	Most considerable losses of lives and properties: • Extensive tsunami inundation; • Public buildings, schools, fisheries, and stores were removed. • Destroyed living and working centres
Top-down vs bottom-up	The upper level operates at the macro level while the local level considers the micro-scale; thus, there is no interaction	Both trends move separately, and there is no feedback or information flow between them
Risk reduction trends	There is no specific correlation between risk reduction's physical and social aspects	The upper level reduces physical risk, and the local level concerns social aspects
Communities' capabilities	Community leaders, volunteers, and supporters assisted with rescue, relief, and evacuation, set up shelters, and improved software	Experts, volunteers, and supporters assisted communities with daily activities, business recovery, and residents' mental health
Emerging challenges	• Top-down approaches • Majority of elderly people • Resuming businesses • Prolonging recovery	• Top-down approaches • Residents' inability • Investment and labour deficiencies • Reconstruction delay

The investigations enabled us to identify incentives and disincentives for the micro-level during recovery, which are the key findings of our study. Such identification is essential because MHEs are somewhat motivational and self-administered, yet they help effectively integrate damage reduction measures at the micro level that lead to sustainable results.

4.5.1 Incentives

Various matters that arise from internal and external factors have motivated MHEs. Individuals are eager to help one another in disaster and cooperate with higher levels to save lives and improve their safety. This is due to their innate nature, but other factors are also at play.

In studied communities, solidarity caused residents to act and operate independently without waiting for outside agents. Residents started rescue and relief efforts, closed floodgates, and provided basic living necessities for one another while everyone was injured and their homes were damaged. In this study, the micro level took responsibility for its safety and security based on its awareness and abilities.

Locational dependencies encouraged affected communities to consider their places' development and cooperate to improve their living conditions by considering safety measures. This is vital in shaping social patterns and relationships, as well as maintaining solidarity and cooperation within a community. As mentioned, younger people cooperated in holding various events in their locations to help their communities' vitality (Caritas Kamaishi, 2017).

Revitalizing local communities, disaster survivors tried to restore local communities from disappearing despite their rapidly declining trends in post-event. Affected communities sought to attract people and visitors from outside to their areas by leveraging their rich natural resources to foster relationships with outsiders and promote their prosperity. Such an incentive led them to request an adjustment to the recovery plan at the city level (Tokumizu, 2017).

Rebuilding victims' livelihoods, the micro level tried to restore livelihoods to protect themselves against potential unfavourable changes. While housing relocations had been ordered in affected areas, local communities helped fishermen safeguard their vested interests and prevent possible changes to fishing areas, thereby preserving the indigenous identity of those settlements (Miura, 2017).

More awareness, micro-level knowledge, and experiences in evacuation or rescue helped them decide when and where to evacuate. At the same time, awareness strengthens motivation. Still, it is a function of the availability of up to date and practical information that upper levels should provide for micro-level consultations. Awareness motivates the micro level to enhance disaster preparedness through drills, training, and workshops.

Engagement in recovery tasks and a micro level of involvement increase the sense of responsibility and accelerate the recovery pace in studied areas. Residents worked alone even when they did not engage in recovery tasks like self-housing reconstruction in Miyagi prefecture (Abe, 2017). The micro level did work in recovery, but if national and prefectural levels also involve the human level then the outcomes could incorporate indigenous knowledge and existing standards.

4.5.2 Disincentives

Disincentives arise from the intensity of disasters and existing trends. In the GEJET, massive damage caused some people to immigrate as they had lost their jobs, living conditions, and housing, and could not resume their work and daily lives in their places of origin. Also, some social, economic, and administrative issues discouraged people.

Physical system failure, high volumes of damage, and systems and functions failure can cause difficulties for the local level in resuming their activities and responsibilities. Extensive physical damages result in human and housing loss that impacts disaster survivors and may even lead to depopulation and structural changes. The GEJET destroyed living and working structures in affected communities. Thereupon, younger people immigrated (Miura, 2017).

Financial constraints, livelihood restrictions, and complex financial conditions can discourage micro-level efforts during recovery, potentially leading to immigration and depopulation that hinder recovery and restoration of functions. The economic constraints of the studied communities have impeded the recovery duration as residents are unable to reconstruct their housing, which is their primary priority.

Top-down approaches are general and uniform but not adaptable to micro-level needs and desires. Affected communities mentioned that prefectural and national levels do not consider their opinions and have limited power to undertake recovery tasks independently (Aoki, 2017; River Meeting, 2016). In such cases, communities may abandon their efforts, resulting in outcomes that lack integrity and compatibility.

Disruption of social ties, the community is a mix of living and working systems preserved by its colonial core. After the GEJET, relocations to safer areas, population immigration, and longer stays in temporary houses affect local dependencies and residents' sense of solidarity. Younger people immigrate to other places, and the remaining residents are mainly elders who require social connections in their familiar environments.

Dangers for volunteers and supporters, affected communities' Shobodan mentioned that their members lost their lives in saving residents, which is unreasonable (Otsuchi Shobodan, 2018). Volunteers in affected areas are helpful, but in events like the GEJET, it is not rational for community organizations to do all tasks alone (River Meeting, 2016).

Considering recovery as a product rather than a process, the recovery process comprises a series of actions to achieve planned results, and such a process governs the direction and condition of its final product. Damage reduction as a product is related to physical aspects, while as a process, it requires micro-level cooperation in incorporating physical damage reduction measures on a micro-scale.

4.6 Conclusion

In conclusion, we go back to our research questions; the primary one is "How does MHE smooth the path toward resilience during recovery?" and the secondary ones are: "How did local communities act to save lives, self-help, and protect themselves against future hazards?" Moreover, "What factors obstruct and motivate them in taking post-event acts and initiatives?"

As mentioned, resilience is the ability of a community to resist, respond, and recover from the effects of a disaster properly and in a planned manner; BBB is a method for enhancing the resilience of communities by leveraging recovery and integrating risk reduction measures across various systems. In a sound recovery process, thinking ahead about hazards, taking responsibility, and maintaining post-event functioning are essential.

In the GEJET recovery experiences, communities made efforts to save lives, provided basic needs, developed recovery plans, attempted to revive disaster-stricken communities, and enhanced local preparedness and response capacity using their available resources. Affected communities' attempts show that they think in advance about future hazards as they hold drills, training, and workshops to increase residents' knowledge and skills; they took responsibility to save themselves and tried to maintain functioning by reviving communities and attracting visitors while their ideas and opinions were not considered by upper levels, which is a clear indication that top-down and bottom-up approaches did not move along each other. MHEs improve element substitution, maintain functioning (through Redundancy), and strengthen communities' capacities (by Resourcefulness), which leads to more rapid restoration of systems (through Rapidity). This, in turn, increases the likelihood of a timely and efficient recovery that is resilient recovery. Also, the ability to withstand stresses and demands without loss of function (Robustness) should be according to the micro level's needs and conditions; otherwise, the results will be inconsistent.

Build back better has primarily focused on structural aspects like seawall construction or housing relocation, which are unsuitable for fishermen, indicating that structural and non-structural elements have been separated. MHEs facilitate building back faster and more inclusively through contingent recovery plans that encompass all population groups. Building back more robust and resistant infrastructures must be based on residents' opinions, as this may influence local businesses.

At the micro level, individuals formed self-protective procedures in the post-event period to save and protect themselves, which demonstrates individuals are self-motivated and can decide and act for their recovery; they are not recipients who wait to be rescued or donated. Our study shows that even vulnerable groups, such as older people attempted to take action for their recovery. Social roots, maintaining communities, and being a part of the recovery process are the main incentives that arise from within communities. In contrast, disincentives mainly arise from recovery trends and policies, as structural damage and financial constraints make residents immigrate. Their social ties also change; top-down approaches consider recovery's final product rather than its process.

Ultimately, the recovery process should be conducted at the micro level to ensure that physical restoration, social development, and economic revival proceed in a complementary manner, resulting in sustainable outcomes.

Notes

1 Tatami is a mat used as a flooring material in traditional Japanese-style rooms. Authors.
2 The 1960 Valdivia earthquake and tsunami was the most powerful earthquake ever recorded, and the resulting tsunamis affected southern Chile, Hawaii, Japan, the Philippines, eastern New Zealand, southeast Australia, and the Aleutian Islands (Valdivia earthquake-Wikipedia, 2023)..

3 Public housing is a type of apartment building or houses of a particular style and design typically built by the government. These houses are cheaper than comparable housing for those who financially cannot afford housing by themselves. Public housing has been provided for affected residents of Tohoku after the GEJET. Authors..

4 Voluntary fire brigades are composed of ordinary citizens with separate main jobs, but they voluntarily defend their community in emergencies and disasters. Their activities include fire extinguishing, rescue, flood control, fire prevention, and lifesaving (FDMA website, 2023)..

5 The GSDF conducts disaster relief, rescue, or lifesaving operations due to large-scale accidents or domestic disasters (GSDF website, 2023).

References

American Planning Association, (2016). "Principles for Preparing a Community's Disaster Recovery Plan", USA.

Australian Disaster Resilience Handbook Collection, (2020). "Community Engagement for Disaster Resilience," Melbourne, Australian Institute for Disaster Resilience.

Burby, R.J. Editor, (1998). "Cooperating with Nature: Confronting Natural Hazards with Land-Use Planning for Sustainable Communities," Washington, D.C., JOSEPH HENRY PRESS.

Cutter, S.L., Boruff, B.J., and Shirley, W.L. (2003). "Social Vulnerability to Environmental Hazards," *Social Science Quarterly*, Vol. 84, No. 2, pp. 242–261.

Global Facility for Disaster Risk Reduction, (2010). "Safer Homes Stronger Communities," The World Bank, Washington D.C., USA.

Global Facility for Disaster Risk Reduction (2018). "Building Back Better: Achieving Resilience through Stronger, Faster, and More Inclusive Post-disaster Reconstruction," The World Bank, Washington D.C., USA.

https://en.wikipedia.org/wiki/2011_Tohoku_earthquake_and_tsunami.

https://en.wikipedia.org/wiki/Kamaishi,_Iwate.

https://en.wikipedia.org/wiki/Otsuchi,_Iwate.

https://en.wikipedia.org/wiki/Miyako,_Iwate.

https://en.wikipedia.org/wiki/1960_Valdivia_earthquake.

https://visitmiyagi.com/.

https://www.fdma.go.jp/.

https://www.japan-guide.com/.

https://www.mod.go.jp/gsdf/english/dro/index.html.

https://www.pref.iwate.jp/.

International Recovery Platform, (2013). "Recovery Status Report, The Great East Japan Earthquake 2011 case studies", Kobe, Japan.

Interview with Akiko Iwasaki, Houraikan Landlady in Kamaishi city, (November 2016), Iwate prefecture.

Interview with Community leaders in Kamaishi city, River Meeting, (November 2016), Iwate prefecture.

Interview with Yuji Sasaki, Secretariat of Hashino District Community Center (November 2016), Kamaishi, Iwate prefecture.

Interview with Junichiro Aoki in Nammita Lab (January 2017), Ogatsu, Miyagi prefecture.

Interview with Hiroshi Miura, Former Branch Manager, Ogatsu General Branch, Regional Division Takayuki, (January 2017), Ogatsu, Miyagi prefecture.

Interview with Certified Specified Non-profit Organization Caritas Kamaishi, (March 2017), Kamaishi, Iwate prefecture.

Interview with Hiroshi Tokumizu, Ogatsu Rose Factory Garden Office, (January 2017), Ishinomaki City, Miyagi prefecture.

Interview with Akinari Abe, Community Reconstruction Working Group Representative (January 2017), Ogatsu, Miyagi prefecture.

Interview with Michiyo Sato, shop owner of the Yaeochi store in Ogatsu (January 2017), Miyagi prefecture.

Interview with Miyako Social Welfare Association (March 2018), Iwate prefecture.

Interview with Shobodan leaders in the Fire Brigade Office of Otsuchi town (March 2018), Otsuchi, Iwate prefecture.

Interview with Unosumai Shobodan (March 2018), Unosumai district, Iwate prefecture.

Interview with Kamaishi Local Autonomous Association Members (March 2018), Iwate prefecture.

Interview with Bureau of Coastal Broader Area Promotion (March 2018), Kamaishi City, Iwate prefecture.

Japanese Red Cross Society, (March 2021), "Japan: Earthquake and Tsunami, Final Report," Guide no. EQ-2011-000028-JPN, Tokyo, Japan.

Koresawa, A. (2012). "Main Features of Government's Initial Response to the Great East Japan Earthquake and Tsunami," *Journal of Disaster Research,* Vol. 7, No. 1, pp. 107–115.

Luchi, K., Johnson, L.A., and Olshansky, R.B. (2013). "Securing Tohoku's Future: Planning for Rebuilding in the First Year Following the Tohoku-Oki Earthquake and Tsunami," *Earthquake Spectra,* Vol. 29, No. S1, pp. S479–S499.

March, A., and Kornakova, M., Editors, (2017), "Urban Planning for Disaster Recovery," Elsevier.

Mazumdar, S., Itoh, S., and Iwasa, A. (March 2021). "Post-Disaster Temporary Housing: An Emic Study of Lived Experiences of Victims of the Great East Japan Earthquake and Tsunami," *International Journal of Mass Emergencies and Disasters,* Vol. 39, No. 1, pp. 87–119.

Mileti, D.S. (1999). "Disasters by Design: A Reassessment of Natural Hazards in the United States," Joseph Henry Press, Washington, D.C., USA.

Pooyan, Z., (2016). "A Study on Emergency Settlement Challenges in Devastating Earthquakes in Iran during last 20 years," Tehran, International Institute of Earthquake Engineering and Seismology.

Pooyan, Z., and Hokugo, A. (2017). "Community Challenges in Resilient Based Disaster Recovery of Tohoku Region," Research Center for Urban Safety and Security, Kobe University, Research Report No. 21, pp. 203–212, Kobe, Japan.

Public Relations Office, Cabinet Office, Government of Japan, Highlighting Japan,(2013). "Cover Story: Lessons from Disasters, Leading Recovery."

Reconstruction Agency, (February 2022). "Status of Reconstruction and Reconstruction Efforts," Created based on the White Paper on Disaster Management FY 2020 and the summary report of the Extreme Disaster Management Headquarters (issued on March 9, 2021).

The United Nations Office for Disaster Risk Reduction, (2015). "Sendai Framework for Disaster Risk Reduction" (2015–2030), Geneva, Switzerland.

Tierney, K. (2014). "Social Roots of Risk, Producing Disasters Promoting Resilience," California, Stanford University Press.

Tokumi, H. (August 2016). "Reconstruction status of Ogatsu district in Ishinomaki city and town planning issues," Tohoku University Volunteer Support, Miyagi Educational University/Tohoku Institute of Technology, Japan.

United Nations Center for Regional Development, (1995). "Comprehensive Study of the Great Hanshin Earthquake," Nagoya, Japan.

UNDRR Terminology, (2023) https://www.undrr.org/drr-glossary/terminology.

Section II

Rethinking Inclusive Redevelopments as a Rebuilding Process

5 Elderly Women and Community Resilience

Nilgün Okay and Ebru İnal Onal

5.1 Introduction

Population ageing is one of the most significant global phenomena of our century. With advances in medical treatments and efforts to protect public health, life expectancy continues to rise, and older people will steadily increase as a proportion of the population. According to the United Nations (UN), the proportion of the world's population aged 65 years or older will reach 11.7% in 2030, up from 9.3% in 2021. This increase is due to the advances in healthcare and living conditions, which have led to longer life expectancies (UN, 2022). Europe and Northern America had the largest proportion of the older population in 2022, with almost 19% aged 65 or over, followed by Australia and New Zealand (16.6%). By 2050, one in every four persons in Europe and Northern America will be 65 or over. Similarly, the proportion aged 65 or over in Eastern and South-Eastern Asia will double to around 26% in 2050 (US Census Bureau International Database projections for 2030). A key component of demographic distribution is aged women. By 2050, the largest population group will be older women.

Globally speaking, the oldest continent in 2050 will be Europe, with the highest ratio of people above 60, estimated at 33.6%. Among regions, the share of women in the population aged 65 or older was the highest in Europe and Northern America (57.5%) in 2022. Japan is currently the only state in the world where the ratio of people above 60 is higher than 30%. The predictions have it that by 2050, there will be another 64 states in the same situation (HelpAge International, 2012; GAWI, 2014; UNDESA, 2014). The age structure of Turkey's population has been changing. The elderly population has increased compared to the population in other age groups. The proportion of the elderly population is expected to be 12.9% in 2030 (TUIK, 2022). In Turkey, women comprise 55.7% of the older population (65 and 79) and 63.34% above 80.

It would seem that most older people live in cities, which suggests that cities with health services and social support for older people may be beneficial. In many developing countries, older people live with their adult children, with at least one grown child often remaining in the family home to support them. The traditional joint family system provided a social safety net for aged women. However, rapid urbanization changed the traditional social system and family relations. In the last several years, the percentage of older people living alone has increased in many

DOI: 10.4324/9781003615903-7

countries while the percentage of those living with their children has decreased. Istanbul is a province with the highest number of older people in Turkey (TUIK, 2022). The 24.1% of households have at least one elderly individual. Women constitute 76.7% of the elderly population living alone; the elderly women whose spouses have died was 50.4%. It seems that older individuals withdraw from social activities and live a life of their minds in the environments they determine themselves. The loss of social status of older women has led to the emergence of physical and mental problems in disasters. The lack of activity of older people due to the pandemic has led to cardiovascular problems (Adepoju et al., 2023a).

5.1.1   Disasters and Elderly

The evolving socio-economic structures and cultural values have brought forth new challenges for our societies. Rapidly expanding urban areas are struggling to cater to the diverse needs of different age groups, especially the elderly. Disasters continue to have a significant impact on our societies, with older women being particularly vulnerable to both the immediate and prolonged effects of such catastrophes (Powell et al., 2009). They consistently have the highest proportion of casualties during disasters. Several researchers have highlighted the additional deaths among women caused by disasters, not just in low and low-middle-income countries, but also in high-income countries (Chowdhury et al., 2022; Dhungel & Ojha, 2012; Drolet et al., 2015). For instance, the largest number of deaths among older women occurred in France due to the 2003 heatwave incident (Pirard et al., 2005). In the 2004 Indian Ocean tsunami, the mortality rate among women was four times higher than that of men (Tuohy & Stephens, 2011). When Hurricane Katrina struck New Orleans in 2005, 71% of the casualties were women (Adams et al., 2020). As for the 2011 Japanese tsunami, 77% of the 15,884 individuals who lost their lives were aged 60 and above (Adams et al., 2020).

Chronic diseases increase the risk of disability, which decreases the physical capacity and quality of life, and leads to higher medical expenses and long-term care needs of the elderly. Disability is not only physical but also includes hearing, sight, and mental disorders, including dementia. These issues cause longer hospitalizations and higher mortality rates among the elderly population. Presently, about 80% of older people suffer from at least one chronic disease, and 50% have at least two (National Center for Chronic Disease Prevention and Health Promotion, 2009). In Turkey, 30% of those over 65 take at least four medications. The excess mortality among elderly individuals relocated to institutions after a nuclear accident revealed that 70% of the deaths occurred among women, with 93% of the fatalities involving individuals aged over 75. After the Hanshin earthquake, 83% of the elderly individuals in overcrowded shelters lost their lives due to social isolation (Tanida, 1996). Spouses, family members, and friends play a crucial role during disasters in the psychological well-being and recovery of the elderly more than other age groups (Fernandez et al., 2002).

The health of older people with medical conditions such as heart disease, respiratory illness, diabetes, and being overweight can be significantly affected by disasters. Extreme weather conditions can trigger heart attacks and strokes in individuals with cardiovascular disease, which can be fatal and also worsen the severity of chronic lung diseases (Madrigano et al., 2013). There was a significant increase in pneumonia cases within the three months following the Tohoku earthquake and tsunami.

The older people are exposed to more injuries due to muscle weakness, exhaustion, and lack of balance. Limited mobility makes evacuation more difficult for them and reduces their capacity to protect themselves from injuries. Deficiencies in hearing, vision, other senses, and cognitive impairment can make it difficult for them to receive warnings and directions during emergencies. Additionally, they may have trouble finding direction in an unfamiliar environment. The prevalence of disabilities among individuals aged 65–74 is 44.6%, then increasing to 63.7% for those aged 75–84 and reaching 84.2% for those over 85 (Age International, 2015). The average age of a person living with disabilities is 69.1 for women.

During emergencies, the elderly face challenges accessing food distribution points, eating, and preparing their meals, making them more vulnerable. Unfortunately, emergency food distribution is seldom designed to meet the specific nutritional needs of older individuals. This puts their health and nutrition at risk. In a study conducted in Turkey, 67% of the elderly face malnutrition problems (Sanlier & Yabanci, 2007). Reasons for this may include poverty, living alone, or age-related disabilities. It is difficult for them to adapt to life in temporary shelters (Okay et al., 2022). Older people do not leave their homes in cases such as evacuation. Disasters often limit their temporary sheltering conditions and increase their vulnerability. For instance, after the Hanshin earthquake, 83% of the elderly living in shelters died. After a disaster, the focus is on first aid, and over the long term, the system needs to respond to the chronic medical needs of older persons.

People have a wrong perception of ageing. The negative image of older people is causing age discrimination, which is more than gender or race discrimination and is often a premise for elder abuse. Older people face discrimination and exclusion because of their age, gender, disability, or health issues. Age discrimination can lead to vulnerabilities and risk factors in disasters . Data shows that 44% of EU citizens consider age discrimination to be a very significant phenomenon, and 35% have reported age discrimination. It is devastating to learn that 57% believe that persons above 70 make no economic contribution to society, and 53% of the interviewees have no friends older than 70 (Age UK, 2011). Although discrimination based on both gender and age is common, the experiences of older women are not visible due to the lack of data disaggregated by gender and age.

The economic status of older women depends on cultural, social, and environmental factors (UNDESA, 2014; Bergstrand et al., 2015). One-third of older women are more likely to be widowed and live alone, compared to only 15% of men (Age International, 2015). Many of them are vulnerable precisely because they lack the livelihoods to have adequate security and self-protection. In the latest earthquakes in Anatolia, tens of thousands of people died due to the collapse of buildings where construction firms had not followed the seismic codes and where inspection was inadequate or corrupt. People also suffer in floods because their homes are not elevated above the flood level, and it is too costly for them to make these necessary mitigation adjustments.

The overall situation of older women is significantly influenced by their marital status, particularly in terms of health and overall life satisfaction. According to UNDESA (2014) older individuals who are married have a lower risk of exhibiting symptoms of depression and are more satisfied with their lives. However, the loss of a partner can make older women more susceptible to poverty, especially in some developing countries where there may be inadequate legislation to protect their right to inherit property from their husbands. Lower-income women often struggle to cope with the financial and social impact of unexpected events due to their lack of resources and assets, leaving them even more vulnerable after disasters.

5.1.2   Resilience

Resilience in disaster risk management is an important concept that involves enhancing preparedness, coping, and adaptive capacities, as well as minimizing vulnerabilities in urban systems infrastructure, economy, and community (Smyth & Sweetman, 2015; Bunce & Ford, 2015; Jamshed et al., 2019; Rana, 2020). When a disaster occurs, women are often less informed about evacuation procedures and are more likely to be victimized due to social and cultural restrictions prohibiting them from evacuating alone. Therefore, self-reliance has become increasingly important in building resilience. A disaster-resilient community is one in which individuals are self-reliant and prepared to adapt and respond to the disaster risks they face (Zhu & Sun, 2017; Astill & Miller, 2018). Health conditions and financial problems are the main challenges to disaster preparedness (Cox & Kim, 2018; Fothergill & Peek, 2004; Okay & Inal, 2019). Disaster preparedness as a socially shared responsibility allows individuals to help other families prepare, thus improving overall community resilience.

Disaster resilience is often perceived as a positive and proactive approach to individual and community engagement with risk reduction (Cutter et al., 2008). The community's building capacity refers to the collective ability in the neighbourhood to focus on good relationships and networks within the community (Okay & Ilkkaracan, 2018). This capacity increases with a high level of information flow and communication infrastructure, which helps disaster resilience within the community (Aldrich, 2012). Therefore, the social dimension of disaster resilience consists of several indicators such as level of education, local knowledge about disasters, emergency training, access to information (using the mobile phone and social media), health status, social status (participating in community meetings), community engagement behaviour (bonding with family members/relatives, bridging with neighbour/friends, linking with NGOs), economic status (average income, assets ownership savings), and resilient capacity (risk reduction/adaptation, preparedness).

5.2 Research Strategy

Disasters are a significant challenge that are studied across various disciplines. The increasing impact of disasters has made traditional research methods difficult. Over the past decade, there has been considerable progress in disaster and resilience research, particularly after establishing links with vulnerability. However, there is a gap in the existing literature regarding disaster preparedness, response, and recovery for older adults. Therefore, this study aims to identify, analyze, and synthesize information from various studies to understand disaster vulnerability and resilience for older women. The study has two objectives: a literature review and a case study analysis. The literature review will focus on vulnerabilities and impacts resulting from disasters. The second objective is to examine the role of women in community resilience, emphasizing their capabilities, efforts, and participation. A case study will highlight the capacity, local knowledge, self-preparedness, and training of older women in achieving community resilience.

5.2.1 Literature Review

The literature search process was conducted in 2022 and involved extracting research articles from Scopus and Google Scholar databases. The analyses did not include the SCI-Expanded and SSCI databases as they do not contain the entire literature of this field. The literature search included studies written in English between 2013 and 2022, aiming to capture a representative set of published research papers on the topic. Scopus and Google Scholar were chosen as the online databases for the search due to their comprehensive coverage of research outputs in all fields.[1] The study was based on the findings of an exploratory rapid review of the evidence base on disasters and local resilience, with a focus on older adults. Only articles containing the selected keywords – older women, ageing, older people, disasters, resilience, vulnerability, and local knowledge – were accessed from the databases.

The objective of the rapid review was to include a diverse range of studies, in contrast to the approach taken in systematic reviews. Initially, the goal was to gather evidence on women's capabilities and their role in developing community resilience in disaster management. The papers examined existing evidence to enhance our understanding of how these initiatives have been implemented at the local level with best practices. Therefore, the objective was to compile a collection of studies that characterized the content and patterns found in the evidence base. The review was limited to studies published in peer-reviewed articles indexed in Scopus that focused on aspects related to social sustainability.

The review of Google Scholar records is provided in Figure 5.1.[2] It helped quickly identify subsequent articles that cite a previously published article on the same topic and focus of our systematic literature review, so it can be manually checked the content and made a decision as to whether to include it or not. This narrative review is a non-systematic review that summarizes the published literature on this concept to reveal a new perspective based on existing knowledge and avoid duplication of research.

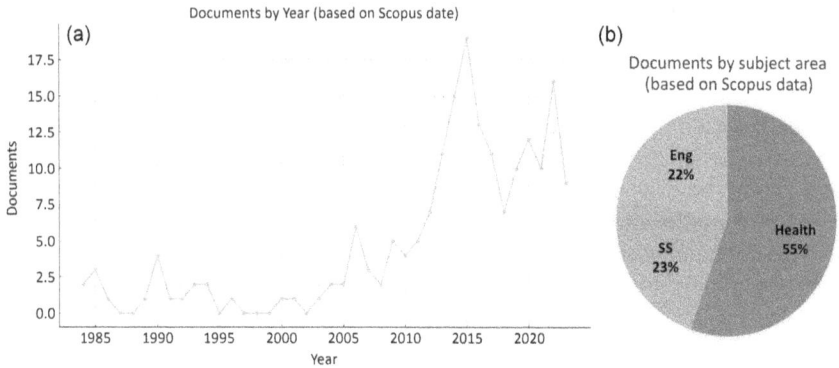

Figure 5.1 (a) illustrates the Trend of the Changes in the Number of Publications in Disaster Research Over Time, and (b) Presents Selected Articles from Various Disciplines

The number of published academic papers is a key metric for assessing the development trend of certain scientific research. After reviewing the literature, the number of articles on disasters is 34,671, elderly people 229, aged women 33, vulnerability 4,409, and resilience 6,089. This data suggests that vulnerability and resilience are the prominent research areas in disaster studies.

The results indicate a rising number of publications on disasters, climate change, and integrated resilience. The research on disasters increased from 436 in 1991 to 4926 in 2012 (Figure 5.1a), showing steady development. Disaster research showed growth after 2005. The analyzed publications began in 1992 and focused on studying climate change adaptation and disaster mitigation. Resilience, in the context of disasters and climate change, is closely linked with disaster risk reduction, as a multidisciplinary phenomenon. The results also revealed articles on disaster and climate change resilience, while no publications were found on integrated resilience.

According to research, a variety of disciplines have studied disaster resilience. From 2013 to 2022, most publications on disaster resilience among the elderly came from the medical and social sciences. Environmental sciences and psychiatry also contributed to the study of disaster resilience during this period (Figure 5.1b). Although there were fewer publications, more disciplines were involved in studying disaster resilience.

A comprehensive literature review from 2013 to the present was conducted to gain insight into the competencies and expertise required for disaster care for the elderly. To ensure the content was both relevant and valid, only articles written and published in or after 2013 were examined in the review. The year 2015 was significant due to increasing publications focusing on the impact of disasters on the elderly population worldwide. A total of 252 articles were analyzed for a comprehensive, full-text evaluation. The search used a combination of keywords related to the experiences of elderly women during and after disasters. After a detailed examination, only 32 articles that met the criteria for inclusion in this research were included in this review. The primary reasons for exclusion were the lack of focus on individual resilience and the absence of specific disaster contexts.

The concept of disaster resilience is rapidly evolving and encompasses various disciplines. However, there has been limited focus on issues related to elderly individuals. While existing literature has extensively addressed the vulnerabilities of women during disasters, research on the elderly, especially older women and other genders, remains scarce. Current research indicates that older adults are disproportionately more vulnerable during and after disasters. Studies primarily emphasize the physical health issues, vulnerabilities, and needs of the elderly during such events. Additionally, the care of elderly individuals during public health emergencies has been a significant concern. Similarly, issues related to elderly care in public health emergencies were highlighted, and the scope of topics discovered in this review is outlined in Table 5.1. Many studies have reported that the health of these vulnerable populations is frequently worsened by disasters, leading to a higher incidence of fatal consequences. Researchers are concerned about the vulnerability of elderly people in disasters. The older age group is more vulnerable to the negative impacts of disasters due to the biological, psychological, and social changes associated with ageing (Cherry et al., 2015; Brockie & Miller, 2017a; Claver et al., 2013; Zhang et al., 2012; Bei et al., 2013). Rafiey et al. (2016) discussed a higher level of positive mental health in disasters rather than the vulnerability of the elderly compared to young people.

The objective of these studies is to gain insight into the factors that contribute to the decline in physical capacity with age and the influence of socio-economic conditions and discrimination on the health and well-being of older individuals in the context of disasters. A review of the literature reveals that older women in disasters worldwide are exposed to a range of adverse experiences, including domestic violence, sexual assault, psychological distress, health problems, and social and financial deprivation. The impact of disasters on women is evidenced by the literature review, which indicates that disasters result in increased mortality, morbidity, and violence against women. Based on the literature analysis, an existing

Table 5.1 The Findings of a Literature Review on the Vulnerability and Capacity of Older Women

Index	n = 32	
vulnerability	19	Bei et al. 2013; Brilleman et al., 2017; Brockie & Miller, 2017; Busapathumrong, 2013; Cénat et al., 2020; Cherry et al., 2015; Claver et al., 2013; Cox & Kim, 2018; Forsman et al., 2013; Gutman & Yon, 2014; Johnson et al., 2015; Kukihara et al., 2014; Pongponrat & Ishii, 2018; Pruchno et al., 2021; Rafiey et al., 2016; Seifi et al., 2018; Stanko et al., 2015; Xu et al., 2015; Wakui et al., 2017; Yazawa et al., 2022
capacity building	13	Adepoju et al., 2023a; Adepoju et al., 2023b; Aldrich & Kiyota 2017; Brockie & Miller, 2017a; Brockie & Miller, 2017b; Cheek et al., 2015; Chowdhury et al., 2022; Howard et al., 2017; Kako & Mayner, 2019; Krishnan et al., 2019; Kwan 2020; Miller & Brockie, 2015; Rich et al., 2018; Timalsina et al., 2021; Touhy et al., 2014; Zhu & Sun, 2017

understanding recognizes the elderly as vulnerable (Table 5.1). Furthermore, the literature also highlights the insufficiencies present among various levels of disaster risk reduction. The inadequacy of community-based disaster education programmes for older adults, health workers, and caregivers, coupled with the lack of a nationwide policy and standardized approach makes individual preparedness challenging. Several studies have been conducted on the social vulnerability of the elderly in disasters (Cherry et al., 2015; Tuohy et al., 2014). Social vulnerability was associated with three key themes, including personal protection, practical preparedness, and social preparedness. Cherry et al. (2015) found that perceived social support has a protective effect on all mental health outcomes, including symptoms of depression and generalized anxiety disorder.

This study is to explore the challenges faced by elderly women in disaster resilience. Limited research is available that evaluates interventions implemented to induce more positive outcomes for older adults (Table 5.1). Specifically, there is a lack of research evaluating best practices for assisting and caring for older adults, as well as the most effective methods for delivering services and resources to them. Older adults demonstrate behavioural resilience during disasters by receiving support from family, friends, and the local community, being assisted in disaster recovery; engaging with social networks to provide support for other victims, and using the event as a source of spiritual growth or personal learning (Miller & Brockie, 2015).

This review highlights that although there is consensus on the challenges faced by women, additional research on interventions is needed to reduce the impacts of disasters on women. It can lead to a better understanding of women's roles and potential in disaster preparedness and response and enhance the safety and resilience of families and communities.

5.2.2   Survey Analysis

Survey analysis was conducted with 36 participants above the age of 65 from different municipalities in Turkey. The data collection took place at various times. Data were gathered through semi-structured interviews. Even though there are limitations in this qualitative study, descriptive findings of the sociodemographic characteristics and capacities of the participants were presented. It is vital to understand these issues in building disaster-resilient communities.

5.2.2.1   Survey Data

Turkey is prone to severe hazards, particularly earthquakes, due to its location at the conjunction of four tectonic plates: the Anatolian, the Eurasian, the African, and the Arabian Plates. Disasters pose a serious threat to people's lives and harm the urban systems, including the physical, natural, and social environments. This study focuses on the districts of Şarköy and Ayvalik in seismically active areas.

Şarköy (Peristasi) is situated west of Tekirdağ in Thrace, along the north coast of the Marmara Sea where the North Anatolian Fault runs through. The area witnessed a devastating earthquake in 1912 that resulted in tsunamis. Şarköy is a coastal town known for wine-making and olive-growing. The population is 3,000, with 29% of the residents aged 65 years and older, 47% in the middle-aged range, and 50% female.

Ayvalik (Cydonia) is a coastal town in the northern Aegean, located opposite Lesbos Island. It is primarily known for its olive cultivation. About 26% of the population in Ayvalik is 65 years and older, with women making up 51% of the total population. In 1944, an earthquake struck the area, killing 30 people and damaging 5,500 buildings. This earthquake was one of the most significant to hit Ayvalik. Following the earthquake, infrastructure in much of the district was destroyed. It took nearly two years to reconstruct the houses, during which time there were migrations from the district.

The interviewees lived in urban and peri-urban areas and were between the ages of 65 and 70 and the ages 70–75 were in the minority (52% in the 65–70 age range, 22% in the 79–84 age range). As for the marital status, mostly married are in the majority (married 55%, widows 29%, single 16%). As for the number of children, the majority of the interviewees had two children and those having one are in the minority (67% with 1–2 children). As for the education level, the majority had a high school degree: finished primary school (21.4%), high school/secondary school (38.6%), and college/university degree (23.6%). About 60% of participants were retired. As for the profession, the responses varied: never worked, housewives, retired teachers, civil servants, and farmers (retired 45%, working 26%, housewife 29%) 61% still engaged in housework.

The story of the unfavourable economic status of the interviewees is wrapped up with the finding that 76% of respondents' income level meets their needs.

a. Regarding the financial assistance to their children's families, there are certain differences between the interviewees with marital status. The majority of inter-viewees who get such assistance are widowed.
b. As for property, 55% have some property, whereas 45% have no property registered in their name. The interviewees do not have any registered property in their name.

The majority of the interviewees live alone in their apartments (33.6%), slightly fewer of them live with their spouse in their apartments (20.7%), then with their son's family in their apartments (16.4%), and none of them in residential care.

a. According to the data, older women help families of their children – through giving care for grandchildren, and financial support.
b. The survey results indicate that the respondents, 68.6%, have provided or cur-rently providing care for their grandchildren.
c. Furthermore, 65.7% of older individuals provide financial assistance to their children's families.

In response to questions regarding their health status and access to medication, 43.6% of the respondents indicated their health status as "neither good nor bad", while 39% considered their health. Participants who feel healthy and do not have severe health problems have a more positive outlook on old age and feel strong in the face of life.

The majority of respondents indicated that they have some hobbies and occupations. Those who live in a family household with other members feel comfortable, and satisfied with their duties, and do not feel overburdened.

a. Participants who receive support from social networks such as family, friends, and neighbours, and who feel healthy and do not have severe health problems have a more positive outlook on old age and feel strong in the face of life.
b. They fear for their children's future, and it was closely followed by fears of earthquakes, illness, as well as the fear of being abandoned and left alone.
c. They stated that age alone does not affect the elderly, but ageing is a problem due to the health problems and limitations that come with it. Participants emphasized that they are self-sufficient.

To assess mitigation activities, participants were asked if they were aware of the hazards that create a high level of risk for the community. They showed a positive attitude towards preparedness. Despite the negativities brought about by health problems, they stated that they are supportive and willing if there are concrete steps to be presented about disaster preparedness.

a. It is noted that the elderly do not feel sufficiently prepared.
b. They need support services to be provided by institutions.
c. They stated that they did not see themselves as vulnerable individuals in disasters.

In terms of taking individual measures, it is seen that they are aware of preparation activities such as attending courses, watching TV broadcasts about disasters, learning protection methods during earthquakes, safety precautions for fires, and insurance.

When asked about the effect of faith on coping with disasters, they stated that faith gives them confidence and peace of mind, provides them the strength to withstand difficulties, and relieves their psychology. They state that no matter what they experience, it is still necessary to take precautions.

Attachment to place was assessed by asking respondents about their willingness to move elsewhere if they were exposed to a disaster. Younger respondents are generally more willing to move than older residents, but even when controlling for age, rural respondents are more attached to their communities. For reasons unknown, the opposite is true, where urban respondents are significantly more attached to their community than those in rural villages.

Despite their status as housewives, participants have a social communication network (51% use social media).

a. About 95% of the respondents own a television; 13% have a laptop or desktop computer in their household; 51% have a smartphone, and 56% do not have an internet connection. It is noted that 69% of the respondents do not use the internet.

b. More than half of the older women (55%) have the WhatsApp application, while Facebook is primarily used for group membership, with 14.5% of the respondents on Facebook.

c. Additionally, only those aged 65–70 can perform e-government/bank transactions.

d. Individuals in the older age group are limited to watching television.

Participants were asked about their preferences for shelter and financial assistance to assess the potential of their social networks to transform into social capital in disasters. A significant portion of the participants talked about the intimate relationships they have developed with their neighbours and friends in NGOs; it was observed that they did not consider these people as support mechanisms in disasters.

a. Depending on the level of education, widowed respondents have a more diverse social network structure. It is possible to say that the intersections of social networks and economic and cultural capital are decisive.

b. While 11 out of 13 participants with secondary school education and above have strong social networks, 7 out of 11 illiterate participants, mostly women, have weak social networks. It is noted that all elderly participants with weak social networks think of staying in official shelters during disasters and expect financial assistance from the state.

c. While 11 out of 18 elderly stated that they would prefer a place provided by the state as their shelter preference in case of a disaster, the other seven responded that they could stay with their children. Among the 15 elderly people in the city, 12 stated that they could stay with their children, and the other three could go to relatives, neighbours, and official shelters. The respondents could apply for financial assistance in disasters.

It is a widely preferred choice to receive care in their homes. Only 4% of low-income individuals expressed a preference for institutional care when they reach old age.

a. Around 31.6% of the respondents would like to live with home care services. When they are too old to care for themselves, 46.0% stated that they would like to stay with their children, and 10.3% would like to go to a nursing home.

b. According to the life satisfaction survey conducted in 2022, 60% of the elderly were from families, 22% were children, 7% were spouses, and 7% were grandchildren.

When the participants were asked whether they needed external support to prepare for disasters, 18 answered yes. They emphasized the need for information support for disaster preparedness, the development of training programmes and neighbourhood organizations, and the importance of the elderly registration system in municipalities.

a.   Interviews with the participants revealed the need for a comprehensive and multifaceted approach to disaster management for older individuals in emergencies to reduce their vulnerability to possible disasters and improve customized service programmes based on their needs.

b.   The research highlights the importance of individuals identifying their own needs instead of relying on experts to determine them. It also emphasizes the significance of developing support services in collaboration.

About 59.2% of respondents indicated that they maintained close relationships with their relatives and could cooperate with them. However, only 14.2% stated, "*I have relations with my friends who are not my relatives, and I can cooperate with them in all matters*" indicating that the respondent always applies this variable. When asked whether they could seek help from individuals outside their immediate family in the case of a disaster, 47.5% answered affirmatively, while 35.4% responded "partially".

The participants stated their connections within both formal and informal networks. Informal relationships within the neighbourhood were considered particularly crucial for disaster preparedness, response, and recovery.

Participants emphasized the importance of women's empowerment in disaster preparedness to reduce their vulnerabilities. A participant from Ayvalik (A2) suggested conducting awareness campaigns to engage the entire community and highlighted the role that people over 65 can play in disaster management. Another participant (A5) stated, "*Most issues can be overcome by introducing some community awareness program on the importance of empowering people in disaster governance*". They suggested the importance of providing capacity-building programmes for older women. They also suggested introducing training and programmes to develop additional skills, to gain knowledge and experience, that will empower women in disaster management.

Two participants from different locations shared their experiences, adding, "*We have not experienced or faced such types of disasters, but our parents did before*". One participant lived through an earthquake in 1999, and they experienced. She explained their recent experience of fire incidents in Ayvalik and how it expanded their knowledge of future disaster preparedness measures.

They like to have good training once a year as training for at least a couple of days. Two participants from Şarköy emphasized the role of the municipality and local NGOs in sharing their knowledge and experience to cope with disasters. One added that women found it very difficult to procure basic needs in disaster situations when faced with shortage of sanitary facilities for women. Luckily, there were women officers at the camps during the daytime who communicated with us. Many women hesitated to come out and talk to male officers. So, they feel more comfortable working with women officers in camps to communicate their issues in person. She explained, *"Women should be represented in the decision-making because half of the population is women. Thus, equal representation should be important, especially in managing disasters. Because most of the disasters affect more women than men"*.

5.3 Discussion

As the world's population ages, alongside that of many countries, there is an increasing number of older individuals who are at risk from extreme weather and earthquakes. Factors such as physical and mental health, disability, social isolation, financial circumstances, lack of access to resources, communication difficulties, and inability to use modern technologies contribute to their vulnerability. While older people are considered particularly vulnerable in disasters, there has been little work done on incorporating older women as key contributors in enhancing community disaster preparedness (Cherry et al., 2015; Brockie & Miller, 2017; Claver et al., 2013; Zhang et al., 2012; Bei et al., 2013; Chowdhury et al., 2022).

The literature analysis has revealed that the concepts of vulnerability were the most frequently used keywords in disaster research (Table 5.1). Much emphasis has been put on understanding and conceptualizing linkages between vulnerability and needs (Ran et al., 2020; Rana, 2020). Women's disaster-associated challenges across the globe are similar. Regardless of women's age, socio-economic or cultural background, their negative consequences during disasters show a distinct pattern of violence, inadequate support, and added pressure to fulfil household responsibilities that affect their well-being around the world (Reynolds & Tyler, 2018; Chowdhury et al., 2022).

5.3.1 Self-preparedness for Disasters

Despite these known vulnerabilities, an older adult's level of risk is related to the individual's self-confidence (or "self-help") in being prepared for a disaster (Brokie, 2017a,b). Although ageing is accompanied by biological changes that increase the risk of illness and disability, many elderly individuals maintain good health. Cox & Kim (2018) found that compared to individuals in the late middle-aged group (51–64), there was no significant difference between the late middle-aged and those aged 65–74.

A strong interest in and awareness of their local communities is evident among older individuals (Howard et al., 2017). For example, adults under the age of 65 and those aged 65 and above demonstrated greater preparedness for medical-related and general events, including the establishment of emergency communication plans and evacuation plans (Tomio et al., 2012). The preparedness of older women for disasters is a significant concern. However, the self-help and self-reliance perspective of disaster recovery and resilience has not been explored through studies.

In this study, research findings identify three key areas where older research (a) participants are willing to train and self-help; (b) social networks and (c) participation in local decision-making and planning.

Older women with higher education levels could have different perceptions of preparedness and barriers. They were more worried about preparing for disasters and had more limited capacity in the face of emergencies. They are more self-sufficient and more confident about their judgement on the perceived probability and consequences of disasters, and they cope and adapt as required. The majority chose to view themselves as survivors rather than as victims of disasters. They explained that they persevere rather than give in to despair. Many shared stories that they had heard from their elders (e.g., earthquakes and war). The participants who identified previous trauma related to the COVID-19 pandemic all linked their narratives with these previous traumas when explaining how they coped with just another experience.

Participants reported low levels of self-preparedness for disasters. They were asked about the strategies and resources that can improve disaster preparedness for older women. Their responses included knowing the risks associated with disasters, being informed about the appropriate measures they should take to keep themselves safe and adopt adequate personal preparations, knowing what to do in an emergency, warnings, evacuations, transportation, communication, shelter, personal care, and medical care, developing a personal emergency support network (family/friends and local community members), and having a stock of medicines and an emergency supply kit. They included a greater need for local/street-level community preparedness to encourage and facilitate support for resilience. They added that community-based disaster preparedness training does not promote behavioural change to increase the low level of public preparedness for disasters.

The survey results show that elderly focused disaster planning is important to set the framework for how communities and organizations move forward in disaster preparation. Therefore, it is necessary to consider functional capacity and abilities rather than age in disaster preparedness planning. Participants wanted to be made aware of their differences and expectations and wanted to be involved in the planning process themselves. Recommendations made include the early reestablishment of community centres as they foster social cohesion and provide opportunities for self-efficacy, coping through volunteerism, and the ability to contribute to community reconstruction. Among recommendations by the elderly is to reconstitute community centres early as they improve social connectedness and offer opportunities for self-efficacy, coping through volunteerism, and the ability to contribute to the rebuilding of the community. These results suggest that community-based disaster preparedness activities are effective methods for risk reduction communication, building resilience, and facilitating behavioural change.

Participants prefer women experts in disaster preparedness and training. They agreed that the community also prefers to communicate with women officers. Their confidence level increases when more women participate in response operations. Most disaster management measures carried out by men focused on disaster response operations. This indicates that women should be part of the response operations. They stated that women work in any situation. They can perform multitasking". Another interviewee responded, "*They have shown very effective in managing overall activities in the division, including disaster management*". One emphasized, "*When women are involved in disaster-related decision-making, they* understand gender-specific issues. Women face many issues staying in temporary shelters. These problems can be well understood and planned by women officers and communicated to the higher authorities".

Participants stated that they are willing to help and support each other. The experience of helping others in a disaster contributes to whether older people are themselves prepared. Older adults tend to display higher levels of resilience in response to trauma than younger persons (Cook, 2002). One factor contributing to older adults' resilience is the influence of past behaviour and experiences, such as prior trauma and disaster experiences. They are positively involved in sharing experiences and stories, and this approach can encourage others to enhance preparations and resilience.

Resilience is also related to beliefs, experiences, attitudes, and behaviours of risk reduction and adaptation (Aldrich, 2021). Many communities have developed their own disaster management techniques and traditions suited to the characteristics of local ecosystems based on the lessons learned from past disaster events over a long history. It is important to note that studies have identified individual beliefs as a resilience factor in disasters (Aida et al., 2023; Alam & Rahman, 2017; Aten et al., 2019; Burnside-Lary et al., 2013; Dev & Manalo, 2023). An individual's religious beliefs play an important role in their psycho-social recovery, provide comfort, and help reduce anxiety (Aten et al., 2019). Spirituality may also influence resilience and can include religious and other social support available to the affected individual as social capital and networks (Chan et al., 2012; Iloka, 2016). Religion also plays a key role in resilience, evidenced by social network connections established by older adults through their places of worship. It appears that having a religious faith and access to religion-based social support help affected individuals cope better with disaster-induced stress.

Disaster experience can be a valuable lesson in the future. This is why the knowledge held by older people is one of the greatest assets. They have lived in past disasters; the elderly have the experience, knowledge, and skills to understand local environmental hazards and their impacts. Few studies have highlighted the usefulness of their experiences for preparedness and response planning (Spurway, 2018). Residents are well-informed about the hazards that affect their communities and their vulnerabilities, and they use this knowledge to mitigate, prepare for, respond to, and recover from disaster impacts. This information can be essential for developing integrated resilience in disaster risk reduction and climate change adaptation strategies (Iloka, 2016; Rana, 2020).

Older women are the primary caregivers for others, including children, the elderly, and people with disabilities. Some older people are not only personally active but also take care of their grandchildren.Study participants who identify as homemakers generally have fewer social interactions, especially mothers who devote their later years to their grandchildren. The significant role of grandmothers in caregiving, observed in many parts of the world, allows younger women to work outside the home, knowing that their children will be cared for. In Turkey, most older women live with or near their children and are cared for by their children according to their needs. Rethinking the methods of caring for older women will become increasingly important, especially when considering their transition from caregivers to care recipients.

Today's world differs from the one older people grew up in, but many older people are better informed than ever. According to the results of the Household Information Technologies Usage Survey, the rate of people in the 65–74 age group using the internet will increase to 32.5% by 2021 due to the pandemic. A gender-based analysis of internet usage among the elderly revealed that 25.9% of elderly women used the internet, as reported by the Turkish Statistical Institute (TUIK, 2022). In Turkey, only a small proportion of older people engage in e-government transactions. Digital inclusion training for the elderly has been conducted by the 65+ Association in cooperation with the municipalities of Bağcılar, Bayrampaşa, Beşiktaş, Şişli, and Zeytinburnu districts in Istanbul.[3] Although limited in number, such training can help the elderly participate in social life. This suggests that if appropriate information and training are provided to the elderly, they will respond effectively and quickly to the messages given, and they can support disaster and emergency risk reduction efforts by organizing at the neighbourhood level.

Aid agencies failed to effectively address the medical needs of the elderly, resulting in many elderly individuals being unable to access medical treatment for chronic and acute conditions. The relief packages have overlooked the dietary restrictions of the elderly, leaving many without access to specialized nutritious diets needed for their health (Mudur, 2005). There is a lack of provision for needs such as walking sticks, hearing aids, and glasses to help the elderly reach aid distribution points during disaster response activities (HelpAge International, 2014). Societal stereotypes about ageing and the perception of older people as a burden often lead to their needs being overlooked by governments and civil society. Treating the elderly as passive recipients of support in disaster preparedness can lead to further discrimination (Howard et al., 2017).

Within the context of the Sendai Disaster Risk Reduction Framework, it is recommended that actions should be implemented to ensure the inclusion and participation of age and gender perspectives in all policies and practices (UN 2020). That is essential for all resilience indicators. There are limited mechanisms to monitor this progress in older people. The Agenda 2030 policy goals are critical to the well-being of older people. By 2030, when the Sustainable Development Goals (SDGs) end, there will be more people aged 60 and over than children under 10.

Societies must adapt their policies and services to respond to the changing age structure of their populations to deliver the promises of the SDGs (Box 1).

Studies on capacity building of the elderly instead of vulnerability in disasters are still new. Although the elderly do not consider themselves vulnerable, the definition of the population has historically been based on age, not functional capacity or capability. Fernandez et al. (2002) argued that age does not make a person vulnerable. Mandatory retirement does not necessarily reflect the true capacity of older individuals. There are no age-related barriers to creativity and contribution. Additionally, over half of the global population over 60 is still economically active, and a significant percentage of older individuals continue to work past the ages of 70 and 75 (IFRC, 2020). Despite the crucial role that women play in disaster resilience, they are often portrayed as victims, depicted as passive and reliant on limited survival, coping, and adaptation abilities. Older women are the world's fastest-growing and least-used asset. They have a lifetime of skills and experience over many years, which could be immensely valuable for society in the context of disaster preparedness activities.

5.3.2 Box 1: Global Goals and Elderly

Global goals emphasize a comprehensive and people-centred approach to disaster risk reduction. The Sendai Framework for Disaster Risk Reduction (SFDRR), the 2030 Agenda for Sustainable Development (SDG), and the Paris Climate Agreement (IPCC) all recognize the need for strong coordination and action on disaster risk reduction (DRR). DRR practices need to be multi-hazard and multi-sectoral, as well as inclusive and accessible, with a focus on involving older persons in the development and implementation of policies, plans, and standards for optimal efficiency and effectiveness. The global goals emphasize the importance of adapting national policies and local strategies to a participatory approach and ensuring the participation of all.

The Sendai Framework outlines priorities to achieve disaster risk reduction and enhance community resilience. These priorities are key strategies for developing and strengthening disaster preparedness to ensure effective response, recovery, and building-back-better reconstruction. They include reducing global disaster mortality, the number of affected people, direct disaster economic losses, disaster damage to critical infrastructure, life services, health, and educational facilities, and developing resilience with national and local DRR strategies by 2030. The SFDRR emphasizes the significant role of traditional knowledge and experience of elders in disaster risk management strategies and the creation and implementation of plans at a global level (UNISDR, 2015).

The 2030 Agenda for Sustainable Development Goals (SDGs) is a global initiative aimed at promoting sustainable development by integrating the environmental, social, and economic dimensions. It emphasizes the need to build the capacity of all countries to reduce risk and adapt to climate change, thus increasing resilience. In particular, the SDGs explicitly address cities (Goal 11) as they face rapidly increasing risks and unmanageable disasters. Cities and communities have to deal with both disasters and sustainable development issues. Additionally, the ageing population is a significant aspect of demographic change in cities. These goals aim to ensure that every older person is included in efforts to leave no one behind (Table 5.2).

The New Urban Agenda (NUA) helps contribute to sustainable development and improve human well-being to enhance disaster resilience and mitigation aspects in urbanization. It supports local authorities' age- and gender-sensitive approaches in urban and regional development decision-making without discrimination based on socio-economic status. Furthermore, the Istanbul Convention adopts a gender perspective on violence against women and gender inequalities.

Table 5.2 How Sensitive are Global Goals with Regard to the Elderly?

Legislation	Actions Related to
SFDRR	• "actions should be implemented in order to ensure the inclusion and participation of gender, age, … in all policies and practices" • "Older persons have valuable knowledge, skills, and wisdom, which are invaluable assets to reduce disaster risk, and they should be involved in the design of policies and plans"
SDGs	Goal 1: End poverty in all its forms everywhere 1.2. By 2030, reduce at least by half the proportion of men, **women and children of all ages** living in poverty in all its dimensions according to national definitions Goal 2: Zero Hunger 2.2. By 2030, end all forms of malnutrition, including achieving, … address the nutritional needs of … women and **older persons** Goal 11: Make cities inclusive, safe, resilient and sustainable 11.2. By 2030, provide access to safe, affordable, accessible and sustainable transport systems for all, improving road safety, notably by expanding public transport, with special attention to the needs of those in vulnerable situations, women, children, persons with disabilities and **older persons**. 11.7. By 2030, provide universal access to safe, inclusive and accessible, green and public spaces, in particular for women and **older persons**
IPCC	Increasing weather and climate extreme events have already exposed millions of people, especially for **elderly people** particularly impacted. Roughly half of the world's population currently experience (IPCC 2022a). Future risks of cardiovascular disease mortality could increase by 47% in the 2050s associated with increasing temperatures (IPCC 2022)
NUA	• adopt and implement disaster risk reduction and management, reduce vulnerability • building urban resilience by reducing disaster risks and by mitigating and adapting to climate change • addressing multiple forms of discrimination faced by … older persons • encouraging the elimination of legal, institutional, socio-economic and physical barriers • in strengthening the interface among all relevant stakeholders, offering opportunities for dialogue, including through age- and gender-responsive approaches, and with particular attention to potential contributions from all segments of society, including men and women, children and youth, older persons • with awareness-raising initiatives, with special attention to the needs of all women, as well older persons • promoting capacity-development initiatives to empower and strengthen the skills and abilities of women and … older persons

It is widely acknowledged that social networks may be an effective instrument in building resilience to disasters. Social capital is key in addressing challenges associated with an ageing population. However, there is limited knowledge on enhancing elders' social capital, especially within the community-based disaster risk management system. This system can encourage communities to improve procedures for gathering and sharing warning information, even if different communities in the same area have policies, as long as the community needs (Iuchi & Mutter, 2020). Social capital as the missing link is identified in several studies in preparing for, responding to, and recovering from disasters (Aldrich, 2012; Aldrich & Meyer, 2014; American Red Cross, 2013; Burnside-Lary et al., 2013). Howard et al. (2017) discussed the engagement and participation of older people in disaster community resilient-building activities in Australia. These networks are helpful to elderly community members who do not have support from family and friends. Despite its proven efficacy, the role of social capital remains unexplored in facilitating resilience.

The elderly population plays an active role in building social capital by engaging in volunteer work and participating in various activities. This study is limited to analyzing whether and how physical and social infrastructure enhanced social capital among elders. Although it varies depending on the level of education, participants have a more diverse social network structure. At this point, it is possible to say that the intersections of social network, economic, and cultural capital are decisive. In general, all participants with weak social networks consider staying in their official shelter during disasters and expect financial aid from the state. During the pandemic, those staying connected with friends and family felt less distress. Individuals with less neighbourhood relations, little social support, and lower levels of social capital experience are more susceptible to depression and sleep problems during quarantine (Adepoju et al., 2023a).

Social capital plays a crucial role in building local capacity for older adults. Bonding capital involves family members and neighbours and also provides a source of trusted information and help. Bridging capital involves practical support from friendly strangers like local community-based organizations (CBOs), and volunteers are instrumental in helping recovery during/after the disasters. Bonding capital provides reliable information and assistance during and after disasters (Brokie & Miller, 2017b). However, disasters can weaken or destroy bonding capital and force reliance on bridging capital. Many individuals have reported depending on bonding capital for assistance in evacuation and bridging capital (Adams et al., 2020; Aldrich & Meyer, 2014). Social capital is considered essential for the needs of older adults. Dynes (2006) emphasized that social isolation can lead to withdrawal from society and increase vulnerability. For instance, women's dependence on male family members for warning information, evacuation instructions, and rescue activities may prevent them from mobilizing in emergencies (Chowdhury et al., 2022). Therefore, older women need social capital to mitigate disaster and build resilience for emotional recovery (Hawkins & Maurer, 2010; Touhy & Stephens, 2012). Studies have shown that community centres have improved social connectedness through involvement with CBOs (volunteering) and have accelerated resilience through elder-led physical and social infrastructure (Henderson et al., 2010; Aldrich, 2012, 2021; Johnson et al., 2015; Aldrich & Kiyota, 2017).

5.3.3 *Planning*

The effectiveness of risk reduction strategies is strongly linked to both women and resilience (Alam & Rahman, 2017; Astill & Miller, 2018; Babatunde-Sowole et al., 2016; Dev & Manalo, 2023; Zaitsu et al., 2018). However, critical issues related to gender and age have been ignored in studies. There is a lack of understanding of gender concerning resilience, and the inequalities that contribute to women's vulnerability and hinder their capacity building have been largely overlooked.

The growing elderly population will increase the demand for disaster and emergency services to meet the basic needs of these individuals, who are at significant risk before and after a disaster. There is a need for community-based integrated services and programmes to support disaster preparedness and response for older women (Kwan, 2020). Planning should be based on specific needs, rather than on age. It is important to note that those aged 75 or older have significantly more barriers to preparedness, making them more vulnerable due to their advanced age. Examining the differences between older adults and younger adults is crucial. Without considering the substantial differences among older adults of different ages may result in an overly optimistic scenario and divert attention from the distinctive vulnerability of older adults (Wakui et al., 2017). Therefore, public disaster education and support for preparedness should consider the vulnerability and resilience of individuals.

Most countries rarely include women in decision-making forums for disaster prevention or recovery planning. Engagement in activities is also strongly linked to mental well-being for the elderly (Forsman et al., 2013). Older women have a crucial role in bridging and bonding social capital across generations. The sharing of resources and experiences is a significant factor in disaster planning. In this study, participants who were already engaged in generating bridging social capital about disaster preparedness stated that they would like to be involved in this kind of activity, as well as local disaster planning.

5.4 Recommendations

Almost everywhere in the world, the number of older people is growing faster than the total population. Countries should improve the sustainability of their health and long-term care systems and adapt them to the growing proportion of older people (Aida et al., 2023). Within the context of the Sendai Disaster Risk Reduction Framework, it is recommended that actions should be implemented to ensure the inclusion and participation of age and gender perspectives in all policies and practices. The UN notes that the lack of gender-disaggregated data and analysis of disasters makes an accurate understanding of disaster impacts and risk reduction problematic. There is a need to fill data gaps with national statistical offices and other relevant stakeholders to improve the production and reporting of local data. It is necessary to develop a data collection system on elderly needs.

In the current social norms, older people tend to be isolated from society, and issues related to ageing are invisible (WHO, 2021). Therefore, older people hardly pass on their experience and wisdom, which are crucial for society, to future generations (Aida et al., 2023). In addition to the loss this represents, isolation puts elders at increased risk of illness and vulnerability in a disaster, while the cost of their care for families and society is growing (Klinenberg, 2016). While nationally there have been efforts to improve disaster planning, recent disasters have demonstrated that elderly focused disaster planning should be developed to move forward in disaster preparation. Disaster care and the need for disaster-specific standards for this population are evident. Their capacity, ability, or competence rather than age should be considered in disaster preparedness. In post-disaster situations, older people's knowledge and experience may be beneficial for coping solutions; therefore, they should be involved in the disaster management cycle. They should be acknowledged as valuable community resources. Nutritional, medical, and caregiving needs of the elderly and women should be addressed in disaster plans.

Survey results outline a strategy for nationwide community-based disaster preparedness education programmes for older adults. Zaitsu et al. (2018) state that special preparation training for older adults develops positive effects. Aldrich & Kiyota (2017) noted that encouraging older people to participate in community preparedness can help them move out of social isolation and increase the resilience of the neighbourhood in general. It is imperative to acknowledge the significance of knowledge in disaster risk reduction. Consequently, there is a pressing need to actively engage local communities and institutions in disaster risk reduction projects.

Older women's kinship relationships are their most valuable social relationships and are the source of social support that strengthens resilience throughout the disaster management cycle. It is also critical to help motivate them to engage in risk reduction, preparedness, and inclusive/participatory planning. Raising awareness against social attitudes and gender misperceptions is an important issue to address in terms of resilience. Local governments, voluntary organizations, and the media are crucial. Establishing neighbourhood preparedness programmes and organizing awareness, planning, and capacity-building programmes for older women are essential to build resilience and protect their independence, dignity, and capacity to rebuild after disasters.

Support women in leadership roles and build trust in their decision-making abilities. Older women's spiritual and religious beliefs can contribute to positive mental health and help them cope with disasters. This makes them more resilient in the face of disasters. Older women should be encouraged to take part in social activities. They should also be involved in planning for temporary shelters. These areas should be designed with older women in mind. When creating facilities for basic needs, it is important to consider the needs of elderly women.

Emergency response planners should be aware of cultural differences and expectations and involve elders in the planning process because elders know what resources they want during response and recovery. Women's participation in decision-making processes is essential not only for ensuring safety in disasters but also for reducing the risks of disasters and building resilience. Crises often expose social problems, inequalities, and discrimination that would otherwise go unnoticed. While eliminating inequalities for women requires putting in place systems to promote women's social inclusion, there is a need to more clearly articulate strategies to increase the disaster capacity of older women. Women's involvement in decision-making and planning processes and their important role during preparedness activities should be included. Therefore, disaster research needs to incorporate these issues into its agenda, as well as explore protective and resilience factors related to enhancing an older adult's self-efficacy during future disasters.

Social infrastructure: Create and implement programmes to improve communication with older people, enabling them to understand their needs and struggles in disasters. Encourage and support the self-organization of older people through establishing self-help groups, and diminish self-neglect and the habits of ignoring their own needs and interests; support activities that contribute to overcoming the prevalent model of self-sacrifice. Social structures will need to be transformed to ensure women's active participation in planning at the community level in which they can contribute. Social infrastructure is seen to help societies build resilience to the challenges of crises. Physical infrastructure helps bind individuals to a particular place and builds social capital, but this approach has not been implemented in community risk management (Aldrich, 2012).

Strengthening infrastructure: During pre-disaster times, older women's experiences of healthcare disparities can contribute to the development or worsening of poor health and well-being, which can hinder their resilience within a disaster context. Although community-based emergency preparedness training classes that have been adapted to address the needs of older adults should maximize the positive impact they have among older adults, healthcare professionals and emergency response personnel should also receive training on providing care relevant to their discipline and appropriate treatments as needed.

Ensuring access to all public systems and services should be the most important strategic step in restructuring resilience. Architecture should be built with accessibility standards to allow access community and public spaces for older people. For the elderly to participate in social life, age-friendly urban transportation and housing projects should be produced by the principles of universally accessible architectural design.

Specific community-based training programmes should be increased to educate older adults and their caregivers about disasters/emergencies affecting their area and how best to prepare for and respond to them. There is also a need for coordinated efforts with the media at all levels to promote understanding that ageing is a normal part of life. Local television channels, which are traditional media, can be used as media and digital literacy training environments for the elderly. Public and local governments should support services based on sustainable city/living standards to keep the elderly in the social environment.

5.5 Summary

By the year 2050, the largest population will be women aged 60 and over. Living in a world with increasing disasters will require older people to be appropriately prepared. There are studies in the literature focusing on the physical and social challenges of the elderly in disasters, but research on the disaster resilience of elderly women is limited. In addition to needs-oriented studies, assessing the capacity of the elderly can be useful in conducting disaster risk management plans. Indeed, dependent and vulnerable old age is being replaced by a more active and independent elderly population. Furthermore, the social relationships of older women can serve as sources of social support and social capital, which can contribute to enhanced disaster resilience. Strong and positive social support facilitates self-help, increases individual resilience, and can lead to rapid recovery after a disaster. In disaster situations, it would be beneficial to utilize the knowledge and experience of older people. It is imperative to adapt urban spaces and public services to the demographic shift towards an ageing population. Furthermore, it is essential to engage older individuals in the planning processes and decision-making about their well-being. Participatory and integrated, more holistic approaches should be employed to enhance the efficacy of disaster and emergency services in creating age-friendly cities.

Notes

1 Scopus (http://www.scopus.com).
2 Google Scholar records (http://scholar.google.com).
3 (https://yaslihaklaridernegi.org/65-icin-dijital-kapsayicilik-ab-projesi-hakkinda/).

References

Adams RM, Evans CM, Mathews MC, Wolkin A, Peek L (2020). Mortality from forces of nature among older adults by race/ethnicity and gender. *J Appl Gerontol.* 1–10. https://doi.org/10.1177/0733464820954676.

Adepoju OE, Smith KL, Shetty S, Taha E-E, Howard DL (2023a). Coping with disasters and pandemics through experience and community: How African American older adults navigate disaster planning, response, and recovery. *Disaster Med Public Health Prep.* https://doi.org/10.1017/dmp.2022.254.

Adepoju OE, Herrera L, Chae M, Han D (2023b). Optimizing disaster preparedness planning for minority older adults: One size does not fit all. *Int J Environ Res Public Health.* 20(1): 401.

Age International (2015). *Facing the facts: The truth about ageing and development.* London: Age International.

Aida T, Kiyota E, Tanaka Y *et al.* (2023). Building social capital with elders' leadership through a community hub "*Ibasho*" in the Philippines and Nepal. *Sci Rep.* 13: 3652.

Alam K, Rahman, MH (2017). The role of women in disaster resilience. In: *Handbook of Disaster Risk Reduction and Management: Climate Change and Natural Disasters. ed. by Madu CN and Kuei CH..* New Jersey: World Scientific Press, 697–719.

Aldrich D (2012). *Building resilience: Social capital in post-disaster recovery.* Chicago: University of Chicago Press.

Aldrich DP (2021). The benefits of Japan's social infrastructure and social ties in uncertain times. *East Asia Forum Q.* 13: 1–4.

Aldrich DP, Meyer AM (2014). Social capital and community resilience. *Am Behav Sci.* 59: 254–269.

Aldrich DP, Kiyota E (2017). Creating community resilience through elder-led physical and social infrastructure. *Disaster Med Public Health Prep.* 11: 120–126

American Red Cross (2013). *Disaster preparedness for seniors by seniors.* Be Red Cross Ready for Disaster. https://www.redcross.org/get-help/how-to-prepare-for-emergencies/older-adults.html.

Astill S, Miller E (2018). "We expect seniors to be able to prepare and recover from a cyclone as well as younger members of this community": Emergency management's expectations of older adults residing in aging, remote hamlets on Australia's cyclone-prone coastline. *Disaster Med Public Health Prep.* 12(1): 14–18.

Aten JD, Smith WR et al (2019). The psychological study of religion and spirituality in a disaster context: A systematic review. *Psychol Trauma: Theory, Research, Practice, and Policy.* 11(6): 597.

Babatunde-Sowole O, Power T, Jackson D, Davidson PM, DiGiacomo M (2016). Resilience of African migrants: An integrative review. *Health Care Women Int.* 37(9): 946–963.

Bei B et al (2013). A prospective study of the impact of floods on the mental and physical health of older adults. *Aging and Ment Health.* 17(8): 992–1002.

Bergstrand K, Mayer B, Brumback B, Zhang Y (2015). Assessing the relationship between social vulnerability and community resilience to hazards. *Soc Indic Res.* 122: 391–409.

Brilleman SL, Wolfe R, Moreno-Betancur M et al (2017). Associations between community-level disaster exposure and individual-level changes in disability and risk of death for older Americans. *Soc Sci Med.* 173: 118–125.

Brockie L, Miller E (2017a). Older adults' disaster lifecycle experience of the 2011 and 2013 Queensland floods. *Int J Disaster Risk Reduct.* 22: 211–218.

Brockie L, Miller E (2017b). Understanding older adults' resilience during the Brisbane floods: Social capital, life experience, and optimism. *Disaster Med Public Health Prep.* 11(1): 72–79.

Bunce A, Ford J (2015). How is adaptation, resilience, and vulnerability research engaging with gender? *Environ Res Lett.* 10: 123003.

Burnside-Lawry J, Akama Y, Rogers P (2013). Communication research needs for building societal disaster resilience. *Aust J Emerg Manag.* 28(4): 29–35.

Busapathumrong P (2013). Disaster management: Vulnerability and resilience in disaster recovery in Thailand. *J Soc Work Disabil Rehabil.* 12(1–2): 67–83.

Cénat JM, Smith K, Morse C, Derivois D (2020). Sexual victimization, PTSD, depression, and social support among women survivors of the 2010 earthquake in Haiti: A moderated moderation model. *Psychol Med.* 50(15): 2587–2598.

Chan KM, Guerry AD, Balvanera P et al (2012). Where are cultural and social in ecosystem services? A framework for constructive engagement. *BioScience.* 62(8): 744–756.

Cherry KE, Sampson L, Nezat PF, Cacamo A, Marks LD, Galea S (2015). Long-term psychological outcomes in older adults after disaster: Relationships to religiosity and social support. *Aging Ment Health.* 19(5): 430–443.

Chowdhury TJ, Kako M, Arbon P, Muller R, Gebbie K, Steenkamp M (2022). Understanding the experiences of women in disasters: Lessons for emergency management planning. *Aust J Emerg Manag.* 37(1): 72–77.

Claver M, Dobalian A, Fickel JJ, Ricci KA, Mallers MH (2013). Comprehensive care for vulnerable elderly veterans during disasters. *Arch Gerontol Geriatr.* 56(1): 205–213.

Cook J (2002). Traumatic exposure and PTSD in older adults: Introduction to the special issue. *J Clin Geropsychol.* 8(3): 149–152.

Cox K, Kim B (2018). Race and income disparities in disaster preparedness in old age. *J Gerontol Soc Work.* 61(7): 719–734.

Cheek C, Piercy KW, Kohlenberg M (2015). Have i ever done anything like this before? Older adults solving Ill–defined problems in intensive volunteering. *Int J Aging Hum Dev.* 80(2): 184–207.

Cutter SL, Barnes L, Berry M, Burton C, Evans E, Tate E et al (2008). A place-based model for understanding community resilience. *Global Environ Change.* 18: 598–606.

Dev DS, Manalo IV, JA (2023). Gender and adaptive capacity in climate change scholarship of developing countries: A systematic review of literature. *Clim Dev.* 15(10), 1–12.

Dhungel R, Ojha RN (2012). Women's empowerment for disaster risk reduction and emergency response in Nepal. Gend Dev. 20(2): 309–321.

Drolet J, Dominelli L, Alston M, Ersing R, Mathbor G, Wu H (2015). Women rebuilding lives post-disaster: Innovative community practices for building resilience and promoting sustainable development. Gend Dev. 23(3): 433–448.

Dynes R (2006). Social capital: Dealing with community emergencies. *Homeland Secur Aff.* 2(2): 1–26.

Fernandez LS, Byard D, Lin CC, Benson S, Barbera JA (2002). Frail elderly as disaster victims: Emergency management strategies. Prehosp Disaster Med. 17(02): 67–74.

Forsman AK, Herberts C, Nyqvist F, Wahlbeck K, Schierenbecks I (2013). Understanding the role of social capital for mental wellbeing among older adults. Ageing Soc. 33(5): 805–825.

Fothergill A, Peek LA (2004). Poverty and disasters in the United States: A review of recent sociological findings. *Nat Hazards.* 32(1): 89–110.

GAWI (2014). *Global age watch index.* London: HelpAge International.

Gutman GM, Yon Y (2014). Elder abuse and neglect in disasters: Types, prevalence and research gaps. *Int J Disaster Risk Reduct.* 10: 38–47.

Hawkins R, Maurer K (2010). Bonding, bridging and linking: How social capital operated in New Orleans following Hurricane Katrina. *Br J Social Work.* 40(6): 1777–1793.

Henderson TL, Roberto KA, Kamo Y (2010). Older adults' responses to Hurricane Katrina: Daily hassles and coping strategies. *J Appl Gerontol.* 29(1): 48–69.

HelpAge International (2012). *Ageing in the twenty-first century: A celebration and a challenge.* United Nations Population Fund (UNFPA), New York, and HelpAge International, London.

HelpAge International (2014). Disaster resilience. In *An Aging World. How to make policies and programmes inclusive of older people.*

Howard A, Blakemore T, Bevis M (2017). Older people as assets in disaster preparedness, response and recovery: Lessons from regional Australia. Ageing Soc. 37: 517–536.

IFRC (2020). *World disasters report.* Gender-Sensitive Approaches For Disaster Management. https://www.ifrc.org/PageFiles/96532/A%20Guide%20for%20Gendersensitive%20approach%20to%20DM.pdf.

IPCC (2022). Summary for Policymakers. In: Climate Change 2022 - Mitigation of Climate Change: Working Group III Contribution to the Sixth Assessment Report of the Intergovernmental Panel on Climate Change. Cambridge University Press; 2023: 3–48.

Iloka NG (2016). Indigenous knowledge for disaster risk reduction: An African perspective. *Jàmbá.* 8(1): 1–17.

Iuchi K, Mutter J (2020). Governing community relocation afer major disasters: Refections on three diferent approaches and its outcomes in Asia. *Prog Disaster Sci.* 6: 100071.

Jamshed A, Rana IA, McMillan JM, Birkmann J (2019). Building community resilience in post-disaster resettlement in Pakistan. *Int J Disaster Resil Built Environ.* 10: 301–315.

Johnson HL, Ling CG, McBee EC (2015). Multi-disciplinary care for the elderly in disasters: An integrative review. *Prehosp Disaster Med.* 30(1): 72–79.

Kako M, Mayner L (2019). The experience of older people in Japan four years after the tsunami. *Collegian.* 26(1): 125–131.

Klinenberg E (2016). Social isolation, loneliness, and living alone: Identifying the risks for public health. *Am J Public Health.* 106(5): 786–787.

Krishnan S, Pappadis MR, Runo R, Graham JE (2019). Experiences and needs of older adults following Hurricane Ike: A pilot study of long-term consequences. *Health Promot Pract.* 20(1): 31–37.

Kukihara H., Yamawaki N, Uchiyama K, Arai S, Horikawa E (2014). Trauma, depression, and resilience of earthquake/tsunami/nuclear disaster survivors of Hirono, Fukushima, Japan. *Psychiatry Clin Neurosci.* 68(7): 524–533.

Kwan C. (2020). Factors and processes in the pre-disaster context that shape the resilience of older women in poverty. Int J Disaster Risk Reduct. 48: 101610.

Madrigano J, Mittleman MA, Baccarelli A, Goldberg R, Melly S, von Klot S, Schwartz J (2013). Temperature, myocardial infarction, and mortality: Effect modification by individual and area-level characteristics. *Epidemiology* (Cambridge, Mass.). 24(3): 439.

Miller E, Brockie L (2015). The disaster flood experience: Older people's poetic voices of resilience. *J Aging Stud.* 34: 103–112.

Mudur G. (2005). Aid agencies ignored special needs of elderly people after tsunami. *BMJ.* 331(7514): 422.

Okay N, Ilkkaracan I (2018). Gender-sensitive disaster risk management. *Resilience.* 2(1): 1–12.

Okay N, Inal E (2019). From vulnerability to building resilience capacity. *Resilience.* 3(1): 85–99.

Okay N, Inal E, Yücel G, Akalın O (2022). Improving resilience capacity of the policies and planning for temporary shelters in crises and disasters. *Handbook of disaster risk reduction for resilience, Vol. 4: Economic vulnerability and recovery programs, Part II: Disaster relief and recovery programs* (ed. S. Eslamian & F. Eslamian). Springer. https://doi.org/10.1007/978-3-031-08325-9_7.

Pirard P, Vandentorren S, Pascal M, Laaidi K, Le Tertre A, Cassadou S, Ledrans M (2005). Summary of the mortality impact assessment of the 2003 heat wave in France. *Eurosurveillance.* 10(7): 7–8.

Pongponrat K, Ishii K (2018). Social vulnerability of marginalized people in times of disaster: Case of Thai women in Japan Tsunami 2011. *Int J Disaster Risk Reduct.* 27: 133–141.

Powell S, Plouffe L, Gorr P (2009) When ageing and disasters collide: Lessons from 16 international case studies. *Radiat Prot Dosimetry.* 134(3–4): 202–206.

Pruchno R, Wilson-Genderson M, Heid AR, Cartwright FP (2021). Effects of peri-traumatic stress experienced during Hurricane Sandy on functional limitation trajectories for older men and women. *Soc Sci Med.* 281, art. no. 114097.

Rafiey H, Momtaz YA, Alipour F et al (2016). Are older people more vulnerable to long-term impacts of disasters? *Clin Interv Aging.* 11: 1791–1795.

Ran J, MacGillivray BH, Gong Y, Hales TC (2020). The application of frameworks for measuring social vulnerability and resilience to geophysical hazards within developing countries: A systematic review and narrative synthesis. *Sci Total Environ.* 711: 134486.

Rana IA (2020). Disaster and climate change resilience: A bibliometric analysis. *Int J Disaster Risk Reduct.* 50: 101839.

Reynolds B, Tyler M (2018). Applying a gendered lens to the stay and defend or leave early approach to bushfire safety. *Aust J Public Adm.* 77(4): 529–541.

Rich JL, Wright SL, Loxton D (2018). Older rural women living with drought. *Local Environ.* 23(12): 1141–1155.

Sanlier N, Yabanci N (2007). The effects of two earthquakes in the Marmara region of Turkey on the nutritional status of adults. *Pak J Nutr.* 6(4): 327–331.

Seifi B, Ghanizadeh G, Seyedin H (2018). Disaster health literacy of middle-aged women. *J Menopausal Med.* 24(3): 150–154.

Smyth I, Sweetman C (2015). Introduction: Gender and resilience. *Gend Dev.* 23: 405–414.

Spurway K (2018). Critical reflections on Indigenous peoples' ecological knowledge and disaster risk management in Australia: A rapid evidence review. *Glob Media J Aust Ed.* 12(1): 1–16.

Stanko K, Cherry K, Ryker K, et al (2015). Looking for the silver lining: Benefit finding after hurricanes Katrina and Rita in middle-aged, older and oldest-old adults. *Curr Psychol.* 34: 564–575.

Tanida N. (1996). What happened to elderly people in the great Hanshin earthquake. *BMJ,* 313(7065): 1133–1135.

Timalsina R, Songwathana P, Sae-Sia W (2021). Resilience and its associated factors among older disaster survivors. *Geriatr Nurs.* 42(6): 1264–1274.

Tomio J, Sato H, Mizumura M (2012). Disparity in disaster preparedness among rheumatoid arthritis patients with various general health, functional, and disability conditions. *Environ Health Prev Med.* 17(4): 322–331.

Touhy R, Stephens C (2011). Exploring older adults' personal and social vulnerability in a disaster. *Int J Emerg Manag.* 8(1): 60–74.

Touhy R, Stephens C (2012). Older adults' narratives about a flood disaster: Resilience, coherence, and personal identity. *J Aging Stud.* 26(1): 26–34.

Touhy R, Stephens C, Johnston D (2014). Older adults' disaster preparedness in the context of September 2010-December 2012 Canterbury earthquake sequence. *Int J Disaster Risk Reduct.* 9: 194–203.

TUIK (2022). The Turkish Statistical Institute. Elderly with Statistics for 2022. https://data .tuik.gov.tr/.

UN (2015). The 2030 Agenda for sustainable development. https://sustainabledevelopment .un.org/post2015/transformingourworld.

United Nations (2022). Population division. World population prospects 2022: Summary of results. Department of Economic and Social Affairs, UN DESA/POP/2022/TR/NO. 3.

United Nations (2020). World population ageing 2020: Living arrangements of older persons (United Nations Department of Economic and Social Afairs, Population Division).

UNDESA (2014). *Population ageing and development.* New York: UNDESA United Nations. http://www.un.org/en/development/desa/population/publications/pdf/popfacts/ PopFacts_2014-4.pdf.

UNISDR (2015). The Sendai framework for disaster risk reduction 2015–2030. United Nations Office for Disaster Risk Reduction, Geneva. Retrieved from http://www .preventionweb.net/files/43291_sendaiframeworkfordrren.pdf.

Wakui T, Agree EM, Saito T, Kai I (2017). Disaster preparedness among older Japanese adults with long-term care needs and their family caregivers. *Disaster Med Public Health Prep.* 11(1): 31–38.

World Health Organization (2021). Global Report on Ageism.

Xu Q, Norstrand JA, Du Y (2015). Effects of living alone on social capital and health among older adults in China. *Int J Aging Hum Dev.* 82(1): 30–53.

Yazawa A, Aida J, Kondo K, Kawachi I (2022). Gender differences in risk of posttraumatic stress symptoms after disaster among older people: Differential exposure or differential vulnerability? *J Affect Disord.* 297: 447–454.

Zaitsu M, Kawachi I, Ashida T, Kondo K, Kondo N (2018). Participation in community group activities among older adults: Is diversity of group membership associated with better self-rated health?. *J Epidemiol.* 28(11): 452–457.

Zhang L, Fu P, Wang L et al (2012). The clinical features and outcome of crush patients with acute kidney injury after the Wenchuan earthquake: Differences between elderly and younger adults. *Int J Care Injured.* 43(9): 1470–5.

Zhu X, Sun B (2017). Study on earthquake risk reduction from the perspectives of the elderly. *Saf Sci.* 91: 326–334.

Understanding "Self-Work/ Labour/Action" Coping Concepts

6 Community Resilience and Micro Human Acts

Recovery after the Great East Japan Earthquake and Tsunami

Ken Tsubouchi, Ryosuke Tomiyasu,
Teruyuki Isagawa, and Shiori Suzawa

6.1 Introduction

While modern disaster recovery is executed by macro-actors who are responsible for planning and organizing activities, the recipients of the rehabilitation act as micro actors as their decisions affect evacuation and relocation (Wilmsen and Webber, 2015). Regardless of whether the planning process is top-down or bottom-up, recovery actors commonly include local and national governments, local and international corporations, development banks, financial corporations, and local communities. In this context, local communities can adaptively manage and respond to extraordinary events, both within and outside the disaster location (Paton, 2006; Norris et al., 2008). However, a community is not a homogeneous entity as it includes many different individuals with diverse agendas. These individuals are mutually a part of and are affected by complex networks of power (Allen, 2006; Cannon, 2008). Therefore, it is important to understand the significance of the micro-activities of individuals on the ground who are embedded in recovery processes that are administrated by macro-actors (Shrestha, 2019).

In Japan, several urban planning techniques and mechanisms have been developed in the context of disaster recovery. These developments have sprung from one of two approaches. The first one is the government-led infrastructure reconstruction since the Imperial Capital Revival Plan of 1923 after the Great Kanto Earthquake and the post-war Revival City Planning of 1945. The second stream of developments is the product of a community-centred participatory process known as "Machizukuri" that emerged after the Great Hanshin-Awaji Earthquake of 1995 (Murakami et al., 2014). Then in 2011, recovery from the Great East Japan Earthquake and Tsunami (GEJET), which devastated hundreds of coastal communities, presented a major challenge in terms of synchronization between macro and micro actors. After GEJET, community-focused reconstruction was the foundation of the recovery efforts (Reconstruction Agency, 2011). However, a strong presence of the national government in urban planning essentially controlled the capacity and funding of the recovery work. The local actors often failed to meet their objectives due to time constraints and lack of planning expertise on top of the unprecedented level of challenges in post-disaster recovery (Iuchi and Olshanky, 2018; Kondo, 2018).

DOI: 10.4324/9781003615903-9

Meanwhile, some practices have successfully addressed different aspects of recovery scenes through the interplay between the activities of micro-actors and local communities. What they have in common is that local actors have made good use of the limited resources around them. Making the most of limited resources in a short timeframe is key in disaster recovery (Olshansky et al., 2012). These practices signal how disaster recovery can be a catalyst for collective measures and the establishment of a new status quo, even in the efforts of micro-actors.

This chapter focuses on several post-GEJET practices where, despite the strong influence of macro-actors, the efforts of micro-actors have been tailored to community-level actions. It further examines the coordination of recovery resources from the perspective of human-environment relations. In Japan, when homes are destroyed in a natural disaster, the residents are sent to an evacuation shelter. Depending on the level of the damage and the situation of DAP, the houses are repaired on an emergency scale or the residents are moved into emergency temporary housing. This temporary arrangement is followed by the reconstruction of residents' homes or purchase of new homes. Therefore, we attempt to understand housing reconstruction in four phases: evacuation, temporary living, relocation, and post-settlement. We first consider relevant perspectives in resources, both human treatment and its nature, to understand how human capacity in disaster recovery is perceived. Next, the research methods applied in the different cases of post-GEJET recovery are discussed. After presenting the research results, the discussion section elaborates on the mechanisms identified in the cases with a focus on relationships between extraordinary events and daily life.

6.2   Theoretical Perspective on Human-Environment Relations in Disaster Recovery

The access model visualizes the interaction between actors in terms of their roles and agency based on the coping strategies they use to adapt to events. In this way, the model is able to depict the network of resource mobilization involved in social events, including disasters. Since the access model provides a dynamic framework for social processes, it helps identify the capacities and strategies of micro-actors, or gaps between them, in the context of overall disaster recovery.

On the other hand, communities are rooted in specific local environments, making it necessary to address spatial aspects as well as social relations. The focus in this chapter on the initiatives of micro-actors in the community requires a perspective that treats human beings and the environment as a set, owing to their interdependence.

Therefore, this chapter examines the efforts of micro-actors at each phase of disaster recovery, using the access model as the basic theoretical foundation, adopting an environmental behavioural perspective that deals with the human-environment relationship as mediated by behaviour.

6.2.1 Access Model Addressing Recovery Resources

The concept of access is used to explain how people benefit from resources and the environment. Access refers to the combination of means, relationships, and processes that enable different actors to benefit from available resources (Peluso and Ribot, 2020). In the context of disaster recovery, the access model attempts to explain the mechanism underlying the social formation of vulnerability triggered by disasters in terms of actor-resource relationships (Blaikie, 2004). Specifically, the model focuses on a specific actor and analyzes the extent to which the actor has or does not have access to resources for the recovery of his livelihood within the social structure and surrounding environment. Resources are broadly defined as the physical and social means to build stable livelihoods, and are stratified according to the relationships between actors. For example, Ribot and Peluso (2003), in their analysis of charcoal trading from Senegalese forests, found that access to forest benefits is not only the consequence of direct access to forests, tools, and markets, but also of access to the state, businesses, and capital; the paper outlines a nested hierarchy in which producers are dependent on traders and traders are dependent on the state. Thus, by mapping the acquisition of access to resources by a single entity within a hierarchical social structure, we can see how formal and informal institutions disproportionately control access to resources and how other mechanisms, such as the rights and decision-making of entities, strengthen or weaken such social structures (Batterbury and Bebbington, 1999). In other words, this model, which carefully assesses resource use and change at different scales, allows us to propose alternative policies or institutions to update macro-social structures together with hidden voices or views of micro-actors.

Access to resources has a chain scale in both space and time, and therefore an empirical approach is adopted. Although the empirical approach has been criticized for its practical difficulties in policy or management (Black, 1990; Hershkovitz, 1993), recent research has focused on a broader appreciation of the complex dynamics and uncertainty in space and time of access (Scoones, 1999). Hence, studies have sought to adopt more qualitative ethnographic and interpretive methods, with research on disaster recovery attempting to illuminate overlooked actors and invisible resources and gain access to social structures (Sou and Webber, 2019; Dalgas, 2018; Artur and Hilhorst, 2012).

6.2.2 Environmental Perspective on Recovery Resources

Environmental Behavior Studies (EBS) is a field that addresses the interdependence of physical environmental systems and socio-cultural systems, encompassing both environmental and human factors. It aims to address the limitations of both environmental design and the social sciences by developing an empirical understanding of the interactions between individuals, social groups, cultures, and their living environments, and using this knowledge for better planning and design of the built environment (Moore, 2004). Typically, research combinations of and triangulations among different approaches are used, depending on the nature of the research question at hand. EBS is by nature multidisciplinary and interdisciplinary, making it necessary to develop the conceptual frameworks (Rapoport, 2008).

In the social sciences, disaster is understood as a phenomenon that combines potentially destructive influences from the natural and/or technological environments with a population in a state of socially and technologically created environmental vulnerability (Oliver-Smith, 1996; Alexander, 2015). Recent research on community recovery has paid attention to people's sense of place to explore the multiple layers of meaning they attach to significant places (Silver and Grek-Martin, 2015). Sense of place is constructed by an individual's personality, life history, values, and interaction with their place, all of which are mediated through their place in the socio-cultural environment (Kaltenborn, 1998). While this concept provides a useful framework for exploring the relationship between people and places, Cox and Perry (2011) propose a more deliberate form of orientation theory in relation to disaster recovery. According to Cox and Perry (2011), a disaster results in the disorientation of a community, both navigationally, in the form of environmental loss, and psychologically, through disruption of home and identity. Reorientation is the process of finding one's psychological and structural bearing after environmental disruption by reconstructing the identity of a familiar landscape in environmental transition.

A similar perspective that focuses more on changes in the physical environment is adopted in environmental transition research. This research centres around the idea that the environment has the greatest impact on the person with the least capacity, particularly in relation to the relocation of older people from their homes to institutions such as care facilities (Schulz and Brenner, 1977; Christenson, 1990). As a result, key findings suggest that it is important to promote people's attitudes towards voluntary relocation and to reduce the degree of social and physical discontinuity between old and new environments to mitigate the potential risks of environmental transitions (Lawton, 1980; Bourestom and Tars, 1974; Fitzpatrick and Tzouvara, 2019). This suggestion has also been reported in the context of disaster recovery, for example in research on relocation to public housing in Japan (Kobayashi et al., 1997).

6.3   Methodology

The research questions for this chapter are as follows:

RQ1: What were the variations in practice through which the efforts of micro-actors led to coordinated action at the community level?

RQ2: How did the micro-actors' sense of place orient/disorient the practice?

RQ3: How were the different resources embedded in these practices connected/disconnected to formal or informal institutions in the larger context?

To capture the rich variation in practice, we adopted a multi-sited ethnography (Marcus, 1995). Ethnography is used not only to understand the culture of an ethnic group but also as a methodology to explain a specific situation, such as a disaster.

This methodology is designed to explore contemporary local change by tracing a cultural formation across and within multiple sites. In designing the methodology, strategies that trace connections, associations, and assumed relationships are important. Hence, we established phases in disaster recovery. The human capabilities brought by disaster recovery are strongly influenced by each specific time-space. By selecting a different site for each phase, we hoped to capture the rich variation between practices and find connections and relationships over time. The geographical locations of cases are shown in Figure 6.1. From here, the four phases

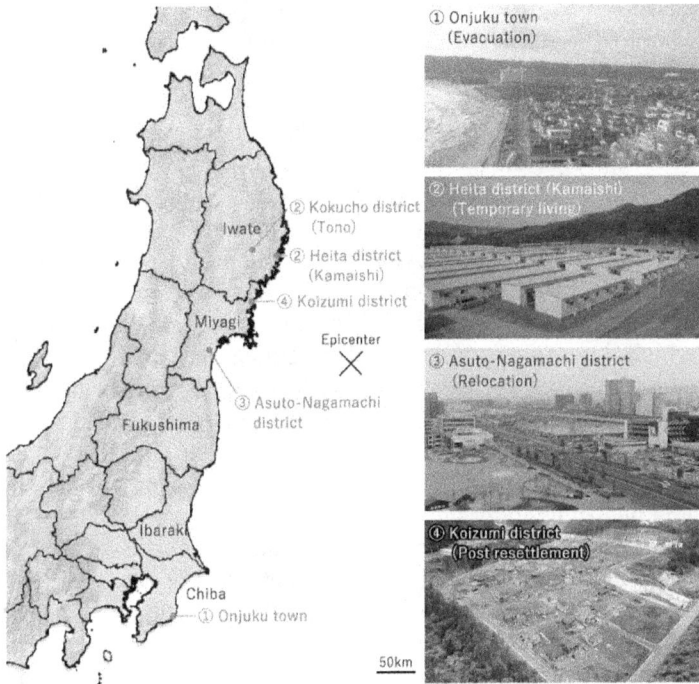

Figure 6.1 Case Study Location (Created by the Authors Based on Map Produced by Geospatial Information Authority of Japan)

Table 6.1 Details of Research Methods

Phase	Method	Period
Evacuation	Interview	November 2012
Temporary living	Interview/ Behaviour Observation	September 2011-November 2012
Relocation	Interview	November 2015
Post-resettlement	Behaviour Observation/ Interview	May-June 2017, June-July 2018

are set out and their characteristics are described, together with an overview of case review and investigation.

6.3.1   Evacuation

The first phase is evacuation. Evacuation after a tsunami is often preceded by the precursor phenomenon of an earthquake, and there is often a lead time before the disaster strikes. Therefore, many researchers have shown that the most effective way to reduce tsunami-related fatalities is early evacuation (e.g., Makinoshima et al, 2020). Here, we take the case of the evacuation behaviour of residents in the coastal area of Onjuku Town, Chiba Prefecture, where a large-scale tsunami warning was issued and evacuation was called for during the Great East Japan Earthquake.

The Onjuku case is appropriate for this phase for two reasons. First, since there was no power outage in Onjuku on the day of the earthquake, disaster information was relatively well communicated. The GEJET resulted in tremors of an intensity of four on the Japanese seismic scale in Onjuku. Three minutes after the earthquake, the meteorological agency issued a tsunami warning for Pacific coastal areas, including Onjuku. At that time, the maximum tsunami run-up in the area was estimated to be two metres high. However, about 25 minutes later, the alert was upgraded to a large-scale tsunami warning, predicting run-ups over 10-metre high. Immediately after the first warning, the local government used an emergency broadcast system and cars with loudspeakers to begin announcing that a tsunami warning was in effect and requested coastal residents to evacuate to higher ground. The first wave of the tsunami struck the Onjuku coast at around 3:20 p.m. According to Tsuji et al. (2011), the flood height was 2.3 m and did not result in human injury or major infrastructural damage. Residents' information acquisition and evacuation behaviour after the earthquake was quantitatively analyzed by Ohno and Isagawa (2012). Second, Onjuku has a relatively solid community foundation. As the town originally developed around fishing ports, many families have lived in the area for generations. In addition, each district has a ward mayor, deputy ward mayor, and other officers, forming an important social unit.

The group interview survey was conducted in November 2012 at the meeting place of each district. The respondents of the 2011 survey were invited to participate. The content of the survey was about the specific information they received and their detailed behaviour on the day of the earthquake (Isagawa, 2014).

6.3.2   Temporary Living

The second phase involves living in Emergency Temporary Housing (ETH). People whose homes were damaged in the tsunami moved to government-provided ETH after staying in shelters or hotels. Approximately 50,000 ETH units were constructed. The people who moved to ETH can be divided into two categories: those who were fortunate enough to retain their previous community of residents, and those whose previous settlements were so disparate that they hardly knew each other when they moved in. This section focuses on two ETH sites in Iwate Prefecture (Kamaishi and Tono), where the DAP was able to stimulate community-building among strangers by utilizing limited resources.

These two sites are selected because they are equipped with spatial features that provide clues for community building, such as a transparent-roofed deck laid on an ordinary and homogeneous alleyway, connecting dwelling units to each other and linking different dwelling buildings (Institute of Gerontology The University of Tokyo, 2011; Nishide et al., 2014). The height of the deck from the ground is the same as the height of the indoor floor so that residents can recognize this outdoor space as part of the ETH's extended space. These designs were experimental and became a spatial resource for the DAP. The author participated in the design as a member of one of the design teams (Mazumdar, 2021).

The fieldwork consisted of behavioural observations and interviews. Behavioural observations were conducted by patrolling all outdoor spaces of the ETH every few days to observe DAP activities. Unstructured interviews were conducted to reconstruct the participants' lives and homes (Tomiyasu, 2014).

6.3.3   Relocation

The third phase is Relocation. This section deals with relocation from temporary housing to post-disaster public housing. Relocation is likely to have a negative impact (relocation effect) on people who do not easily adapt to environmental changes, such as the elderly (Schulz and Brenner, 1977). Therefore, relocation processes and methods that consider environmental transition are important.

This case study examined the relocation of a temporary housing community in Sendai City to nearby post-disaster public housing (Arai, 2014). The target area is a highly convenient area with many shops and hospitals. After four years of living in temporary housing (233 units), a community was formed among the affected households who came from different backgrounds. Subsequently, using the local government's system of application for residence in a group, approximately 80 households moved into three buildings of post-disaster public housing (327 units) constructed within 800 m of the temporary housing.

Such relocation, which results from a temporary living environment, is expected to maintain the physical and social environment and reduce the burden of environmental transition (Suzawa et al, 2018). In terms of MHE, relocation based on a temporary living environment is expected to maintain the physical and social environment and reduce the burden of environmental transition.

6.3.4   Post-Resettlement

During post-resettlement, the fourth phase, changes from the pre-disaster period play an important role because they are often assessed by residents who have been disconnected from their previous communities and local socio-economic activities (Iuchi and Mutter, 2020).

The case in focus is the planned relocation of Koizumi district in Kesennuma City, which was carried out with the strong involvement of residents and a community-centred planning approach. The relocation site adopted the Radburn concept with a loop lane on a head-cut elevation, housing clusters grouped by a cul-de-sac road, and a central green belt of the same size as the common space in the previous district. This case demonstrates how individual behaviours triggered by spatial characteristics can be situated in pre- and post-disaster community relationships.

Behavioural observations were conducted by patrolling set routes and plotting the activities observed at the relocation site. Quantitative data obtained from these observations have also been reported in a previous study (Tsubouchi et al., 2023). Semi-structured interviews were conducted to understand the residents' cognition and psychological response to the relocation process and post-resettlement.

6.4   Results

We established the four phases of the post-disaster process. In each phase, topics related to MHE were found based on the findings of the research. These topics guide the discussion (Figure 6.2).

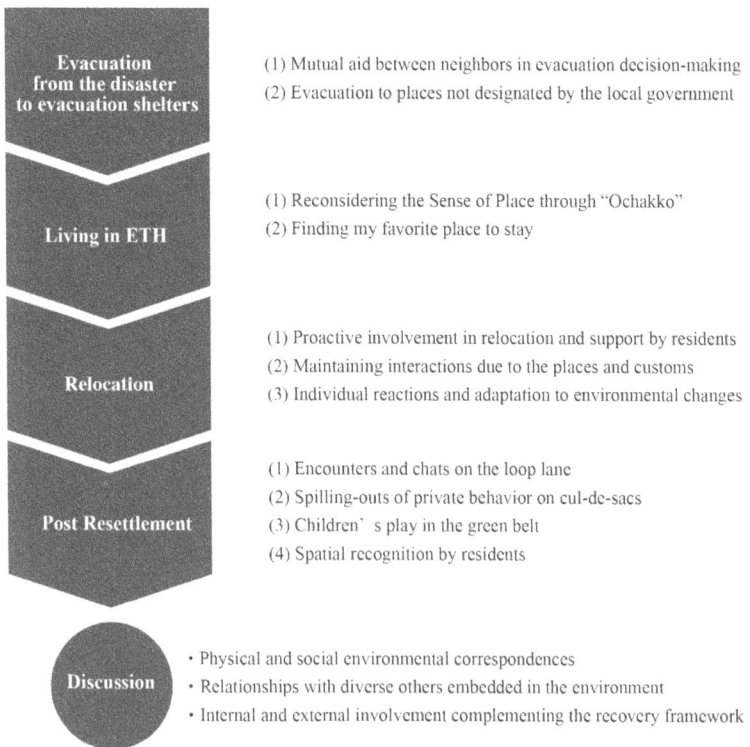

Evacuation from the disaster to evacuation shelters
(1) Mutual aid between neighbors in evacuation decision-making
(2) Evacuation to places not designated by the local government

Living in ETH
(1) Reconsidering the Sense of Place through "Ochakko"
(2) Finding my favorite place to stay

Relocation
(1) Proactive involvement in relocation and support by residents
(2) Maintaining interactions due to the places and customs
(3) Individual reactions and adaptation to environmental changes

Post Resettlement
(1) Encounters and chats on the loop lane
(2) Spilling-outs of private behavior on cul-de-sacs
(3) Children's play in the green belt
(4) Spatial recognition by residents

Discussion
• Physical and social environmental correspondences
• Relationships with diverse others embedded in the environment
• Internal and external involvement complementing the recovery framework

Figure 6.2 Composition of This Chapter through the Post-disaster Process

6.4.1   *Evacuation from the Disaster to Evacuation Shelters*

When an earthquake occurs and a tsunami is expected to strike, local governments call on residents to evacuate to shelters. Some residents evacuate at the call of their neighbours or family members before the local government's evacuation information is issued. Often, they evacuate to non-designated sites.

6.4.1.1   *Mutual Aid between Neighbours in Evacuation Decision-Making*

In the questionnaire survey, residents who had evacuated were asked when they took the decision to evacuate. The most common response was "when I heard that the initial alert was upgraded to a large-scale tsunami warning" (approximately 30%), followed by "when my family or acquaintances recommended evacuation" (Ohno and Isagawa, 2012).

The information acquisition and sequence of evacuee behaviour on the day of the earthquake can be understood from the accounts of Residents A and B. Resident A (seventies, female) revealed that a neighbour came to her house, got her into a car, and evacuated her to higher ground. In this case, the person quickly evacuated with her emergency kit without obtaining any specific information about the tsunami, and only later recognized it as an emergency when she saw the tsunami. In contrast, Resident B (seventies, female) was unaware that a tsunami was coming and had no intention of evacuating, but was persuaded by her family to do so. Thus, although evacuation during disasters is often understood as a cognitive process triggered by disaster information, as in Perry's warning response model (Perry, 1979), actual evacuation may occur without clear decision-making.

From these examples, we can highlight the effectiveness of behaviours such as talking to family members and neighbours and taking the elderly in their cars as MHE in the early phases of a disaster.

Author: What was the situation when the earthquake occurred?
Resident A: The TV shook so much that I was startled and held it down.
Author: Did you know that a tsunami warning was issued immediately after the earthquake?
Resident A: I don't remember. A neighbour came to call me and gave me a ride. I drove to Onjuku-dai. I ran away immediately without listening to the TV or radio.
Author: Did you know about the upgraded tsunami warning?
Resident A: I don't remember.
Author: Did you know about the expected tsunami height?
Resident A: No, I didn't. I didn't think about the height. I just knew that a tsunami was coming.
Author: Did you know the estimated time of the tsunami?
Resident A: I didn't know. The sea was receding, so I knew a big one was coming.
Author: Is there anything you did before evacuating?
Resident A: I usually pack water, candy, bank books, money, and other important things in a backpack. I evacuated with it.

[Interview conducted on 12 November 2012.]

Author: What was the situation when the earthquake occurred?

Resident B: I was with my son and his wife, so I felt completely safe. We were on the first floor and didn't feel much shaking.

Author: Did you know that a tsunami warning was issued immediately after the earthquake?

Resident B: No, I didn't.

Author: Did you know about the upgraded tsunami warning?

Resident B: I didn't worry about it. I left it to others and didn't think it was scary, so I didn't know about the tsunami. My son and his wife said, "Mom, enough, let's evacuate", and we did.

Author: Is there anything you did before evacuating?

Resident B: I didn't take anything with me.

[Interview conducted on 12 November 2012]

6.4.1.2   *Evacuation to Places Not Designated by the Local Government*

Approximately 30% of evacuees first evacuated to high ground at designated temporary evacuation sites, 20% to designated evacuation sites (schools, etc.), less than 20% to specially opened evacuation sites, and the remainder to non-designated sites including local meeting places, temples or shrines, and nearby high ground.

Onjuku Town Hall was not designated as an evacuation site but was opened as an additional evacuation site for up to 85 people because of the large number of evacuees. Because the town hall building (Figure 6.3), located on high ground, functioned as a landmark and a familiar place, many people headed there, especially those who had not decided on an evacuation site in advance. Some respondents also stated that they found it easier to obtain information there.

The Rokkenmachi Youth Center (Figure 6.4) was also not a town-designated evacuation site; however, residents voluntarily evacuated there as it is located on high ground. On the day of the earthquake, approximately 50 people evacuated, spending their time watching TV and gazing at the sea. Resident C (70s, male), a member of the community association, reported that when he observed that the number of evacuees was low, he personally went to several elderly people's homes in the neighbourhood to spread the word that a tsunami was coming and that they should evacuate.

Based on the above examples, we can point to the flexible acceptance of evacuees in places not designated by the local government and the voluntary call for evacuation by community association officers to surrounding residents as effective MHEs to ensure the safety of people during the evacuation phase.

6.4.2   *Living in Emergency Temporary Housing*

There are a few acquaintances in ETH who have just moved in. Through the information-sharing practice of "ochakko", we try to highlight the difficulty of maintaining community links. The use of outdoor benches show that different people have different ways of communicating and settling down, and maintaining diversity in outdoor spaces is important.

Figure 6.3 Onjuku Town Hall Located on High Ground

Figure 6.4 Rokkenmachi Youth Center, Chiba Prefecture

6.4.2.1   Reconsidering the Sense of Place through "Ochakko"

When people meet, they greet each other even if they are unacquainted. When they get to know each other, they stand and talk. When both parties have spare time, they sit in chairs and enjoy chatting. If there is something to drink nearby, the conversation will broaden, and the time will be more enjoyable. As this communication blossoms, the community takes shape. The practice of enjoying conversation over a cup of tea is also quite natural in the Tohoku region, where it is called "Ochakko". "Ocha" means "drinking", and "kko" is a playful suffix. However, the place they visit is not a restaurant like an Italian bar or a French café, but a neighbour's house. People go to each other's houses and gossip about their families, what happened in the village, and other trivial matters that contribute to the cohesion of the local community.

At the Kamaishi ETH site, "Ochakko" was held on the deck in front of ETH, as intended by the designers. The roof over the deck was a safe place to relax in even when it rained. The alley is a space mainly for traffic but has been transformed into a second lounge area, where residents lay out chairs and tables and enjoy drinks with neighbours (Figure 6.5).

The Kamaishi ETH site also received a community centre built with corporate donations, where a community café was operated by a volunteer group of residents (Figure 6.6). There was also a sports facility for children that was highly

Figure 6.5 Chatting and Drinking on the Deck in Front of ETH

Figure 6.6 Community Cafe in the Community Centre

appreciated by young families. Having multiple spaces at ETH sites where residents can unwind and chat is important for supporting residents' recovery from the mental and physical stress and trauma caused by disasters (Iwasa, 2012).

Some residents preferred not to visit the community café at the community centre. Resident D (60s, female) told us a symbolic story about the relationship between interaction and place among residents at the Kamaishi ETH site.

Before the earthquake, she lived with her family in a fishing village with a close-knit community. She was engaged in business, and she liked to get to know her neighbours and frequently held "Ochakko" gatherings with them. She said she had only been to the community centre once. Therefore, we asked her:

    Author: Why don't you go to the community centre?
Resident D: Because we don't have the habit of going to cafes and restaurants to drink and talk. "Ochakko" is something you do at your neighbour's house.
    Author: So why don't you go to your friends' houses in the ETH to talk?
Resident D: Everyone in the ETH comes from different areas. Unlike the people in the village where they used to live, we have nothing in common, so we don't have much to talk about, and they don't seem to have a lot of humanity. And even though everyone seems to be in good spirits, I think we are tired inside. Going to other people's houses to talk with

them can be very tiring, can't it? That's why it's easier to stay at home and remain private. And the small rooms in the ETH may be another reason for being cautious.

Author: So, do you still "Ochakko" with people from your former village by visiting each other's homes?

Resident D: Since we live in different places, we don't have much to talk about. In the past, if we met outside, we would greet each other and talk about the sea, fishing, fields, etc., but now we just greet each other and that's it. The conversation doesn't continue.

[Interview conducted on 23 November 2012]

For Resident D, the community café felt like a formal place, and even though there was no set amount, having to pay money to enjoy conversations with fellow residents, unlike in an "Ochakko", seemed to keep her away from the café. She is an outgoing person who knows many ETH residents. However, she was too self-conscious to "Ochakko" at ETH and communicated with others less frequently. There are two reasons for this finding.

The first is the lack of conversation topics. Unlike in their home villages, people at the ETH site have not spent much time together and do not have many shared experiences, so there are no exciting topics of conversation. Furthermore, even though they are all survivors, they have experienced different degrees of pain; therefore, they do not know how far they can go and are cautious about the topics they can discuss. Another reason is that, at the ETH, the places for serving guests and sleeping overlapped. Even if the people who invite guests do not mind, the people who are invited to the ETH are cautious and hesitate to come into the ETH to chat. Additionally, because the people she knew from her previous community lived in different places, Resident D was unable to communicate with them.

Of course, some people can communicate as they did before. However, from this case study, it is clear that communication is necessary for community building, and for that, sharing time, place, and experience – in other words, sharing one's life – is essential.

6.4.2.2   *Finding My Favourite Place to Stay*

ETH in Japan is small. The average floor area of a house in Japan is 120 m^2 (Statistics Bureau Ministry of Internal Affairs and Communications Japan, 2018), whereas in the ETH it is 30 m^2. Therefore, instead of remaining indoors, residents prefer to sit in the outdoor spaces of the ETH. However, the outdoor spaces are typically homogeneous. As ETH needs to be built in large numbers in a short period of time, for the sake of speedy planning and construction, a uniform design is applied. As a result, ETH units of the same size are placed parallel and at the same distance from each other, and the alleys have the same landscape regardless of where you walk.

The government and the NPO/NGO could easily imagine such a DAP mentality and decided to distribute benches in the hope that a place to sit down in the outdoor spaces of the ETH would lead to communication between residents. Benches were given to almost all ETHs in Iwate and placed in alleys and in front of the community centres. They hoped that the elderly and young people with children would leave their homes and enjoy chatting. The initiative generally worked well and became a place for chatting, except during cold winter months (Figure 6.7).

Resident E (70s, female) lived with her son in his 40s at the ETH. As they only had one bedroom, the son slept in the living room and she slept in the bedroom. She lost her house in the tsunami, and her husband was in the hospital, so she had a lot to think about and had a stifling life. Therefore, on sunny days when her son was at work, she would sit alone on a bench outside and look out at the children playing in the park (Figure 6.8). The covered deck and benches became comforting places where she could be alone but feel safe and peaceful. Not everyone is sociable or always wants to chat with someone. This confirms the value of a place outside one's home where one can feel calm and secure. Thus, residents have spaces to relax due to the combination of the mindful roofed deck design by the designer, the small mechanisms of the government, and the NPO/NGO that provided the benches.

6.4.3 Relocation

In this case study, the relocation was conducted from the ETH to three nearby buildings in the DPH (Figure 6.9). This section clarifies the details of the relocation process and introduces issues related to the activities of micro actors.

Figure 6.7 Chatting on a Bench Beside ETH

Figure 6.8 Sitting Calmly on a Bench

6.4.3.1   *Proactive Involvement in Relocation and Support by Residents*

Because the relocation was to a neighbourhood and the transition period with both keys was approximately three months, the transition was proactive and gradual, with some residents moving their belongings multiple times. In addition, as they proceeded with the relocation process, some residents, such as elderly people who lived alone, were supported by the former chairperson of the neighbourhood association of the ETH, who provided counselling, helped with paperwork, and assisted with the move. This proactive involvement in the transition process and the support system provided by residents is considered to have reduced the burden of environmental transition.

6.4.3.2   *Maintaining Interactions Due to the Places and Customs*

The persistence of familiar environmental elements is an important factor in environmental transitions (Toyama, 1988.). Even after relocating to the DPH, residents continue to interact with each other by visiting places and maintaining customs formed when they lived in the ETH. The details are as follows.

Even after moving from ETH to DPH, residents continue to use nearby places, such as supermarkets and clinics (Figure 6.10). These supermarkets have become places where they greet and chat with former ETH neighbours. For example, some

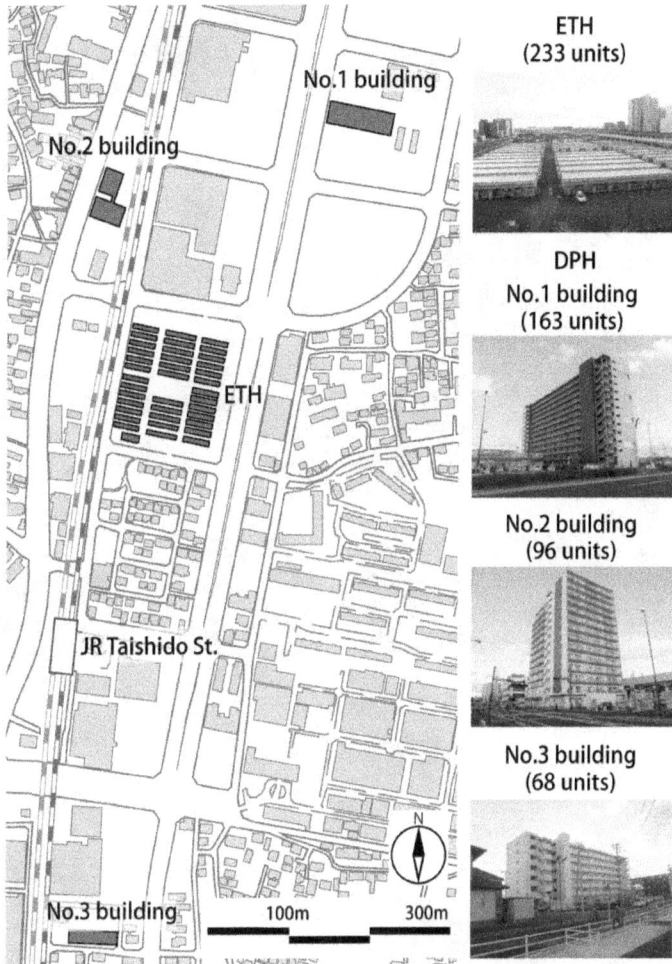

Figure 6.9 A Map of Nagamachi District, Sendai (Created by the Authors Based on Map Produced by Geospatial Information Authority of Japan)

residents would go to a supermarket that was not the nearest one so that they could meet acquaintances who had moved to another DPH.

When the residents lived in the ETH, performing radio exercises in the open spaces of the ETH was a daily routine (Figure 6.11). After moving to the DPH, this activity was moved to a park next to the public housing, and participating in radio exercises became an opportunity to meet ETH friends. However, some residents said that they no longer participated in the radio exercises because the park was too far away. Thus, when the location changes, the distance from the residence is an important factor in determining whether to continue a social activity.

Figure 6.10 A supermarket in the Neighbourhood

Figure 6.11 Open Space in the ETH Where the Radio Exercises Were Held

Events were held daily at meeting locations in the ETH by external support groups (Figure 6.12). Although the frequency of events decreased, some events continued to be held at the meeting place in the ETH for approximately a year after the relocation to DPH. Some residents stated that they looked forward to the knitting classes and tea-drinking parties held once or twice a month, even after moving out. In addition, annual reunions of ETH residents and memorial gatherings for the disaster are held, providing an opportunity to meet friends.

Neighbourhood associations and self-governing activities by residents in Japan play important roles in the recovery process (Okada et al, 2018). In this case, residents' awareness of neighbourhood associations increased owing to their ETH experiences. Therefore, active participation in neighbourhood associations continued even after moving into the DPH. Some residents also commented that participating in the DPH neighbourhood association provided them opportunities to meet acquaintances and friends.

6.4.3.3 *Individual Reactions and Adaptation to Environmental Changes*

This section introduces the residents' narratives about how they felt and adapted to the environmental changes that accompanied their relocation.

Figure 6.12 Events Held at the Meeting Place in the ETH

Resident F   In the DPH, I quickly became friends with a woman on the same
(seventies   floor and talked with her often, but once inside her house, I felt
female, No.1   lonely and discouraged when she was not feeling well. In ETH,
building)   chatting while sitting on a bench was a natural way to interact.
If I don't take a walk, I have no contact with the outside world.
Even acquaintances and friends from the ETH feel disconnected
from those who have moved into the second and third housing
units. Therefore, when returning from an outing, I sometimes
venture off the bus early, go shopping at the supermarket in
front of No.3 building, and chat with acquaintances.

[Interviews conducted in November 2015]

In the case of relocation, it seems natural that they would maintain their relationship with the residents who relocated together to the DPH in the neighbourhood of the ETH. However, maintaining these relationships and interactions is not necessary. As Resident F's narrative shows, the DPH is divided into three different locations, and the space settings in the ETH and DPH are quite different (Figures 6.13 and 6.14).

Figure 6.13 ETH Environment: Easy to Interact with Neighbours

Figure 6.14 DPH Environment: Not Easy to Interact with Neighbours

Relationships were maintained through ingenuity and positive efforts at the individual and community levels. Though the design of common spaces in the buildings needs to be considered, it can be said that the "neighbourhood x community-based" relocation method promotes MHE and reduces negative effects of relocation.

6.4.4 Post-Resettlement

The spatial characteristics and perceptions of the relocation site were examined through the activities and conversations of residents in the loop lane, cul-de-sacs, and green belts.

6.4.4.1 Encounters and Chats on the Loop Lane

Older adults often walk around loop lanes during afternoon hours. If they run into someone else, it becomes a great place to chat (Figure 6.15). What makes this space unique is that it has a stable temporary nature owing to the high frequency of specific settings in a large space. Actually, the loop lane was not designed for chatting. Residents turned it into a socializing space by sitting on retaining walls, kerbs, or wheels. By arranging their own settings, they created a temporary private space called "our chat space" within the public space of the loop lane. It is important here to note that these private spaces do not exclude other residents. Improvised settings on the street allow passers-by to join in the natural chatter. Second, it makes it easier for several residents to encounter each other because the loop lane is a regular walking route for older people. Filling a large space with a specific behaviour gives the loop lane a unique quality.

The quality of the place described above is particularly evident in the space by the park (Figure 6.16). This location has high visibility owing to the absence of buildings. This makes it easier for the residents to see each other while walking or chatting. It is also important to note that the number of movable benches is small compared to the scale of the park.

The loop lane and its associated spaces are tailored to semi-public places, where moderate human relationships can be established. In fact, quantitative data show that this space has become the most frequent place of communication for residents who were members of different neighbourhood associations before relocation.

Figure 6.15 Chatting in the Loop Lane

Figure 6.16 Chatting in the Space by the Park

Figure 6.17 Activities around the Cul-de-sac and the Housing Site

6.4.4.2   *Spilling-Outs of Private Behaviour on Cul-de-sacs*

Many residents perform activities such as car washing, playing, and gardening on the cul-de-sac rather than performing the activities only at housing sites (Figure 6.17). These spillover behaviours result in the road being used as an extension of residential areas. This is a consequence of the nature of the cul-de-sac with its restricted access.

Furthermore, performing these activities outside stimulates chats between residents (Figure 6.18). When residents are active around the boundaries of their housing sites, it leads to spontaneous conversations with other residents moving through the cul-de-sac. It is important to note that these chats on the cul-de-sac take place over residents' belongings such as flower beds and kitchen pots. Residents' chatter would surely be about their possessions, such as how the plants are flowering and how to fertilize them. The quality of these conversations differs from those occurring on the loop lane as these are generally mediated by objects (Tsubouchi et al., 2023).

Therefore, the cul-de-sac is tailored as a semi-private place where private activities spill over and neighbourhood socialization flourishes. In fact, quantitative data

Figure 6.18 Chatting about Residents' Belongings on the Cul-de-sac

Figure 6.19 Children Playing in the Green Belt

shows that communication naturally occurs between residents who live in housing clusters constrained by cul-de-sacs (Tsubouchi et al., 2023).

6.4.4.3 *Children's Play in the Green Belt*

Behaviour in the green belt is infrequent, but children can be seen playing in this space (Figure 6.19).

The types of behaviours described above, such as socializing in the loop lane and cul-de-sacs, are more suitable for adults, and children are less likely to behave in the same way in these spaces. In this sense, the green belt is an ideal space for children. Large open spaces with few behaviour-inducing spatial elements do not arise in stable settings; rather, they make the space suitable for children's free play. In addition, unpaved fields are often avoided by adults, which gives children the freedom to play.

The behaviours of adults and children are made more distinct because they are in different spaces. This division of behaviour and utilization is the result of the two sides of both the cul-de-sac and green belt provided by the Radburn concept of residential land design.

6.4.4.4   Spatial Recognition by Residents

Residents' spatial recognition of the above utilizations was relatively negative. We interpreted the following two sets of symbolic interview data.

First, the residents told stories about their relocation sites by borrowing expressions from outsiders. Specifically, one resident expressed dissatisfaction with the relocation site because outsiders had commented to her that the road structure created by the cul-de-sac was confusing.

Resident G: After all, everyone has moved in and settled down, so at times like Obon and New Year, many of the residents' relatives visit the relocation site but don't know the home location. I have had people come to my house and ask me to tell them where their relatives live. I then ask them how they came. If they say they came by car, I say, "Excuse me, please go outside and then go around the loop lane", while if they come on foot, I say, "Please walk from here".

Author: So, you ask them to plough through the footpath, don't you? Yes, yes. I see. I remember when I spoke to you last year, you told me you were disappointed that cars couldn't plough through in the relocation site. How do you feel now that you've been here for about a year?

Resident G: I am still disappointed.

[Interview conducted on 22 June 2018]

Second, many residents feel that they are struggling with community depopulation and this less positive recognition dominates. However, when the author presented one resident with a positive evaluation of the relocation site by a newcomer who had moved some time after relocation, he/she looked back and re-evaluated the planning process.

Resident H: As I said, there are so many elderly people in the district. Many elderly people! So, make sure that many young people come as soon as possible.

Author: Hahaha. I see…

…

Author: I talked to a newcomer from the Oya district (district next to the Koizumi district) the day before yesterday. The Oya district also conducted community relocation, didn't it?

Resident H: Yes, yes.

Author: I asked why he didn't relocate in his origin district, and then he answered, "Koizumi's relocation site is good".

…

Author: He told me that he thought he could live comfortably for spatial leeway since there was a green belt in the centre.

Resident H: Oh, hahaha. I got it.

…

Resident H: After all, we have confirmed in the workshops that a car-centred relocation site was not good, and it was good when it has a spatial leeway.

Author: Yes. Yes. Exactly. So, I think there was much worth that you residents
considered what the relocation site should have been.

Resident H: Truly. Oh yes.

[Interview conducted on 5 July 2018]

6.5 Discussion

In this chapter, multiple practices after the GEJET at different sites during each
recovery period revealed that micro actors utilized the environmental resources
around them to engage in community-level activities. The following sections discuss the coordination of recovery resources from the perspective of human-environment relations while responding to the research questions.

6.5.1 *Physical and Social Environmental Correspondences*

In all recovery periods, the correspondence between the physical and social environments improved the level of environmental utilization from the individual to
the community. First, during evacuation activities, the presence of familiar people plays an important role in decision-making. This means that residents know
what kind of people live where in the community and that community evacuation
activities are achieved by residents sharing information with each other. In addition, private routes based on the daily lives of residents played an important role
in the actual evacuation. Second, in emergency housing, sharing daily activities
is important in the process of transforming temporary housing into communities. Semi-public spaces, such as porches and window decks, function as places
where people can chat and check on each other. This can be understood as the
emergence of community customs specific to temporary housing. Third, after
relocation, former ETH residents continued to interact with each other, bonded
by shared places and customs, such as conversations in the supermarket, daily
radio calisthenics, and other community activities. Fourth, during resettlement,
residents engaged in graded private/public behaviour in response to the hierarchical scale of the relocation site. Residents have tailored spaces depending on
the objects and their contexts.

Although the community is primarily based on a specific local environment
positioned by geographic space, the social and physical environments of modern
communities are mismatched owing to the diversification of lifestyles and sophis-
tication of mobility. However, many of the communities affected by the GEJET
were rural villages where the social and physical environments still matched. In all
cases, despite the difficulty in coordinating the efforts of micro actors in community practices due to the extent of the damage, it was possible to embed community
practices in a way that was specific to each disaster recovery situation by drawing on the potential of the environment. It is important here that these everyday

socializations have not taken place in specially created places, but in ordinary places. The emergence of daily customs in ordinary places has not allowed the efforts of micro actors to stand alone, but has elevated them to community recovery activities through the mediation of the environment. Therefore, we need to learn more deeply about the different actors with which the environment connects during disaster recovery.

6.5.2   Relationships with Diverse Others Embedded in the Environment

The correspondence between physical and social environments strengthens an individual's sense of place through interactions with others. Looking at cases in relation to others, it is striking that residents demonstrate a sense of place with others rather than themselves. For example, during the evacuation and relocation phases, a sense of place created through relationships between residents guided disaster recovery practices. First, the residents' knowledge of who lived where had a direct impact on community evacuation activities. Second, the sense of being able to meet people they knew at the neighbourhood supermarket, which was fostered in temporary housing, was maintained after relocation and encouraged people to go out. On the other hand, outsiders can play an important role in the residents' sense of place. In temporary living, it was important for the realization of neighbourhood chats to have external experts who tailored daily places, rather than a community café set up by external supporters. In addition, residents' perceptions after resettlement were based on borrowed evaluations from outsiders, in contrast to the community-centred planning process.

According to place theory, disasters cause a loss of community orientation both in terms of the navigational aspect of environmental loss and the psychological aspect of disrupted experiences of place and identity (Cox and Perry, 2011). Reorientation is an attempt to recover from disorientation caused by disaster recovery experiences. In this study, it is important to note that not only day-to-day accumulation but also the presence of others is important for reorientation. The built environment has the power to generate and visualize people's environmental relationships, and people perceive themselves in relation to others embedded in the environment (Suzuki, 1996). In disaster recovery, which oscillates between ordinary and extraordinary, it is important to establish relationships with diverse others, which may be the key to the stable environmental transition of micro actors.

6.5.3   Internal and External Involvement Complementing the Recovery
Framework

In all phases, the efforts of the micro actors complemented the macro disaster recovery response through community initiatives. While the use of resources by micro actors is commendable, it is important to view it from a macroscopic perspective. The administrative system was supplemented by residents calling on neighbours during evacuation and by the opening of non-designated evacuation centres. External experts also introduced careful placemaking in temporary housing as a voluntary initiative. In relocation, the planning of public housing in relation to the proximity of temporary housing was proposed by the residents with experts' support. After resettlement, dialogue with external researchers helped restore a sense of community from the dominant influence of depopulation and reconstruction frameworks. These practices can be evaluated as a reorientation to improve residents' sense of place, with internal and external involvement centred on the community. When considering such practices at the macro level, it is important that micro actors have adequate access to policies. This study has shown that, in many cases, external experts are responsible for this access.

Recovery practices in the GEJET were achieved through polycentric governance, which was not guaranteed by existing institutions because of unprecedented damage (Aoki, 2016). Many expert interventions exist in this context. Such interventions by experts, especially researchers, have historical and social pathways in Japan that are not confined to disaster recovery. In Japan, the cycle of research and practice feedback arises from social imperatives to resolve the turmoil of lifestyles in postwar modernization, which has developed in its own unique discipline known as architectural planning studies (Funahashi, 1996). Although expert interventions in this study can be considered socially rooted when viewed as a conventional practice of architectural planning studies, it is necessary to consider, for more stable access, how to involve appropriate external experts, and for how long.

First, while community-based interventions by experts present the advantage of reflecting different local realities, they also face macro challenges such as dealing with issues of wide scope and versatility across a large number of affected areas. In fact, only a minority of GEJET cases have promoted disaster recovery initiatives through collaboration with local communities and external experts. Such ad hoc practices are referred to as the guerrilla model (Onoda, 2012; MAK Centre for Art and Architecture, 2014). This model expresses the characteristics of tailor-made access bridging the micro and macro by local people and experts themselves, and can be said to indicate the possibilities and limits of expert intervention with a bottom-up style.

Second, disasters affected by human factors are not simply a matter of solving short-term technical problems. In particular, "slow-onset hazards" associated with social, political, and economic change, such as the shrinkage of Japan demonstrated in the post-resettlement period, require external engagement over a long period of time (Wilson, 2012). However, external experts providing disaster recovery services tend to focus more on the project itself and pay less attention to the time before and after it (Abram and Weszkalnys, 2013). The involvement of town planning professionals, such as architectural planners, is certainly favourable for recovery because it coordinates various stakeholders and allocates limited resources as public projects in compressed times (Iuchi, 2014; Olshansky and Chang, 2009). However, there are concerns that this could institutionalize or fragment the supposedly comprehensive livelihood recovery process (Tsubouchi et al., 2021). This study shows that residents suffer from disorientation during disaster recovery due to depopulation. Long-term external involvement is necessary to resolve these problems. It is necessary to establish a macrostructure that allows for the long-term involvement of experts familiar with the relationship between humans and the environment.

6.6   Conclusion

This chapter explored the efforts of micro actors tailored to community-level actions through four practices that responded to the disaster recovery periods after the GEJET. The cultural and contextual lessons revealed that the micro actors who stepped in to fill a communal communication gap are people who are typically considered vulnerable groups, such as the elderly, women, and children. Instead of marked vulnerability under normal circumstances, these groups exhibited micro-activism under disaster circumstances, and other groups responded positively to their micro-activities. In each practice, the social and physical environment meshed and tailored the everyday place, thereby developing the behaviour of micro actors at the community level. In addition, the discovery of a sense of place in relation to others, especially external professionals, resulted in stable access that bridged the micro and macro. These were not institutionally committed to the GEJET but resulted only from the voluntary activities of experts. Therefore, there are challenges in terms of sustained efforts and comprehensive or pluralistic livelihood reconstruction. Future disaster recovery will require more effort to link the efforts of these micro actors to the macro level with further empirical and long-term research.

Acknowledgement

We would like to express our sincere gratitude to all the research participants for their cooperation and for telling us about their recovery efforts to support our fieldwork in their own warm way.

References

Abram, S., Weszkalnys, G. (2013). *Elusive Promises: Planning in the Contemporary World.* Berghahn.

Alexander, D. E. (2015). *Disaster and Emergency Planning for Preparedness, Response, and Recovery.* Oxford University Press.

Allen, K. M. (2006). Community-based disaster preparedness and climate adaptation: Local capacity-building in the Philippines. *Disasters,* Vol. 30, No. 1, pp. 81–101.

Aoki, N. (2016). Adaptive governance for resilience in the wake of the 2011 Great East Japan Earthquake and Tsunami. *Habitat International,* Vol. 52, pp. 20–25.

Arai, N. (2014). More community design toward an after recovery —At Asuto-Nagamachi temporary housing in Sendai. *Journal of Architecture and* Building *Science,* Vol. 1661, pp. 28–29. http://jabs.aij.or.jp/earthquake/eq_bt_201408.pdf.

Artur, L., Hilhorst, D. (2012). Everyday realities of climate change adaptation in Mozambique. *Global Environmental Change,* Vol. 22, No. 2, pp. 529–536.

Batterbury, S. P., Bebbington, A. J. (1999). Environmental histories, access to resources and landscape change: An introduction. *Land Degradation & Development,* Vol. 10, No. 4, pp. 279–289.

Black, R. (1990). "Regional political ecology" in theory and practice: A case study from Northern Portugal. *Transactions of the Institute of British Geographers*, Vol. 15, No. 1, pp. 35–47.

Blaikie, P. (2004). Access to resources and coping in adversity. In Blaikie, P., Cannon, T., Davis, I., Wisner, B. (Eds.), *At Risk: Natural Hazards, People's Vulnerability and Disasters*, Routledge, pp. 87–124.

Bourestom, N., Tars, S. (1974). Alterations in life patterns following nursing home relocation. *The Gerontologist*, Vol. 14, No. 6, pp. 506–510.

Cannon, T. (2008). *Reducing People's Vulnerability to Natural Hazards Communities and Resilience*, UNU WIDER Research Paper No. 2008.34 [Online]. United Nations University.

Christenson, M. A. (1990). Designing for the older person by addressing environmental attributes. *Physical & Occupational Therapy in Geriatrics*, Vol. 8 No. 3–4, pp. 31–48.

Cox, R. S., Perry, K. M. E. (2011). Like a fish out of water: Reconsidering disaster recovery and the role of place and social capital in community disaster resilience. *American Journal of Community Psychology*, Vol. 48, pp. 395–411.

Dalgas, K. (2018). Translocal disaster interventions: The role of individual relief channels in Philippine disasters. *Journal of Contingencies and Crisis Management*, Vol. 26, No. 3, pp. 377–384.

Fitzpatrick, J. M., Tzouvara, V. (2019). Facilitators and inhibitors of transition for older people who have relocated to a long-term care facility: A systematic review. *Health and Social Care in the Community*, Vol. 27, pp. e57–e81.

Funahashi, K. (1996). Transactional perspective, design, and "Architectural Planning Research" in Japan. In Wapner, S., Demick, J., Yamamoto, T., Takahashi, T. (Eds.), *Handbook of Japan-United States Environment-Behavior Research*, Springer, pp. 355–364.

Hershkovitz, L. (1993). Political ecology and environmental management in the Loess Plateau, China. *Human Ecology*, Vol. 21, pp. 327–353.

Institute of Gerontology, The University of Tokyo. (2011). Temporary Housing in Tono. Shinkenchiku, December. pp. 166–171.

Isagawa, T. (2014). An environment-behaviour studies on tsunami evacuation based on the survey for the residents before and after the Great East Japan Earthquake, The Tokyo Institute of Technology. Ph.D.thesis (in Japanese).

Iuchi, K. (2014). Planning resettlement after disasters. *Journal of the American Planning Association*, Vol. 80, No. 4, pp. 413–425.

Iuchi, K., Mutter, J. (2020). Governing community relocation after major disasters: An analysis of three different approaches and its outcomes in Asia. *Progress in Disaster Science*, Vol. 6, p. 100071.

Iuchi, K., Olshanky, R. (2018). Revisiting tohoku's 5-year recovery: Community rebuilding policies, programs and implementation. In Santiago-Fandiño, V., Sato, S., Maki, N., Iuchi, K. (Eds.), *The 2011 Japan Earthquake and Tsunami: Reconstruction and Restoration Insights and Assessment after 5 Years*, Springer, pp. 91–112.

Iwasa, A., Hasegawa, T., Shinkai, S., Shinozaki, M., Yasutake, A., Kobayashi, K. (2012). A practical approach to temporary housing for disaster victims. *Journal of Asian Architecture and Building Engineering*, Vol. 11, No. 1, pp. 33–38.

Kaltenborn, B. P. (1998). Effects of sense of place on responses to environmental impacts: A study among residents in Svalbard in the Norwegian high Arctic. *Applied Geography*, Vol. 18, No. 2, pp. 169–189.

Kobayashi, M., Miura, K., Maki, N. (1997). Environmental transition and natural disaster: Restoration housing for the Mt. Unzen Volcanic Eruption. In Wapner, S., Demick, J., Yamamoto, T., Takahashi, T. (Eds.), *Handbook of Japan-United States Environment-Behavior Research*, Springer, pp. 209–234.

Kondo, T. (2018). Planning challenges for housing and built environment recovery after the great East Japan earthquake: Collaborative planning and management go beyond government-driven redevelopment projects. In Santiago-Fandiño, V., Sato, S., Maki, N., Iuchi, K. (Eds.), *The 2011 Japan Earthquake and Tsunami: Reconstruction and Restoration Insights and Assessment after 5 Years*, Springer, pp. 155–169.

Lawton, M. P. (1980). Environmental change: The older person as initiator and responder. In Datan, N., Lohmann, N. (Eds.), Transitions of aging, Academic Press, pp. 171–193.

MAK Center for Art and Architecture (2014). *Groundswell: Guerilla Architecture In Response To The Great East Japan Earthquake*. https://www.makcenter.org/exhibitions /groundswell-guerilla-architecture (Accessed 20th June 2024).

Makinoshima, F., Imamura, F., Oishi, Y. (2020). Tsunami evacuation processes based on human behaviour in past earthquakes and tsunamis: A literature review. *Progress in Disaster Science*, Vol. 7, p. 100113.

Marcus, G. E. (1995). Ethnography in/of the world system: The emergence of multi-sited ethnography. *Annual Review of Anthropology*, Vol. 24, No. 1, pp. 95–117.

Mazumdar, S., Itoh, S., Iwasa, A. (2021). Post-disaster temporary housing: An emic study of lived experiences of victims of the great East Japan earthquake and tsunami. *International Journal of Mass Emergencies & Disasters*, Vol. 39, No. 1, pp. 87–119.

Moore, G. T. (2004). Environment, behaviour and society: A brief look at the field and some current EBS research at the University of Sydney. In *The 6th International Conference of the Environment-Behavior Research Association* Tianjin, China.

Murakami, K., Wood, D. M., Tomita, H., Miyake, S., Shiraki, R., Murakami, K., Itonaga, K., Dimmer, C. (2014). Planning innovation and post-disaster reconstruction: The case of Tohoku, Japan/ Reconstruction of tsunami-devastated fishing villages in the Tohoku region of Japan and the challenges for planning/Post-disaster reconstruction in Iwate and new planning challenges for Japan/Towards a "network community" for the displaced town of Namie, FukushimaResilience design and community support in Iitate Village in the aftermath of the Fukushima Daiichi nuclear disaster/Evolving place governance innovations and pluralising reconstruction practices in post-disaster Japan. *Planning Theory & Practice*, Vol. 15, No. 2, pp. 237–242.

Nishide, K., Otsuki, T., Tomiyasu, R. (2014). Proposal and examination of 'Community-care Temporary-housing'. *MERA Journal*, Vol. 16, No. 2, pp. 24–28.

Norris, F. H., Stevens, S. P., Pfefferbaum, B., Wyche, K. F., Pfefferbaum, R. L. (2008). Community resilience as a metaphor, theory, set of capacities, and strategy for disaster readiness. *American Journal of Community P sychology*, Vol. 41, pp. 127–150.

Ohno, R., Isagawa, T. (2012). How do coastal residents behave after a big earthquake?: A questionnaire survey after the Great East Japan Earthquake at Onjuku, Chiba Prefecture. *Proceedings of the 9th International Conference on Urban Earthquake Engineering/ 4th Asia Conference*, pp. 1923–1930.

Okada, T., Howitt, R., Haynes, K., Bird, D., McAneney, J. (2018). Recovering local sociality: Learnings from post-disaster community-scale recoveries. *International Journal of Disaster Risk Reduction*, Vol. 31, pp. 1030–1042.

Oliver-Smith, A. (1996). Anthropological research on hazards and disasters. *Annual Review of Anthropology*, Vol. 25, No. 1, pp. 303–328.

Olshansky, R., Chang, S. (2009). Planning for disaster recovery: Emerging research needs and challenges. *Progress in Planning*, Vol. 72, No. 4, pp. 200–209.

Olshansky, R. B., Hopkins, L. D., Johnson, L. A. (2012). Disaster and recovery: Processes compressed in time. *Natural Hazards Review*, Vol. 13, No. 3, pp. 173–178.

Onoda, Y. (2012). White Knight or Guerrilla: What can architects do in disaster reconstruction? *Shinkenchiku*, Vol. 87, No. 19, pp. 43–49 (in Japanese).

Paton, D. (2006). Disaster resilience: Integrating individual, community, institutional and environmental perspectives. In Paton, D. and Johnston, D. (Ed.), *Disaster Resilience: An Integrated Approach*, Charles C Thomas Publisher, Ltd, Springfield, Illinois, pp. 305–318.

Peluso, N. L., Ribot, J. (2020). Postscript: A theory of access revisited. *Society & Natural Resources*, Vol. 33, No. 2, pp. 300–306.

Perry, R. W. (1979). Evacuation decision-making in natural disasters. *Mass Emergencies*, Vol. 4, No. 1, pp. 25–38.

Rapoport, A. (2008). Environment-behabior studies: Past, present, and future. *Journal of Architectural and Planning Research*, Vol. 25, No. 4, pp. 276–281.

Reconstruction Agency (2011). *Seven Principles for the Reconstruction Framework*. https://www.cas.go.jp/jp/fukkou/english/pdf/7principles.pdf (Accessed 20th June 2024).

Ribot, J. C., Peluso, N. L. (2003). A theory of access. *Rural Sociology*, Vol. 68, No. 2, pp. 153–181.

Schulz, R., Brenner, G. (1977). Relocation of the aged: A review and theoretical analysis get access arrow. *Journal of Gerontology*, Vol. 32, No. 3, pp. 323–333.

Scoones, I. (1999). New ecology and the social sciences: What prospects for a fruitful engagement? *Annual Review of Anthropology*, Vol. 28, No. 1, pp. 479–507.

Shrestha, A. (2019). Which community, whose resilience? Critical reflections on community resilience in peri-urban Kathmandu Valley. *Critical Asian Studies*, Vol. 51, No. 4, pp. 493–514.

Silver, A., Grek-Martin, J. (2015). "Now we understand what community really means": Reconceptualizing the role of sense of place in the disaster recovery process. *Journal of Environmental Psychology*, Vol. 42, pp. 32–41.

Sou, G., Webber, R. (2019). Disruption and recovery of intangible resources during environmental crises: Longitudinal research on 'home' in post-disaster Puerto Rico. *Geoforum*, Vol. 106, pp. 182–192.

Statistics Bureau Ministry of Internal Affairs and Communications Japan (2018). *Statistical Handbook of Japan*. Statistics Bureau Ministry of Internal Affairs and Communications Japan.

Suzawa, S. et al. (2018). Efficacy of community-based relocation in a neighboring area from temporary housing to disaster public housing. *Journal of Architecture and Planning* (Transactions of AIJ) Vol. 83, No. 750, pp. 1391–1401. https://doi.org/10.3130/aija.83.1391

Suzuki, T. (1996). Mode of being in places. In Wapner, S., Demick, J., Yamamoto, T., Takahashi, T. (Eds.), *Handbook of Japan-United States Environment-Behavior Research*, Springer, pp. 113–129.

Tomiyasu, R. (2014). *A Study on Residential Environment for the Elderly in the Process of Reconstruction after the Great East Japan Earthquake*. The University of Tokyo. Ph.D .thesis (in Japanese).

Toyama, T. (1988). *Identity and Milieu: A Study of Relocation Focusing on Reciprocal Changes in Elderly People and their Environment*, KTH Royal Institute of Technology doctoral thesis.

Tsubouchi, K., Mori, S., Nomura, R. (2023). Actual conditions and a planning review of collective relocation site from the view of changes in neighborhood relationships: Focusing on the collective relocation project for disaster prevention in Koizumimachi district, Kesennuma city, Japan. *Japan Architectural Review*, Vol. 6, No. 1, p. e12335.

Tsubouchi, K., Okada, T., Mori, S. (2021). Pathway of adaptation to community relocation: Prospects and limitations of community-centred planning. *International Journal of Disaster Risk Reduction*, Vol. 66, p. 102582.

Tsuji, Y., et al. (2011). Tsunami height in Ibaraki and Chiba coasts, The website of the Earthquake Research Institute, The University of Tokyo. https://www.eri.u-tokyo.ac.jp/TOPICS_OLD/outreach/eqvolc/201103_tohoku/eng/#tsunami%20height (Accessed 20th June 2024). https://doi.org/10.15083/0000032415

Wilmsen, B., Webber, M. (2015). What can we learn from the practice of development-forced displacement and resettlement for organised resettlements in response to climate change? *Geoforum*, Vol. 58, pp. 76–85.

Wilson, G. A. (2012). *Community Resilience and Environmental Transitions*. Routledge.

7 Building New Community in the Emergency Temporary Housing

Focusing on Women's Group Activities

Mitoko Nakashima

7.1 Introduction

Japan has experienced numerous massive earthquakes over the past 30 years, from the 1995 Great Hanshin-Awaji Earthquake to the 2004 Niigata-Chuetsu Earthquake, the 2011 Great East Japan Earthquake and Tsunami (hereinafter GEJET), the 2016 Kumamoto Earthquake, and the 2024 Noto Peninsula Earthquake. Through such experiences, Japan has learned a great deal about disaster recovery. Numerous studies have been conducted on housing during the recovery process, particularly in architecture and urban planning. One of the issues highlighted in these studies is how to rebuild communities and local social ties that have been dismantled and weakened in the process of disasters and subsequent recovery.

Existing studies on the 1995 Great Hanshin-Awaji Earthquake have examined the relationship between social isolation and the residential environment in temporary housing and disaster public housing (Shiozaki et al. 2009) and the continuity and formation of communities in the process of transitioning from temporary housing to disaster public housing (Itoh 2015). In the case of the 2011 GEJET, it has been pointed out that relocation from temporary housing to disaster public housing based on the temporary housing community may reduce the burden of the environmental transition (Suzawa et al. 2018). It is necessary to reconstruct the care environment for the vulnerable, such as the elderly and people with disabilities, by utilizing existing community resources, such as families, relatives, and local communities, which have been responsible for community care (Maeda et al. 2020).

These studies have pointed out the necessity of utilizing existing local resources, such as communities that existed before the disaster and at the time of temporary housing, as well as the family and kinship relationships of the victims themselves. However, there is a limit to utilizing these existing local resources for disaster victims whose existing social relationships have been severed or dismantled by repeated relocations from the evacuation shelter to temporary housing and then to disaster public housing, collective relocation, and the rebuilding of independent houses (Figure 7.1).[1] Through the relocation process, existing local communities are dismantled, and the elderly and other vulnerable disaster victims face the risk of social isolation.

Considering this problem, studies on collective housing and community reconstruction in disaster public housing after the 1995 Great Hanshin-Awaji Earthquake

DOI: 10.4324/9781003615903-10

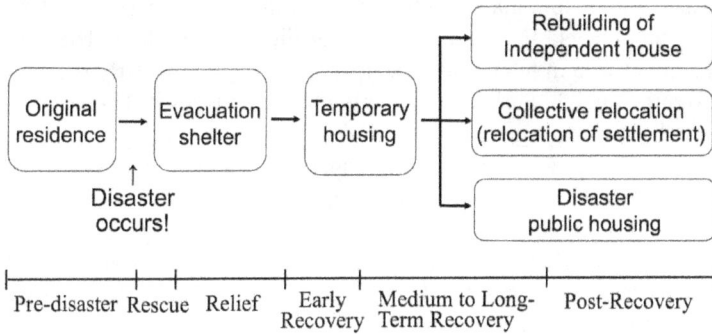

Figure 7.1 Relocation Process of the Disaster Sufferers and Stages of Disaster Recovery

are instructive. For example, studies on Hyogo Recovery Collective Housing point out that it was an attempt to create a new way of residence through cooperative living by organizing meals and events in the common room, but it did not necessarily lead to the formation of a proactive community by residents (Sasaki and Ueno 2003; Koyabe 2005; Inami 2009). Furthermore, Itoh (2018) suggested that although community organizations of neighbourhood associations were newly started and various events were held in the assembly halls of disaster public housing, the highly prepared organizations made it difficult to create autonomous communities, and some people were left out of the organized networks. Thus, despite the efforts of several existing studies, the conditions for creating new social relations and rebuilding communities in the process of disaster recovery have not yet been fully elucidated.

The author examined the possibility of creating new social interactions and relations through the use of assembly halls in disaster public housing in the Mabi-cho area, Okayama Prefecture, which was damaged by the 2018 Western Japan flood. The results of the study indicated that the conditions for creating new social interactions and relations through the use of assembly halls are by no means uniform and that further detailed analysis is needed, particularly considering the social context of each residential setting in the recovery process (Nakashima 2024). Focusing on the community activities of a women's group in the temporary housing of Ofunato City, Iwate Prefecture, one of the areas damaged by the 2011 GEJET, this chapter examines their attempt to create new social interactions and a new community in temporary housing by cooperating with each other, rather than relying solely on existing local resources.

After the 2011 GEJET, many towns were swept away by the tsunami and many temporary housing units were built, in which rebuilding communities became an urgent task. In many temporary housing units, various households moved from different districts, resulting in households living next door who did not know each other at all. In the temporary housing studied in this chapter, some female residents organized themselves into self-help groups and began to engage in various community activities such as distributing support supplies, accepting volunteers, and holding events at the assembly hall. Their activities played a major role in temporary housing, especially in the early recovery stage when no formal neighbourhood association had been formed. This chapter examines how the women's group was organized, how they engaged in activities in temporary housing, how they changed their role in temporary housing after the establishment of the neighbourhood association, and what kind of changes were brought about in the temporary housing community. Through an analysis of the significance of this group of women in temporary housing, this chapter attempts to elucidate the possibilities and limitations of Micro Human Efforts (MHE) for self-help activities by disaster-affected persons in recovery from disasters. As Subasinghe et al. (2021) noted, the MHE can become a developmental model for community-based disaster recovery. However, the possibilities and limitations of the MHE in the recovery processes are not fully examined. Examining the relationship between the MHE and formally organized community activities and gender differences in the MHE, this chapter attempts to elucidate the significance of disaster recovery processes.

The contents of this chapter are based on the results of the author's field research, particularly participant observations and in-depth interviews conducted for five and a half years from July 2011 to October 2016 at temporary housing, and a supplementary interview in April 2024 at the disaster public housing in Ofunato City, Iwate Prefecture. As suggested in Table 7.1, participant observations were conducted through the participation of the author and students as volunteers in various support activities such as open-air café, open-air wedding party, shaved ice stall in the open air, café at assembly hall, and other irregular events held by residents and outside support groups. The author and students participated in the first support activity, an open-air café in July 2011, as volunteer staff for a support activity by an outside support group; however, the shaved ice stall in the open air and the café at the meeting place were organized by the author and students themselves.

Table 7.1 Outline of Research Method

Research Period	*July 2011 – October 2016*
Participant observations	• Open-air café (July 2011) • Open-air wedding party (November 2011) • Shaved ice stall in the open air (every July 2012–2016) • Café at assembly hall (every March 2013–2016) • Additionally, we participated in other irregular events held by residents and outside support groups
In-depth interviews	We interviewed a total of more than 80 residents of temporary housing who consented to be interviewed in the questionnaire survey conducted during approximately 40 days from September to November each year
Investigation participants	The author and a total of 15 graduate and undergraduate students of Kagawa University (2–6 students per year)

In addition to these activities, the author and students also participated in irregular support activities by the residents' association of temporary housing and outside support groups as needed. The author participated in all of these activities and personally interacted and communicated with temporary housing residents. All descriptions in the following sections are based on the author's own experiences and do not include observations made by the students.

With regard to the in-depth interviews, the author and students interviewed more than 80 residents of temporary housing who consented to be interviewed in the questionnaire survey[2] conducted during approximately 40–50 days from September to November each year. Although a small number of these interviews were conducted by students, all the interview data used for the analyses in this chapter were obtained from the author's own interviews.

Ōfunato City, the subject of this study, is located in the southeastern part of Iwate Prefecture along the Sanriku Coast (Figure 7.2). Half of the city centre on the western shore of Ōfunato Bay was devastated by the tsunami caused by the 2011 Tōhoku Earthquake. Ofunato City's human casualties from the earthquake and tsunami included 354 dead and 79 missing, while 2,789 houses were totally destroyed and 1,148 were half-destroyed (Ofunato City 2015:53). Immediately after the earthquake and tsunami on 11 March 2011, 64 evacuation shelters were

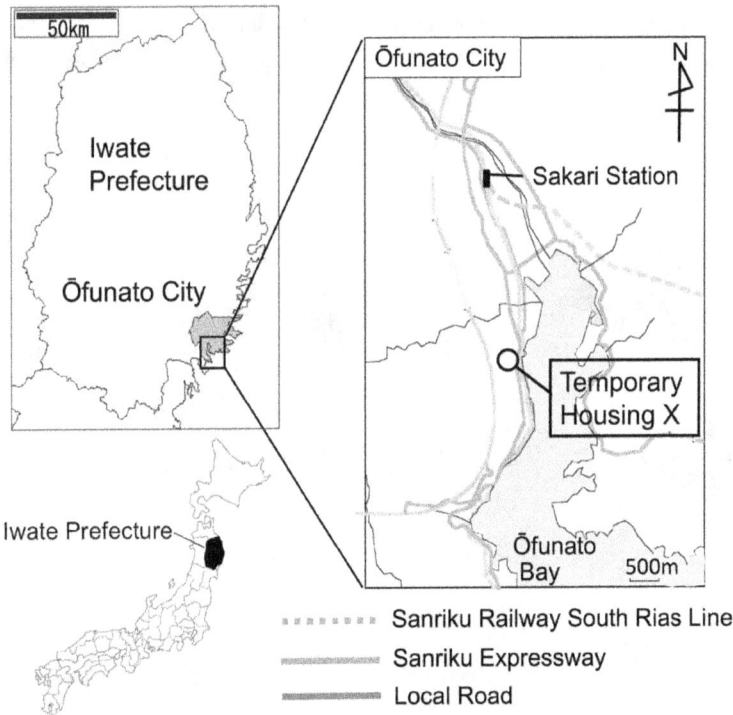

Figure 7.2 Study Area

set up throughout Ofunato City, and at its largest, 8,737 evacuees stayed in the shelters (Ofunato City 2015:89). By the end of July of the same year, 1,801 houses in 37 housing complexes of emergency temporary housing (hereinafter temporary housing)[3] were constructed in Ofunato City as a whole (Ofunato City 2017). Most of the temporary housing was prefabricated with electricity, water, gas, and other infrastructure in place,[4] and air conditioners, televisions, refrigerators, and washing machines were installed in each unit. The layouts varied from 1-bedroom to 3-bedroom types but were basically row-house types (Figure 7.3).

Ofunato City had a population of approximately 40,000 before the earthquake[5] and was a local city with fishing, fish processing, and commerce industries as its core industries. According to the National Census, the rate of owner-occupied houses in Ofunato City as of 2010, the year before the disaster, was 74.7%, which was considerably higher than the national average of 61.9% for the same year. Therefore, most temporary housing residents who had lived in their own detached houses were not accustomed to living in housing complexes and faced various problems such as privacy, daily life noise, small residential spaces, relationships with neighbours, and other restrictions in the lives of temporary housing.

In this chapter, Temporary Housing X is considered a case study of 37 housing complexes in Ofunato City. The Temporary Housing X is the second largest temporary housing in Ofunato City, with 138 units at its largest in 2013. The 37 temporary housing complexes in Ofunato City vary in size, location, and the surrounding environment. However, Temporary Housing X is a relatively urban-type temporary housing complex built on the playground of a municipal junior high

Figure 7.3 Constructed-Type Temporary Housing

(This Row-House Consists of Six Housing Units.Photographed by the Author on 12 October 2013)

school (Figure 7.4) located on the high ground close to the city centre, and its residents are composed of people from various districts in and outside Ofunato City.

The residents began moving into the Temporary Housing X in May 2011, then the assembly hall was constructed in August, and the residents' association of the Temporary Housing X was founded in September of the same year under the support of the city government (Table 7.2). After the assembly hall was set up, in addition to various support events organized by outside supporters, the residents themselves began holding salons, exercise classes, tea parties, and other events, and community activities gradually became more active, which made Temporary Housing X one of the most active temporary housings in Ofunato City.

7.2 Reconstruction Process of the Community in Temporary Housing

The period of occupancy of temporary housing was set at two years by the Disaster Relief Act, but in areas affected by the 2011 GEJET, the period was often longer than the prescribed two years. The Temporary Housing X began to be occupied in May 2011 and remained a place where disaster victims lived for five and a half years until it was closed in November 2016. A sixth-grade elementary school girl living in the Temporary Housing X, whom the author met during the first survey in July 2011, was already a second-year high school student by November 2016, when the Temporary Housing X was closed. The temporary housing community has undergone significant changes in form and nature through the long process of reconstruction in Temporary Housing X. This section describes this process with a

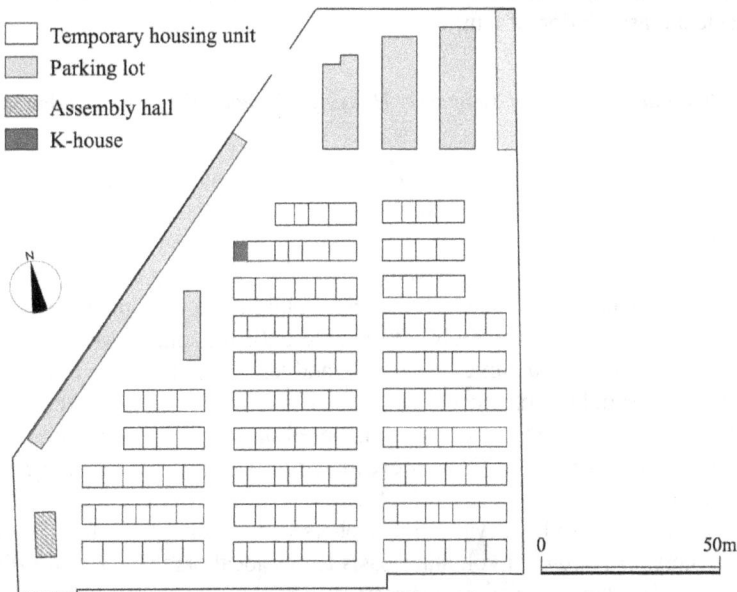

Figure 7.4 Layout Map of the Temporary Housing X

Table 7.2 Outline of the Temporary Housing X

Temporary Housing X	
External appearance (Photographed by the author on 16 July 2011)	
Number of households	138 (October 2013)
Beginning of residing	May 2011
Meeting facility	Assembly hall
Foundation of Residents' Association	September 2011 (promoted by the city government)
Original hometown of residents	Various settlements from extra-local different areas

focus on the development and changes in women's group and its relationship with the residents' association of temporary housing.

7.2.1 Preliminary History of Temporary Housing: Communities in Evacuation Shelter

Temporary Housing X was constructed on the playground of a municipal junior high school. From the day of the 2011 GEJET, the gymnasium of the junior high school served as an evacuation shelter for many disaster victims living nearby. According to Ofunato City (2015), during the first week after the earthquake and tsunami, approximately 500 disaster sufferers huddled in this junior high school gymnasium shelter, approximately 200 people until the end of March, approximately 100 people until the middle of May, and less than 20 people in early July. Since the author did not conduct field research at this junior high school gymnasium shelter, the following information is based on my interviews with the residents of Temporary Housing X who evacuated to the same shelter as well as on archived documents.

The management style of evacuation shelters varied from shelter to shelter, with some shelters operated on a voluntary basis led by local organizations for disaster prevention and community centre directors, while others were led by stationed government officials (Ofunato City 2015:90). The management of the junior high school gymnasium shelter is the responsibility of the evacuees themselves, who decide on the division of roles among them and manage the evacuation shelter by themselves.[6] The evacuees were assigned various roles in running the shelters, such as allocating space for evacuees; making lists of evacuees; bringing in, sorting, and distributing relief supplies such as food, clothes, and other necessities; cleaning rooms; posting notices; supporting information from the local government; posting messages from evacuees; and information about those who were missing. The evacuees organized themselves into subgroups to take on these roles and took on their work in the management of the shelter. Some of the female evacuees who were members of the actual working group in the management of the shelter moved into Temporary Housing X, built on the adjacent ground, and played leading roles in community building there.

7.2.2 Beginning of Temporary Housing Community: Birth and Development of the K-Ladies

According to the interviews with the residents of Temporary Housing X, of the 138 total households in Temporary Housing X, more than 30 households have moved from the junior high school gymnasium shelter. Of these 30 households in Temporary Housing X, a self-help organization of temporary housing "K-Ladies" was organized by seven women who had been involved in the management of the junior high school gymnasium shelter. K-Ladies played an important role in the early stages of community rebuilding in Temporary Housing X.

The birth of K-Ladies in Temporary Housing X was triggered by the creation of miçanga (woven bracelet). This was part of the "Miçanga on the beach" project, which aimed to restore work and confidence in women who had lost their jobs due to the disaster by making handmade miçangas from the fishing nets of tsunami-devastated fishermen.[7] Ms A, one of the leading persons of the K-Ladies, and her friends, who worked together at the junior high school gymnasium shelter on operational tasks, engaged in this miçanga project at Ms A's house in Temporary Housing X. Ms A put a sign on the window of her temporary house that read "Miçanga Project, looking for collaborators", then several women living in Temporary Housing X decided to participate in the project. Initially, as noted above, the miçanga making was done at Ms A's house, but later it was done at K-House (Figure 7.4), which used one of the vacant houses in Temporary Housing X.

As shown in Table 7.3, all members of the K-Ladies were women in their 40s and 50s. Although the majority were housewives at the time of their inception, their previous occupations ranged from housewives to self-employed individuals and part-time workers.[8] Characteristically, about half of them were working in the shopping district of the city centre that was devastated by the tsunami, and some knew each other to some extent. Furthermore, their children were classmates, current students, or graduates of junior high school, where gymnasiums and playgrounds became the evacuation shelter and site of the temporary housing, so they also had contact with one another.

Table 7.3 Members of the K-Ladies (at the time of July 2011)

Member	Age	Present Job	Previous Job
A	50s	housewife	self-employed (laundry)
B	50s	housewife	unknown
C	40s	housewife	self-employed (flower shop)
D	40s	housewife	self-employed (fish shop)
E	40s	housewife	part-time worker (canning work)
F	40s	housewife	housewife
G	40s	housewife	housewife

Source: The author's interviews with the members

K-Ladies' activities included receiving and distributing relief supplies, communicating with support groups, accepting and managing volunteers, and organizing various events. Above all, the reception and distribution of relief supplies played a significant role in temporary housing during the early recovery stage. In the early recovery stage, when no formal residents' association of temporary housing had been organized, the K-Ladies served as the receiving body for relief supplies and distributed them to temporary housing residents. At first, there was no list of residents of Temporary Housing X, and it was impossible to know who lived in the house. When an international NGO offered to provide clothes as relief supplies to temporary housing residents, the K-Ladies members went door-to-door to interview the residents to determine the number of persons, gender, and age of the family members in each household, and to compile a list of temporary housing residents for distribution of relief supplies of clothing to each household. Although the K-Ladies was neither an officialized sub-group of the residents' association nor an authorized private group, there was no alternative group to distribute relief supplies in the stage of early recovery, so the K-Ladies could operate as a self-help group in temporary housing.

Ms A, one of the leading members of K-Ladies, actively expanded her personal connections with outside support groups and volunteers, and she began to serve as a point of contact for temporary housing.[9] The larger her personal connections expanded, the more support groups and volunteers began to visit Temporary Housing X to provide various support activities for residents. In July 2011, for example, the author and students visited the Temporary Housing X to conduct an open-air café and learning support for the children, which was hosted by the K-Ladies. We set up a tent at the Temporary Housing X site and opened an open-air café (Figure 7.5) offering free hot and cold drinks to create a space for residents to interact with each other.[10] We also used K-House (Figure 7.4) to provide learning support for children living in temporary housing, although in reality, K-House became a playroom for the children. Through the support activities at this café and K-House, the residents of the temporary housing, their children, and outside volunteers had the opportunity to interact with each other (Figure 7.6).

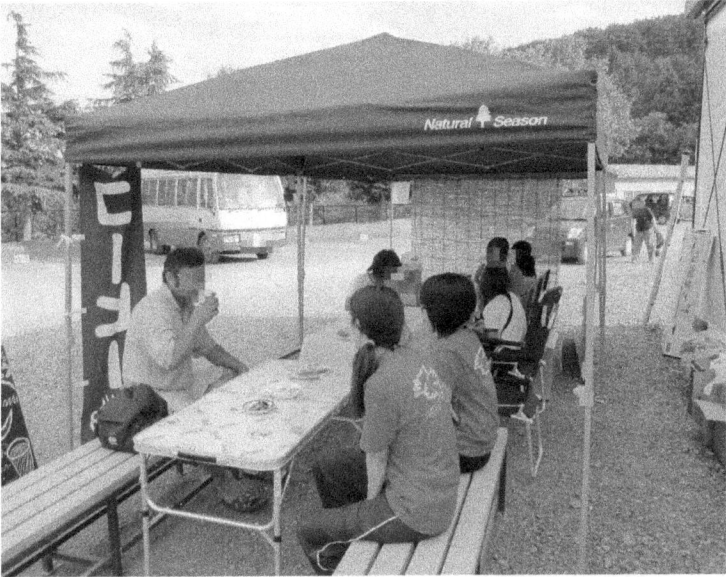

Figure 7.5 The Open-Air café at the Temporary Housing X (Photographed by the Author on 14 July 2011)

Thus, the K-Ladies played a significant role in building new communities in temporary housing during the early recovery stage. The K-Ladies was a completely private and voluntary organization with no president or membership system. Anyone who wished to participate in its activities, and there was no particular obligation to do so. This was both a strength and a weakness of the K-Ladies. While it was a voluntary, private organization that allowed for free activities, it also had limitations in terms of the representation of temporary housing residents. This was evident in the subsequent stages.

7.2.3   Development and Problematics of the Temporary Housing Community: Discrepancies between the Residents' Association and the K-Ladies

In August 2011, three months after the Temporary Housing X was opened, an assembly hall was finally constructed in a corner of the temporary housing site (Figure 7.4). The following month, in September, the residents' association for Temporary Housing X was officially organized with the support of the Ofunato City office. Furthermore, in September 2011, Ofunato City introduced a new system of temporary housing support staff (hereinafter, support staff),[11] who were selected among temporary housing residents and assigned to each temporary housing complex to provide community support, such as building communities in temporary housing and identifying problems faced by temporary housing residents in collaboration with the residents' association of temporary housing. Thus, various

Figure 7.6 Social Interactions between the Residents, the Children, and Volunteers
(Photographed by the Author on 17 July 2011)

institutions that support communities in temporary housing have gradually developed. In conjunction with these processes, the residents' association came to the forefront as the main actor of community activities in Temporary Housing X. In this sense, the recovery process has gradually shifted from the stage of early recovery, when people leave the stage of emergency relief and begin the first steps towards independent living, to the stage of medium- to long-term recovery, when daily life is restored, and the social infrastructure of the community is strengthened.

The Japanese government's position on the management of temporary housing strongly urges the formation of residents' associations in each temporary housing complex.[12] The actual role of the residents' associations was as an accepting body in each temporary housing unit for the distribution of relief supplies from the government, provision of administrative services, provision of information related to recovery, and promotion of social interaction among the residents of the temporary housing. In other words, the residents' association was regarded as an official organization representing temporary housing residents. This led to discrepancies between the K-Ladies and the residents' association in Temporary Housing X.

As noted above, the K-Ladies was a completely private and voluntary organization, and it did not represent the entirety of temporary housing residents. This has led to problems with community activities. In July 2013, the author and students once again opened a volunteer café in the Temporary Housing X in collaboration with a local coffee wholesaler. We decided to use the assembly hall of the temporary housing for the café. I contacted Ms A of the K-Ladies in advance and asked her to give permission to hold the café and give our best wishes to other members of the K-Ladies. Of course, she readily agreed, and gave me a reassuring reply, "I am looking forward to seeing you again". However, when we visited the assembly hall of the Temporary Housing X on the day of the café with drinks, foodstuffs, coffee machines, etc., the president of the residents' association of the Temporary Housing X told us, "I was not told that the café would be held at the assembly hall today, and we have already received another reservation of footbath services from the Kobe University volunteer team for the use of the assembly hall today". We were surprised to hear this and replied that we had already received permission to hold the café through Ms A. The president said, "I have not given such permission to you. If you want to use the assembly hall, you should properly apply to the residents' association". We apologized for failing to contact the president of the residents' association and asked him to allow us to conduct café activities at the assembly hall. After consulting with the Kobe University volunteer team, we decided to hold a café and footbath at the assembly hall in collaboration with each other, and these activities were successfully welcomed by temporary housing residents (Figure 7.7). Since then, the author has made sure to send applications for volunteer work in temporary housing to both Ms A and the president of the residents' association.

According to the authors interviews with both Ms A of the K-Ladies and the president of the residents' association, the lack of proper communication between Ms A and the president of the residents' association was the direct reason for this

Figure 7.7 The Café at the Assembly Hall of the Temporary Housing X

(Photographed by the Author on 9 March 2013)

problem. However, as suggested in this case, the activities of the K-Ladies and the residents' associations sometimes overlapped, and the two parties had a competitive relationship with the initiatives in community activities, such as receiving volunteers from outside support groups, accepting and distributing various relief supplies, and organizing various events by temporary housing residents. After the introduction of the support staff system in Temporary Housing X in September 2011, the support staffs were stationed during the daytime at the assembly hall of the temporary housing, and they became the point of contact for receiving volunteers, relief supplies, and coordinated community activities, acting as a bridge between the residents' association and the K-Ladies, especially Ms A. As a result, relief supplies from municipal governments and public organizations were to be distributed by the support staff, while those from individuals and private organizations were to be distributed by the K-Ladies. In addition, applications for volunteers from outside aid organizations went through the support staff, but some of the organizations often directly contacted the K-Ladies members through their personal connections without going through the support staff.

Although the residents' associations had gradually taken the initiative in community activities such as distribution of relief supplies, summer festivals, exercise classes, recovery counselling sessions, residents' meetings, and so on, individual residents and informal organizations were also active in activities such as tea parties and various hobby circles of cooking, calligraphy, and folk songs at the assembly hall. Furthermore, outside support groups were active in volunteer activities and various events. They repeatedly visited Temporary Housing X to hold a variety of events and expanded their networks through personal connections with K-Ladies, including Ms A and other residents. In this sense, it can be said that in Temporary Housing X, community activities developed through the coexistence of official and personal networks. In both networks, assembly halls of temporary housing played an important role as centres of community activities.

Although the status of the K-Ladies in the temporary housing community declined in relative terms, they did not become a subordinate organization of the residents' association, nor were they absorbed into it. They remained in a parallel relationship and played different roles in receiving relief supplies and volunteers, as described above. The K-Ladies themselves gradually reduced their activities as a group around 2013. Due to friction among members, they began to pursue their own individual activities, and the group's activities ended.

7.2.4 Gender Bias in Community Rebuilding: Beyond the Gender Gap

The fact that women's self-help groups, such as the K-Ladies, played a significant role in the early recovery stage in temporary housing is very suggestive when considering gender issues in community rebuilding after the disaster. Most major cities along the Sanriku coast of the Tohoku area were severely damaged by the tsunami and many people lost their places of work. There were no significant differences between men and women. Both men and women lost their jobs. However, there were significant differences between men and women in subsequent responses. Many men sought work and went to employment security offices to look for gainful employment, but most of the jobs they found were manual labour, such as clearing rubble, demolishing houses, and restoring roads and infrastructure, and not many of these jobs were easily accessible to women. It was difficult for women to find new employment opportunities. Under such circumstances, the Miçanga project described in the second section was one of the few attempts to create cash income opportunities for women affected by the disaster.

On the other hand, women still had to assume their share of housework, childcare, and care for the elderly even after the disaster. Even if they did not have cash jobs, they worked in temporary housing homes doing housework, childcare, and nursing care. In this respect, it can be said that they are in line with the context of the typical gendered division of labour in provincial cities of Northeastern Japan. When we first visited Temporary Housing X to volunteer at the open-air café in July 201, all of the K-Ladies members were busy housewives cleaning, doing laundry, cooking three meals a day, and taking care of the elderly at home. Furthermore, they also participated in self-help community activities in temporary housing and even took care of volunteers. Many of them spent most of their day in temporary housing, and it is thought that by interacting with the residents of temporary housing, they became aware of the problems and needs of temporary housing residents.

When we visited the Temporary Housing X during the daytime on weekdays in 2011, we could see only preschool children, women, and the elderly, not adult men of the working generation. Of course, not all men go out to work during the day. There must have been a certain number of men who could not find work or who could not engage in manual labour because of their health problems. However, they are rarely seen in temporary housing during the daytime. According to the interviews with some of the K-Ladies members, this is because some of these men went out to play pachinko (Japanese pinball game) or drank alcohol during the daytime in their temporary housing rooms. It is understandable that many people who lost their families, homes, or jobs in the tsunami were depressed by mental shock and stress and were unable to maintain a positive attitude. When we were working in the open-air café at the Temporary Housing X in July 2011, a middle-aged man, obviously drunk, wandered up to our café in the daytime and approached a female volunteer student. A member of the K-Ladies, who was standing nearby, interrupted him and said to us, "Stay away from him. He is danger!" After he walked away from us, she grumbled, "There are sometimes these kinds of drunks in our temporary housing. It's so troubling". Of course, it is assumed that she made these actions and statements because she was concerned that the female students would be in danger. However, I felt a sense of helplessness when I was present at this scene.

As a result, in the early recovery stage, some women were quick to become involved in self-help activities in temporary housing and build many social networks, whereas men were not. This is evident in the fact that there were no male groups or individuals engaged in community activities, such as those of the K-Ladies, in the early recovery stage. Of course, as noted above, the background for these women's involvement in community activities was their participation in a working group in the junior high school gymnasium shelter. They realized the necessity of self-help activities in running temporary housing as well as shelter. However, it can be said that women's active participation in self-help activities in temporary housing is influenced by the gendered division of labour, in which they have been excluded from wage labour and engaged in domestic work such as housework, childcare, and nursing care. The various self-help activities of the K-Ladies were informal, based on the personal relationships of the K-Ladies members constructed through their ordinary lives. Therefore, these women were free to carry out their own activities, regardless of their position or occupation. However, this means that the K-Ladies could not culminate in formal organizational status and would remain as an informal self-help group as long as it depends on the personal relationships of the K-Ladies members.

In the medium- to long-term recovery stage, when residents' associations were formed and the formal organization of the temporary housing community was established, men instantly began to take the initiative. A man in his 70s became the president of the residents' association, and two out of the four support staff members were also men. Thus, as the temporary housing community became more organized and institutionalized, men began to appear on stage as major actors. Unlike the K-Ladies, the residents' association of Temporary Housing X became an organization that officially represented temporary housing residents and became a leading organization in subsequent community activities.

However, even in the medium-to long-term recovery stage, there were few men as general participants in community events, rather than board members of the residents' association. According to the author's observations, even at tea parties, hobby circle gatherings held at the assembly hall, and various social events organized by outside groups and volunteers, most participants were middle- and old-aged women, and men were rarely seen. In the author's interviews with K-Ladies members, one member shared two interesting stories about the participation of male residents in community activities. When a member of the K-Ladies asked one old-aged male resident of the temporary housing why he did not participate in the event at the assembly hall, he replied, "Because the participants are all women, which makes it difficult for me to attend, and because I am not very talkative and reserved, so I would only cause trouble if I attended the tea party". On the other hand, when the K-Ladies asked another elderly man, who once worked in the construction industry and had never attended any events at the assembly hall, to build benches around the assembly hall for people to rest and to make wooden planters for flower seedlings from a support group, he accepted their request without hesitation and worked silently to build the benches and planters.

This episode suggests that the feeling that one can be of service to the community is a catalyst for participation in community activities. In light of the above, it is necessary not only to encourage men to participate in events, but also to provide opportunities for both men and women to get involved in the community in a variety of ways, taking advantage of the characteristics of each resident, regardless of gender.

7.3 Conclusion

This chapter traced the reconstruction process of the community in the temporary housing of Ofunato City, focusing on the activities of a women's group, the K-Ladies, in the temporary housing. This group of women played a significant role in rebuilding the community in temporary housing, particularly during the early recovery stage. Without any official organizations, such as residents' associations in temporary housing, the K-Ladies, which began with making miçanga to create cash income opportunities for women, laid the foundation for rebuilding the temporary housing community in many ways, from receiving and distributing relief supplies to compiling a list of residents, receiving support groups, and communicating and coordinating with support groups.

What made these diverse activities possible was the accumulation of a variety of social relationships, such as those built through the operation of evacuation shelters, those formed through work and community ties before the disaster, and those formed through children and schools. These connections were not necessarily a continuation of the pre-disaster community, but rather an attempt to build new social relationships in temporary housing by connecting partial connections and, in this sense, to create a new community. Furthermore, by expanding their personal networks with outside support groups, K-Ladies attracted a variety of support activities for residents from outside groups. It was also an attempt to enrich the community activities of temporary housing by actively connecting them to the outside world.

While the completely private and voluntary nature of the K-Ladies allowed for free community activities unrestricted by the systems and rules of the community, it also had limitations in terms of representation of all temporary housing residents. In the medium- to long-term recovery stage, as communities became more organized and institutionalized, the role of residents' associations as formal resident organizations grew, whereas the initiative of the K-Ladies as private organizations declined. However, private organizations and individual residents were also active in conducting various activities at the assembly hall. In this sense, community activities developed through the coexistence of both official and personal networks.

The fact that women's groups such as the K-Ladies played an important role in rebuilding the temporary housing community in the early recovery stage is inextricably linked to the fact that women were kept away from cash income opportunities. Furthermore, women had to take on housework, childcare, and nursing care, and therefore, they were never separated from their "homes" in the temporary housing. Consequently, women's involvement in temporary housing communities is thought to have been significant. In this sense, the role of women in temporary housing communities suggests a gender bias in community rebuilding.

The findings obtained through the examination of women's group activities in temporary housing may provide insight into the significance and limitations of MHE in disaster recovery. In the early recovery stage, when the existing community was dismantled and the social infrastructure of the community was still not

constructed, voluntary activities of the MHE based on small-scale, informal relationships, such as self-help activities of the K-Ladies, played a major role in recon-
necting separated disaster sufferers and giving them the opportunity to take the
first steps towards community living through mutual aid. In a situation lacking an
underlying community organization, such as a residents' association, informal self-
help activities based on personal relationships provide the first clue to rebuilding a
community. However, the MHE of informal self-help activities is deeply embedded in the existing gendered division of labour, in which women are excluded from
wage labour and engaged exclusively in domestic work. Furthermore, such activities of MHE are mainly based on the informal relationship of specific residents
and cannot represent temporary housing residents. In the case of the K-Ladies, this
led to a conflict between the K-Ladies and the residents' association of temporary
housing. In this sense, it can be said that there is a need for cooperation and coordination between informal self-help organizations such as the K-Ladies and formal
community organizations such as residents' associations in temporary housing.

The role of MHE, such as the self-help activities of the K-Ladies in community
rebuilding, has not yet ended with the closure of temporary housing. The various
social capitals built in the process of community rebuilding in temporary housing will be carried over to subsequent disaster public housing, disaster prevention
collective relocation sites, and other types of reconstructed housing, where social
capital is expected to lead to the construction of new communities once again. In
this sense, it is necessary to examine in detail the actual conditions of MHE in community rebuilding that takes place during each process of recovery from disasters.

Notes

1 This relocation process does not necessarily coincide with the disaster recovery stages.
  For example, during the period of temporary housing, there is a transition from early
  recovery, when people leave the stage of emergency relief and begin the first steps
  towards independent living, to medium- to long-term recovery, when daily life is
  restored and the social infrastructure of the community is strengthened.
2 The results of the analysis of the questionnaire survey were published in a series of
  papers titled "Study on the Prevention of Social Isolation of the Elderly in the Temporary
  Housing Units, Part 1-4" (Nakashima et al. 2013, 2014, 2015, 2017).
3 Emergency temporary housing must be set up by local governments under the Disaster
  Relief Act and is classified into two types: newly constructed temporary housing and
  rented temporary housing that is converted from existing housing. In Ofunato City, more
  than 90% of temporary housing was newly constructed because of the small existing
  rental housing stock and the fact that most were destroyed by the tsunami.
4 In temporary housing, there is no obligation to pay rent, but residents must pay their own
  water, sewer, gas, and electricity bills.
5 According to the Ofunato City Statistical Book, the population of Ofunato City was
  40,737 in 2010 but decreased to 32,453 in 2023.
6 Of course, there was support from local government officials, but the number of local
  government officials was limited, and there were not enough staff to cover all evacuation
  shelters in Ofunato City.
7 The "Missanga on the beach" project began with the efforts of a women's group in
  Sanriku Town, Ofunato City under the support of the "Jobs for Sanriku" project launched

by some broadcasting stations in Tohoku and an advertising agency in Tokyo, and later spread to other areas of the tsunami-affected Sanriku coast (Executive Committee of the "Jobs for Sanriku" Project official website).

8 Most of the former workplaces of the K-Ladies members were damaged by the tsunami, and the members lost their jobs after the disaster.

9 When I volunteered at Temporary Housing X, I first contacted Ms A and asked her to accept our activities at the temporary housing.

10 When we conducted this activity in July 2011, the Temporary Housing X did not have an assembly hall, and there was no space in the temporary housing for residents to interact with each other. Therefore, we wanted this café to be used as an exchange space for the residents.

11 This support staff system started in September 2011 with the support of Kitakami City, and up to 81 support staff were assigned to 37 temporary housing complexes in Ofunato City. After support from Kitakami City ended, the programme has been operated under the direct management of Ofunato City since 2014, with the financial support of the Japanese government's recovery support staff system.

12 The interim report of the "Project Team for Housing Environment of Emergency Temporary Housings" established in the Ministry of Health, Labor and Welfare states, "In order to build a 'community' in each temporary housing complex, it is first necessary to establish a residents' association based on each housing complex, and to collect information on issues faced by the residents in temporary housing, and to proactively solve the issues on their own" (Ministry of Health, Labor and Welfare 2011).

References

Executive Committee of "Jobs for the Sanriku" Project. "Jobs for Sanriku" Project. http://www.sanriku-shigoto-project.com (Last accessed June 26, 2024).

Inami, N. 2009. The possibility of collective housing for the elderly: A case study of Hyogo Recovery Collective Housing. *Soshioroji* 53(3): 21–37.

Itoh, A. 2015. Temporary housing, recovery public housing and local community. *The municipal problems: The journal of the Tokyo Institute for Municipal Research* 106(1): 27–32.

Itoh, A. 2018. Community development and problems of disaster recovery public housing in the process of disaster reconstruction after the Great Hanshin-Awaji Earthquake. *The Annual Reports of the Tohoku Sociological Society* 47: 37–47.

Koyabe, I. 2005. Challenges for new residence: Hyogo Recovery Collective Housing. *Urban Housing Sciences* 49: 54–65.

Maeda, M., Tsukuda, H., Onoda, Y., Takada, M., Amakusa, H. and Nakamura, K. 2020. A study on house and life restoration with household separation and reorganization in group resettlement: The case of Tamaura-West district in Iwanuma City, Miyagi Prefecture in the Great East Japan Earthquake of 2011. *Journal of Architecture and Planning: Transactions of AIJ* 85(770): 793–803.

Ministry of Health, Labor and Welfare. 2011. *Actions based on the results of the questionnaire survey on the living environment of emergency temporary housing: The interim report of the project team for Housing Environment of Emergency Temporary Housings.* https://www.mhlw.go.jp/stf/houdou/2r9852000001svlt-att/2r9852000001svq9.pdf (Last accessed June 27, 2024).

Nakashima, M. 2024. A study on the living conditions of residents of disaster public housings in Mabi-cho, Okayama Prefecture: Focusing on the assembly hall and the state of interactions. *Journal of Social Safety Science* 44: 1–8.

Nakashima, M., Anabuki, S. and Kobayashia, A. 2013. A study on the prevention of social isolation of the elderly in temporary housing units. Part 1: Focusing on exchange relationships and community activities in the temporary housing units of Ofunato City. *Architectural Institute of Japan Proceedings of the Housing Studies Symposium* 8: 25–34.

Nakashima, M., Furuya, R. and Ozaki, R. 2014. Study on the prevention of social isolation of the elderly in the temporary housing units, part 2 -With focusing on the exchange relationships and the consciousness on the recovery public housing in Ofunato City. *Architectural Institute of Japan Proceedings of the Housing Studies Symposium* 9: 133–142.

Nakashima, M., Koizumi, T. and Tatsu, K. 2015. Influence of the use of support centers for the elderly on the exchange relationships of the elderly in temporary housing units: A study on the prevention of social isolation of the elderly in temporary housing units, Part 3. *Architectural Institute of Japan Proceedings of the Housing Studies Symposium* 10: 101–110.

Nakashima, M., Ozawa, T., Kusu, T., Okudaira, S., Hirao, T. and Myojin, Y. 2017. Role of the support center for the elderly in the temporary housing units of Ofunato City: A study on the prevention of social isolation of the elderly in temporary housing units. Part 4. *Architectural Institute of Japan Proceedings of the Housing Studies Symposium* 12: 265–274.

Ofunato City. 2015. *Ofunato-shi, Higashinihon Daishinsai Kirokushi (Ofunato City, The Great East Japan Earthquake Record Book)*. Ofunato: Ofunato City.

Ofunato City. 2017. *Unpublished documents from the second meeting of the Ofunato City Recovery Plan Promotion Committee*. Ofunato: Ofunato City.

Sasaki, S. and Ueno, K. 2003. On the change in the residents' living style in public collective housing for the elderly: Based on a four-and-a-half-year continuous survey of the residents living in Hyogo Revival Collective Housing. *Urban Housing Sciences* 43: 54–59.

Shiozaki, Y., Tanaka, M., Meguro, E. and Horita, Y. 2009. Study on the change of characteristics of residential space and the social "isolation" of the residents of the disaster restoration public housing: Case of the great Hanshin-Awaji earthquake. *Journal of Architecture and Planning: Transactions of AIJ* 74(642): 1813–1820.

Subasinghe, C., Sutrisna, M. and Olatunji, O. 2021. Multidisciplinary perspectives of Micro Human Efforts in post-disaster recovery. *International Journal of Mass Emergencies and Disasters* 39(1): 1–10.

Suzawa, S., Arai, N., Iwasa, A., Kurono, H., Otsuki, T. and Imoto, S. 2018. Efficacy of community-based relocation in a neighboring area from temporary housing to disaster public housing: Verification from viewpoints of the environmental transition. *Journal of Architecture and Planning: Transactions of AIJ* 83(750): 1391–1401.

Section IV

Synthesizing Isolated/ Interrelated "Self-Work/Labour/ Action" for Socio-economic Outcomes

8 Enhancing Micro-human Efforts through Livelihood Assistance for Women in Post-disaster Recovery in Sri Lanka

Yamuna Kaluarachchi, Menaha Thayaparan, and Kalindu Mendis

8.1 Introduction

Globally, there has been a rise in disasters and their severities over the past decade, contributing to increased numbers of deaths and economic and social casualties (Chhotray, 2022). The destructions that accompany disasters create an urgent need to rebuild the lives of the affected communities within a short time. The United Nations Development Programme (UNDP, 2009) has tried to make this rebuilding programme an opportunity to "Build Back Better (BBB)", where the built environment responds to the needs of the affected community and long-term sustainability, contributing to the resettlement and healing process of the displaced. To safeguard a resilient and sustainable recovery, the Sendai Framework for Disaster Risk Reduction (United Nations Office for Disaster Risk Reduction [UNDRR], 2015) and, more broadly, the Sustainable Development Goals (United Nations [UN], 2015) emphasize that Disaster Risk Management and development planning should be inclusive of all fragments of society comprising gender, disabled, vulnerable and marginalized (King et al., 2019). Even though the international community has attempted to embrace this resilience and inclusion, in practice, these segments of society and their needs are often overlooked throughout the rebuilding process (Robles, 2019).

In Post-Disaster Rebuilding (PDR) programmes in South Asia, adequate gender-desegregated data is hard to come by (Drolet et al., 2015). Given this context, any initiative to promote and support the inclusion of women must undertake measures to understand conditions that enable or hinder the participation of women in PDR. Moreover, disasters have direct and indirect impacts on the livelihoods of those affected, where interruptions and dislocations of livelihood tend to have severe effects on poor and marginalized households, mostly women (Lord et al., 2016). According to Eadie et al. (2020), shelter and livelihood are the two main criteria that play a critical role in the lives of individuals in their post-disaster recovery, especially in the perception of the most marginalized who will need specific shelter and job opportunities.

Micro-human efforts are based on the physical and psychological resources of people in disaster-affected communities (Astill & Miller, 2018; Wild et al., 2013). Such efforts have described personal tacit inner psychological, trait, motivational,

DOI: 10.4324/9781003615903-12

and material resources as essential criteria for individual recovery. Thus, individual micro-human efforts collectively become an integral and holistic mechanism for communities to adapt to achieve a post-disaster new normal and beyond.

Livelihood assistance is of the highest importance to women in the recovery context after a disaster, as it plays a crucial role in enabling and empowering them to gain micro-human efforts such as self-reliance, self-management, self-improvement, self-therapy, self-reinforcement, self-confidence, self-support, and self-optimization (Oloruntoba & Asare-Doku, 2021). It demonstrates that assistance to improve livelihoods not only empowers women but also strengthens community resilience and enhances the broader trajectory of recovery outcomes. Despite the international community's efforts to embrace resilience and inclusion, vulnerable groups, especially women and their needs are often overlooked during the PDR processes in Sri Lanka (Mendis et al., 2022). Hence it is a unique opportunity to initiate research that contributes to the broader "BBB" programme and gender inclusion in PDR. Even though there are studies on PDR "BBB" programmes worldwide, less attention has been paid to gender inclusion with a particular focus on livelihood development, which ultimately helps to gain post-disaster recovery benefits while strengthening micro-human efforts. This study aims to investigate this neglected yet significant area of study and builds on previous research on gender inclusion in post-disaster development BBB programmes (Kaluarachchi, 2021; Mendis et al., 2020) in Sri Lanka. The research adopts qualitative research methods that help reveal interrelationships between localized and transformative practices of individuals, families, and social groups and their more expansive socio-cultural, physical, and economic environments. Using Preferred Reporting Items for Systematic Reviews and Meta-Analyses (PRISMA) (Page et al, 2021), an extensive systematic literature review, including published and unpublished reports and case studies, was conducted to establish theory related to micro-human efforts and place the study in the current context. Stakeholder processes and related governance mechanisms concerned with the assistance offered in the post-disaster setting were examined and mapped to identify influential roles and responsibilities and any gaps in the support system to improve the livelihoods of women. Primary data was gathered from stakeholder interviews and focus group discussions, and the collected data was analysed using qualitative content analysis to identify challenges, barriers, and opportunities for women during the post-disaster phase. The study identifies inclusive strategies for promoting livelihoods to achieve micro-human efforts and recommends enhancing livelihoods for women.

8.2   Literature Review

8.2.1   Disaster Impacts on the Livelihoods of Women

Natural disasters severely affect the livelihoods of women (Eadie et al., 2020; Lord et al., 2016). A livelihood is more than a pay cheque or a job; it refers to the diverse ways individuals and communities sustain themselves (Roy & Mathbor, 2021). Moreover, the loss of livelihoods and income reflects the emotional and psychological consequences of disasters. It can take a significant amount of time, sometimes a year, to start the building back process of livelihoods and income sources, illustrating how household food security and income are highly subject to the vagaries of climate and disasters (Clissold et al., 2020).

Using the PRISMA approach in the literature review, the authors identified the impact of disasters on women's livelihoods in the global context while recognizing the barriers they face to engage in livelihood-related activities and livelihood-related opportunities. Table 8.1 presents an in-depth analysis of these findings from 30 literature sources.

Twenty-five criteria were identified as barriers through the literature review and the information gathered via interview findings. Among these, the five most cited critical barriers faced by women are social negligence (B11), lack of financial support to start livelihoods and training from the government (B2), being expected to perform unpaid or poorly paid labour (B8), lack of livelihood options (B5), and underestimation of capabilities (B9).

In many instances, as the primary carer of the family, women's livelihood opportunities are jeopardised in Sri Lanka as they are required to perform unpaid care work (B8), which influences their involvement in post-disaster resource allocation and in many instances their productive contributions go unrecognized, unaccounted, and underpaid. However, according to Tanyag (2018), women's caregiving and unpaid labour are an invisible safety net to help families and communities cope. Besides, adhering to cultural norms (B14) where women take a subordinate role would frequently jeopardise women's economic recovery after a disaster.

Women tend to suffer more injuries, die more frequently in most disasters (Tanyag, 2018), and become unemployed or underemployed in the aftermath of a disaster (Roy, 2021). Women have comparatively negligible access to post-disaster livelihoods because they suffer intense care work burdens of the family, limited mobility, threats of sexual and gender violence, social negligence, and pre-existing vulnerability to economic exploitation (Bang & Few, 2012; Roy, 2021). Even though Sri Lanka has made significant progress towards achieving gender equality recently, in the face of structural barriers and societal norms perpetuating gender stereotypes, many women and girls continue to suffer discrimination and violence in disaster situations (UNDP, 2021).

Further, women are significantly affected when they fall under intersectional marginalization, for instance, disabled women. It is widely recognized that disabled people are disproportionately affected by disasters due to high levels of poverty, limited resources, and lack of welfare benefits, often combined to reinforce their vulnerability (Lee & Chen, 2019; Stough et al., 2016). Historically, gaining employment has been a challenge for people with disabilities (Cobley, 2015). In addition, Stough et al. (2016) claimed that after disasters, finding new employment opportunities was more challenging for the intersectional community of disabled women. These communities lack such opportunities due to the physical, attitudinal, and systemic barriers that limit their participation in society (Cobley, 2015). Individuals with disabilities who have informal or sporadic jobs accommodating

Table 8.1 Impact of Disasters on the Livelihoods of Women

Impact on Livelihood in the Post-disaster Context		Literature Sources	Number of Citations		
			Quantity	%	Rank
Barriers	B1. Lack of skills	(Lord et al., 2016; Perera-Mubarak, 2013; Stough et al., 2016; Zayas et al., 2017)	4	13.33%	8
	B2. Lack of financial and training support from the government	(Clissold et al., 2020; Cobley, 2015; Eadie et al., 2020; King et al., 2019; Lord et al., 2016; Roy, 2021; Stough et al., 2016; Zayas et al., 2017)	8	26.67%	2
	B3. Less opportunities to develop adaptation capacity	(Cobley, 2015; Greenough, 2018; King et al., 2019)	3	10.00%	10
	B4. Lack of sustainable livelihood options	(Eadie et al., 2020; Zayas et al., 2017)	2	6.67%	14
	B5. Lack of livelihood options	(Badayos-Jover, 2017; Eadie et al., 2020; Lord et al., 2016; Sohrabizadeh, 2016; Stough et al., 2016)	5	16.67%	5
	B6. Inadequate and unsafe housing	(Eadie et al., 2020; Zayas et al., 2017)	2	6.67%	14
	B7. Inadequate provision of utilities	(Cobley, 2015; Eadie et al., 2020; Sohrabizadeh, 2016)	3	10.00%	10
	B8. Expected to perform unpaid/low-paid labour	(Chhotray, 2022; Eadie et al., 2020; Greenough, 2018; Lord et al., 2016; Perera-Mubarak, 2013; Roy, 2021; Stough et al., 2016; Tanyag, 2018)	8	26.67%	2
	B9. Underestimation of capabilities	(Badayos-Jover, 2017; Chhotray, 2022; Eadie et al., 2020; Sohrabizadeh, 2016; Zayas et al., 2017)	5	16.67%	5
	B10. Non-recognition and non-quantification of livelihood activities	(Chhotray, 2022; Cuaton, 2019a; Lord et al., 2016)	3	10.00%	10
	B11. Social negligence	(Chhotray, 2022; Eadie et al., 2020; Khankeh et al., 2013; King et al., 2019; Lord et al., 2016; Phibbs et al., 2014; Roy, 2021; Sohrabizadeh, 2016; Stough et al., 2016; Tanyag, 2018)	10	33.33%	1

(Continued)

Table 8.1 (Continued)

Impact on Livelihood in the Post-disaster Context	Literature Sources	Number of Citations		
		Quantity	%	Rank
B12. Unwillingness to engage in livelihoods	(Perera-Mubarak, 2013)	1	3.33%	22
B13. Threats of sexual and gender violence	(Tanyag, 2018)	1	3.33%	22
B14. Distance to Livelihood opportunities	(Eadie et al., 2020; Tanyag, 2018)	2	6.67%	14
B15. Barriers to continuing traditional household livelihood options	(Eadie et al., 2020)	1	3.33%	22
B16. Cultural barriers	(Chhotray, 2022; Perera-Mubarak, 2013; Roy, 2021; Tanyag, 2018)	4	13.33%	8
B17. New geographical setting	(Perera-Mubarak, 2013)	1	3.33%	22
B18. Exclusion from important land-use transformations	(Chhotray, 2022)	1	3.33%	22
B19. Force to join the sex industry	(Tanyag, 2018)	1	3.33%	22
B20. Limitations in reproductive roles	(Fajarwati et al., 2016; Tanyag, 2018)	2	6.67%	14
B21. Increase in domestic work	(Fajarwati et al., 2016; Tanyag, 2018)	2	6.67%	14
B22. Home life changes	(Fajarwati et al., 2016; Perera-Mubarak, 2013; Tanyag, 2018)	3	10.00%	10
B23. Changes in interactions with neighbours	(Fajarwati et al., 2016; Tanyag, 2018)	2	6.67%	14
B24. Lack of priority for completing physical care	(Khankeh et al., 2013; Tanyag, 2018)	2	6.67%	14
B25. Lack of disability-sensitive support	(Zayas et al., 2017)	1	3.33%	22
Opportunities O1. Development of micro-human efforts	(Bang & Few, 2012; Cobley, 2015; Cuaton, 2019b; Pakjouei et al., 2021; Perera-Mubarak, 2013; Renuka & Srimulyani, 2015; Roy, 2021; Roy & Mathbor, 2021)	8	26.67%	2

their disabilities found employment in post-disaster situations particularly challenging (Stough et al., 2016) as they had to adapt to a new context with new sets of conditions. Even though these marginalized segments of communities' recovery is a long-term process in the post-disaster context, job opportunities and income generation can act as accelerators that can have many societal and economic benefits (Cuaton, 2019a; Eadie et al., 2020; Roy & Mathbor, 2021; Stough et al., 2017).

In the aftermath of a disaster, many household income-generation activities are derailed by the destruction of related assets. Although men tend to resume their livelihoods early, their incomes are invariably insufficient to meet post-disaster expenditures. Therefore, women are expected to be engaged in various economic activities within these parameters with positive outcomes (Perera-Mubarak, 2013). Many disabled women are eligible for social security income benefits from the government (Cobley, 2015; Lee & Chen, 2019; Phibbs et al., 2014), and the majority rely on this income as their primary source of income. However, this income is insufficient, and there is a need to subsidise this income with other means (Stough et al., 2016; Zayas et al., 2017). In addition, government and Non-Governmental Organizations (NGOs) provide livelihood support to women with disabilities, replacing productive assets lost in the disaster or providing grants to replace lost merchandize (Cobley, 2015).

The study identified overarching opportunities that empower the livelihoods of women in post-disaster situations. As shown in Table 8.1, most of the authors have stressed that while there are many barriers to women engaging in livelihoods, they will get the opportunity to develop micro-human efforts with the engagement of livelihoods in the PDR. With the support for their livelihoods, women gain access to the resources, skills and opportunities for self-employment and self-sufficiency (Cobley, 2015; Pakjouei et al., 2021; Renuka & Srimulyani, 2015; Roy, 2021; Roy & Mathbor, 2021). These assistances may take various forms, including vocational training, access to credit and financial services, support for business development, market links and access to productive assets such as tools and equipment. Women with a secure livelihood are better positioned to contribute to the recovery process actively. They can invest their skills and efforts in creating small businesses, agricultural activities, and providing services in their communities. This empowerment not only helps to rebuild their lives but also contributes to the overall recovery and resilience of the community (Pakjouei et al., 2021; Perera-Mubarak, 2013). As a result, further research on the impacts and strategies to enhance livelihoods in order to improve the micro-human efforts of women is required to reap the maximum benefits of post-disaster programmes in the Sri Lankan context.

8.2.2 Strategies to Promote Livelihoods for Women in the Sri Lankan Post-Disaster Context

People require a regular income and access to a stable source of livelihood in addition to a place to reside to settle and continue with their lives (Sadiqi et al., 2017). Restoring livelihood sources in affected communities is crucial for both people's safety and the long-term viability of PDR efforts. Moreover, post-disaster livelihood strategies should be able to function once some sense of normalcy has been restored (Eadie et al., 2020). Table 8.2 depicts 14 distinct strategies for strengthening the livelihoods of women in the post-disaster context in Sri Lanka. All 14 suggested strategies are essential and can be applied to improve the livelihoods of both women and disabled women.

Several identified strategies are related to skills, knowledge and capacity development and training opportunities for the vulnerable community groups (S1, S2, S3, S4, S7). New knowledge and skills acquired from the training programmes will build capacity and provide an alternative means of generating income after the community is re-established (Sadiqi et al., 2017). Mainstreaming gender inclusion within the PDR policies, structures and livelihood opportunities are identified as key strategies (S5, S6, S8, S9) to address the gender issues in livelihoods in the post-disaster context (King et al., 2019; Lord et al., 2016; Pakjouei et al., 2021; Pincha, 2016; Racioppi & Rajagopalan, 2016; Renuka & Srimulyani, 2015; Sohrabizadeh, 2016). The most serious issue raised by many respondents is the absence of gender inclusion in the Sri Lanka Disaster Management Act (2005), which is the primary legal document for disaster management in Sri Lanka. While respondents revealed that the Sri Lankan policy environment has shortcomings in terms of operationalizing "inclusion", global policies and influences that are associated with funders can be used to motivate national and local governments, as well as other stakeholders, to ensure access, participation, and non-discrimination of women in PDR programmes. Further, promoting sustainable livelihood approaches (S5) can provide a valuable opportunity for women to mitigate societal attitudinal barriers (S14). Empowering collaboration (S11) and involving communities in decision-making (S13) are essential strategies.

8.3   Research Methodology

This study adopts a qualitative research approach. Initially, a narrative literature review was carried out to provide the basis for the study, followed by a systematic literature review by adopting Preferred Reporting Items for Systematic Reviews and Meta-Analyses (PRISMA) (Page et al., 2021), mainly to explore the research question "What are impacts on the livelihood options of women in the post-disaster context?" which was developed using the PICO (Population, Intervention, Comparison, and Outcomes) approach (Richardson et al., 1995). The PICO approach offers a solid foundation for developing the research question and establishing the key terms for the literature review based on the research question terms. Following the PICO approach, the first step was to create a logic grid and conduct an initial search utilizing the grid's key terms, as displayed in bold italics in Table 8.3. Alternative terms for the key terms were then found by evaluating the titles and abstracts of the papers obtained in this first search, which were used to construct a comprehensive logic grid. According to Melnyk and Fineout-Overholt (2011), "Comparison" is the only optional component in the PICO approach. Consequently, the Comparison component was neglected as there is no comparator, an alternative to compare with the intervention in the research question.

Table 8.2 Strategies to Overcome the Barriers Attached to Livelihoods Development in the Post-disaster Context

Strategies	Literature Sources	Number of Citations		Rank
		Number	%	
S1. Promote skill identification programmes	(Cuaton, 2019b; Eadie et al., 2020; Jamshed et al., 2019; King et al., 2019; Lord et al., 2016; Pakjouei et al., 2021; Renuka & Srimulyani, 2015; Sadiqi et al., 2017; Zayas et al., 2017)	9	30%	1
S2. Promote vocational training programmes	(Cuaton, 2019b; Eadie et al., 2020; Jamshed et al., 2019; Lord et al., 2016; Pakjouei et al., 2021; Sadiqi et al., 2017)	6	20%	7
S3. Capitalize the resources and knowledge available within communities	(Cuaton, 2019a, 2019b; Eadie et al., 2020; Lord et al., 2016; Pakjouei et al., 2021; Sohrabizadeh, 2016; Zayas et al., 2017)	7	23%	5
S4. Promote livelihood transformation programmes	(Cuaton, 2019b; Eadie et al., 2020; Lee & Chen, 2019; Lord et al., 2016; Pakjouei et al., 2021; Renuka & Srimulyani, 2015; Roy, 2021; Roy & Mathbor, 2021)	8	27%	3
S5. Promote sustainable alternative livelihoods	(Cuaton, 2019b; Eadie et al., 2020; Renuka & Srimulyani, 2015; Zayas et al., 2017)	4	13%	11
S6. Introduce women/ disability-sensitive livelihood opportunities	(Eriksson et al., 2017; Lord et al., 2016; Zayas et al., 2017)	3	10%	12
S7. Promote skill/ capacity-building programmes	(Chhotray, 2022; Cobley, 2015; Cuaton, 2019b; Greenough, 2018; Lord et al., 2016; Pakjouei et al., 2021; Renuka & Srimulyani, 2015; Roy & Mathbor, 2021; Sohrabizadeh, 2016)	9	30%	1
S8. Strengthen policies and social structures	(Cuaton, 2019a, 2019b; King et al., 2019; Lee & Chen, 2019; Phibbs et al., 2014; Renuka & Srimulyani, 2015; Roy & Mathbor, 2021; Sohrabizadeh, 2016)	8	27%	3
S9. Mainstream gender inclusion	(King et al., 2019; Lord et al., 2016; Pakjouei et al., 2021; Pincha, 2016; Racioppi & Rajagopalan, 2016; Renuka & Srimulyani, 2015; Sohrabizadeh, 2016)	7	23%	5
S10. Mobilize kin networks	(Clissold et al., 2020; Cuaton, 2019b; Perera-Mubarak, 2013; Phibbs et al., 2014; Stough et al., 2017)	5	17%	10

(Continued)

Table 8.2 (Continued)

Strategies	Literature Sources	Number of Citations		Rank
		Number	%	
S11. Empower and enhancing collaboration with government and non-government organizations	(Clissold et al., 2020; Lord et al., 2016; Roy, 2021)	3	10%	12
S12. Lobby for needs and rights	(Clissold et al., 2020; Lord et al., 2016)	2	7%	14
S13. Involve them in the decision-making process	(Cuaton, 2019b; King et al., 2019; Lord et al., 2016; Renuka & Srimulyani, 2015; Roy & Mathbor, 2021; Sohrabizadeh, 2016)	6	20%	7
S14. Mitigate attitudinal barriers in the society	(King et al., 2019; Lord et al., 2016; Pincha, 2016; Racioppi & Rajagopalan, 2016; Renuka & Srimulyani, 2015; Sohrabizadeh, 2016)	6	20%	7

Table 8.3 Logic Grid for Key Terms with Alternative Terms

Population	Intervention	Comparison	Outcome
Post-disaster Context	Women	–	Livelihood Options
Post-disaster phase	Gender		Livelihood
Post-disaster phase	Woman		Income-generation
Post-disaster situations	Women		Income-generating options
	Female		Economic activities
Post-disaster period			Job opportunities
Post-disaster period			Employment
Post-crisis			
Post-crisis			
Disaster response			
Disaster recovery			
Disaster rebuilding			
Disaster reconstruction			
Disaster rehabilitation			
Disaster relief phase			
Disaster early recovery			

The search strategy illustrated in Figure 8.1 was developed using the terms identified in Table 8.3. In the search strategy, quotation marks (" ") were used to derive the articles to match the exact terms used within, and the wildcard characters (* and ?) were used to identify different variations of a specific term. Moreover, the identified terms are combined using Boolean operators: "OR" and "AND".

(livelihood* OR "livelihood option*" OR "income generation" OR "income generate* option*" OR job* OR "job opportunity*" OR employment) AND (gender OR woman OR female*) AND ("post-disaster" OR "post-crisis" OR "post-disaster" OR "post-crisis" OR "disaster response" OR "disaster recovery" OR "disaster rehabilitation" OR "disaster rebuilding" OR "disaster reconstruction" OR "disaster relief" OR "disaster early recovery")

Then, the literature search focused on articles from two highly recognized databases, Web of Science and Scopus. Utilizing the developed search strategy, the literature search was carried out under some filter options, as displayed in Table 8.4.

All records generated from the databases were imported to Mendeley software for screening purposes. The complete search found 68 articles: 27 and 41, respectively, from the Web of Science and Scopus databases. Moreover, 11 relevant articles found from "out of the search system" (such as reports) were manually added. Three screening processes were initiated to collect the necessary resources for the systematic literature review. In the first screening, 16 duplicates were removed; in the second screening, 11 irrelevant to the context were removed; in the third

---

(livelihood* OR "livelihood option*" OR "income generation" OR "income generate* option*" OR job* OR "job opportunity*" OR employment) AND (gender OR woman OR female*) AND ("post disaster" OR "post crisis" OR "post-disaster" OR "post-crisis" OR "disaster response" OR "disaster recovery" OR "disaster rehabilitation" OR "disaster rebuilding" OR "disaster reconstruction" OR "disaster relief" OR "disaster early recovery")

Figure 8.1 Final Search Strategy

Table 8.4 Utilized Filter Options

Category	Filters
Years	2012–2022
Article type	Research articles, Proceedings papers, Early cite/Articles on early access, books
Search fields	Title, Abstract, Keywords
Language	English

screening, 22 articles were removed as they did not specifically focus on women's livelihoods following disaster situations. Hence, 30 articles were derived for the qualitative analysis at the end of the screening process, as illustrated in Figure 8.2.

According to Ritchie et al. (2014), a qualitative research approach is ideal for gathering opinions and information from people based on their experience and will be helpful in situations where an in-depth analysis of the gathered primary data is necessary. Merriam (2019) found that interviews are ideal for two-way information exchanges. Interviews are one of the best ways of data collection in a qualitative study because they facilitate the generation of new ideas and perceptions linked to a particular matter (Azungah, 2018). In this study, the interviewees were selected using purposive sampling based on their knowledge and experience of facing and handling post-disaster situations as stakeholders and their willingness to participate in the interviews. Naderifar et al. (2017) claimed that no specific sample size is required in a qualitative study. Therefore, in this study, the sample size was determined based on saturation principles, a process by which researchers collect and analyse the data until no new details emerge (Sohrabizadeh, 2016). Data saturation

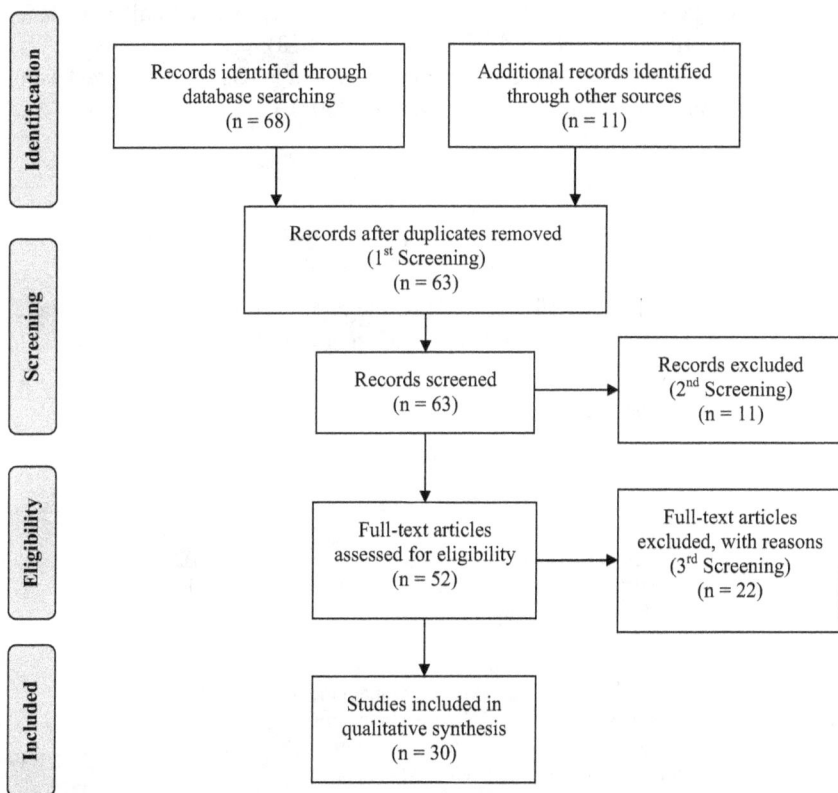

Figure 8.2 Study Selection Flow Diagram

was reached after the 16th interview, but one additional interview was done to ensure no new findings came to light. As such, 17 interviews were (R1–R17) conducted with key stakeholders, as shown in Table 8.5.

According to Rowley (2012), semi-structured interviews allow the participants to explain the significance of a subject through their thoughts, experiences, and viewpoints. In this research, each semi-structured interview (via physical visits/online meetings/telephone conversations) lasted 60–90 minutes.

In addition, a Focus Group Discussion (FGD) consisting of purposefully selected ten women participants (WFG1 – WFG10) from a flood-prone area (Wennawatta, Sri Lanka) was carried out to get insights from the women about their livelihood. Focus Group Discussion (FGD) is commonly used as a qualitative approach to grasp social issues thoroughly (Nyumba et al., 2018). This method is an excellent approach to bringing people from similar backgrounds or experiences together to discuss a specific topic of interest. Focus groups gather information on collective opinions and the meanings underpinning such opinions (Mishra, 2016). Although it is generally accepted that between six and eight participants are sufficient in an FGD (Krueger & Casey, 2000), Fern (1982) and Mendes de Almeida (1980) had reported as few as four and as many as fifteen participants. Ten participants are thus regarded as significant enough to obtain a range of opinions while small enough not to become disordered or fractured (Nyumba et al., 2018).

The collected data from stakeholder interviews and FGDs were analyzed using code-based content analysis (Hsieh & Shannon, 2005).

8.4   Findings and Discussion

8.4.1   Stakeholders and the Governance Process in Promoting Livelihoods for Women in the Sri Lankan Post-disaster Context

In Sri Lanka, according to all respondents, the commanding line between stakeholders was found to be a top-down approach that originates from the national to

Table 8.5 Profile of the Interview Respondents

Respondent	Type of Organization/Area focused/Position of the interviewee	Years of experience
R1	National/Disaster/Top Management	12
R2	National/Disaster/Top Management	02
R3	National/Disaster/Top Management	13
R4	NGO/Disaster/Top Management	16
R5	National/Disaster Research/Scientist	09
R6	National/Disaster Research/Top Management	25
R7	Divisional/Disaster/Middle Management	14
R8	Divisional/Disaster/Middle Management	12
R9	National/Women/Top Management	25
R10	National/Disabled/Middle Management	07
R11	INGO/Women and Disabled/Top Management	22
R12-R17	Local/Community Representation	N/A

the local level. However, information is transferred from the local to the national levels via a bottom-up approach. Figure 8.3 depicts the command and communication lines between national-level stakeholders and the community in the post-disaster governance process to boost women's livelihoods. In Figure 8.3, national, district/provincial, and local stakeholders are represented by red diamonds, green boxes, and yellow circles, respectively.

As demonstrated in Figure 8.3, if there is two-way communication between stakeholders, those stakeholders are linked by a double arrow-headed line. All respondents declared that top-down and bottom-up approaches should be used in tandem to maximize the effectiveness of PDR programmes in promoting livelihood assistance. Respondent 2 (R2) emphasized that *"both these approaches are needed to manage post-disaster situations, while the information coming from the bottom level is important to improve rebuilding activities and resilience"*. R3 stressed that *"communication within and between the levels should be strengthened to accomplish the PDR needs"*. Accentuating that the needs and capabilities of women are usually overlooked in most of the post-disaster livelihood rebuilding programmes in Sri Lanka, R7 critiqued, *"there is a loophole in community participation in decision making associated with PDR programmes. Even though the community has many valuable opinions, practitioners only consider the top-level orders"*. Adding to the conception that many PDR programmes are not as successful as expected, R10 stated, *"While some livelihood rebuilding initiatives include women, their long-term viability is uncertain since the initiatives are not tailored to support their real needs and capacities"*. As such, the findings reveal the current governance process is inadequate to improve the livelihoods of vulnerable community groups and further emphasize that a proper mechanism for increasing community

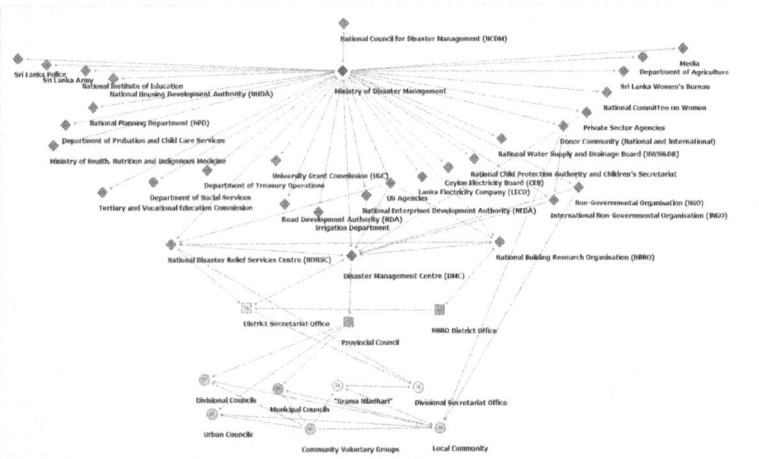

Figure 8.3 Current Communication and Commanding Lines between the Stakeholders Involved in PDR

engagement in decision-making should be established to meet the post-disaster livelihood needs of women successfully.

8.4.2 Barriers Faced by Women in Engaging Livelihoods Following a Disaster in Sri Lanka

According to Lord et al. (2016), disasters have direct and indirect impacts on the livelihoods of those affected, and interruptions and dislocations of livelihoods tend to have more severe effects on women. One of the critical barriers collectively mentioned by the FGD participants was the lack of sustainable job opportunities. It was mentioned that many of them are forced into low-paying jobs or are limited to traditional roles, which do not provide a stable income. Agreeing with that, WFG6 stressed that *"as women, we have to bear the burden of domestic and caregiving responsibilities, leaving little time for income-generating activities"*.

In addition, different ethnic communities in Sri Lanka navigate their day-to-day lives based on different social class positionings, and class hierarchies are likely to further influence the restrictions to engage in livelihoods. R13, a man from the Malay (minority Muslim) community, emphasized that *"women's inability and unwillingness to involve even in home-based economic activities (B4) can be due to cultural norms in this society"*. This kind of alienation from the community has increased household financial difficulties following disasters. In contrast, Tanyag (2018) stressed that despite cultural barriers, many women and young girls chose to engage in sex work (B20) as a source of income in the post-disaster setting, a topic seldom acknowledged in the Sri Lankan context. Sex work is considered a coping mechanism in these contexts because it is utilized to assure survival, not just the survival of the women involved as a livelihood but also the survival of their dependents, especially in widowed households. However, no empirical results were revealed concerning sex work as a means of livelihood. People with disabilities experience enhanced physical and livelihood problems after disasters. According to all respondents, there is a lack of attention in PDR programmes in Sri Lanka for comprehensive physical care for disabled women. Zayas et al. (2017) claimed that with their functional limitations, people with disabilities found it even more challenging to overcome this situation due to limited opportunities to access employment and a lack of disability-sensitive support (B4) to rebuild their livelihoods in the post-disaster recovery phase.

The fundamental cause of most barriers is the government's failure to prioritize women's inclusion in PDR efforts. R5 stated that *"these initiatives will not succeed until it is listed as a high priority action or a cross-cutting matter"*. However, according to most respondents, some NGOs successfully targeted women due to their close collaboration with grassroots communities. R4 stated that *"as an NGO, gender and disability inclusions are two cross-cutting themes for our organisation. Therefore, we cannot avoid these two complementary themes in any of our projects. Even in the COVID-19 response, those two aspects were always prioritised"*. Though there is livelihood support, women, especially the disabled, face practical limitations and find it extremely difficult to juggle their limitations with the training and livelihood support offered by PDR programmes (Eadie et al., 2020; Zayas et al., 2017). Hence, sustainable livelihood strategies must cater for these diverse needs.

8.4.3 *Enhancing Micro-human Efforts of Women via Livelihood Opportunities in PDR in Sri Lanka*

Strengthening women's micro-human efforts through livelihood opportunities in the PDR context in Sri Lanka is an important and influential initiative. Women's empowerment and participation in economic activities are essential for their own well-being and the overall development and resilience of communities and nations.

It was revealed that prior to the 2017 severe flood incident in Sri Lanka, several women did not leave their homes for work. However, in the aftermath of the disaster, many women received tailoring and sewing training with the help of government and non-government organizations, which resulted in them engaging in self-employment and earning as much as their male counterparts. WFG2 stated, *"I used to feel so dependent before, but now, with my small sewing business, I have my own source of income"*. These livelihood support programmes serve as crucibles where women's self-reliance is formed. As women acquire skills that enable income generation, a profound change was visible. In addition to financial benefits, this new self-reliance stimulated autonomy and improved control over their destinies.

Similarly, Renuka and Srimulyani (2015) stated that, after the tsunami in Indonesia, some women lost their livelihoods and were compelled to start new types of employment to earn money for their daily life needs due to the support and motivation that came from their families and networks with other affected women. They further state that, in many instances, religion has acted as the best source of strength for the survivors who had lost their families and properties. However, all the participants in the FGD claimed that the continuation of the support given by the authorities with necessary resources for the improvement of their livelihoods is lacking. WFG5 stated that *"as a self-employed person, I create paper cards. Nevertheless, after the disaster, everything got ruined, and I did not get any support to restart my employment. The government also took our information, but no one got back to us until now"*. Results illustrated that the lack of support to restart employment after the disaster can have long-term economic consequences for individuals and their families. It is also essential to support self-employed individuals to help them rebuild their livelihoods after a disaster. Astill and Miller (2018) claim that one aspect of micro-human efforts, self-help, refers to communities with the material and psychological resources necessary to be resilient in the context of the PDR. Therefore, to leverage such micro-human efforts of women, the continued support with necessary resources from the government and NGOs is crucial in the PDR context in Sri Lanka.

Perera and Mubarak (2013) claimed that some women could not resume their traditional income-generation activities in the post-tsunami development stage in Sri Lanka and were also disadvantaged in commencing alternative economic activities. While acknowledging this, R17 asserted that the changing geography of post-disaster relocation had affected women's access to livelihoods. Moreover, due to a lack of awareness of the importance of incorporating gender inclusion into rebuilding, local authorities do not consider gender inclusion in rebuilding to be a priority in PDR programmes. Further, the community is not engaging and demanding their essential needs but simply accepting the aid given by the government, even if it is not benefiting their livelihoods. For instance, R1 mentioned,

> *A partially disabled woman, a tailor before the disaster, stated that she had requested a sewing machine from local officers to restart her livelihood but was given a goat. This resulted in her finding a way to earn money to feed the goats, which was an additional burden for her.*

R1 added that corruption in the local governance system contributed to the mismatches between community demands and supplies and that the local-level governance takes a top-down approach ignoring the real needs of the grassroots communities.

In contrast, R3 stated that *"due to the accountability in the system, committing any fraudulent activities by the government officers are highly restricted. The work carried out by government and NGOs are officially reported to UN agencies, which are then validated for accuracy and accountability"*. These responses also show contradictory opinions among the stakeholders who are implementing the policies, but there is also evidence that disasters can sometimes create opportunities for new and different livelihood strategies for women (Perera-Mubarak, 2013).

8.4.4   Strategies to Promote Livelihoods for Women to Enhance the Micro-human Efforts in the Sri Lankan Post-disaster Context

Micro-human efforts include individual efforts, particularly from women, to actively engage in various self-directed activities and practices that contribute collectively to disaster recovery and development in the community. These efforts enable individuals to become agents of change and resistance, enabling them to shape their futures in the face of difficulties. Therefore, livelihood engagement is of the highest importance to women in post-disaster recovery situations, as it plays a crucial role in enabling and empowering them to develop micro-human efforts.

As elaborated by many of the respondents (both stakeholders and FGD participants), the identified strategies related to skills, knowledge and capacity development and training opportunities (S1, S2, S3, S4, S7 [refer Table 8.2]) act as essential tools for empowering women to become self-reliant. When women gain skills for earning money, it brings about a significant change in their lives. This newfound ability to support themselves not only contributes financially but also enhances their independence and gives them more control over their lives. This positive development can also help them face difficulties in future disaster events. In addition, when women are engaged with a proper livelihood and get a sustained income, they gain confidence, which sets them on a path of self-empowerment. This personal growth often has external positive effects. According to R3, *"empowered women become leaders of their communities, contribute to better recovery discussions and achieve both comprehensive and long-lasting outcomes".*

However, in Sri Lanka, the road to exploiting the potential of aid to livelihoods to improve micro-human efforts is filled with many challenges and strengthening policies and social structures, mainstreaming gender inclusion, empowering and enhancing collaboration with government and NGOs can primarily ameliorate the existing status to develop micro-human efforts of disaster-affected women.

8.5 Conclusions and Recommendations

This study investigated enhancing the micro-human efforts of women via livelihood opportunities in the post-disaster rebuilding context in Sri Lanka while exploring the barriers that women face, opportunities, stakeholder engagement, and the existing governance process in promoting livelihoods in post-disaster contexts. In the empowerment process, women needed to be facilitated for micro-human efforts. Since PDR can offer opportunities to build disaster-resilient communities, it is wise to seek hidden resilience displayed by communities affected by disasters themselves.

A significant challenge for the study was the lack of disaggregated data related to the livelihoods of women for specific locations and regions; in this instance, Sri Lanka and South Asia. This is a broader problem common to the region and is critical to advance in-depth research and gain insights into the problems associated with gender inclusion in post-disaster development strategies.

Strategies to promote livelihoods were identified through literature analysis and primary data considering the status of the post-disaster context and the associated governance process. The findings revealed that the government's inability to incorporate and, in some instances, prioritize gender inclusion in PDR efforts is the root cause of most of the barriers to involving women in Sri Lanka's livelihood opportunities. Though the government offers post-disaster livelihood assistance, the practical constraints that women face are not given attention.

Promoting inclusive livelihood assistance is vital to hasten the recovery of women in post-disaster settings. Limited gender-sensitive initiatives in Sri Lanka illustrate that women's recovery is multifaceted, gradual, complex, and require long-term continued support. If women are not protected from risk, they are in danger of falling back into poverty. The study also recommends the following:

a. Formulation of national policies that make gender concerns central in post-disaster development programmes.
b. Developing sex-disaggregated data that would effectively help address the concerns of women at every stage of the relief and reconstruction efforts.
c. Inclusivity of vulnerable communities' needs in recovery planning and post-disaster development.
d. Identification of specific needs and vulnerabilities of females, including female-headed households to provide adequate support.

e. Supporting community organizations, including local grassroots societies and networks to contribute to local decision-making processes so that the vulnerable community perspectives are included in mainstream development processes.

f. Informing both women and men and all local stakeholders on the importance of the inclusion of gender considerations in post-disaster development

The knowledge generated by this study, the proposed strategies, and recommendations can have significant implications for decision-makers such as disaster management policymakers in developing countries like Sri Lanka, as well as international development and aid agencies working globally to improve gender inclusion in the post-disaster context.

References

Astill, S., & Evonne, M. (2018). The trauma of the cyclone has changed us forever: Self-reliance, vulnerability and resilience among older Australians in cyclone-prone areas. *Ageing and Society, 38*(2), 403–429.

Azungah, T. (2018). Qualitative research: Deductive and inductive approaches to data analysis. *Qualitative Research Journal, 18*(4), 383–400. https://doi.org/10.1108/QRJ-D-18-00035

Badayos-Jover, M. B. P. (2017). Security in adversity: Highlighting coastal women's agency and efforts to organise after Haiyan. *Asian Fisheries Science, 30*(Special issue), 303–312.

Bang, H. N., & Few, R. (2012). Social risks and challenges in post-disaster resettlement: The case of Lake Nyos, Cameroon. *Journal of Risk Research, 15*(9), 1141–1157.

Chhotray, V. (2022). A supercyclone, landscapes of 'emptiness' and shrimp aquaculture: The lesser-known trajectories of disaster recovery in coastal Odisha, India. *World Development, 153.* https://doi.org/10.1016/j.worlddev.2022.105823

Clissold, R., Westoby, R., & McNamara, K. E. (2020). Women as recovery enablers in the face of disasters in Vanuatu. *Geoforum, 113*, 101–110.

Cobley, D. S. (2015). Typhoon Haiyan one year on: Disability, poverty and participation in the Philippines. *Disability and the Global South, 2*(3), 686–707.

Cuaton, G. P. (2019a). A post-disaster gendered value chain analysis on seaweed farming after Super Typhoon Haiyan in the Philippines. *Journal of Enterprising Communities, 13*(4), 508–524. https://doi.org/10.1108/JEC-11-2018-0091

Cuaton, G. P. (2019b). A post-disaster study of a women-led handicraft industry in rural Philippines. *Journal of Enterprising Communities-People and Places in the Global Economy, 13*(4), 489–507.

Drolet, J., Dominelli, L., Alston, M., Ersing, R., Mathbor, G., & Wu, H. (2015). Women rebuilding lives post-disaster: Innovative community practices for building resilience and promoting sustainable development. *Gender and Development, 23*(3), 433–448.

Eadie, P., Atienza, M. E., & Tan-Mullins, M. (2020). Livelihood and vulnerability in the wake of Typhoon Yolanda: Lessons of community and resilience. *Natural Hazards, 103*(1), 211–230.

Eriksson, H., Albert, J., Albert, S., Warren, R., Pakoa, K., & Andrew, N. (2017). The role of fish and fisheries in recovering from natural hazards: Lessons learned from Vanuatu. *Environmental Science and Policy, 76*, 50–58.

Fajarwati, A., Mei, E. T. W., Hasanati, S., & Sari, I. M. (2016). The productive and reproductive activities of women as form of adaptation and post-disaster livelihood strategies in Huntap Kuwang and Huntap Plosokerep. In V. K. Siswanto & U. F.

Kurniawati (Eds.), *Cities 2015: Inteligent planning towards smart ciities* (pp. 370–377). CRC Press.

Fern, E. F. (1982). The use of focus groups for idea generation: The effects of group size, acquaintanceship, and moderator on response quantity and quality. *Journal of Marketing Research, 19*(1), 1. https://doi.org/10.2307/3151525

Greenough, K. M. (2018). Pastoralists shifting strategies and perceptions of risk: Post-crisis recovery in Damergou, Niger. In W. L. Filho & J. Nalau (Eds.), *Climate change management* (pp. 129–142). Springer.

Hsieh, H.-F., & Shannon, S. E. (2005). Three approaches to qualitative content analysis. *Qualitative Health Research, 15*(9), 1277–1288.

Jamshed, A., Rana, I. A., McMillan, J. M., & Birkmann, J. (2019). Building community resilience in post-disaster resettlement in Pakistan. *International Journal of Disaster Resilience in the Built Environment, 10*(4), 301–315.

Kaluarachchi, Y. (2021). Gender inclusion and the impact on women's lives in post disaster build back better programmes in Sri Lanka. *International Journal of Mass Emergencies and Disasters, 39*(1), 43–64.

Khankeh, H., Nakhaei, M., Masoumi, G., Hosseini, M., Parsa-Yekta, Z., Kurland, L., & Castren, M. (2013). Life recovery after disasters: A qualitative study in the Iranian context. *Prehospital and Disaster Medicine, 28*(6), 573–579.

King, J., Edwards, N., Watling, H., & Hair, S. (2019). Barriers to disability-inclusive disaster management in the Solomon Islands: Perspectives of people with disability. *International Journal of Disaster Risk Reduction, 34*, 459–466.

Krueger, R. A., & Casey, M. A. (2000). *Focus groups: A practical guide for applied research* (4th ed.). SAGE Publications. https://doi.org/10.1037/10518-189

Lee, H.-C., & Chen, H. (2019). Implementing the Sendai Framework for disaster risk reduction 2015–2030: Disaster governance strategies for persons with disabilities in Taiwan. *International Journal of Disaster Risk Reduction, 41*, 101284.

Lord, A., Sijapati, B., Baniya, J., Chand, O., & Ghale, T. (2016). *Disaster, disability, & difference: A study of the challenges faced by persons with disabilities in post-earthquake Nepal*. United Nations Development Programme.

Melnyk, B. M., & Fineout-Overholt, E. (2011). *Evidence-based practice in nursing & healthcare: A guide to best practice*. Wolters Kluwer/Lippincott Williams & Wilkins.

Mendes de Almeida, P. F. (1980). A review of group discussion methodology. *European Research, 8*(3), 114–120.

Mendis, A. P. K. D., Disaratna, V., Thayaparan, M., & Kaluarachchi, Y. (2022). Policy-level consideration on marginalised communities in the post-disaster context: A desk study. In Y. G. Sandanayake & K. G. A. S. Waidyasekara (Eds.), *Proceedings of the 10th World Construction Symposium* (pp. 668–681). Ceylon Institute of Builders.

Mendis, A. P. K. D., Thayaparan, M., & Kaluarachchi, Y. (2020). Gender and disability inclusion in post-disaster rebuilding 'Build Back Better' programmes in Sri Lanka: A literature review. In Proceedings of the 13th FARU International Research Conference 2020 (pp. 81–88). Faculty of Architecture Research Unit (FARU), University of Moratuwa.

Merriam, S. B. (2019). *Qualitative research in practice: Examples for discussion and analysis* (S. G. Robin (ed.)). John Wiley & Sons, Inc.

Mishra, L. (2016). Focus group discussion in qualitative research. *TechnoLearn: An International Journal of Educational Technology, 6*(1), 1. https://doi.org/10.5958/2249 -5223.2016.00001.2

Naderifar, M., Goli, H., & Ghaljaie, F. (2017). Snowball sampling: A purposeful method of sampling in qualitative research. *Strides in Development of Medical Education, 14*(3), 1–4.

Nyumba, T. O., Wilson, K., Derrick, C. J., & Mukherjee, N. (2018). The use of focus group discussion methodology: Insights from two decades of application in conservation.

Methods in Ecology and Evolution, 9(1), 20–32. https://doi.org/10.1111/2041-210X.12860

Oloruntoba, R., & Asare-Doku, W. (2021). Self-reliance in disaster recovery: A systematic literature review 1990–2019. *International Journal of Mass Emergencies & Disasters, 39*(1), 11–42. https://doi.org/10.1177/028072702103900102

Page, M. J., McKenzie, J. E., Bossuyt, P. M., Boutron, I., Hoffmann, T. C., Mulrow, C. D., Shamseer, L., Tetzlaff, J. M., Akl, E. A., Brennan, S. E., Chou, R., Glanville, J., Grimshaw, J. M., Hróbjartsson, A., Lalu, M. M., Li, T., Loder, E. W., Mayo-Wilson, E., McDonald, S., ... Moher, D. (2021). The PRISMA 2020 statement: An updated guideline for reporting systematic reviews. *Systematic Reviews, 10*(1), 89. https://doi.org/10.1186/s13643-021-01626-4

Pakjouei, S., Aryankhesal, A., Kamali, M., Seyedin, H., & Heidari, M. (2021). Positive effects of earthquake from the perspective of people with physical disability in Iran. *International Journal of Disaster Resilience in the Built Environment, 12*(2), 157–169.

Perera-Mubarak, K. N. (2013). Positive responses, uneven experiences: Intersections of gender, ethnicity, and location in post-tsunami Sri Lanka [Respuestas positivas, experiencias desparejas: Intersecciones de género, etnicidad, y ubicación en el Sri Lanka post tsunami]. *Gender, Place and Culture, 20*(5), 664–685.

Phibbs, S., Good, G., Severinsen, C., Woodbury, E., & Williamson, K. (2014). What about us? Reported experiences of disabled people related to the Christchurch earthquakes. *Procedia Economics and Finance, 18*, 190–197.

Pincha, C. (2016). Gender differential impacts of the 2004 tsunami. In L. Racioppi & S. Rajagopalan (Eds.), *Women and disasters in South Asia: Survival, security and development* (1st ed., pp. 24–63). Taylor and Francis.

Racioppi, L., & Rajagopalan, S. (Eds.). (2016). *Women and disasters in South Asia: Survival, security and development* (1st ed.). Taylor and Francis.

Renuka, R., & Srimulyani, E. (2015). Women after the tsunami: Impact, empowerment and changes in post-disaster situations of Sri Lanka and Aceh, Indonesia. *Asian Journal of Women's Studies, 21*(2), 192–210. https://doi.org/10.1080/12259276.2015.1062277

Richardson, W. S., Wilson, M. C., Nishikawa, J., & Hayward, R. S. (1995). The well-built clinical question: A key to evidence-based decisions. *ACP Journal Club, 123*(3), 12–13.

Ritchie, J., Lewis, J., Nicholls, C. M., & Ormston, R. (2014). Analysis in practice. In *Qualitative research practice: A guide for social science students and researchers* (pp. 295–343). SAGE Publications Ltd.

Robles, C. P. Q. (2019). *Gender equality and women's empowerment in disaster recovery.* https://www.gfdrr.org/recovery-hub

Rowley, J. (2012). Conducting research interviews. *Management Research Review, 35*(3/4), 260–271.

Roy, S. (2021). *Climate change and gendered livelihoods in Bangladesh.* Routledge.

Roy, S., & Mathbor, G. M. (2021). Post-cyclone (Aila), transforming lives and gendered relations in Bangladesh. *Community Development Journal, 56*, 463–479.

Sadiqi, Z., Trigunarsyah, B., & Coffey, V. (2017). A framework for community participation in post-disaster housing reconstruction projects: A case of Afghanistan. *International Journal of Project Management, 35*(5), 900–912.

Sohrabizadeh, S. (2016). The neglect of women's capacities in disaster management systems in Iran: A qualitative study. *Indian Journal of Gender Studies, 23*(3), 467–480.

Sri Lanka Disaster Management Act, No. 13 of 2005, Parliament of The Democratic Socialist Republic of Sri Lanka. Gazette of The Democratic Socialist Republic of Sri Lanka

Stough, L. M., Ducy, E. M., & Holt, J. M. (2017). Changes in the social relationships of individuals with disabilities displaced by disaster. *International Journal of Disaster Risk Reduction, 24*, 474–481. https://doi.org/10.1016/j.ijdrr.2017.06.020

Stough, L. M., Sharp, A. N., Resch, J. A., Decker, C., & Wilker, N. (2016). Barriers to the long-term recovery of individuals with disabilities following a disaster. *Disasters, 40*(3), 387–410. https://doi.org/10.1111/disa.12161

Tanyag, M. (2018). Resilience, female altruism, and bodily autonomy: Disaster-induced displacement in post-haiyan Philippines. *Signs: Journal of Women in Culture and Society, 43*(3), 563–585. https://doi.org/10.1086/695318

United Nations. (2015). *Transforming our world: The 2030 agenda for sustainable development*. https://www.unfpa.org/sites/default/files/resource-pdf/Resolution_A_RES _70_1_EN.pdf

United Nations Development Programme. (2009). *Sri Lanka national report on disaster risk, poverty and human development relationship*. United Nations Development Programme.

United Nations Development Programme. (2021). *Gender equality*. https://www.lk.undp .org/content/srilanka/en/home/gender-equality.html

United Nations Office for Disaster Risk Reduction. (2015). *The sendai framework for disaster risk reduction 2015–2030*. https://www.undrr.org/publication/sendai-framework -disaster-risk-reduction-2015-2030

Wild, K. J. L., & Wiles, A. R. E. S. (2013). Resilience: Thoughts on the value of the concept for critical gerontology. *Ageing & Society, 33*(1), 137–158.

Zayas, J., Garcia, J.C., Lacsamana, L., Garcia, F.D. and Alburo-Cañete, K.Z. (2017). Building back better: making inclusion work in disaster recovery in the aftermath of Typhoon Haiyan. Rizal: Women with Disability LEAP to Economic and Social Progress.

9 The Creation of Self-Resiliency Through Neighbours Helping Neighbours

An Example of Micro-Human Efforts in Disasters

Kevin Kupietz

9.1 Introduction

9.1.2 Populations Face Increasing Risk from Disasters

Disasters are not a new phenomenon in the world. After all a popular belief of the earth's beginning is a one big explosion that created the known universe (Wall, 2022). A popular theory later in history is that a large asteroid hit the earth with so much force that it obscured the sun. Consequently, it caused the occurrence of an ice age that killed off more than 50% of the planet's life, including all the dinosaurs (Than, 2017). Later one unexpected volcanic eruption from Mount Vesuvius destroyed the cities of Pompeii and Herculaneum (Bagley, 2017). The list can go on and on. In fact, there are multiple historical natural disasters that have happened that have taken tens of thousands of lives. When looking at technology or man-made disasters, such as war and conflict, the numbers rise even faster and further. While modern history has not seen extinction-level disasters such as the asteroid that killed the dinosaurs, the National Oceanic and Atmospheric Administration (NOAA) does show that the number of naturally occurring events has become more severe and more frequent in recent years (NOAA, 2022). See Figures 9.1 and 9.2.

It is easy to watch the evening news and dismiss the daily discussions and consequences of disasters as happening in other places, as they do not have a direct impact on the local community. Though factually, NOAA (2022) shows that all states have been directly affected by at least one or more of these major natural events (see Figure 9.3). Some disasters such as the COVID-19 pandemic of 2019–2022 have affected every community in the country. Other disasters, such as Hurricane Maria, which had a pronounced effect on Puerto Rico and other areas in 2017, left an indirect effect on the entire country, as the pharmaceutical industry in Puerto Rico was destroyed, causing shortages of lifesaving IV fluid bags across the country (Waleca, 2018). The bottom line is that all disasters are local and have the greatest effects locally as they occur, and no one is immune from potential devastating disasters.

In more than 60 years of data, there have been more than two thousand federally declared disasters in the United States, with the numbers continuing to rise (FEMA, 2022a). Every state in the country has been affected directly by a disaster at one point or another, as have most communities. Increasing trends in climate

DOI: 10.4324/9781003615903-13

1980-2021 United States Billion-Dollar Disaster Event Cost (CPI-Adjusted)

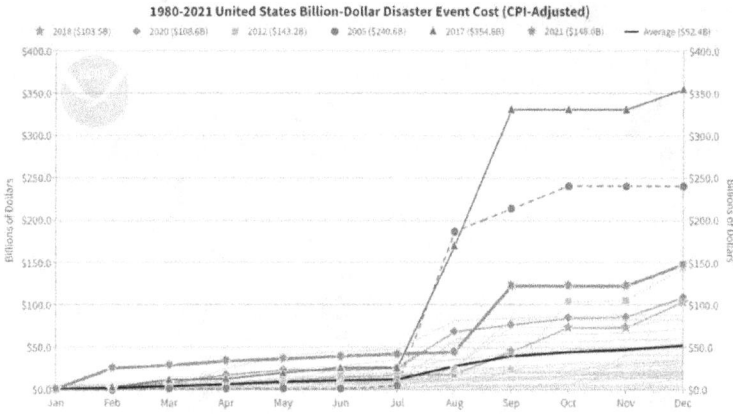

Figure 9.1 NOAA Graph of Billion-Dollar Events in the US by Year (Updated 8 April 2022). NOAA National Centers for Environmental Information (NCEI) US Billion-Dollar Weather and Climate Disasters (2022). https://www.ncei.noaa.gov/access/billions/, DOI: 10.25921/stkw-7w73

United States Billion-Dollar Disaster Events 1980-2021 (CPI-Adjusted)

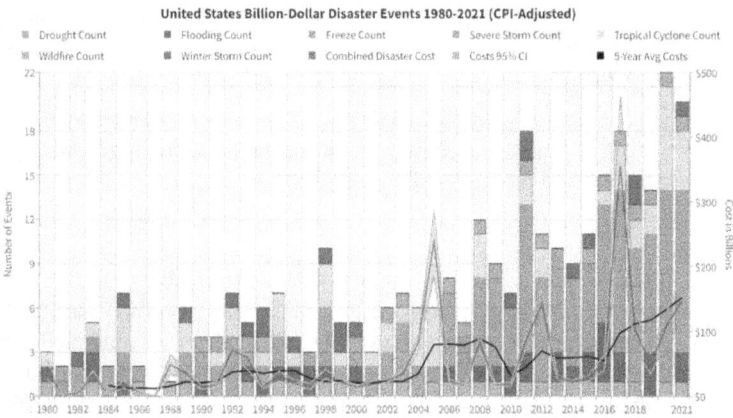

Figure 9.2 This shows a Breakdown of the Different Natural Events Since 1980 in Correlation to Their Adjusted Damages Per Year. NOAA National Centers for Environmental Information (NCEI) US Billion-Dollar Weather and Climate Disasters (2022). https://www.ncei.noaa.gov/access/billions/, DOI: 10.25921/stkw-7w73

change, population, technology, and other factors will result in these numbers continually rising through generations to come. FEMA has a public domain listing of all declarations, which will give the reader the disasters by state but also down to the county level (FEMA, 2022a) as well. Seeing the past declarations of an area can help people better assess the risk of an area through historical data. FEMA also maintains a public domain website of the daily situational report, where anyone can

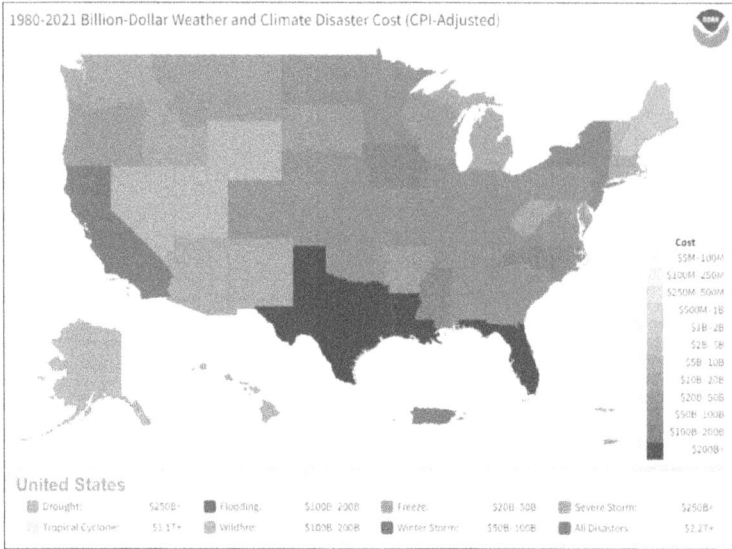

Figure 9.3 Graph by State of the Total Cost of Naturally Occurring Disasters from 1980–
2021. NOAA National Centers for Environmental Information (NCEI) US
Billion-Dollar Weather and Climate Disasters (2022). https://www.ncei.noaa
.gov/access/billions/, DOI: 10.25921/stkw-7w73

look and see what activities FEMA is monitoring and participating in on any given
day to better understand the risks (FEMA, 2022b).

*** Learning Activity *** Most people do not realize all the resources available to the public to help themselves as well as others before, during, and
after a disaster. One of those resources is the FEMA Daily Situational Report.
This report will show the reader what activities FEMA is monitoring and participating in, as well as show risk factors from things such as heat, weather,
and other known hazards. Go to FEMA Daily Situation Report Archive 2022
(disastercenter.com) and look at the situational report for today. Just for fun,
pick a past day such as your birthday and look to see what was happening on
that day. It is almost guaranteed that you will not find an empty day. ****

A survey by AICPA (2022) showed that while 61% of the American population
believed that they would be impacted by a natural disaster in the next 3–5 years,
37% admitted they were not sure what the financial implications to them would
be, and 71% stated the disaster would have a major or moderate effect on their
financial situation. These kinds of numbers demonstrate that the average person
will need help when faced with a disastrous situation. The question then becomes,
where does that help come from? Many people falsely believe that the help will

come from the federal government. While they will provide assistance with federally declared disasters, this help will take time to stage up and arrive. Once the help arrives, they do not take over the scene as seen in most disaster movies. They are there to help the state and local authorities and provide support within their areas of authority.

9.2   Volunteers to the Rescue

The average person thinks that in the event of a disaster, hordes of trained professionals will swoop down on their communities and save the day, making everything right again. While there are trained professional disaster responders who will come in and do their best, they cannot do it alone. With the frequency and severity of disasters increasing and the number of professional disaster workers on the decline, there are not enough career disaster workers to solve all the community's disaster dilemmas on their own (Goodrick, Waltermire, Anderson, and Gravius, 2019). In some areas, such as the number of professional firefighters, the US is seeing an increase in the number of paid responders, but this is occurring to overcome the declining number of volunteer firefighters in the system. While the number of paid firefighters in the country has gone up from below 20% to above 30% in the past couple of decades, the fire service still only has an estimated 1,080,800 firefighters. Of this approximately 358,000 are paid with the remaining 722,800 being volunteers, donating their skills in their free time with no pay (NFPA, 2021). The volunteer firefighters are more prevalent in rural areas with some counties in the United States having no paid firefighters on staff. With cutbacks in government budgets, as well as a recently noted shrinking candidate pool for emergency responders, the country is seeing a decline in professional responders.

This trend can be seen in most large disasters with most disaster-related professions. The National Guard and power companies are examples of a paid workforce that is called in to help support the disaster responders from outside the disaster area. This workforce is limited, though, often leaving a need for more help. There are many volunteer organizations that also step up and send resources such as the American Red Cross, Team Rubicon, Salvation Army, faith-based groups, and civic organizations such as the NAACP. There are also many civilian volunteers who will self-deploy to disasters to offer their help, but this can be more problematic than helpful if not done properly within the command-and-control system of the local authorities at the disaster site.

History has shown that incidents such as the Oklahoma bombing, where more than 12,000 volunteers showed up, can be problematic (Souza, 2009). Volunteers outside the control system can cause safety and accountability concerns as well as consume vital resources needed for the incident response leading to inefficiency. Volunteer responders who are not properly briefed can walk unprepared into extremely dangerous areas. A hero for wanting to do the right thing and help, Doris Needham, a registered nurse who rushed to the scene of the Oklahoma bombing, was killed when she was struck in the head by a falling piece of concrete from the unstable building (Kifner, 2005). Good intentions do not protect would-be rescuers from harm. In fact, the nature of disasters often misrepresents the sense of urgency which increases the risk-taking of responders. Other research validates the idea that volunteers must be folded into the existing disaster accountability and coordination systems to remain safe and effective (Persson and Uhnoo, 2021).

9.2.1 Volunteers and Human Nature

Unlike movies that show people self-centred on survival, which is often seen in (Thormar et al, 2010) emergencies and disasters, there is the human capacity for wanting to help others. Staub (2014) points out that even infants a day after birth show signs of empathy towards the other infants they are housed with. The problem with helping is that the average person is not sure what to do to help or has incorrect ideas of how to help based on their experiences, normally from media platforms. Research has shown that helping others is often a function of motivation and confidence in the ability to help others (Staub, 2014). Meaning that if properly trained, the average person is more likely to step in and render help and do it safer and more efficiently.

The volunteer pool can make significant strides in helping themselves, their families, and their communities in disasters. When they are properly trained and come together in a coordinated effort while putting their unique talents and skillsets to bear on the problem at hand, individuals can certainly be effective on their own by being prepared to take care of themselves and their families in times of disaster. Under normal conditions, this will allow them to be self-sufficient for the FEMA (2022c) recommended 3–5 days. By not requiring outside assistance, this allows responders more time and resources to concentrate on those in more distress or who have lost more. If the self-sufficient individual is properly trained, they can coordinate with other resources, so they do not require assistance but are actually able to render aid to others allowing for a more efficient recovery for the community as a whole. As disasters continue to grow in severity and frequency, and organizations such as FEMA advocating for personal preparedness, one would think that the American population would be prepared for disasters. Unfortunately, research and observation does not support this idea. To make this more problematic is that as factors such as income and education level go down or functional needs go up the level of preparedness is less (Tala et al., 2014). This does provide an area for greater growth within the MHE idea of making efforts to strengthen self and family resilience, which allows more individual resources to volunteer and help others who may not be as prepared or able to help themselves.

In some respects, there will be differences in the views between how individuals and teams see their roles and resources when volunteering. For example, a rural group may find that they have more of a need for self-resilience than their suburban or urban counterparts due to the availability of formal infrastructure and resources (Flint and Stevenson, 2010). These differences allow volunteers to be better equipped to manage their local needs during an emergency (Souza, 2009). This helps cement the idea that all disasters are local, meaning that the organized volunteers who live in the area are going to know the people, the culture, and the issues better than outside help. They will know better who may need extra help, who is resistant to ask for help and know who the needed resources or skills may have to solve problems during emergencies than what out of the area responders would.

9.3 More to Disasters Than Just Response

When the average person thinks about helping in an emergency or disaster situation, the thought is normally about right then, when the fire is raging, or the flood waters are in the homes, etc. Helping people in disasters is much more than that though. In the Emergency Management (EM) field, we typically think of disasters in four phases: Mitigation, Preparedness, Response, and Recovery (see Figure 9.4). The response phase is the action phase of rescuing people and property from the event. The recovery phase is usually the most resource-intensive phase, and this involves bringing the community back to a sense of normalcy or to a pre-incident condition. This phase can take years for a full recovery to occur. Prior to the event, there is the mitigation phase, where actions are taken to eliminate or reduce the hazards from a future event. The mitigation phase is where the most efficiency can be accomplished. For example, a community that spends thousands of dollars to build a levee to protect it from flooding will save millions of dollars that a future flood could cause in structural damage alone. The fourth traditional phase is preparedness. In the preparedness phase, the community and individuals are becoming prepared to survive the future disaster. This is arguably the most important phase for the concept of neighbours helping neighbours, as in this phase they train on how to help each other, they provide stores of emergency supplies to get them through the disaster, develop plans for their families and more. A fifth phase that is becoming more popular in EM discussions is Prevention (see Figure 9.5). The prevention phase takes mitigation one step further and tries to prevent the disaster from

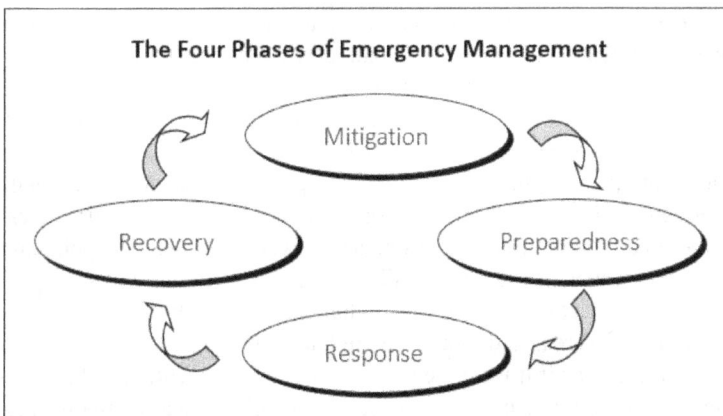

Figure 9.4 The Four Traditional Phases of Emergency Management. Figure from FEMA IS 10 Course is10comp.pdf (fema.gov)

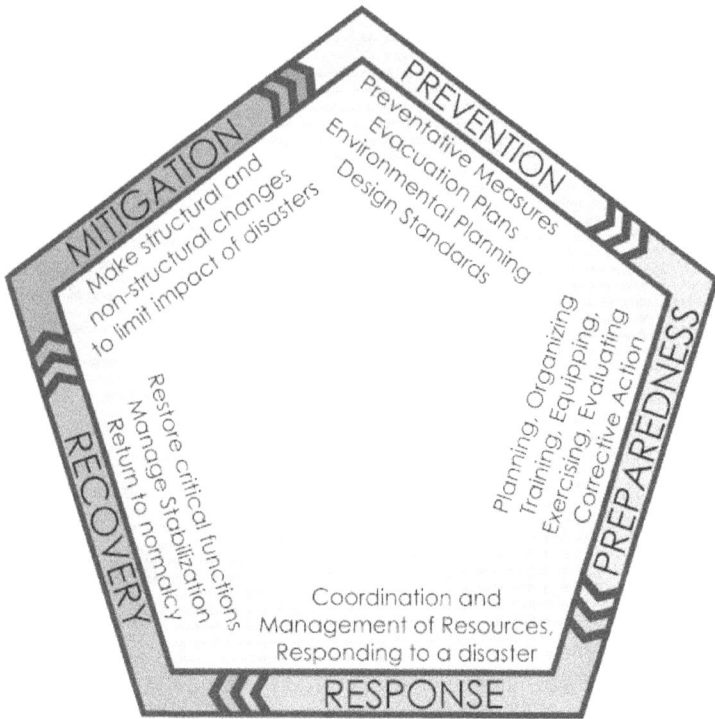

Figure 9.5 Five Phases of Disaster – Showing the Element of the Prevention Phase into the Newer Version of the Five Phases of the Disaster Cycle. Fig from Bexar County Texas EM the Five Phases of Emergency Management | Bexar County, TX – Official Website

happening at all. For example, a community that does not allow building on known floodplains is preventing homes from being destroyed there by future floods.

In discussing how individuals and communities can be more resilient, it is important to be able to talk about the actions that individuals can take in each of these stages to increase the overall effectiveness of micro human efforts in disaster resilience. For example, in the mitigation and prevention stages, individuals who are better educated in the hazards and corrective actions can use their voices more efficiently in community planning processes as well as support the political agendas that will best make for a more resilient community. In these phases, advocacy is an important concept. Japan's efforts to build a sea wall that stretches more than 14 feet tall in some areas and protects more than 220 miles of shoreline are still as controversial today as if it were the proper mitigation/prevention technique to utilize (Onishi, 2011). Some of the Japanese people believe that the sea wall is more distracting to the natural views than it will do good in the event of a major tsunami like the one that struck the coast in 2011 (Matanle, Littler, and Slay, 2019).

Preparedness phase is probably where the individual can make the most difference in the protection of themselves, their families, and community. In this phase, one would become educated on what needs to be done in the event of an emergency. They would begin to stock needed supplies while making and practising plans for disasters. This is also the phase where individuals can have the greatest impact by helping to pass this knowledge on to others and to advocate for proper preparedness techniques among their family and neighbours as the more people that are properly prepared for a disaster in the community, the more resilient the entire community becomes. As part of a volunteer organization, public education becomes a key tactic in helping others understand the importance and steps to take to be prepared.

For individuals to follow the recommendations of disaster preparedness experts such as FEMA ready.gov (2023) to do things such as stockpile emergency supplies to last at least 72 hours, have one gallon of drinking water on hand for each person per day, and have an emergency "go bag" ready for quick evacuation, etc. would all be great examples of individual micro-human efforts. These may seem like small and common-sense efforts, but the more people that are ready to be self-sufficient for 72 hours, the more resources and efforts by the rescue committee can be focused in other areas in order to have a quicker recovery time. Knowing what to do in a disaster is an important concept and can be another great example of MHEs. These educational opportunities could be as simple as a child teaching their grandparents how to use technology such as cellular phones to stay up to date with emergency announcements for a disaster. Other more complex skills can be incorporated such as people taking and/or teaching others how to administer basic first aid in order to save lives with delays in emergency response personnel.

Response phase is the phase that most people associate with disaster management. It is certainly an important phase as this is when life and property are in the most danger. In a disaster, the top three priorities in order are always: Life Safety, Incident Stabilization and Property Conservation. That means we protect all life, including those of the responders first and above all else. We take steps to keep the incident from getting any worse than it already is, and sometimes this means doing nothing that might make it worse such as injuring a responder. Finally, we try to protect property from further damage if possible. Properly trained individuals can do a lot to help in the accomplishment of these three priorities in emergencies and disasters, demonstrating the MHE concept. Take for example, an everyday occurrence of a person having a cardiac arrest where their heart stops. It is known that without oxygen, brain damage begins within 4–6 minutes. A couple of these minutes will be taken with the call to 911 for help and for emergency crews to get to their vehicle and enroute, then there is the drive time and the time to get to the patient, etc. Nationally, the benchmark response time for emergency personnel in normal circumstances is seven minutes. In rural areas, heavy traffic conditions, bad weather, disaster situations, etc., this time can be stretched out much longer. Even at seven minutes, brain damage begins to occur in the patient, and the chance of survival is going down every minute that chest compressions are not being performed. The solution is simple, though, and that is for bystander CPR to be performed while waiting for the emergency crew(s) can greatly enhance the survivability of the patient. Bystander CPR is a simple skill that can be learned in 10 minutes when properly taught. Simple acquired skills and knowledge with the confidence to use these skills allows the average person to be able to help their family, friends, and neighbours in the gap of time between the incident and the arrival of professional help. These heroic steps taken by everyday citizens are often the difference in a person living a normal life and not. When individuals work as part of an organized volunteer group, their outcomes become greatly increased as they can be deployed in force to areas that need help or the potential for help may be needed.

Recovery Phase is often the longest, most complex, and expensive phase of a disaster. In this phase, the primary goal is to bring a sense of normalcy back to those involved in the disaster. In many cases, this may take years. It is often seen that after a disaster the proper recovery steps are not taken causing cascading events. For example, a disaster can be an emotionally traumatic event that without proper care may cause issues for the survivor(s) for the rest of their lives. In the case of a building, if it is not properly rebuilt or fixed it could cause issues years later. For example, flooded structures must have water-damaged materials properly replaced or treated in order to keep from mold developing and long-term health effects happening to the building inhabitants years after the incident. Individuals properly educated on recovery efforts can not only make better choices in the recovery process for themselves and their families but can offer a wide array of helpful services to their communities. This help could be from manual labour helping people clear debris from their property, helping with rebuilding property, providing food, and sheltering, to helping people fill out documentation for federal or insurance aid.

It is known by emergency management experts that disaster response and recovery are expensive. The National Institute of Building Sciences (NIBS, 2018) report that for every one dollar spent on mitigation saves the US six dollars in disaster costs. This is an important but often overlooked point in the recovery process, as it is often more expensive to build an item back up more resilient rather than in the way it was. Hurricane Maria wreaked havoc on the poorly maintained island's electrical grid in Puerto Rico. It took almost an entire year to get power back to the entire island. While FEMA allocated over nine billion dollars to the system and the local utility earmarked another 12 billion, five years later Hurricane Fiona caused another island-wide power outage (Blaustein, 2022). Many believe that with a more proactive mitigation plan for the power grid as it was being rebuilt following Hurricane Maria, future damage from storms such as Fiona would have been minimized.

One of the common issues with a community in recovery is that outside help slows long before the need goes away. Volunteer organizations that take on community recovery missions can help the community through their actions but also through reminding everyone else of the needs of the community to get back to that pre-incident way of life.

A great example of recovery MHEs is the collection of donations. In disasters during the recovery phase often large collection pots of donations can be seen in surrounding communities as well as nationally and in some instances internationally.

While the "things" being donated are nice and needed, the things are a logistical problem to collect, transport to the scene, and disburse. The cold, hard truth is that a monetary donation to a reputable organization that can then can use that money to purchase needed supplies is almost always a better way. The combined donation can buy necessary items in bulk at a fraction of the cost of what the average person can buy and donate. The large purchase will also include the logistics of getting the supplies to the area in an organized fashion so that the receivers know exactly what is in the shipment and how to distribute the items most efficiently for use. The idea of monetary donations is a good example of how individuals can utilize their micro human effort combined with others to make a significant overall difference in the recovery of a community. These individual contributions are a significant part of the total recovery money allocated to an area and are often are the fastest to arrive and quickest to make a difference to the communities affected. The CDP (2019) reported in their study of US household giving that 30% of households reported giving monetary contributions to disasters and 12% of households reported volunteering in disasters during the study time frame. It should be noted that the study did find that this time of giving was time-sensitive in that only 5% of the participants gave to the ongoing recovery efforts the year after, and only 2% two years later. Often, money gathered for disaster aid is collected by non-governmental organizations (NGOs) rendering aid and/or assistance to the victims, but recently there has been an increase in local grassroots crowdfunding efforts gaining popularity due to their ease of giving. The CDP study (2019) showed the growing support of crowd funding with 10% of the respondents indicating that they gave their money through crowdfunding sources and that more than a third had positive perceptions of crowdfunding in disaster aid efforts, showing a growing trend in how people utilize their efforts to help others.

Mitigation Phase can sometimes be the hardest to understand and implement, but it is merely the stage in which action is taken to eliminate the hazard altogether or at least minimizing the effects of the hazard. Eliminating the hazard may be as simple as not building in a floodplain area so there are no structures at risk from flooding. An example of reducing the impact of a risk might be the great Japanese sea wall that has the intent of not stopping a tsunami from coming, but protecting the communities behind the wall from most tsunamis, thereby reducing the risk of living in those communities (Anders et al, 2016).

Previously, it was discussed that money spent on mitigation has an overall saving on the cost of recovery. This can be looked at from the micro human effort as well. This can be highlighted in the wildland fires in Maui in 2023 when one lone home trended on social media as being the lone survivor in the neighbourhood, with all of the other homes around it totally destroyed by the fire. This home, over 100 years old, had fire-resistant characteristics incorporated into the remodelling of the home, such as a metal roof and no trees or bushes within six feet of the structure (Farberov, 2023). These same simple tactics can be employed by individuals in their homes. Instead of using combustible materials such as pine straw or tree bark around the home, use non-combustible materials such as rock or gravel. Plan carefully where to plant new trees around a structure. Adult trees and shrubs may catch fire jeopardizing the house but depending on the situation, they may also cause issues if broken due to high winds or the roots can even weaken nearby structural components.

9.4   Community Emergency Response Teams (CERT): An Example of Neighbours Helping

9.4.1   Neighbours

A notable example of a volunteer group that can be mobilized to help from within a specific or be deployed from neighbouring communities is the nationally supported, locally implemented groups, Community Emergency Response Teams better known by their acronym CERT (FEMA, 2022c). These groups are comprised of local volunteers from all walks of life who come together in a coordinated effort to help their communities survive and recover from disasters. The critical activities of these groups allow the limited number of professional responders to focus on the more complex tasks of the disaster efforts. It is important to point out that for Micro-Human Efforts to be truly effective, they all must collectively connect to create a whole effort to more resilient communities. CERT programmes working in conjunction with efforts from local families and neighbourhoods all the way to the federal level have shown that these MHEs can help communities respond to and recover from disasters quicker than merely relying on governmental agencies to solve the problems in the community created by disasters.

The CERT model was first introduced in Los Angeles in the 1980s to mobilize local volunteers as a response capability to devastating earthquakes after local LA officials examined the actions of volunteer efforts in Japan and Mexico. In 1993, the Federal Emergency Management Agency (FEMA) expanded the CERT programme to an all-hazards approach and made it available to all communities nationally (Canal, 2019). Following the 9/11 terror attacks on the US, CERT saw an increase in involvement as more resources were put into the formation and training of CERT programmes across the country. Today CERT programmes can be seen in different forms in different types of communities including Campus – CERT on colleges and universities and Teen CERT in high schools in all the states and territories (FEMA, 2022c).

CERT Members see themselves in roles able to help and support traditional responders, but just as important, they have a critical role in helping to build capacity in non-disaster functions to better help their communities become more resilient (Flint and Stevenson, 2010). While community CERT programmes are made up of individuals from across the community of all different age groups, Teen and Campus CERTs specifically target the younger students at their respective high schools or college campuses. These teams are organized to provide coordinated efforts in the community and are led to teach lifesaving and preparedness skills while teaching the students teamwork, leadership, and community stewardship. Once started these tend to be continuing cycles for the students and many take on disaster roles long after their graduations.

An example of how capacity can be built for MHE in the education of the young is the teen and campus CERT programmes, as they teach disaster skills while instilling a sense of positive community stewardship as well. Summer camps for Teen CERT programmes have been popular and highly successful in teaching students to be able to help others in times of need, as well as showing them good community stewardship (Ready, 2019). These outlets have worked to teach and mentor students but also to provide useful and worthwhile activities for students on breaks. In some cases, these activities have been responsible for giving students a new purpose that previously could not be seen as to how they fit in to help. For example, CERT programmes working with underprivileged and at-risk teens have found success in motivating the participants to learn how to help others, as reported from a CERT programme working with high-risk teens in the Watts area of Los Angeles (Ossey, Sylvers, Oksuzyan, et al, 2017). Another programme that conducted the first coordinated CERT training camp for American Indian tribal communities saw similar success (Ready.gov, 2019). These types of programmes are breaking the traditional view of what a disaster worker looks like to the more modern concept that anyone can help in a disaster using their individual talents and efforts to help.

9.5 Campus CERT

Campus life is traditionally a time for young adults to set out on their own and experience different life opportunities. While campuses encourage students to try new experiences and learn new things, they do not always put the emphasis on learning how to help others in disasters. However, the numbers indicate that life-saving and preparedness skills should be treated as more of a mainstay than an outlier. The National Center for Research on Epidemiology of Disasters reports that natural disasters affect 218 million people worldwide, claiming 68,000 lives, and that droughts affect more than one billion people (Covington, 2021). They also report that in the last 25 years there have been almost 7,000 natural disasters that have killed more than 1.35 million people, showing that this is not a localized phenomenon in time. These incidents not only have a significant impact on life but also a significant impact on the economy of the communities and the families. The Insurance Information Institute reported that natural disasters caused estimated losses of 74.4 billion dollars for 2020 alone and that more than 20% of people have no emergency funds to help recover or rebuild after an event (Covington, 2021).

9.5.1 *Case Study for Campus CERT to Harness and Teach MHE in Emergency/ Disaster Management*

A Campus Community Emergency Response Team (Campus-CERT) could very well be the thing to help not only teach students about personal preparedness but also practice how to be advocates for more resilient communities. This is the belief of several university campuses, such as Elizabeth City State University (ECSU) in North Carolina. ECSU is a small Historically Black College and University (HBCU) campus in rural Northeast NC that is part of the University of North

Carolina System (UNC). In 2018, ECSU chartered its Campus CERT programme with the intent to utilize the programme to provide hands-on training for the university's newly formed Emergency Management undergraduate programme. Due to student support and interest, though, the programme quickly grew to something much larger. The following couple of years were hard for most academic organizations due to COVID-19 pandemic restrictions, but the ECSU CERT programme utilized this period of time as an opportunity to gain experience on how to help their communities. While the students still worked on their normal CERT skills, such as how to set up local hurricane shelters, CPR/First Aide etc. they branched out to help with the COVID-19 relief missions. ECSU CERT members helped with COVID-19 testing in the early stages and later wrote and received two COVID-19 safety grants, where students provided educational messaging on safety during a pandemic. Later, the students worked with another grant to help to provide emergency go bags that they handed out during COVID-19 testing and vaccination sites on and off campus. At one point during the pandemic, the students were notified about a local county school system that was not able to hold their annual elementary school safety fair due to virtual learning restrictions from COVID-19. The students brainstormed some ideas and created their own YouTube page where they posted homemade safety videos for children to view.

One of the remarkable things about a Campus CERT is the specialized resources and skills that a university has over other community groups. In the case of the ECSU CERT programme, it was well represented by more than 60 students from across the campus with a variety of skill sets by the summer of 2022, despite COVID-19. The group used these specialized skill sets to form subgroups within the team consisting of students with specialized skills. For example, one group specializes in the use of Unmanned Aircraft Systems (UAS) and works with students with skills in logistics, engineering, computers, etc., to start a Damage Assessment Response Team (DART). This asset was formed to be able to deploy at the request of a jurisdiction to provide damage assessments and infrastructure inspections from the air with a wide array of different drones and sensors. The team(s) can analyze the results in the mobile Command Van, which is outfitted with specialized computer analysis and communication equipment, or beam data back to the university lab where additional teams can help analyze the data. After attending specialized training with counter UAS through the Department of Homeland Security and FEMA, the team is now pursuing the technology and ability to provide counter UAS protection to area planned events. Other students have honed their skills in public education to help teach others how to prepare for emergencies and disasters, while other groups of students have focused their skills on business continuity and risk management to be able to help local organizations better prepare for disasters. Each student in the CERT programme is encouraged to follow their passions and those things they find meaning in to make communities safer. These micro-efforts have ranged from obtaining secure medication drop boxes for expired medication to disaster preparedness shows in the planetarium to planting trees and working with outdoor environmental use and resiliency projects. Each of these individual inspired projects gathered support from others within the CERT programme and turned into larger, more meaningful projects for community health and welfare.

The ECSU CERT programme saw many great accomplishments from helping with university and community events to unique training with US Marine and Coast Guard response aircraft, to developing university plans to respond to disasters (see Figure 9.6). Probably the greatest thing that the team has done to date was to offer a helping hand to other campuses wanting to start their own Campus CERT programmes. The CERT programme joined and became an active member in the HBCU EM Workforce Consortium with the goal of increasing the number of HBCU CERT members. Even the ECSU Chancellor engaged in the movement when she personally sent a letter recommending Campus CERT programmes and offered the help of her campus team to anyone that asked for it. ECSU is just one example of many success stories from everyday students and citizens with the desire to make a difference. The key to this success is the desire to help coupled with proper training and the coordination with the existing disaster management efforts.

The COVID-19 pandemic was a time when many organizations slowed or even came to a stop in their activities of micro-human efforts, but for others such as CERT groups, it was an opportunity for them to think outside of the box to provide care and services in new and different ways. The ECSU CERT programme, for

Figure 9.6 ECSU CERT – ECSU CERT Students Showing off Their New Shirts Donated to Them by a Benefactor. The Van in the Background Is the ECSU Damage Assessment Response Team (DIRT) Command Vehicle Serving Double Duty for COVID-19 Mitigation Activities. Photo by Kevin Kupietz

example, was able to thrive in their help to the community during this time through public education, helping with COVID-19 testing and vaccination efforts, as well as continuing their work in the more traditional disaster arenas. Working in small groups with the appropriate safety measures in place, the group demonstrated the micro-human effort ideology by conducting specialized public education through social media as well as in person. For example, the ECSU CERT students applied for and received two different COVID-19 mitigation mini-grants through the American College Health Association (ACHA) (see Figure 9.7). The first money, pre-COVID-19 vaccination availability, was utilized to help with a social media campaign and the initiation of the ECSU "Candy for COVID-19" project, where students in small groups went out and talked to people about pandemic safety. Those who engaged in conversation with the students were rewarded with candy. The programme was very effective in educating people about pandemic safety and local resources. A second grant awarded to the students by ACHA allowed for the Candy for COVID-19 project to continue with the addition of "COVID-19 Warrior" coins being awarded to participants who, in the conversation, mentioned that they had received their COVID-19 vaccination. Utilizing techniques like this and guidelines such as the ACHA (2022) COVID-19 guidelines for campuses, the ECSU CERT team was able to help the university not only open for face-to-face courses sooner than other institutions but also to keep the COVID-19 numbers low at the university.

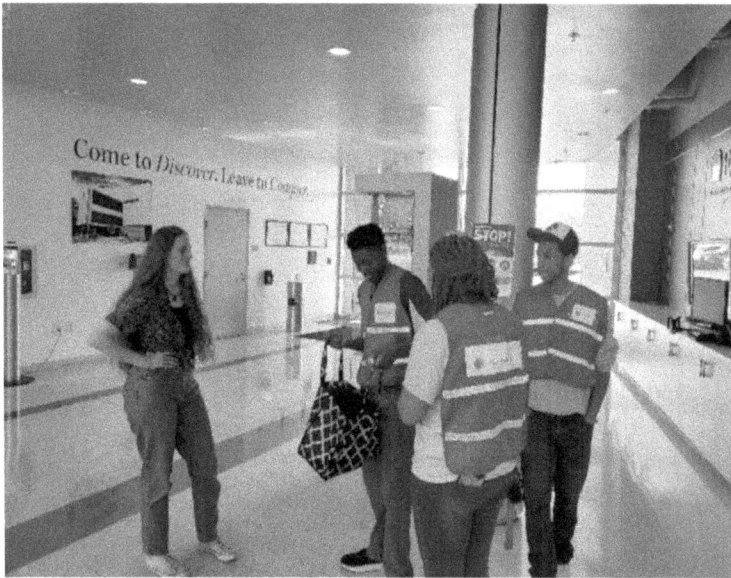

Figure 9.7 Public Education – ECSU CERT Students Conducting Door-to-Door Public Education on Campus. This Is One of the Many Activities that the Students Regularly Undertake to Increase the Disaster Preparedness Knowledge. Photo by Kevin Kupietz

9.6 The Future of Volunteers and Disasters Response

The United States was founded on the principles of volunteerism, from the volunteer Revolutionary War soldiers to the recognized father of the American Volunteer Fire Service, Benjamin Franklin, and on. Even though Congress stepped in for some individual events, such as the Portsmouth, New Hampshire, fire of 1803, where they passed a temporary law suspending the collection of bonds from merchants who suffered from the conflagration, the federal government did not have a comprehensive disaster programme (New Hampshire, 2022). The modern form of federal response did not see an organized response for 150 years, until the Disaster Relief Act of 1950, and then in 1979, the creation of the Federal Emergency Management Agency (FEMA) (HUD, 2015). FEMA was developed as support for local authorities in disasters never with the intent to take over or to compensate for all the losses of a disaster. The need for professional responders, as well as organized volunteers to aid in disaster response has always been needed. Following the 9/11 terror attacks, President Bush and later President Obama both strongly encouraged Americans to help in the war on terror by volunteering their time and services to their local communities. As the times change, so do certain aspects of society, which make volunteering more of a challenge. Current levels of volunteerism are seeing a decline across the board. There are fewer people volunteering on a regular basis and the hours they are able to give are typically lower than a few decades ago. This does become problematic for communities as disasters in recent years are increasing in severity and frequency.

There is hope for an increase in the pool as the nature of disaster management is becoming better understood. It is becoming a widely accepted fact that it takes a village to overcome a disaster, meaning that it takes a wide variety of skills, talents, and knowledge to build and rebuild resilient communities. Everyone has something to offer to help their family and community fight disasters. No matter the skill or trade, there is likely a place for them within an organized volunteer group to make a positive difference in their communities fight for disaster resilience and survival. Not everyone needs to be out putting bandages on people or rebuilding structures. There is also a need for people to plan, educate others, help others with documentation, help people with their psychological well-being, help entertain to take their minds off the bad things, people to give hope, and so much more. The COVID-19 pandemic has taught us several valuable lessons for disaster response, recovery, and preparedness, but it also taught us methods to overcome traditional limitations. For example, prior to COVID-19 tradition dictated that to help at a disaster, a person had to be physically there. Now it is known that many of the tasks needed to be completed in disaster response and recovery can be done virtually or in smaller pods of volunteers hundreds of miles away. This idea has opened the door to an entirely new way of thinking about how groups can volunteer to make a difference in disasters. Volunteers have not gone away, and communities cannot fend off disasters without the help of volunteers. This need will continue the perpetuation of volunteer groups. The question is how modern society conveys to the youth the importance and value of volunteering in organized and properly trained groups in order to help others?

9.7 Conclusion

This chapter has examined how small investments, such as those seen in campus and community CERT programmes, can result in large community rewards by taking individual time and talents, making them more powerful through the coordination with others in an organized group(s). It is human nature to want to help others, but this desire must be tempered with appropriate actions and coordination. It has been observed that during times of emergencies and disasters that people want to help; they just often do not know how. In some cases, this may just make the help inefficient; in other cases, it may lead to no action and in others, unfortunately, it makes the situation worse. The answer then comes in the form of training and organization. It is true that one person can make a difference, but for that to be a positive difference everyone must be rowing the boat in the same direction.

This chapter has laid out the case for how micro-human efforts can make a difference in every phase of emergency/disaster management. It has provided examples of how MHEs can make a difference to the individual, family, and community levels of resiliency and survivability. There is still much work to be done in this area, though. Large sections are not properly prepared for a disaster if it were to happen today. It has been shown that the number of unprepared goes up when looking at more vulnerable groups or those with more functional and access needs, such as health issues, age, and poverty. It is the hope that this chapter has not only laid out the case for why micro-human efforts are important in emergency and disaster response but has also inspired, energized, and equipped others with foundations for creating their own MHEs for more resilient communities to emergencies and disasters.

9.8 Starting a CERT Programme in Your Community or Campus

The following is a quick guide put together by the author to help Historically Black Colleges and Universities (HBCUs) develop Campus CERT programmes on each university campus. This same quick guide can be used for communities (CERT), high schools (Teen CERT), or other college campuses (Campus CERT). For more information, contact your local state/territory CERT programme or FEMA CERT directly.

9.8.1 Starting a Campus CERT

Maybe you have been thinking about it before, or this chapter has motivated you to think that you would like to start a Campus or Community Emergency Response Team (CERT). CERT is a FEMA-originated organization that is organized through local and state Emergency Management organizations. The purpose of CERT is to train volunteers in preparedness and disasters so that they can help to train others as well as respond in a coordinated method to help others in time of need within their level of training. https://www.ready.gov/community-emergency-response -team The following is a list of things to take into consideration as you begin the trek on forming a fun, exciting, meaningful, and sustainable CERT programme in your community or campus.

a.   Research the CERT programme as to the opportunities and the help available from state and local resources. See CERT Starters Guide. https://www.fema .gov/media-library/assets/documents/118914 or https://www.fema.gov/media -library-data/1470339607110-e31f7c7086431f7f8fba48bf6f3dd9fe/Campus _CERT_Starter_Guide_Final.pdf

b.   In most areas, CERT is considered to be an extension of the local Emergency Management organization. Begin conversations with them early. Here is a list of state point of contacts for CERT: https://www.fema.gov/faq-details/ Locating-my-State-CERT-Coordinator/cert

c.   Once you have decided that you want to move forward with a CERT pro- gramme, begin conversations with your community, university and/or high school leadership, especially the legal department(s). Some of the biggest questions that they will have are volunteer safety, liability injury insurance, disaster-related tasks, recruitment, and chain of command. Have responses ready for these types of questions in your discussions. See the following link for some ideas on these answers. https://www.ready.gov/community-emer- gency-response-team   /   (https://www.fema.gov/media-library/assets/docu- ments/28051},

d.   Look at other CERT programmes to get ideas to help develop your programme to be strong and efficient. You will find the CERT community very friendly and willing to help others develop successful programmes. https://community .fema.gov/Register/Register_Search_Programs

e.   Develop bylaw drafts and any specialized policies or procedures that you may need to meet your university requirements. Some examples of these include https://police.ucsf.edu/system/files/ermp_non-confidential_annexes_cj_edit _0.pdf or https://www.emich.edu/publicsafety/emo/documents/ccert_bylaws .pdf

f.   Once permission has been granted by leadership to move forward, plan to recruit members and arrange for meeting(s). See link for example of proposed meeting. http://www.ecsu.edu/calendar/index.php?eID=693 Things that may help with recruitment may include public education as to what CERT does, lifesaving training for members, helping students to meet university volun- teer requirements, specialized training/events, etc. The addition of a university website and/or social media outlets can help explain the programme to poten- tial   volunteers   https://www.bc.edu/emergency/how-to-prepare/safety_and _emergencytraining/c-cert.html

g.   Have all members register for a Federal Student Identification Number (SIDs). This is a lifelong number that is needed for anyone to register for a FEMA course. https://cdp.dhs.gov/femasid

h.   Make meetings with members fun and meaningful. Encourage members to begin their training on their own with FEMA Independent Study (IS) classes.

These classes are needed for all first responders, including CERT members. These classes also are meaningful on resumes, help the credibility of the team and if integrated appropriately into college courses as homework assignments can be useful recruiting tools. All members should start with IS 317 CERT training, which is a good introduction to the CERT community and basic life-saving skills. https://training.fema.gov/is/courseoverview.aspx?code=IS-317 All members should take IS 100 https://training.fema.gov/is/courseoverview .aspx?code=is-100.c and IS 200 https://training.fema.gov/is/courseoverview .aspx?code=IS-200.c Later, encourage students to take classes such as IS 700 and 800. There are many other exceptionally good courses to take from the FEMA IS program. All courses are free and open to everyone. https://training .fema.gov/is/crslist.aspx

i. Work with your state Emergency Management CERT programme manager to set up the initial CERT course for your team. The initial training is approximately 40 hours and will teach basic lifesaving skills. https://www.fema.gov /media-library/assets/documents/27368 Your state agency can help you find instructors for the course. It is advisable to eventually get university staff to take the train-the-trainer course to be able to help with the training. https:// www.fema.gov/media-library/assets/documents/27475. Since COVID-19, another option is that many states will now accept the didactic part of CERT training from the University of Utah's online programme, which is at this time free to participants. Community Emergency Response Team (CERT) | School of Medicine | University of Utah Health.

j. Also work with the University Services for the CERT members to help in planning and execution of campus drills and exercises. https://www.fema.gov /hseep

k. There are many other things to consider when looking into building a community or campus CERT programme, but this is a good start. Remember there often is not a perfect answer that works for all organizations, so you may have to adapt some of these ideas to fit your needs. If you try new ideas and they work, be sure to share them with others. One of the remarkable things about CERT is the sense of family within the organizations.

References

ACHA (2022, August 15). *COVID-19 considerations for institutions of higher education, Fall 2022*. ACHA. Retrieved from https://www.acha.org/documents/Resources/ Guidelines/ACHA_COVID_Considerations_for_IHEs_Fall_2022.pdf.

AICPA (2022). *Majority of Americans believe they are likely to be impacted by a natural disaster, few are financially prepared: AICPA survey*. AICPA. Retrieved from https:// www.aicpa.org/news/article/majority-of-americans-believe-impacted-by-a-natural -disaster.

Anders Blok, Moe Nakazora and Brit Ross Winthereik (2016). Infrastructure environments. *Science as Culture*, 25(1), 1–22. https://doi.org/10.1080/09505431.2015.1081500.

Bagley, Mary (2017, December 19). Mount Vesuvius & Pompeii: Facts and history. *Live Science*. Retrieved from https://www.livescience.com/27871-mount-vesuvius-pompeii .html.

Blaustein, A (2022). How to protect Puerto Rico's power grid from hurricanes. *Scientific American*. Retrieved from https://www.scientificamerican.com/article/how-to-protect -puerto-ricos-power-grid-from-hurricanes/.

Canal, Bonnies (2019). History of community emergency response team (CERT) program. *Resiliency Institute*. Retrieved from https://theresiliencyinstitute.com/history-of -community-emergency-response_10/.

CDP (2019). US Household Disaster giving. Center for disease Philanthropy. Retrieved from https://www.issuelab.org/resources/34757/34757.pdf.

Covington, Taylor (2021, August 9). Natural disaster statistics in 2021. *The Zebra*. Retrieved from https://www.thezebra.com/resources/research/natural-disaster-statistics/.

FEMA (2022a). Disaster declarations. *FEMA*. Retrieved from https://www.fema.gov/ disaster/declarations.

FEMA (2022b). Daily situational reports. *FEMA*. Retrieved from https://www.disastercenter .com/FEMA Daily Situation Report Archive 2022.html.

FEMA (2022c). Find a CERT. *FEMA*. Retrieved from https://community.fema.gov/Prepare dnessCommunity/s/cert-find-a-program?language=en_US.

Ferberov, snejana (2023, Aug 21). Owner of viral red house thinks this is why it survived the Maui wildfires that turned everything else to ash. *New York Post*. Retrieved from https://nypost.com/2023/08/21/owner-of-mauis-unscathed-red-house-explains-why-it -survived/.

Flint, Courtney and Stevenson, Joanne (2010). Building Community disaster preparedness with volunteers: Community Emergency response teams in Illinois. *Natural Hazards Review*. Retrieved from https://d1wqtxts1xzle7.cloudfront.net/46564707/Building _Community_Disaster_Preparedness20160617-14159-badwn1-with-cover-page-v2.pdf ?Expires=1657396086&Signature=V9SpmgWps2J6EDHf3M0627OAbaHLq4YbQcj 5PHHbCdYcg1kmiX8C2uMR2E9KiJvS9qV5EDe7YbK72B7HUw~qZClMLuPnXNR 2l8xR~uJDEElKX7boCdX8SyPk4MpK~WcrtpXK182qWKouzR5KuO1TIV6hLNt wpDDs7NFww~gmQOcM7gU7N~jhpv7RRN2x5d5pQKLnPEdlh3~gBDpy3y7D4gD QLV4HQ2lL1MtfZNCBeUdT2IvKKvbwF0vQv1nZv0nToY7A20nkS-t3gIiOns5huTpj 0eba6xq4PTiGOtpVnPRULV96Xj0p9GjcWtlWq7qQ2kSmeuJRSJNr9pbdyyTr5Q__ &Key-Pair-Id=APKAJLOHF5GGSLRBV4ZA.

Goodrick, Jake, Waltermire, Bridgette, Anderson, Natalie and Gravius, Christian (2019, August 13). Everybody is a first responder in disaster, police and firefighters say. *State of Emergency*. Retrieved from https://stateofemergency.news21.com/everybody-is-a-first -responder-in-disasters-police-and-firefighters-say/.

HUD (2015). Evidence matters. *HUD*. Retrieved from https://www.huduser.gov/portal/ periodicals/em/winter15/highlight1_sidebar.html.

Kifner, John (2005, April 20). 10 years after the bombing, Oklahoma City remembers. *The New York Times*. Retrieved from https://www.huduser.gov/portal/periodicals/em/ winter15/highlight1_sidebar.html.

Matanle, P. Littler, J. and Slay, O. (2019). Imagining disasters in the era of climate change: Is Japan's seawall a new Maginot Line? *The Asia-Pacific Journal: Japan Focus*, 17(13), 1–29.

New Hampshire (2022). The Portsmouth fires that turned the city to brick. *New England Historical Society*. Retrieved from https://www.newenglandhistoricalsociety.com/the -portsmouth-fires-that-turned-the-city-to-brick/.

NFPA (2021). US fire department profile 2019. *NFPA*. Retrieved from https://www .nfpa.org/-/media/Files/News-and-Research/Fire-statistics-and-reports/Emergency -responders/osFDProfileTables.pdf.

NIBS (2018, January 11). *National Institute of Building Sciences issue new report on the value of mitigation*. National institute of Building Sciences. Retrieved from https://www .nibs.org/news/national-institute-building-sciences-issues-new-report-value-mitigation.

NOAA (2022). *Billion-dollar events*. National Oceanic and Atmospheric Administration. Retrieved from https://www.ncei.noaa.gov/access/monitoring/billions/.

Onishi, Normitsu (2011, March 13). Seawalls offered little protection against tsunami's crushing waves. *The New York Times*. Retrieved from https://www.npr.org/sections /parallels/2014/03/11/288691168/in-tsunamis-wake-fierce-debate-over-japans-great -wall.

Ossey, Shamika, Sylvers, Sharon, Oksuzyan, Sona, et al. (2017, April 11). *Community Emergency Response team (CERT) training of high-risk teens in the community of Watts, South Los Angeles, 2013–2014*. Disaster Medicine and Public Health Preparedness, Cambridge University Press. Retrieved from https://www.cambridge.org/core/journals /disaster-medicine-and-public-health.

Persson, S., & Uhnoo, S. (2021). Dilemmas and discretion in complex organizations: Professionals in collaboration with spontaneous volunteers during disasters. *Professions and Professionalism*, *11*(2). https://doi.org/10.7577/pp.3961.

Points of Light foundation (2002). Preventing a disaster within the disaster: The effective use and management of unaffiliated volunteers. *Points of Light Foundation*. Retrieved from https://www.ojp.gov/pdffiles1/Archive/202852NCJRS.pdf.

Ready (2019, November). Summer camps turn teens into preparedness leaders. *FEMA*. Retrieved from https://community.fema.gov/story/Summer-Camps-Turn-Teens-into -Preparedness-Leaders?lang=en_US.

Souza, Andrew (2009). Wasted resources: Volunteers and disasters. *Naval Post graduate School*. Retrieved from https://apps.dtic.mil/sti/citations/ADA514418.

Staub, Ervin (2014, November 22). Why people help strangers and risk their lives for strangers. *HuffPost*. Retrieved from https://www.huffpost.com/entry/why-do-people -help-strang_b_5863494.

Tala M. AI-Rousan, Rubenstein, Linda M. and Wallace, Robert B. (2014). Preparedness for natrual disasters among older US adults: A nationwide survey. *American Journal of Public Health*, 104, 506–511. https://doi.org/10.2105/AJPH 2013.301559.

Than, Ker (2017, November 8). What killed the dinosaurs? *National Geographic*. Retrieved from   https://www.nationalgeographic.co.uk/history-and-civilisation/2017/11/what -killed-the-dinosaurs.

Thormar, S. B., Gersons, B. P., Juen, B., Marschang, A., Djakababa, M. N., & Olff, M. (2010). The mental health impact of volunteering in a disaster setting: A review. *The Journal of Nervous and Mental Disease*, 198(8), 529–538.

Waleca, Konrad (2018, February 12). Why so many medical shortages months after Hurricane Maria. *CBS News*. Retrieved from https://www.cbsnews.com/news/why-so -many-medicines-arel-in-short-supply-after-hurricane-maria/.

Wall, Michael (2022). The Big Bang: What really happened at the universes birth? *Space .com*. Retrieved from https://www.space.com/13347-big-bang-origins-universe-birth .html.

10 Self-Governance as Agency in Post-Disaster Recovery

Richard Oloruntoba and Winifred Asare-Doku

10.1 Introduction

The adverse impacts of natural disasters are reducible and human-made disasters are avoidable. However, emphasis has mostly been on response and recovery based on government and public sector intervention (Chamlee-Wright and Storr, 2010; Cunin and O'Hara, 2019; Oloruntoba and Asare-Doku, 2021). In recent times, researchers have begun to go beyond conventional public sector-led approaches to recovery to examine the role of self-governance, self-help and self-reliance in disaster recovery and management (Grube and Storr, 2014). Self-governance is the ability of a person, actor or societal group to exercise all necessary functions of regulation without intervention from an external authority (Rasmussen, 2011). Self-governance may refer to personal conduct or to any form of institution, such as family units or social groups (Kooiman and Van Vliet, 2000). It is about the capacity of social entities to govern themselves autonomously. Self-governance is closely related to various philosophical and socio-political concepts such as autonomy, independence, and self-control and could be relevant and necessary at various levels – national, regional, state, city, village, neigborhood, or other (Kooiman and Van Vliet, 2000). Self-governance could be the difference between people who successfully recover from the aftermath of disasters and those who do not (Grube and Storr, 2014). Self-governance in the context of disaster recovery is the ability of a person or group of persons to function and lead themselves out of disaster autonomously with little external influence (Grube and Storr, 2014; Rubin, 2019; Oloruntoba and Asare-Doku, 2021). How individuals and communities self-reorient, self-reorganize and use their resources and abilities to rebuild their lives and communities after a disaster is a critical factor in recovery at a collective level (Liu and Ni, 2021).

Research shows that individuals possess certain internal resources and strengths that they may not be aware of that can enhance and facilitate their resilience and functioning (Sheldon and King, 2001; Manyena, 2006; Cano-Calhoun, 2021). For instance, positive emotions, positive psychology, happiness, and emotional well-being have been shown to enhance resilience and functioning (Pellerin and Raufaste, 2020). Similarly, the psychological capital (PsyCap) literature emphasizes the role of positive psychological resources of hope, efficacy, resilience, and optimism (HOPE) in enhancing resilience and functioning (Finch et al., 2020). It

DOI: 10.4324/9781003615903-14

is therefore likely that unawareness, unrecognition, or under-recognition of such resources by individuals and disaster managers means such resources are often not drawn upon in disaster recovery efforts at an individual and agency level. As a result, the challenge of identifying the internal resources and mechanisms that might buffer post-disaster recovery problems and promote faster rebuilding and recovery in affected populations remains a significant one for disaster managers, researchers, educators, and policymakers. One set of micro-human resources that has demonstrated strong evidence in positively influencing performance outcomes for adults is psychological capital (PsyCap) (Luthans et al., 2004; Luthans, 2002) but this has often not been drawn upon in recovery efforts.

Hence, this chapter aims to (1) discuss the concept of self-governance, self-help, self-reliance and positive psychology in the disaster recovery process, and (2) discuss the key facilitators of self-governance approaches to recovery from the literature.

Towards these aims, the rest of the chapter is structured as follows: Section 2 provides a brief overview of natural disasters and their impacts. Section 3 explains the more modern integrated view of disasters as extending beyond mere management of physical hazards and impacts of disaster (i.e. "acts of god") to managing less dramatic issues of intergenerational social and economic vulnerability (i.e. "acts of man") as well as "technological/industrial" disasters (Kapucu, 2007; Perrow, 2007). Section 4 addresses the interplay of pre-existing geographical, geological and meteorological hazards in the environment in which people live and susceptibility to those hazards arising from pre-disaster social vulnerability (i.e. from poverty, economic status, social class, ethnicity, race, and gender). Section 5 discusses self-governance, positive psychology and psychological resilience in the disaster recovery process, while section 6 discusses the key facilitators of self-governance in post-disaster recovery from the literature. Section 7 goes further to discuss the key facilitators of self-governance, self-help and self-reliance, while section 8 summarizes and concludes the discussion.

10.2   Natural Disasters and Impacts

The term "disaster" has been conceptualized in a range of ways in the literature (Alexander 2002; Cutter 2005a; Schenker-Wicki, Inauen and Olivares, 2010). However, the term is usually reserved for "a serious disruption of the functioning of society, causing widespread human, material or environmental losses which exceed the ability of the affected people to cope using *only their own* resources" (Asian Disaster Reduction Centre, 2005; United Nations, 2004a b c, 2006; United Nations Development Programme 2004, 2008). Quarantelli and Dynes (1977) define the term "disaster" as the disruption to society after the "event". Altay and Green (2006, p. 476) argue that disasters are "intractable problems that test the ability of communities, nations, and regions to effectively protect their populations and infrastructure, to reduce both human and property loss, and to rapidly recover after the event".

Kapucu (2007) asserted that disasters are occurrences that are notable, rare, unique and profound in terms of their impacts, effects, or outcomes. From this range of definitions, it seems that disasters almost always have to do with "disruption", with "losses", and "challenges" to the ability to recover rapidly. These disaster definitions demonstrate how and why the inherently disruptive nature of disasters relates to self-governance and the need for self-governance in individuals and communities, and how self-governance assists in post-disaster recovery. Conventionally, relevant governments, public sector disaster management agencies (PSDMAs) and others must act to reduce the impact of disasters, their disruption, effects, losses and outcomes (Boin, 2008; Hood, 1991; Kapucu and Van Wart, 2006). Governments and their PSDMAs in particular must act to reduce disruption to the functioning of society (Boin, 2008; ISDR, 2004; Kapucu and Van Wart, 2006; Schenker-Wicki, Inauen and Olivares, 2010). In this chapter, we define a disaster as an unforeseen event that causes great damage, destruction, and human suffering or even death to a large number of people, which in turn overwhelms the response capacity of local communities, often necessitating urgent requests for external assistance on a national, regional or international scale.

Scholarly definitions of disasters have historically focused on the physical features of disasters and the impacts of physical agents such as wind and water in cyclones and floods (Kapucu, 2007). Such historical definitions differentiated between "acts of god" and "acts of man" as well as "technological" disasters (Kapucu, 2007; Perrow, 2007). Later on in the early literature, disasters appear to be seen as phenomena that result in significant disruptions of social life that may not even involve a physical agent or physical hazard of any kind such as an earthquake, volcano, or cyclone (Drabek and McEntire, 2003).

Since the 1990s and up until now, it appears a more integrative view of disasters has emerged in which disasters are considered to be social in their nature, origin, manifestation, or consequence (Drabek and McEntire, 2003). Disasters are seen as explicit manifestations of hidden societal vulnerabilities and weaknesses in social structures or systems (Kreps, 1989; Warner and Loster, 2006; Oliver-Smith, 2009).

As a result of such an integrative view of disasters, many disaster scholars and sociologists are now choosing to abandon the distinction between "natural", "technological", or "man-made" disasters derived from early notions of "acts of god" and "man-made" happenings. For example, the impact of disasters, whether the causative agent is man (as in war) or nature (as in an earthquake), remains the same: they all produce "social disruption", "losses", and "challenges" to the ability of individuals and communities to rapidly recover. Hence, disasters may also result from subtle, mundane, non-spectacular, non-dramatic everyday social processes such as racism (Cutter, Boruff and Shirley, 2003), lack of opportunity, and poverty that render individuals, communities, and areas vulnerable and susceptible to the impact of natural hazards (Cutter, Boruff and Shirley, 2003; Kapucu, 2007, 2008).

Nevertheless, some scholars still argue that the distinction between "man-made" and "natural" disasters is necessary (Bellgarde-Smith, 2011; Quarantelli, 2003a b; Young et al., 2006). Such scholars often argue that man-made disasters, such as wars are still inherently different from disasters arising from natural hazards and agents, such as earthquakes especially in their origins, developmental paths, manifestations, and consequences. They note that in "natural" disaster events, there are no conscious and deliberate human attempts to bring about negative effects, such as social disruption, as there are in war and conflict situations (Bellgarde-Smith, 2011; Young et al., 2006). Hence, there appears to be no unified view on whether to differentiate between natural or man-made disasters. However, differentiation helps classify disasters in our attempts to study and understand them.

10.2.1   Physical and Social Impacts

Disasters often manifest as: (1) intrinsic or direct features such as physical damage from the event itself to houses, farms and infrastructure; and human injuries and loss of life; (2) secondary indirect or extrinsic features such as resulting food shortages, overwhelmed hospitals and a general sense of community confusion (see Table 10.1 for the general types of disaster impact). In addition to damaging housing, infrastructure, the environment, and other physical impacts, disasters disrupt daily social routines and everyday social coping mechanisms (Drabek and McEntire, 2003). Therefore, disasters often cause significant stress in and to affected communities (Drabek and McEntire 2003). In summary, impacts arising from disasters could be categorized as (1) *physical impacts* (Lindell and Prater, 2003; Verschuur et al., 2020) i.e. physical damage and destruction to property, buildings and human life; (2) *social and sociological impact* (Quarantelli, 1989; Fothergill and Peek, 2004; Arcaya et al., 2020) *and (3) psychological impact and stress* (Norris and Elrod, 2006; Norris et al., 2008; Easterwood and Saeed, 2020).

10.2.2   Disaster Response and Recovery

Disasters often trigger a community response first, where neighbours and victims help each other before external parties arrive to assist (Drabek and McEntire, 2003).

Table. 10.1 Disaster Impact Types and Impact Types Requiring Disaster Recovery (Oloruntoba, 2013)

General Disaster Impacts	Disaster Impacts Relevant to Responsiveness and Thesis Aims
• Increased risk of communicable diseases • Economic loss • Damage to housing • Damage to livestock and crops • Damage to water systems • Damage to infrastructure • Community disruption and sociological damage • Adverse personal and community health impacts e.g. mental health issues and climatic exposure • Damage to the environment	• Population movements and displacement • Demand for relief and assistance exceeds local capacity • Food shortage • Mortality, serious injuries and missing persons

Subsequently external parties respond and arrive to help, and these arriving helpers also experience part of the collective stress in the affected community because of the chaos and the significant and urgent needs in the affected community (Drabek and McEntire, 2003). Arriving responders often include government(s) and their agencies such as public sector disaster-mandated agencies (PSDMAs), the military, voluntary groups, charities, public and private sector organizations, transportation firms, the media, individual volunteers, and others.

Responders help by undertaking rescue and salvage, delivering and distributing relief, and caring for the injured and those who are emotionally damaged by the disaster (Thomas, 2003; Thomas and Mizushima, 2005). For this thesis, I define disaster response as the goal-directed actions and activities of government(s) and their PSDMA, militaries, various public agencies, communities, and other non-governmental organizations (NGOs) that are undertaken in the aftermath of a disaster that aim to reduce the impact of disasters, their effects, and outcomes. Such goal-directed actions serve to reduce losses and disruption to the functioning of the community and society, and enable rapid community recovery and rehabilitation. Response to disasters usually takes place during, and immediately following a disaster unless an early warning was received, in which case, preparations take place before the disaster occurs (Alexander and Klein, 2009).

Disaster response activities may include search and rescue (SAR) activities, putting out fires, triage of the injured, setting up emergency hospitals, stabilization of houses and other public infrastructure, and the provision of immediate disaster relief such as food, water, first aid, medical care, and other relief services needed for life sustenance. Those persons undertaking such disaster relief tasks have often been referred to as "first responders" (Alexander and Klein, 2009).

Disaster relief is, however, often conceived as a much narrower concept than disaster response as it mainly involves the provision of disaster relief goods for the immediate sustenance of life and short-term reduction of human suffering, grief, trauma, and death usually in the immediate aftermath of a disaster (Coppola, 2011; Thomas, 2003). Such disaster relief goods often include food, water, temporary shelter, and first aid. Sometimes, it may include medical care and other relief services such as search and rescue (SAR) and immediate counselling. Disaster relief is undertaken during the immediate "emergency" phase of a disaster, which is usually up to 96 hours to two weeks after the disaster event depending on the context (Coppola, 2011; Thomas, 2003). Disaster relief processes and operations (DRPOs) have the aim of alleviating immediate suffering and prevent further loss of life (Coppola, 2011; Thomas, 2003).

10.3 Natural Hazards and the Interplay of Hazards and Vulnerability

A natural hazard is a natural phenomenon that might have a negative effect on humans and other animals, or the environment (Shaluf, 2007). A natural hazard is a risk factor that may be categorized as originating from (1) internal (beneath the earth's surface), (2) external (on the earth's surface), (3) weather-related (meteorological or hydrological), and (4) biological phenomena such as pandemics

Before the Disaster	After the Disaster
Strategic planning Mitigation activities Preparedness/response & relief planning, training & disaster early warning & communication systems activities Multi-organisational planning Prevention, hazard, risk & vulnerability analysis Continuous surveillance & monitoring activities	Response activities such as needs & damage assessments, resource mobilisation to site Search & rescue (SAR) activities Disaster relief activities, sustenance distribution Triage & first aid activities Financial aid Debris removal & clean-up & salvage Recovery/rebuilding/rehabilitati on & resettlement activities Long term sustainability planning

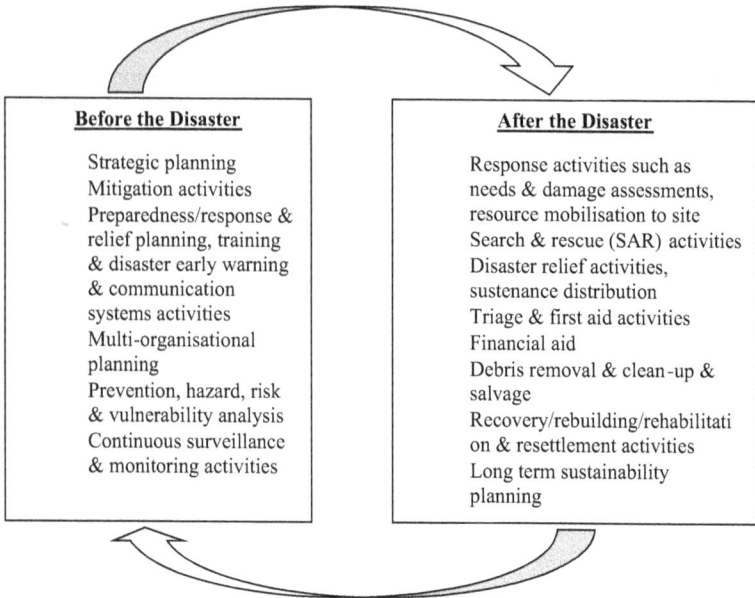

Figure 10.1 Disaster Management Cycle. Source: Adapted from Oloruntoba (2013)

(Shaluf, 2007). Natural hazards are features of physical causative agents for disasters (Singh and Pande, 2011). Examples include active and dormant volcanoes, landslides, hurricanes, and earthquakes (Singh and Pande, 2011). The geographical environment may also be a source of hazards, with human settlements as sources of hazards, and due to population growth and concentration around the world, the potential for risk and disaster has increased.

Vulnerability is the quality or state of being exposed to the possibility of being harmed physically or emotionally. Social vulnerability is the susceptibility of social groups to the adverse impacts of natural hazards, including disproportionate death, injury, loss, or disruption of livelihood. It refers to potential harm to people. Social vulnerability involves a combination of factors that determine the degree to which someone's life and livelihood are put at risk by a discrete and identifiable hazard event in nature or in society (e.g. ethnicity, race, gender, financial status) (Kuhlicke et al., 2011; Singh et al., 2014; Spielman et al., 2020). Existing vulnerability may be a greater determinant of disaster than hazards themselves (Kuhlicke et al., 2011; Singh et al., 2014; Spielman et al., 2020). Only the individual person can determine his/her degree of vulnerability.

A hazard on its own cannot produce a disaster unless it interacts with an existing vulnerability (Bergstrand et al., 2015). Pre-existing individual vulnerabilities include social status, race, health status, age, gender, culture, class, homelessness, poverty, inequity, and a lack of economic/social opportunities, all of which contribute to disaster vulnerability; racism and discrimination in disaster relief; ethics in disaster assistance.

Natural disasters can result from natural hazards interacting with pre-existing social, human or community vulnerability (Bellgarde-Smith, 2011; Cutter et al., 2003; Drabek and McEntire, 2003). Hence, an interplay of hazard and vulnerability can result in adverse impacts (Weichselgartner, 2001), though the impact of disasters varies from person to person, group to group and community to community depending on prior vulnerability and resilience (Oloruntoba and Asare-Dokubo, 2021). As a result, disaster prevention ideally should be based on hazard removal and/or vulnerability reduction, and removal is not always possible. Hence, novel recovery strategies such as self-governance and psychological resilience are required.

10.4 Self-governance, Positive Psychology and Psychological Resilience in the Disaster Recovery Process

There are diverse strategies and mechanisms for recovery and rebuilding after disaster. However, the emphasis has traditionally been on national and local governments and non-governmental organizations to act as agencies and instigators of recovery (Sobel and Leeson, 2006). However, in recent times, these "top-down" approaches to disaster recovery and management have been less than effective (Blackman et al., 2017). Furthermore, there has been a limited focus on studies of internal human resources available for disaster recovery, such as the concept of self-governance. Self-governance is the ability of a person or group to function and lead themselves with little external influence (Grube and Storr, 2014). At a collective level, how individuals and communities self-reorient, self-reorganize and use their resources and abilities to rebuild their lives and communities after a disaster is a critical factor in recovery and thriving (Grube and Storr, 2014). Research shows that individuals possess certain strengths of which they may not be aware of that can enhance their resilience and functioning (Miller and Smith, 2017), and the greater a community's capacity for self-governance, the better able it is to deal with complex challenges such as recovering after a disaster (Miller and Smith, 2017).

The self-help literature in cultural and psychological studies argues that individuals can exercise control and mastery over themselves and their lives, another personality trait that helps individuals against the impact of adversity or traumatic events such as disasters (Rimke, 2000). Under the self-help concept, individuals are fully responsible for their failures as well as their successes, their despair as well as their happiness (Rimke 2000). Similarly, self-reliance is defined as "relying on one's own abilities, decisions, and resources rather than depending on assistance from others" (Astill and Miller, 2018:7).

There are several variations of the concept in disaster recovery and resilience building, and individual models of self-reliance in recovery have been variously referred to as: self-labour, self-work, self-dependence, self-management, self-transformation, self-practices, self-provisioning, self-therapy, self-improvement, self-support, self-reinforcement, self-employment, self-optimization, and micro-human efforts (Oloruntoba and Asare-Doku, 2021). The focus on self-reliance has also been referred to as the *self-help* approach to disaster and emergency management (Abramson et al., 2010). This view originates from the thinking that a disaster-resilient community is one in which individuals and communities should be self-reliant and prepared to adapt or respond to the risks and hazards they live with (Astill and Miller, 2018; COAG, 2011). The definition is based on the view that those adversely impacted by disasters, for instance, have the skills, capacity, and agency to stand on their own and sustain themselves without depending on external humanitarian aid (Easton-Calabria and Omata, 2018; Omata, 2017). Although, those who are often affected by disasters are often the most vulnerable in our unequal world. The self-reliance perspective moves disaster management responsibility from the government and places it firmly with the individual. It assumes that individuals have the required material and psychological resources within them to be adaptive and resilient.

Micro-human efforts, including self-help, self-reliance or self-governance approaches to recovery, have been said to be based on the physical and psychological resources of individuals in communities impacted by disasters (Estill and Miller, 2018; Wild, Wiles, and Allen, 2013). Such models of self-help, self-governance and self-reliance have described personal tacit inner psychological, trait, motivational, social capital as well as material resources as essential criteria for individual recovery (Grube and Storr, 2014). Leveraging such micro-human efforts, inner motivations, and resources is assumed to enable impacted and displaced individuals to proactively take responsibility and find urgent solutions and resources to facilitate quicker personal recovery, and ultimately, collective or community recovery and allied processes (Fast, 2019).

An important aspect of self-help, self-governance and self-reliance, in addition to material and physical resources are psychological resources such as resilience and trait resilience (Fletcher and Sarkar, 2013). Resilience refers to the capacity of an individual or a community to absorb the impact of a disturbance, return to the state that existed before the disturbance, and advance to a more capable position through learning and adaption (Cutter et al., 2008; Oloruntoba, 2015). This suggests that resilience facilitates a quicker recovery. These internal resources are crucial for quicker and more effective disaster recovery under the increasing intensity and frequency of disasters, as communities do not have to await government's traditional "top-down" approach that often does not reflect the long-term needs of a recovering community.

Psychological resilience at the individual micro-human level has been defined as effective coping and adaptation in the face of adversity (Ogińska-Bulik and Michalska, 2020). It is the ability to bounce back or recover from stress. Individual psychological resilience is manifested as persistence and flexible adaptation to the demands of life, the ability to take remedial actions in difficult situations, and a tolerance of negative emotions and failures (Ogińska-Bulik and Michalska, 2020). The terms individual resilience and psychological resilience are often used interchangeably in the literature and share similar characteristics. Trait resilience is a commonly used term in the psychology and mental health literature (Bensimon, 2012; Hu et al., 2015; Waugh et al., 2011). The term often relates to psychological resilience and individual resilience regarding mental health and overall individual resilience (Bensimon, 2012; Hu et al., 2015; Waugh et al., 2011). This trait perspective of individual and psychological resilience suggests that resilience is a personal trait that helps individuals cope with adversity and achieve good adjustment and development (Hu et al., 2015). Scholars who support this view see resilience as a personality trait that protects individuals against the impact of adversity or traumatic events such as disaster recovery contexts (e.g., Connor and Davidson, 2003; Ong et al., 2006). These qualities may be acquired or learned by individuals and communities. Thus, it makes sense for governments to build on these qualities.

The facilitators of self-help, self-governance, self-reliance, and individual resilience, according to Oloruntoba and Asare-Doku (2021), Chester and Duncan (2010) and Chester et al., (2008) include (1) faith, religion, religiosity, and availability of religious social support; (2) humour, mindfulness, and a positive outlook; (3) physical and material resources; and (4) strength of social networks and social capital.

10.4.1 Faith, Religion, Religiosity, and Availability of Religious Social Support

Pre-disaster religiosity has been found to predict higher levels of post-disaster social resources, optimism, and sense of purpose (Chan et al., 2012; Clarke, 2006). It seems having a religion, or faith, and having access to religion-based social support (e.g., helpers from churches, temples, or mosques) helps affected individuals to cope better with disaster-induced stress. Also, it seems religious social support (e.g., Salvation Army, World Vision) and greater religiosity within the individual would mitigate the strength of the relationship between individual loss of resources and stress symptoms (Chan et al., 2012; Clarke, 2006). Thus, resulting in less stress and an ability to recover quicker. Greater religiosity and religious social support have also been found to result in higher individual resilience and/or an ability to demonstrate self-help and self-reliant behaviour, which together may help the community to be more resilient and thus facilitate a faster recovery.

Almost any type of faith, spirituality, or religion has been shown to enhance resilience, from Hindu (Kasim and Nurdin, 2021) to Islam (Ettengoff and Rodriguez, 2022), Christianity (Alawiyah et al., 2011; Chester and Duncan, 2010) and others. Various studies have repeatedly identified spirituality, faith and religion as individual resilience factors in disasters (Abbott, 2019; Ager et al., 2015; Aten et al., 2019; Davis et al., 2019; Llamas, 2014; Niaz, 2006; Wilkinson, 2015). The roles spirituality, religion, and faith communities are often ignored in disaster management (Chester and Duncan, 2010; Chester et al., 2008; Clarke, 2006). Overlooking the role of faith, religiosity, and spirituality often reflects "modernist" approaches that position cultures and religions as hindrances to development, rather than seeing them as resources, assets, or strengths of existing societies (McGregor, 2010). Even within the context of increasing recognition of the importance of local culture and customs, the influence of religion and faith is often overlooked and unexplored. Donors and humanitarian organizations with secular worldviews have often failed to connect with disaster-affected groups due to a lack of appreciation of the importance of faith traditions (Clarke, 2006; McKaughan, 2017). In many contexts, the exclusion of faith-based communities means disaster management agencies do not take advantage of a significant resilience resource within affected communities.

Such individual resilience factors mitigate against stress and depression and facilitates quicker recovery through the ability to undertake self-help activities and be more self-reliant. For example, praying to "God" was described as a resource in the aftermath of a disaster (Mitchell, 2003). Self-help and how some communities have used spirituality, faith and religiosity successfully in recovery is also good for the environment, other species, and the people. Although, much of the published empirical research are methodological case studies. This means that theories and ideas from other places may need to be evaluated for relevance, and irrelevant ones identified as such.

Several scales have been developed to measure spirituality (e.g., Makkar and Singh, 2021), faith (e.g., Plante and Boccaccini, 1997) and religiosity (e.g., Chamberlain, 2010). For instance, the *Duke Religion Index* (Chamberlain, 2010) measures how much religious social support is available to an individual after a traumatic or disaster event. The Spiritual Support Scale (Cherry et al., 2018), and the Religious Support-Short Form (Chamberlain, 2010) measure similar religiosity factors. In relation to faith and religion, some studies have described hope as a personal resilient factor or resource in coping (Alawiyah et al., 2011; Niaz, 2006).

Other studies describe optimism as a resource in being resilient (Aaliyah et al., 2011; Chan et al., 2012; Iacoviello and Charney, 2020; Maltais and Gauthier, 2009; Mann et al., 2018; Marks et al., 2009; Niaz, 2006). Yet still believing in God and meaning-making in the loss are considered contributory to individual resilience (Augustine, 2009), all of which may individually and collectively contribute to self-reliance through self-help activities. Hence, a quicker recovery after disasters.

10.4.2   *Humour, Mindfulness, and Positive Outlook*

There are other individual-related characteristics that can contribute towards self-help and self-reliance, and thus individual resilience in the disaster recovery process. The adaptive coping strategies and emotion-focused coping resources found in post-disaster individual resilience include humour and a humorous outlook on life and what has just been experienced (Cherry et al., 2018). A humorous approach entails cognitive flexibility, which is a process of reappraising and reframing stress or trauma for growth (Iacoviello and Charney, 2020). Other personal characteristics and dispositions that contribute to self-help, self-reliance, and individual resilience include mindfulness (Kono and Burton, 2019); gratification/gratitude (Kono and Burton 2019; Marks et al., 2009); authenticity (Kono and Burton 2019); virtuousness (Kono and Burton, 2019); perseverance (Llamas, 2014; Niaz, 2006); acceptance (Mason, 2019); meditation (McGeehan, 2014); and intellectual resources (Niaz, 2006).

Each of these facilitators was drawn from the literature on positive psychology or the psychology of optimal functioning, the Leisure and Well-being Model [LWM] (Carruthers and Hood, 2007; Hood and Carruthers, 2007; 2016)]. The LWM model includes five leisure enhancement mechanisms: savouring an experience, gratification, authenticity, mindfulness, and virtuousness. These were adapted and tested in the disaster aftermath context and found to enhance coping and individual resilience (Carruthers and Hood, 2007; Hood and Carruthers, 2007, 2016). Mindfulness means taking more leisure or unoccupied time for calmness and emotional healing and intermittently taking the mind of disaster-related issues, such as house reconstruction or relocation plans (Kono and Burton, 2019).

Gratification is the feeling of the joy of connection to other people character-ized by harmony, sharing, and a sense of belonging (Hood and Carruthers, 2007, 2016; Kono and Burton, 2019). It allows individuals to re-energize and re-motivate themselves by connecting with something larger than the current version of self and to grow to be a better version of self, like the concept of self-help (Hood and Carruthers, 2007). Savouring is said to trigger positive emotions through rec-reational activities after disasters, which can evoke positive affect. Furthermore, a sense of gratitude and appreciation towards ordinary activities brings affected individuals back to their normal lives disrupted by disaster with the aim of trigger-ing positive emotions.

Authenticity is said to be therapeutic for individuals affected by disasters because the disasters severely challenged their sense of self. Individuals affected by disasters can thus regain a sense of their identity and who they were pre-disaster through play and recreational activities, and through jokes and laughter (Kono and Burton, 2019).

10.4.3 *Physical and Material Resources*

Studies have found significant correlations between the availability of, and expo-sure to social resources, and a sense of optimism and sense of purpose, as well as exposure to stress, depression, and feeling of hopelessness and helplessness (Foa and Foa, 2012). Likewise, physical and material resources such as property and funds. Physical and material resources are tangible resources such as money, information, goods, and services. Availability of such resources helps to manage psychological distress. They also can contribute towards self-help and self-reliance if available on a timely basis, thus enhancing individual resilience and faster recov-ery in disasters. Scales such as the Social Provisions Scale (Chan et al., 2012) are tools designed to measure how much social resources are available to individuals to help them recover in the aftermath of a disaster.

10.4.4 *Strength of Social Network and Social Capital*

An individual's social network is indeed an important protective factor that buffers from experiencing significant symptoms of distress and helplessness in recovery (Aldrich, 2011a; 2012; Patel et al., 2017). Such social networks may be termed social capital and may include instrumental support such as money and the offer-ing and acceptance of emotional support. An absence of a social network can potentially can be a significant risk factor for post-traumatic stress symptoms in response to disasters (Bokszczanin, 2012). A lack of social connectedness may deny an individual the external resources they may need to unleash their internal resources needed for undertaking and demonstrating self-help and self-reliance in a post-disaster context. Strong and positive social support, social capital, and social embeddedness enhance individual resilience to stress and the ability to recover quicker. It can also facilitate self-help and self-reliance after a traumatic experience such as disasters (Aldrich, 2010; 2011b). Similarly, Patel et al (2017) argue that the connectedness of an individual to a social network based on social relationships might be relevant to enhance overall community resilience (Ozbay et al., 2007; Patel et al., 2017).

In this section, we further discuss the key facilitators of self-governance, self-help and self-reliance and provide examples from the literature.

10.4.4.1   Faith and Religiosity

Religiosity, religion or having a faith may be described as having complete trust or confidence in something, someone, or a strong belief in a deity. It is an important facilitator for many, and it is personal and individualized. Many studies show that faith and religiosity are major factor in promoting resilience and self-governance and helping to overcome adversities and existential crises (Davis et al., 2019; Niaz, 2006). Spirituality is an essential source of resilience, especially in a disaster. Faith in God was a critical resource in helping survivors cope with the aftermath of the disaster, while also making meaning of events (Augustine, 2009; McGeehan, 2014; Wilkinson, 2015). Faith was considered important for personal strength, facilitating recovery and resilience. Faith in prayers offered to God and the reading of the Bible were vital to survival and helped individuals bounce back (Niaz, 2006). For others, acceptance of one's fate (karma) was considered an element of resilience (Fernando, 2012). Faith in God and spiritual beliefs were found to be coping mechanism for survivors of Hurricane Katrina in the United States. In developing resilience and supporting recovery (Henderson et al., 2010). An individual's religious beliefs play an important role in their psycho-social recovery. Although it might appear intangible, faith and religious beliefs provide comfort and help reduce anxiety (Baidhawy, 2015).

10.4.4.2   Religious Practices

This theme refers to rituals practised to help in post-disaster recovery. Religious coping is the most effective and consistent coping strategy among natural disaster survivors (Mesidor and Sly, 2019). The studies reported religious or spiritual practices such as prayer, meditation, and reading the Bible (Alawiyah et al., 2011; Matais and Gauthier, 2009; McGeehan, 2014). These practices provide comfort and serve as an active way of coping. Prayer was not only frequently mentioned and the most salient religious practice in most studies, but it was also reported as powerful and pervasive (Aaliyah et al., 2011; Fernando and Hebert, 2011; Tausch et al., 2011).

Prayer was also an effective coping mechanism practiced by survivors of all ages, contributing to resilience. Many studies have reported reading the Bible and quoting verses of scripture that were considered encouraging (Tausch et al., 2011). The effect of these practices and spiritual activities were a positive part of recovery, which helped people to adjust in the aftermath of the disasters. A study in Nepal found that participants who engaged in religious practices such as prayer in the aftermath of an earthquake expressed more resilience than those who did not (Jang et al., 2018).

10.4.4.3 *Psychological Capital*

Psychological capital describes factors within a person including self-efficacy, hope, and optimism (Luthans et al., 2007). Positive psychology emphasizes developing inner strengths, such as hope, optimism, and courage (Seligman 2002a, 2002b). These personal-psychological traits were coping resources in achieving resilience. They are subjective attributes that are often associated with resilience (Hobfoll et al., 2003). Survivors demonstrated resilience by maintaining optimism and hope. Hope was sustained by not dwelling on negative thoughts that emerged as a facet of resilience (Fernando, 2012).

Optimism was negatively associated with post-disaster distress; thus, the more optimistic survivors were, the more resilient they became (Chan et al., 2012; Maltais and Gauthier, 2009). Optimism is an adaptive way of coping in uncertainty hoping for situations to improve (Maltais and Gauthier, 2009). Engaging in activities and hobbies was reported in some studies as helping to maintain hope and well-being (Mann et al., 2018). In addition to optimism, gratitude, perseverance were also mentioned as enhancing resilience (Fernando, 2012; Niaz, 2006). Cognitive flexibility – the ability to reappraise traumatic experiences – can reframe thoughts about an event leading to acceptance and resilience (Iacoviello and Charney, 2020). According to Iacoviello and Charney (2020), optimism and cognitive flexibility can enable an individual to develop resilience.

10.4.4.4 *Social Capital and Social Embeddedness*

Social capital and social embeddedness have to do with whether an individual has access to external resources that they can access if and when needed to help temporarily bolster their ability to cope, adapt, and be resilient to disaster trauma and stress (Akbar and Aldrich, 2018). Such external resources could enable the demonstration of self-help and self-reliance initiatives and facilitate the demonstration of individual resilience. Collectively, the sum aggregation of such atomized, autonomous, and self-governing individual personal resilience(s) (which may draw from outside resources) may together contribute towards community resilience and quicker individual and community recovery; drawing upon Rimke (2000) and Patel et al. (2017).

10.4.3   How Local People May Help Themselves

The willingness of local people to express and provide input to recovery processes and outcomes with and without government is key. Where there are formal government recovery efforts, the government must serve the people and not vice versa, and there should be community participation in running disaster recovery programmes. Where there is little or no government effort, local communities can organize and coordinate with stakeholders such as emergency services, religious groups, corporate bodies, associations, national and international NGOs, voluntary organizations, social activists, political parties, and others. However, local communities should participate in and coordinate disaster recovery efforts. For instance, local communities that are unaffected or little affected by a disaster would attempt to rescue those who have been affected by using available resources. Community members should participate in deciding what assistance is needed most.

Community solidarity, collectivism and social capital are necessary for disaster recovery programmes as well as cooperation within and between social networks. This social capital is very important as the community knows best its social characteristics and the needs of community members. For example, the community can build their houses with their own designs and materials as community members best know the requirements for disaster-resistant houses. Community solidarity is another form of self-help for example through assisting one another in rebuilding their houses. On completing one house, the community then builds another person's house. Community participation and solidarity in recovery will minimize potential conflict and hasten recovery (see Carstensen et al., 2021; Rosse, 1993).

The community members can create activities that relate to disaster awareness since the local community has a lot of influence on efforts associated with disaster mitigation policy. Hence, communities can pre-identify vulnerable areas for action either by themselves or by the government. Various studies have stressed that participation and ownership by the local people can result in significant achievements through "self-help" and placing the local community at the forefront of the recovery process. The values of cooperation and solidarity among individuals, their social networks, and other members of the community are important social capital. Likewise, resilience and dignity involve not to depend on government assistance but undertaking self-help. Where there is a government response, the community must decide on the type of rehabilitation that best meets local needs.

For instance, community members who were much poorer or older than others could be prioritized for receiving assistance while other, more resilient less vulnerable members could wait. Hence, undertaking recovery in a shared and collective manner. Also, community members may work voluntarily in rebuilding houses for the neediest families where necessary using any of the building materials that could be salvaged from the debris to save time and avoid buying expensive new materials. This is different from waiting for a housing contractor to build the house. Overall, intangible self-help resources such as resilience, trust, social networks and shared values in a community can improve the speed and efficiency of disaster recovery

10.5   Conclusion

In summary, intangible self-help resources such as resilience, faith, trust, social networks and shared values, faith, religious practices, psychological, and social capital are important in developing resilience for self-governance and self-help in recovery situations. Faith-induced hope and optimism can facilitate post-disaster recovery. Religious practices such as praying and reading the Bible seem to enhance the relationship with God and might have helped to overcome the trauma associated with a disaster and spurred self-help and self-reliance initiatives in achieving a relatively faster recovery.

Likewise, other psychological factors also contribute to resilience for self-governance and self-help post-disaster, such as social capital and social connectedness from which external resources may be drawn. The sum of such individual self-help and self-reliance/personal resilience may collectively contribute towards aggregate community resilience and thus quicker individual and community recovery. Overall, we must also leverage the pre-existing motivational and psychological strengths and resources of individuals, such as their abilities, faith, capacities, knowledge, and social capital, to enhance faster recovery.

References

Abramson, D. M., Stehling-Ariza, T., Park, Y. S., Walsh, L., & Culp, D. (2010). Measuring individual disaster recovery: A socioecological framework. *Disaster Medicine and Public Health Preparedness, 4*(S1), S46–S54.

Abbott, R. P., & White, R. S. (2019). *Narratives of faith from the Haiti earthquake: Religion, natural hazards and disaster response.* Routledge.

Ager, J., Fiddian-Qasmiyeh, E., & Ager, A. (2015). Local faith communities and the promotion of resilience in contexts of humanitarian crisis. *Journal of Refugee Studies, 28*(2), 202–221.

Akbar, M. S., & Aldrich, D. P. (2018). Social capital's role in recovery: Evidence from communities affected by the 2010 Pakistan floods. *Disasters, 42*(3), 475–497.

Alawiyah, T., Bell, H., Pyles, L., & Runnels, R. C. (2011). Spirituality and faith-based interventions: Pathways to disaster resilience for African American Hurricane Katrina survivors. *Journal of Religion & Spirituality in Social Work: Social Thought, 30*(3), 294–319.

Aldrich, D. P. (2010). Fixing recovery: Social capital in post-crisis resilience. *Journal of Homeland Security,* Forthcoming. Available at SSRN: https://ssrn.com/abstract =1599632

Aldrich, D. P. (2011a). The power of people: Social capital's role in recovery from the 1995 Kobe earthquake. *Natural Hazards, 56*(3), 595–611.

Aldrich D. P. (2011b). The externalities of strong social capital: Post-tsunami recovery in Southeast India. *Journal of Civil Society, 7*(1), 81–99.

Aldrich, D. P. (2012). Social, not physical, infrastructure: The critical role of civil society after the 1923 Tokyo earthquake. *Disasters, 36*(3), 398–419.

Alexander, D. (2002). *Natural disasters.* Routledge.

Alexander, D. A., & Klein, S. (2009). First responders after disasters: A review of stress reactions, at-risk, vulnerability, and resilience factors. *Prehospital and Disaster Medicine, 24*(2), 87–94.

Altay, N., & Green III, W. G. (2006). OR/MS research in disaster operations management. *European Journal of Operational Research, 175*(1), 475–493.

Arcaya, M., Raker, E. J., & Waters, M. C. (2020). The social consequences of disasters: Individual and community change. *Annual Review of Sociology, 46,* 671–691.

Asian Disaster Reduction Centre. (2005). Total disaster risk management: Good practices. http://www.adrc.or.jp/publications/TDRM2005/TDRM_Good_Practices/PDF/Chapter3 _3.3.2-1.pdf Samarajiva: Mobilizing ICTs for disaster warnings745 viewed 1 July 2021.

Astill, S., & Miller, E. (2018). 'The trauma of the cyclone has changed us forever': Self-reliance, vulnerability and resilience among older Australians in cyclone-prone areas. *Ageing & Society, 38*(2), 403–429.

Aten, J. D., Smith, W. R., Davis, E. B., Van Tongeren, D. R., Hook, J. N., Davis, D. E., ... & Hill, P. C. (2019). The psychological study of religion and spirituality in a disaster context: A systematic review. *Psychological Trauma: Theory, Research, Practice, and Policy, 11*(6), 597.

Augustine, J. (2009). The effects of individual, family, and community factors on adult resilience: A study on the tsunami survivors of 12/26/2004, Electronic Theses and Dissertations. 754. University of Denver, Colorado. https://digitalcommons.du.edu/ etd/754

Baidhawy, Z. (2015). The role of faith-based organization in coping with disaster management and mitigation: Muhammadiyah's Experience. *Journal of Indonesian Islam, 9*(2), 167–194.

Bellegarde-Smith, P. (2011). A man-made disaster: The earthquake of January 12, 2010—A Haitian perspective. *Journal of Black Studies, 42*(2), 264–275.

Bensimon, M. (2012). Elaboration on the association between trauma, PTSD and posttraumatic growth: The role of trait resilience. *Personality and Individual Differences, 52*(7), 782–787.

Bergstrand, K., Mayer, B., Brumback, B., & Zhang, Y. (2015). Assessing the relationship between social vulnerability and community resilience to hazards. *Social Indicators Research, 122,* 391–409.

Boin, R. A. (2008). *Crisis management: A three volume set of essential readings.* Sage Publications Ltd, USA, ISBN: 9781847870889.

Blackman, D., Nakanishi, H., & Benson, A. M. (2017). Disaster resilience as a complex problem: Why linearity is not applicable for long-term recovery. *Technological Forecasting and Social Change, 121,* 89–98.

Bokszczanin, A. (2012). Social support provided by adolescents following a disaster and perceived social support, sense of community at school, and proactive coping. *Anxiety, Stress & Coping, 25*(5), 575–592.

Cano-Calhoun, C. (2021). *Community and agency perspectives on local self-reliance in disasters.* University of Washington.

Carruthers, C. P., & Hood, C. D. (2007). Building a life of meaning through therapeutic recreation: The leisure and well-being model, part I. *Therapeutic Recreation Journal, 41*(4), 276.

Carstensen, N., Mudhar, M., & Munksgaard, F. S. (2021). 'Let communities do their work': The role of mutual aid and self-help groups in the Covid-19 pandemic response. *Disasters, 45,* S146–S173.

Chamlee-Wright, E., & Storr, V. (2010). Expectations of government's response to disaster. *Public Choice, 144*(1–2), 253–274.

Chamberlain, A. K. (2010). *"Long-term relationships between religiousness and posttraumatic stress response following resource loss from Hurricane Katrina.* Ph.D. Dissertation, University of Southern Mississippi, Hattiesburg, MS.

Chan, C. S., Rhodes, J. E., & Pérez, J. E. (2012). A prospective study of religiousness and psychological distress among female survivors of Hurricanes Katrina and Rita. *American Journal of Community Psychology, 49,* 168–181.

Cherry, K. E., Sampson, L., Galea, S., Marks, L. D., Stanko, K. E., Nezat, P. F., & Baudoin, K. H. (2018). Spirituality, humor, and resilience after natural and technological disasters. *Journal of Nursing Scholarship, 50*(5), 492–501.

Chester, D. K., & Duncan, A. M. (2010). Responding to disasters within the Christian tradition, with reference to volcanic eruptions and earthquakes. *Religion, 40*(2), 85–95.

Chester, D. K., Duncan, A. M., & Dibben, C. J. (2008). The importance of religion in shaping volcanic risk perception in Italy, with special reference to Vesuvius and Etna. *Journal of Volcanology and Geothermal Research, 172*(3–4), 216–228.

Clarke, G. (2006). Faith matters: Faith-based organisations, civil society and international development. *Journal of International Development: The Journal of the Development Studies Association, 18*(6), 835–848.

Connor, K. M., & Davidson, J. R. (2003). Development of a new resilience scale: The Connor-Davidson resilience scale (CD-RISC). *Depression and Anxiety, 18*(2), 76–82.

Coppola, D.P. (2011). Introduction to International Disaster Management, 2nd edition, Elsevier Butterworth-Heinemann, Burlington, MA.

Council of Australian Governments (COAG). (2011). *National strategy for disaster resilience: Building the resilience of our nation to disasters.* COAG.

Curnin, S., & O'Hara, D. (2019). Nonprofit and public sector interorganizational collaboration in disaster recovery: Lessons from the field. *Nonprofit Management and Leadership, 30*(2), 277–297.

Cutter, S. (2005a). *The geography of social vulnerability: Race, class, and catastrophe.* Discussion organized by SSRC on 'Understanding Katrina: Perspectives from the Social Sciences'.

Cutter, S. L., Barnes, L., Berry, M., Burton, C., Evans, E., Tate, E., & Webb, J. (2008). A place-based model for understanding community resilience to natural disasters. *Global Environmental Change, 18*(4), 598–606.

Cutter, S. L., Boruff, B. J., & Shirley, W. L. (2003). Social vulnerability to environmental hazards. *Social Science Quarterly, 84*(2), 242–261.

Davis, E. B., Kimball, C. N., Aten, J. D., Hamilton, C., Andrews, B., Lemke, A., ... & Chung, J. (2019). Faith in the wake of disaster: A longitudinal qualitative study of religious attachment following a catastrophic flood. *Psychological Trauma: Theory, Research, Practice, and Policy, 11*(6), 578.

Drabek, T. E., & McEntire, D. A. (2003). Emergent phenomena and the sociology of disaster: Lessons, trends and opportunities from the research literature. *Disaster Prevention and Management: An International Journal, 2*(12), 97–112.

Esterwood, E., & Saeed, S. A. (2020). Past epidemics, natural disasters, COVID19, and mental health: Learning from history as we deal with the present and prepare for the future. *Psychiatric Quarterly, 91*, 1121–1133.

Easton-Calabria, E., & Omata, N. (2018). Panacea for the refugee crisis? Rethinking the promotion of 'self-reliance' for refugees. *Third World Quarterly, 39*(8), 1458–1474.

Etengoff, C., & Rodriguez, E. M. (2022). "At its core, Islam is about standing with the oppressed": Exploring transgender Muslims' religious resilience. *Psychology of Religion and Spirituality, 14*(4), 480.

Fast, J. (2019). James Bohland, Jack Harrald and Deborah Brosnan. The disaster resiliency challenge: Transforming theory to action. *Journal of Homeland Security and Emergency Management, 16*(2). https://doi.org/10.1515/jhsem-2019-0005

Fernando, D. M., & Hebert, B. B. (2011). Resiliency and recovery: Lessons from the Asian tsunami and Hurricane Katrina. *Journal of Multicultural Counseling and Development, 39*(1), 2–13.

Fernando, G. A. (2012). Bloodied but unbowed: Resilience examined in a South asian community. *American Journal of Orthopsychiatry, 82*(3), 367.

Finch, J., Farrell, L. J., & Waters, A. M. (2020). Searching for the HERO in youth: Does psychological capital (PsyCap) predict mental health symptoms and subjective wellbeing in Australian school-aged children and adolescents? *Child Psychiatry & Human Development, 51*, 1025–1036.

Fletcher, D., & Sarkar, M. (2013). Psychological resilience. *European Psychologist, 18*(1), 12–23.

Foa, E. B., & Foa, U. G. (2012). Resource theory of social exchange. In K. Törnblom & A. Kazemi (Eds.), Handbook of social resource theory: Theoretical extensions, empirical insights, and social applications (pp. 15–32). Springer.

Fothergill, A., & Peek, L. A. (2004). Poverty and disasters in the United States: A review of recent sociological findings. *Natural Hazards, 32*, 89–110.

Grube, L., & Storr, V. H. (2014). The capacity for self-governance and post-disaster resiliency. *The Review of Austrian Economics, 27*, 301–324.

Henderson, T. L., Roberto, K. A., & Kamo, Y. (2010). Older adults' responses to Hurricane Katrina: Daily hassles and coping strategies. *Journal of Applied Gerontology, 29*(1), 48–69.

Hobfoll, S. E., Johnson, R. J., Ennis, N., & Jackson, A. P. (2003). Resource loss, resource gain, and emotional outcomes among inner city women. *Journal of Personality and Social Psychology, 84*(3), 632.

Hood, C. (1991). A public management for all seasons? *Public Administration, 69*(1), 3–19.

Hood, C. D., & Carruthers, C. P. (2007). Enhancing leisure experience and developing resources: The leisure and well-being model part II. *Therapeutic Recreation Journal, 41*(4), 298.

Hood, C. D., & Carruthers, C. P. (2016). Strengths-based TR program development using the Leisure and Well-Being Model: Translating theory into practice. *Therapeutic Recreation Journal, 50*(1).

Hu, T., Zhang, D., & Wang, J. (2015). A meta-analysis of the trait resilience and mental health. *Personality and Individual differences, 76*, 18–27.

Iacoviello, B. M., & Charney, D. S. (2020). Cognitive and behavioral components of resilience to stress. In *Stress resilience* (pp. 23–31). Academic Press.

Jang, M., Ko, J. A., & Kim, E. J. (2018). Religion and mental health among Nepal earthquake survivors in temporary tent villages. *Mental Health, Religion & Culture, 21*(4), 329–335.

Kapucu, N (2007). Non-profit response to catastrophic disasters. *Disaster Prevention and Management: An International Journal, 16*(4), 551–561.

Kapucu, N. (2008). Culture of preparedness: Household disaster preparedness. *Disaster Prevention and Management: An International Journal, 17*(4), 526–535.

Kapucu, N., & Van Wart, M. (2006). The evolving role of the public sector in managing catastrophic disasters: Lessons learned. *Administration & Society, 38*(3), 279–308.

Kasim, F. M., & Nurdin, A. (2021, January). Religion as a social capital in realizing disaster resilience in Aceh. In *International conference on social science, political science, and humanities* (ICoSPOLHUM 2020) (pp. 222–228). Atlantis Press.

Kuhlicke, C., Scolobig, A., Tapsell, S., Steinführer, A., & De Marchi, B. (2011). Contextualizing social vulnerability: Findings from case studies across Europe. *Natural Hazards, 58*, 789–810.

Kono, S., & Burton, S. (2019). The applicability of therapeutic recreation to post-disaster lives: The leisure and well-being model perspective. *Therapeutic Recreation Journal, 53*(3), 193–209.

Kooiman, J., & Van Vliet, M. (2000). Self-governance as a mode of societal governance. *Public Management an International Journal of Research and Theory, 2*(3), 359–378.

Kreps, G. A. (Ed.). (1989). *Social structure and disaster; symposium on social structure and disaster, college of William and Mary, Williamsburg, Virginia, 15–16 may 1986*. University of Delaware Press.

Lindell, M. K., & Prater, C. S. (2003). Assessing community impacts of natural disasters. *Natural Hazards Review, 4*(4), 176–185.

Liu, W., & Ni, L. (2021). Relationship matters: How government organization-public relationship impacts disaster recovery outcomes among multiethnic communities. *Public Relations Review, 47*(3), 102047.

Llamas, J. D. (2014). *Resilience in the aftermath of a technological disaster: A community-based mixed methods research study.* University of California.

Luthans, F. (2002). Positive organizational behavior: Developing and managing psychological strengths. *Academy of Management Perspectives, 16*(1), 57–72.

Luthans, F., Youssef, C. M., & Avolio, B. J. (2007). Psychological capital: Investing and developing positive organizational behavior. *Positive Organizational Behavior, 1*(2), 9–24.

Luthans, F., Luthans, K. W., & Luthans, B. C. (2004). Positive psychological capital: Beyond human and social capital. *Business Horizons, 47*(1), 45–50. https://doi.org/10.1016/j.bushor.2003.11.007

Makkar, S., & Singh, A. K. (2021). Development of a spirituality measurement scale. *Current Psychology, 40*, 1490–1497.

Maltais, D., & Gauthier, S. (2009). Long-term impacts on personal and spiritual values for French Canadian elderly victims of a flood in Quebec, Canada. In Eugene, Dominique & Kalayjian, Ani (Eds). *Mass Trauma and emotional healing around the world: Rituals and practices for resilience and meaning-making,* 193. Bloomsbury.

Mann, C. L., Gillezeau, C. N., Massazza, A., Lyons, D. J., Tanaka, K., Yonekura, K., ... & Katz, C. L. (2018). Fukushima triple disaster and the road to recovery: A qualitative exploration of resilience in internally displaced residents. *Psychiatric Quarterly, 89*, 383–397.

Manyena, S. B. (2006). The concept of resilience revisited. *Disasters, 30*(4), 434–450.

Marks, L. D., Cherry, K. E., & Silva, J. L. (2009). Faith, crisis, coping, and meaning making after Katrina: A qualitative, cross-cohort examination. In K. E. Cherry (Ed.), *Lifespan perspectives on natural disasters: Coping with Katrina, Rita, and other storms* (pp. 195–215). Springer.

Mason, L. (2019). *Displaced children of Katrina 10 years later: A phenomenological study of post-disaster coping.* Psy.D. Dissertation, Clinical Psychology, William James College, Ann Arbor, MI.

McGeehan, K. M. (2014). *Religious narratives and their implications for coping, recovery, and disaster risk reduction.* Ph.D. Dissertation, University of Hawaii at Manoa, Manoa, HI.

McGregor, A. (2010). Geographies of religion and development: Rebuilding sacred spaces in Aceh, Indonesia, after the tsunami. *Environment and Planning A, 42*(3), 729–746.

McKaughan, D. J. (2017). On the value of faith and faithfulness. *International Journal for Philosophy of Religion, 81*, 7–29.

Mesidor, J. K., & Sly, K. F. (2019). Religious coping, general coping strategies, perceived social support, PTSD symptoms, resilience, and posttraumatic growth among survivors of the 2010 earthquake in Haiti. *Mental Health, Religion and Culture, 22*(2), 130–143.

Miller, W., & Smith, D. J. (2017, November 4). *The emergence, restoration, and resiliency of self-governance.* http://dx.doi.org/10.2139/ssrn.3065327

Mitchell, J. T. (2003). Prayer in disaster: Case study of Christian clergy. *Natural Hazards Review, 4*(1), 20–26.

Niaz, U. (2006). Role of faith and resilience in recovery from psychotrauma. *Pakistan Journal of Medical Sciences, 22*(2), 204.

Norris, F. H., Stevens, S. P., Pfefferbaum, B., Wyche, K. F., & Pfefferbaum, R. L. (2008). Community resilience as a metaphor, theory, set of capacities, and strategy for disaster readiness. *American Journal of Community Psychology, 41*, 127–150.

Norris, F. H., & Elrod, C. L. (2006). *Psychosocial consequences of disaster: A review of past research.* The Guilford Press.

Ogińska-Bulik, N., & Michalska, P. (2020). The relationship between emotional processing deficits and posttraumatic stress disorder symptoms among breast cancer patients: The mediating role of rumination. *Journal of clinical psychology in medical settings, 27*(1), 11–21.

Ogińska-Bulik, N., & Michalska, P. (2021). Psychological resilience and secondary traumatic stress in nurses working with terminally ill patients—The mediating role of job burnout. *Psychological Services, 18*(3), 398.

Oliver-Smith, A., (2009). Sea level rise and the vulnerability of coastal peoples: responding to the local challenges of global climate change in the 21st centruty, viewed 8 August 2005, http://www.ehs.unu.edu/file/get/4097

Oloruntoba, R. (2013). *The implications and limitations of commercial supply chain management process models for disaster relief.* PhD Dissertation. University of Newcastle, New South Wales, Australia. August.

Oloruntoba, R. (2015). Resilience and adaptive capacities in Cyclone Larry. In J. Mackee & H. Giggins (Eds.), Proceedings of the 5th International Conference on Building Resilience (pp. 548–567). University of Newcastle.

Oloruntoba, R., & Asare-Doku, W. (2021). Self-reliance in disaster recovery: A systematic literature review 1990–2019. *International Journal of Mass Emergencies & Disasters, 39*(1), 11–42.

Omata, N. (2017). *Studies in forced migration.* Vol. 36, *The myth of self-reliance: Economic lives inside a liberian refugee camp.* Berghahn Books.

Ong, A. D., Bergeman, C. S., Bisconti, T. L., & Wallace, K. A. (2006). Psychological resilience, positive emotions, and successful adaptation to stress in later life. *Journal of Personality and Social Psychology, 91*(4), 730.

Ozbay, F., Johnson, D. C., Dimoulas, E., Morgan Iii, C. A., Charney, D., & Southwick, S. (2007). Social support and resilience to stress: From neurobiology to clinical practice. *Psychiatry (Edgmont), 4*(5), 35.

Patel, S. S., Rogers, M. B., Amlôt, R., & Rubin, G. J. (2017). What do we mean by 'community resilience'? A systematic literature review of how it is defined in the literature. *PLoS currents, 9.*

Pellerin, N., & Raufaste, E. (2020). Psychological resources protect well-being during the COVID-19 pandemic: A longitudinal study during the French lockdown. *Frontiers in Psychology, 11*, 590276.

Perrow, C. (2007). Disasters ever more? Reducing US vulnerabilities. *Handbook of disaster research,* 521–533. New York, Springer.

Plante, T. G., & Boccaccini, M. T. (1997). The Santa Clara strength of religious faith questionnaire. *Pastoral Psychology, 45*(5), 375–387.

Quarantelli, E. L. (1989). Conceptualizing disasters from a sociological perspective. *International Journal of Mass Emergencies & Disasters, 7*(3), 243–251.

Quarantelli, E. L. (2003a). *A half century of social science disaster research: Selected major findings and their applicability,* viewed 20 April 2022, http://dspace.udel.edu:8080/dspace/handle/19716/297.

Quarantelli, E. L. (2003b). Urban vulnerability to disasters in developing countries: Managing risks. In A. Kreimer, M. Arnold, & A. Carlin (Eds.), *Building safer cities: The future of disaster risk.* p.211 The World Bank, Washington.

Quarantelli, E. L., & Dynes, R. R. (1977). Response to social crisis and disaster. *Annual Review of Sociology, 3*(1), 23–49.

Rasmussen, C. E. (2011). *The autonomous animal: Self-governance and the modern subject.* University of Minnesota Press.

Rimke, H. M. (2000). Governing citizens through self-help literature. *Cultural Studies, 14*(1), 61–78.

Rossé, W. L. (1993). Volunteers and post-disaster recovery: A call for community self-sufficiency. *Journal of Social Behavior and Personality, 8*(5), 261.

Rubin, C. B. (2019). Introduction: 110 years of disaster response and emergency management in the United States. In *Emergency Management* (pp. 1–10). Routledge.

Schenker-Wicki, A., Inauen, M., & Olivares, M. (2010). Unmastered risks: From crisis to catastrophe: An economic and management insight. *Journal of Business Research, 63*(4), 337–346.

Seligman, M. E. (2002a). Positive psychology, positive prevention, and positive therapy. *Handbook of Positive Psychology, 2*(2002), 3–12.

Seligman, M. E. (2002b). *Authentic happiness: Using the new positive psychology to realize your potential for lasting fulfillment.* Simon and Schuster.

Shaluf, I. M. (2007). Disaster types. *Disaster Prevention and Management: An International Journal, 16*(5), 704–717.

Sheldon, K. M., & King, L. (2001). Why positive psychology is necessary. *American Psychologist, 56*(3), 216–217. https://doi.org/10.1037/0003-066X.56.3.216

Singh, R., & Pande, R. K. (2011). Morphometry of landslides in Garhwal Himalaya, India. *Disaster Prevention and Management: An International Journal, 20*(4), 355–362.

Singh, S. R., Eghdami, M. R., & Singh, S. (2014). The concept of social vulnerability: A review from disasters perspectives. *International Journal of Interdisciplinary and Multidisciplinary Studies, 1*(6), 71–82.

Sobel, R. S., & Leeson, P. T. (2006). Government's response to Hurricane Katrina: A public choice analysis. *Public Choice, 127*, 55–73.

Spielman, S. E., Tuccillo, J., Folch, D. C., Schweikert, A., Davies, R., Wood, N., & Tate, E. (2020). Evaluating social vulnerability indicators: Criteria and their application to the Social Vulnerability Index. *Natural Hazards, 100*, 417–436.

Tausch, C., Marks, L. D., Brown, J. S., Cherry, K. E., Frias, T., McWilliams, Z., ... & Sasser, D. D. (2011). Religion and coping with trauma: Qualitative examples from Hurricanes Katrina and Rita. *Journal of Religion, Spirituality & Aging, 23*(3), 236–253.

Thomas, A & Mizushima, M (2005). Logistics training: necessity or luxury? *Forced Migration Review, 22*, 60–61.

United Nations *International Strategy for Disaster Risk Reduction* (UN-ISDR). (2004a). *Living with risk, a global review of disaster reduction initiatives*, UN Sales Publication, Geneva, Switzerland.

United Nations Office for Disaster Risk Reduction (UNISDR). (2004b). Terminology, viewed 10 September 2010, http://www.unisdr.org/eng/library/lib-terminology-eng-p.htm.

United Nations. (2004c). Core terminology of disaster reduction. In K. Thywissen (Ed.), Towards disaster resilient societies, 2–3. United Nations University Press.

United Nations. (2006). Core terminology of disaster reduction. In K. Thywissen (Ed.), *Towards disaster resilient societies*, 2004. United Nations.

United Nations Development Programme. (2004). Core terminology of disaster reduction. In K. Thywissen (Ed.), *Towards disaster resilient societies*, 2004. United Nations.

United Nations Development Programme. (2008). Core terminology of disaster reduction. In K. Thywissen (Ed.), *Towards disaster resilient societies*, 2004. United Nations.

Verschuur, J., Koks, E. E., & Hall, J. W. (2020). Port disruptions due to natural disasters: Insights into port and logistics resilience. *Transportation Research Part D: Transport and Environment, 85*, 102393.

Waugh, C. E., Thompson, R. J., & Gotlib, I. H. (2011). Flexible emotional responsiveness in trait resilience. *Emotion, 11*(5), 1059.

Weichselgartner, J. (2001). Disaster mitigation: The concept of vulnerability revisited. *Disaster Prevention and Management: An International Journal, 10*(2), 85–95.

Wild, K. Wiles, J.L., & Allen,, R.E (2013). Resilience: thoughts on the value of the concept for critical gerontology. *Ageing & Society*, *33*(1), pp.137–158.

Wilkinson, O. (2015). *Faith and resilience after disaster: The case of Typhoon Haiyan.* Misean Cara. http://www. miseancara. ie/faith-resilience-disaster.

Young, O. R., Berkhout, F., Gallopin, G. C., Janssen, M. A., Ostrom, E., & Van der Leeuw, S. (2006). The globalization of socio-ecological systems: An agenda for scientific research. *Global Environmental Change*, *16*(3), 304–316.

11 Conclusion

11.1 Disaster Chronology – An Example from Japan

The damage, harm, losses, and problems caused by the occurrence of a natural or other disaster including the death and destruction it wrought can take up significant human, psychological, physical, community, environmental, infrastructural, technological, and financial/economic attention, resources, time, and energy. It is therefore necessary to develop scholarship that can assist in the development of alternative scenarios, approaches, and models that may be more effective, efficient, and satisfactory to disaster-affected persons (DAP).

For illustration below, we take as an example disasters in Japan, where encounters with disasters are among the highest in the world. And Japan is among the most advanced in disaster research, prediction, mitigation, preparedness, response, and recovery. Japan's cultural and contextual conditions may constitute a special and good case for learning about resilience. Moreover, it is worth periodically examining how the entirety of disaster recovery could be understood better. An overriding question is what would be meaningful and useful to disaster-affected persons (DAP).

A prevalent model of post-disaster recovery in Japan, for example, consisted of the following (see also Mazumdar, Itoh, & Iwasa 2021). After a disaster that affected life and property an initial step was moving away from the disaster-affected area to temporary shelters (TS). These could be with relatives, friends, or nearby initial temporary accommodations provided by the local authorities, mostly in large structures, such as stadiums, schools, and municipal or religious buildings. In TS, individuals and families could be apportioned small amounts of space as temporary shelter. As DAP could select a space for themselves within the shelter building, relatives and friends could possibly stay together in close proximity and render aid and comfort to each other. Such highly temporary accommodations were supposed to be only for the brief duration of a few days to a few weeks when governmental authorities could provide or DAP could find more appropriate longer-term accommodations.

The next step for DAP was to move to emergency temporary housing (ETH). These were assigned by the government mostly based on one or more lotteries. In this assignment system, relatives or friends were not likely to receive accommodations together or nearby, which negatively affected mutual reliance and aid.

DOI: 10.4324/9781003615903-15

These ETH were similar to pre-manufactured trailer homes. Japan's Disaster Relief Act (1984/1947) limited ETH to those whose houses were completely destroyed or severely damaged, though prefectural governments were allowed some discretion in local implementation.[1] Moreover, DAPs were not permitted to exchange one ETH unit for another identical or similar one, for example, to be close to relatives.

When permanent housing became available the government assigned DAP to specific units mostly based on a lottery, which was viewed as fairer than other modes of assignment due to the equal opportunity a lottery afforded and the reduced possibility of the authorities favouring or discriminating.

11.1.1   Emergency Temporary Housing – Provision and Allocation

The lottery system did not give consideration to mutual aid among relatives and close friends. Co-coping with family, relatives, or friends was not fostered. DAP mostly had to rely on their own individual efforts (i.e. MHE) for most survival needs. Even though this system might have seemed fair, it may not have assisted disaster victims (DV) in day-to-day life becoming more comfortable. For example, a person could not easily leave a child or dependent with a relative or close friend in order to go and purchase necessities or run errands. The above is a distant and aggregate view adopted mostly by planners and authorities and could be referred to as a top-down view.

Though prevalent, this system could have several potential problems. Even provincial authorities could be physically and socially distant from and unfamiliar with the disaster zone. Autochthonous conditions and context may not be known in detail; social systems and regional needs may not be fully or correctly understood, situated knowledge may not be used, and resources and products may not be considered for utilization. Non-resident outsiders without this local knowledge could be treated as experts, whose ideas could be privileged and implemented over the ideas or objections of knowledgeable residents. Imported foreign products may not be suitable or sustainable for local conditions, such as climate (e.g. humidity, heat, dust, etc.), technological requirements (e.g. stable non-spiking electric supply), and underlying language and cultural assumptions (Mazumdar 2024a; 2024b). These could cause dissatisfaction, damage, rifts, and conflicts, besides privileging foreign products and economies, while downgrading local products; even though these may be more appropriate and sustainable, and it could leave the local people indebted to one or more foreign "benefactors" and contribute to upsetting the local system and economy.

Housing the population left unhoused by a disaster becomes a primary task for the authorities. Usually, governments do not have within their jurisdiction an available stock of housing to be assigned in the event of a disaster. Unencumbered open space is mostly not available for ETH to be constructed or installed. Consequently, existing housing must be found (for which a list could be maintained), or new ETH must be constructed. Thus, the location and amount of space for ETH can turn out to be a difficult problem.

This is not one of Karl Popper's (1966) simple "clock problems" that can be analyzed into its constituent parts to which solutions can be easily found. Counting the numbers of housing units needed and ordering them is an oversimplification of a more complex task into a simple "clock problem". Increasing the types of units, working out the numbers of each and configuring their designs so that these are physically, socially, culturally, and religiously suitable (Mazumdar & Mazumdar 1993; Mazumdar 2024a,b) to unknown potential residents makes the problem less parametric, more complex, multidimensional and unpredictable and therefore closer to Karl Popper's "cloud problem". Simplification of complex cloud problems into more analyzable, tractable ones may not help resolve all the nested problems and thus is inherently likely to encounter more difficulties and fail in part or whole. Nevertheless, simplifications are common.

In Japan,

> Social workers learned from the Kobe Earthquake in 1995 that simply providing new housing is not enough. There, people who lost their homes, became depressed after moving to places where they didn't know anybody. In the five years after the quake more than 200 elderly people died solitary deaths in temporary housing.
>
> (Facts & Details 2014: https://factsanddetails.com/japan/
> cat26/sub161/item1744.html)

Furthermore, even though stays in ETH were supposed to be temporary, lasting a few weeks to a few months, sometimes this time stretched to years; ten years after GEJET some people were still in ETH. What can be considered a reasonable time period is a pertinent question.

A bottom-up view would be that of DAP seeking a place to restart life anew after losing family and friends, and some or nearly all belongings in the disaster. Their search for existing affordable housing units could be severely hampered by their attempts to obtain food and necessities and file applications with the authorities while concurrently trying to obtain food and necessities for the family with the limited resources immediately available while in an ETH (see also Mazumdar, Itoh, & Iwasa 2021).

It is noteworthy that several of these procedures are changing as part of an ongoing effort to make the disaster recovery process more apt for DAP. A new changed scenario is emerging. Following the January 2024 Noto earthquake in Japan, for example, greater variety, sizes, and more comfortable ETH designs were offered (The Japan News, 01 March 2024, https://japannews.yomiuri.co.jp/society /noto-peninsula-earthquake/20240301-172033/). Some ETH in Suzu in Ishikawa prefecture are not industrially produced, are two-storied, made of wood, and are reportedly better; these were designed by renowned architect Shigeru Ban, an innovator in ETH designs.[2] Also, the selection criteria for DAP receiving ETH in Wajima, Ishikawa prefecture, included consideration of the amount of damage suffered, families with elderly and children, and elderly, among others.[3] Many other conscientious designers have offered solutions (e.g. Dalton 2017) and experimental ideas (e.g. pre-manufactured products like geodesic domes (Oliver 1987).

Moreover, since the 1995 Kobe earthquake disaster "An effort was made to keep communities intact and relocate ent(i)re (sic) towns and districts to the same place" (Facts & Details 2014: https://factsanddetails.com/japan/cat26/sub161/item1744.html).

Thus, now more interplay is developing between top-down policies and efforts and the needs of the bottom. Nevertheless, not usually factored into the recovery process discussions and discourses are efforts made by individuals and very small groups, which we have labelled micro human efforts (MHE) (see also Subasinghe, Sutrisna & Olatunji 2021). The poignant invisibility of such efforts in the larger scheme of grand efforts makes them micro.

11.2   The Need for Considering MHE

In academia, a common practice is to reach for, derive, or develop theories, for-mulae, or statements with statistical generalizability or broad universal applicabil-ity. In this, characteristics of the small, different and variant are ignored. What might be ignorable as only minor variations or blips from the distance of scient-ism can turn out to be highly important or significant to others. Therefore, we are unable to neglect, avoid, or overlook the special, unusual, numerically insignificant and small but must consider these also as important. Consequently, micro human efforts or MHEs are essential and indispensable. While "micro-human" has been a clinical term in some disciplinary and interdisciplinary fields, it has hardly been a speculative term in disaster studies (Subasinghe, Sutrisna & Olatunji 2021).

Although people under post-disaster circumstances respond creatively and react constructively to changes in their surrounding environments, such instantaneous and intuitive individual and small group initiatives have not been seen as an inte-gral part of the grand projects normally done by local and international agencies. This results in devaluation and disregard for efforts crucial to the lives and func-tioning of DAP.

Suppose for a moment that, in the context of disasters, MHEs were disallowed and did not exist. What would be the result? Nearly all activities and efforts would occur only on the initiative, request or order of a leader, authority or organization. For all needed actions, DAP would have to await decisions, approvals, and actions from such higher levels. This could forestall quick action and preclude many small and homegrown projects. There would be little to write about regarding MHEs. But this hypothetical scenario did not occur. Consequently, MHEs are significant for and in this book.

11.3   MHE Theory

The top-down approaches described above were criticized for being elitist, non-democratic, not very effective or efficient, and for leaving some sections of society without receiving the assistance they needed and were dependent on. These DAPs had lost much, possibly including family, relatives, friends, pets, sacred objects, legacy items, meaningful and favourite things, equipment, tools, belongings, income/jobs, and many more. Moreover, in this mode, at a crucial time of vulnerability and helplessness, due consideration was not given to some sets of DAP, the purported beneficiaries. For this, some blamed the societal structures and relationships, whereas others felt that administrative structures, regulations, and rules were hindrances to timely aid distribution. It could be both. DAPs were reliant on distant others, whose knowledge of local conditions could be lacking or scant. Disaster recovery efforts were at the mercy of national, prefectural, and municipal governments or administrative units. In the absence of adequate research on local DAPs, situated and even personal knowledge or experience on which to base decisions could be lacking. This left DAP to figure out for themselves what to do and how to do it.

There was another narrative, however, one dealing with the small efforts made by DAP to help themselves and sometimes others. Though these MHE may have been crucial, they were going unattributed, unrecognized, and unaccounted. This meant that there was hardly any administrative or governmental support for these endeavours. Nor were these efforts being coordinated or factored into overall plans or policies. Interestingly, the contributions of some non-governmental organizations (NGOs) are now being recognized in a few places, but this still overlooks the MHE by local DAPs.

Ontologically, MHE seems to be a special entity. It consists of the small and possibly the different and variant. It appears to be ubiquitous. The micro or small is part of the large, but in its undeconstructed entirety, the large may not be part of the small. And, as discussed in the introduction, *micro* transcends location and geographical boundaries just as disasters do. The various studies in this book attempted to identify and develop concepts, terms, and some emerging theories, a few borrowed from the discourse on equity, power, balance, and impact literature.

It is almost inevitable that MHE will occur as people act on the urge to take care of themselves and their families. Moreover, some populations and their efforts may be ignored, e.g. women (Okay & Onal) and the elderly (Kaluaracchi, Thayaparan & Mendis; Okay & Onal). Conceivably, in other circumstances, the efforts of youth, men, minorities, and others could be downgraded or ignored. This initial examination of MHE was needed in order to start the process of arriving at a deeper understanding of it.

11.4 Varieties of MHE

In their quotidian lives, DAPs engage in many and various MHE. These small projects could be for themselves or for neighbours in the same geographical area. Many MHE projects are based on the skills, experience, or knowledge of the DAP; examples include residents helping other residents with needs, chores, driving (e.g. for the elderly & children), providing childcare (babysitting), cleaning, making, cooking, sewing, tailoring, knitting, teaching, shopping, doing carpentry, plumbing, electrical work, painting, etc. Through such activities using their own efforts DAPs help other DAPs (Iwasa 2011, 2012; Iwasa, Hasegawa, Shinkai, Shinazaki, Yasutake, & Kobayashi 2012) see also Nakashima; Tsubouchi et al.; Okay and

Onal in this volume. These may be part of an exchange or informal non-monetary and even monetary economy.

MHE can occur in all phases of a disaster. In the pre-disaster consciousness phase, ritualized actions can make people aware of the need for preparation. Preparation for disaster can be individual and psychological (Oloruntoba & Asare-Doku) or organizational and community-oriented (Kupietz). Actions during disaster are noted by Tsubouchi, Tomiyasu, Isagawa, and Suzawa. MHE during disasters has not received as much attention, though it is known to occur (as in using boats to rescue people and other heroic actions as people try to save others from impending disaster covered by news media (see Criss 2017 for an MHE example). Post-disaster actions are usual (e.g. Nakashima), as are post-disaster rituals (Stewart and Strathern). Post-disaster analyses are abundant (e.g. Kaluarachchi, Thayaparan & Mendis; Okay & Onal; Pooyan & Hokugo).

11.4.1   MHE – Kinds

Several kinds of MHE are revealed in this book. Examples are: age-based MHE (Okay & Onal); Gendered MHE (Okay & Onal; Kaluarachchi, Thayaparan, & Mendis); Individual person-oriented (Oloruntoba & Asare-Doku); Issue-oriented (Okay & Onal; Kupietz); and Product-oriented (Silva, Subasinghe & Ballinger; Kupietz). Conceivably, there could also be professionally oriented and policy-oriented ones (but for a professionally oriented example see Silva, Subasinghe & Ballinger).

Though these are described and presented here in the context of post-disaster rebuilding, such MHE may also occur in neighbourhoods in non-disaster contexts as well.

11.4.2   MHE Actions

Five major actions are identified and described briefly below:

a) *Dealing*: DAP, those who survive the disaster, have to deal with the disaster. This implies staying alive through it and its effects. In order to do this, they take several MHE, conquer their fears, react successfully to an unexpected and unusual occurrence, and handle the contingencies that arise (for example, a disaster can lead to the closure of a familiar and known exit route). Some of these can foil the best laid plans, and alternatives may have to be found without much time, resources, or help available.

b) *Coping*: Unexpected disasters present many problems that require individuals and small groups to use whatever resources are available to manage adequately. This may also require helping those who require assistance in coping. Coping has a slight edge over dealing as it enables eyes on others.

c) *Adjusting*: The disaster-changed situation requires adjusting to which in turn may need reorientation to the changed situation. For example, things may move and become more precarious, routes may change, usual landmarks may not exist, and dangers may underlie what seems regular.

d) *Rebuilding*: In the new situation and status quo, rebuilding may be quite different from the pre-disaster conditions. There may be a shortage of resources, such as building materials, due to unusual demand. Familiar products may not be available, and what is available may be of a different standard and quality.

e) *Resilience*: The desire to deal with, cope, adjust to, and rebuild may require renewed, strengthened, and heightened resourcefulness, social connectivity, preparedness, and familiarity with actions needed. This phase is transformative as it enables the autonomous functioning of an incorporated unit.

All of the above require the belief that one's own micro-level efforts, no matter how small or insignificant, will eventually lead or contribute to an acceptable new life. Of course, the micro-level efforts may be seen as definitive steps leading to the accomplishment of the larger tasks and goals. Importantly, these MHE are within an individual's control and agency and could be independent of the assistance of others.

11.4.3 Views of MHE

Negative and critical views of MHE were taken by many governments, administrators, and planners. MHE may be viewed as mostly unsupervised by authorities, which might imply that their quality is not verifiable or supportable, and may be unreported. Authorities commonly prevented MHEs in the past (Subasinghe 2013). They precluded MHE because these were viewed as unplanned, informal, confusing, unhealthy, of low-quality, unsafe, messy, and unprotectable during dangers (because these mostly were not planned to enable access for safety equipment such as fire engines, trucks, hook-and-ladders, etc.). MHEs were viewed negatively by those who disliked unorganized, uncontrolled efforts.

MHEs were ignored by several governments who did not actively prevent them and did not act to remove them. This does not imply a neutral position.

A positive view appeared in the 1970s when some scholars and practitioners began to write about the value and benefits of MHE (though they were not referred to as such at the time). Examples include Turner (1976) who in contrast to authoritarianism and technocratism (of authorities), focused on self-build in a way that could be categorized as MHE. Caminos and Goethert (1978) proposed to provide sites and services to enable people to use their own efforts to build houses for themselves on the serviced lots they promoted. Goethert, Hamdi, and Gray's (1988) microplan is another example. These successfully made self-efforts and MHE more acceptable. MHE signalled freedom from state intervention, which could be a liability or an asset. Though governmental authorities could encourage MHEs, this was not prevalent, except for some examples noted.

11.4.4 Valuation of MHE

MHE may not be valued or viewed negatively. Disregarding small efforts characterizing MHE and privileging large ones is common. MHEs could be seen as not having consistency, logic or control, as unplanned, unapproved, hastily constituted, low-quality, unreliable, and perhaps even dangerous (e.g. fire or other hazards). From such a position, it may seem best to stop or eradicate these efforts and occasionally, informal settlements were forcibly removed by authorities (although there sometimes were hidden agendas behind these ostensible reasons). Removal or demolition of such work meant that these efforts could amount to naught, which could put rather heavy strains on the under-resourced, who would have to bear the costs of multiple attempts.

A neutral stance is also possible. Authorities with this position do not take an active role in either assisting or preventing MHEs from happening and could ignore them. In many jurisdictions, MHE was being ignored. As people need to take care of families, restart their work/jobs if possible, send children to school, and re-establish their disrupted lives, MH efforts occur and are likely to continue.

MHE could be viewed positively and recognized as useful, important and contributing to rebuilding, physical and economic development without external support. When seen as beneficial, authorities occasionally provide aid. MHE efforts are sometimes seen as supplying valued products and services, creating jobs, and contributing taxes, i.e. as productive entities or efforts.

MHE is mostly not monetized. That is, usually monetary value is not imputed to it, which may result in non-comparison and non-consideration in financial discussions. MHE may be valuable to those who are engaged in it. Lack of monetization might result in no taxes and lack of financial or economic support.

MHE can be facilitated by attention to several important factors. A positive psychological attitude can be of great benefit to the individuals involved (Oloruntoba & Asare-Doku). Without a positive outlook and initiative, the activities may become dull, uninteresting, and worthless. Non-recognition of the contributions of sections of society, such as women (Okay & Onal; Kaluaracchi, Thayaparan & Mendis; Nakashima), elderly (Okay & Onal), youth, and lower-income people can result in their non-participation, alienation, and exclusion. This implies that actively seeking participation of all sectors is crucial to a sense of caring, ownership, and full participation.

11.4.5 MHE – Chapter Contributions to This Book

In their chapter, Stewart and Strathern point to MHE in the formation of new rituals and ritual spaces as memorials of a disaster, lest future generations forget the disaster victims, and considerations such as human deaths, demise of animals including pets, loss of significant trees, as well as destruction and devastation caused by the event.

Grief rituals, memorial rituals, and remembrance rituals go beyond usual cultural rituals to create new ones. Grief rituals can be temporary, such as appropriating a small amount of (mostly public) space to place photographs, posters, flowers, candles, and other objects, and may disappear or be cleared away after a period of time, sometimes by the mundane need for cleaning. They are sometimes are made permanent.

Importantly, as Stewart and Strathern describe, participation in many of these rituals constitutes micro human efforts. These may have the potential to become macro human efforts when the rituals draw many to participate.

Silva, Subasinghe, and Ballinger examine the involvement of professional architects in the process of post-disaster housing. They claim that there is "dissonance between the architects' design intentions and the evacuees' expectations" (p. 11) and believe that architects design housing on the basis of their own notions about the nature and form of housing. They show that evacuees make modifications to the houses at their own expense indicating that they are dissatisfied with the designs of the houses they are provided, and that the designs fail to "integrate self-improvement in rehousing" (p. 11). The current designs and policies thus end up thwarting MHEs by DAP. As the designs produced by architects, often hired by the funding/aid agencies, fail to satisfy DAP, they suggest "design review" (p.4) at a pre-construction phase as a possible remedy.

Pooyan and Hokugo studied the aftermath of the Great East Japan Earthquake and Tsunami (GEJET) and describe the micro human efforts and roles that assisted in the reestablishment of a new post-disaster "normalcy" including the incentives that helped in MHE and the disincentives. They reviewed global concepts and ideas such as the UN's Sendai Framework for Disaster Risk Reduction and Build Back Better to see how MHE could operate with those in the background, under what conditions they could be useful and under which they could not. Even when few resources are available, MHE could be operative due to the actions micro actors take.

Recognition of such self-recovery efforts would be the first step to including and supporting them as being among the repertoire of options possible for rebuilding and resuming normalcy. For the policies to be implemented, even a top-down approach by any governmental, semi-governmental, or non-governmental organization requires agents on the ground, i.e. MHE by DAP, which could potentially be part of the overall approach. Pooyan and Hokugo conclude that after a disaster, recovery could be triggered with or without grand schemes like BBB or external agents, but likely by a combination of self-directed MHE unaided or aided by others. DAP themselves might wish to become more resilient so that future disastrous events would be less damaging or harmful, and that recovery would be swift, and in a manner that would reduce some identified problems of previous disasters and of life as it existed then.

Okay and Onal focus on the possible roles played by women, especially elderly women, in post-disaster recovery. Based on demographics, they claim that elderly women may be the largest group. As such, they need disaster protection. In many cases, women do not get important roles in disaster protection; yet, they are mostly capable of not only helping themselves but also contributing to the community as well. The authors suggest an expanded role for women (especially those aged 65–75 years old) because they are healthy and financially well-positioned.

Tsubouchi, Tomiyasu, Isagawa, and Suzawa's surprising finding was that among those normally considered vulnerable, such as the elderly, women, and children, there were some who provided help during gaps in communication. The authors suggest that "Future disaster recovery will require more effort to link the efforts of these micro actors to the macro level with further empirical and long-term research".

Nakashima describes the formation of MHE by women in a post-disaster emergency temporary housing (ETH) area. These women, the K-Ladies, were taking care of several immediate needs of the residents in the ETH.

Kaluarachchi, Thayaparan, and Mendis describe the barriers preventing MHE after disasters. Primary among these is inadequate assistance for women to obtain gainful employment and start or continue enterprises. This is exacerbated for the intersectional marginalized, such as women with disabilities. Societal normative expectations and longstanding policies that led to the entrenchment of norms or lack thereof have led to women not receiving post-disaster recovery aid, especially for livelihood activities. As a result, MHEs, especially those by women, are isolated, invisible, unsupported, under-resourced, and face numerous barriers. They conclude by suggesting policies for change.

Kupietz remarks, as have others, that after disasters, many people offer and show up to volunteer to help DAP.[4] He suggests, as have some others, that a disaster is a combination of external and internal factors. He draws inspiration from Emergency Management (EM) in which disasters are seen by the Federal Emergency Management Agency (FEMA) as being of four phases, viz: (1) mitigation (severity reduction) and prevention; (2) preparation/preparedness, (3) response, and (4) recovery. He also mentions another model with five phases: (1) mitigation, (2) prevention, (3) preparation/preparedness, (4) response, and (5) recovery. As is evident, the two are not significantly dissimilar; the difference is in the discreteness of stages.

Kupietz would like to have people be prepared for most expectable disasters. He notes that many people volunteer to help DAP and concludes by suggesting that the effectiveness and efficiency of volunteers can be increased through training, such as Community Emergency Response Teams (CERT), which is a training programme for volunteers to increase the resilience of communities. He presents a case study of a CERT in a university campus and concludes that investments in training have value, especially in times of emergency and disasters.

Kupietz's phases of disaster management could be recategorized as follows. A pre-disaster phase could include mitigation, prevention and preparation/preparedness sub-phases, all prior to a disaster striking. The disaster event phase could include the response sub-phase. This would be followed by a post-disaster phase and would include a recovery sub-phase.

Oloruntoba and Asare-Doku focus on the psychological make-up of DAPs, what they call self-governance. By this, they mean the ability as well as the ways in which persons take and implement decisions without intervention by others. Accordingly, they discuss ideas and themes related to individuals' and small groups' self-governance, including self-response and self-awareness. Self-resilience or self-psychological resilience, they believe, can be aided by positive psychology or focusing on positive aspects of life, events, and outcomes. Self-psychological resilience, they claim, can come from self-decision-making, self-deciding, self-acting, and not depending on others for higher or lower-level decisions or for action. Personal and individual resilience may depend on an individual's personality and having a positive psychological outlook. They conclude that religiosity, faith, and prayer can help bolster personal resilience, which can contribute to community resilience.

The contributions in this book point out a few of the deficiencies of current approaches. Together, these chapters indicate the meagre scholarship on the topic of MHE, their variety, cultural and contextual conditions, overlooked aspects (such as the contributions of women and the difficulties they encounter), the lack of understanding of the issues facing and faced by governmental and administrative staff, and more.

11.4.6 Planning for Disasters with MHE in Mind

The unpredictability and relative rarity of disasters make pre-thinking and pre-planning for these seem to many people like daydreaming and an unproductive use of time. Using existing housing stock for disaster housing may present logistical problems. For cities without excess funds, allocating amounts for government-built housing may seem unsupportable until a disaster strikes and even then adequate funds may not be available. Leaving government-built housing unused for use in the event of a disaster may not be politically acceptable. If in use during non-disaster times, hurriedly un-housing those housed there to accommodate DAP may not be possible. Nevertheless, forethought and pre-planning are necessary even for tricky cloud problems like housing. For example, ETH solutions in various materials and sizes have been proposed[5] and some cities (e.g. Irvine, California, a planned city) have pre-planned and constructed deep flood channels for draining water quickly in the event of sustained heavy rains.

It is worth noting that not all external factors, such as earthquakes, result in major disruption and losses, i.e. in becoming disasters. Disasters are a combination of external factors (events) as well as internal ones, such as not being prepared for the events. Similarly, Disaster Risk is a result of the interactions of the factors: Hazard, Exposure, and Vulnerability. Exposure and vulnerability can be reduced by preparation. For flooding risk, for example, houses built on the ground are more vulnerable than houses raised on stilts or columns.

Discussions of disasters from an afterthought second-chance point of view are necessary as these could hasten the work of recovery along the above-noted ideas. After GEJET 2011, in order to increase safety, several municipalities in Japan decided to raise the ground level to protect against flooding. For example, in Rikuzen-takata (Iwate Prefecture), the ground of the entire contiguous urban area was raised by approximately 30 feet, and additional measures were taken to make the area more disaster resistant[6] (for e.g. see Schauwecker 2016; Spencer 2025). Irrespective of the merit or appropriateness of these solutions, these indicate that pre-planning and early actions are possible.

It is useful to develop forethought for future disaster occurrences. Build Back Better (BBB) and the Sendai Framework for Disaster Risk Reduction (SFDRR 2015–2030), which claims to have helped some 123 countries develop organizations by 2022 for implementing disaster risk reduction strategies, are two options. For those unfamiliar with post-disaster recovery efforts, these frameworks BBB (Pooyan & Hokugo; Kaluarachchi et al.), and SFDRR (Pooyan & Hokugo; Okay & Onal) might provide initial ideas and a brief general sense of what might be required. However, it is useful to remember that these general suggestions may sometimes not be applicable in specific examples, conditions, contexts, and cultures different from the ones considered, or if they lacked input into the development of these, e.g. different time horizons, resource availability, etc. Moreover, these may undergo revisions and changes, sometimes not in a manner advantageous to DAPs. Although developed with international participation, the limitations, cautions, and criticisms of these general schemes (Maly 2018) indicate that they may not help solve all core problems.

Importantly, early thought, proactive preparation, and familiarity with procedures and actions to take in emergency scenarios can assist in dealing with the suddenness, unexpectedness, intensity, magnitude, and speed of the disaster event and consequent harm. Awareness of techniques that work can lead to being prepared psychologically and physically, and in a state of readiness for containment and reduction of harm. As discussed in the introduction, vita activa or making an effort to be inactive to find time and atmosphere to absorb the impact of a disaster is an indispensable step towards harm reduction. Across cultures and contexts, this status of inactivity is seen as a spiritual endeavour of introspection or mental memorialization, as discussed in the Stewart and Strathern chapter.

In all of these, although neglected in the past, the potential role of MHE needs to be factored in. As Pooyan and Hokugo point out, DAPs are not passive aid-recipients waiting for the governmental authorities or other agencies to carry them across an imaginary line to a comfortable post-disaster life. DAPs take actions to save their lives, move away from the disaster, find or devise solutions, and implement these on their own so that they can start living again, independently if possible.

There can be advantages and benefits of the superior and deep-grounded knowledge of local conditions, resources, culture, geography, and the appropriateness of solutions that may inform local MHE. This together with scientific and broad scholarly knowledge, can lead to more informed and possibly wise decisions. Neglect of either can be problematic. Importantly, MHE can be crucial in all steps of disaster recovery. Acknowledgement of MHE's role can lead to its incorporation into disaster planning generally, as well as in specific instances as necessary steps towards resilience. Viewing MHE as essential can also direct general approaches, policies, and procedures to become more responsive to the grounded cultural and contextual realities in the field.

Examples of MHE by DAP can include the following. They may check on relatives, friends, and neighbours; share information on whether to evacuate, the urgency of evacuation, or the amount of time available and therefore what to pack and take; where to evacuate to, on open and available exit routes from their familiarity with exit routes as congestion and obstructions can occur on exit routes, which can cause problems (Isagawa & Ohno 2018). People may listen to relatives and friends over general advice from the government, or others. DAPs may make micro human efforts to help others, e.g. family, relatives, friends, neighbours, elderly, children, persons with disabilities (e.g. blind, sick/unwell), those with mobility problems, and who need help evacuating. Helping others effectively and efficiently in times of urgency can be improved by preparation and training for disasters – i.e. knowing what to do (Kupietz).

11.4.7   MHE's Workability, Cost, and Evaluation

It is useful to consider MHE's workability. MHE is likely to work effectively when DAP have a few basic essentials. For example, if tools are made available (e.g. for carpentry), many small needs can be accomplished at the ETH site (Iwasa 2011, 2012; Iwasa, Hasegawa, Shinkai, Shinazaki,Yasutake, & Kobayashi 2012). MHE is less likely to be useful when policies, regulations, and governmental reticence disable, disallow, discourage, or prevent mutual or self-help. Several efforts and adjustments have been described in the chapters (e.g. Silva, Subasinghe, and Ballinger).

It is helpful to evaluate MHE's costs and disadvantages. Conceivably, among DAPs there could be a lack of knowledge and experience to act. There could be divergent ideas, a lack of agreement, disagreement, conflict, incomplete thoughts, personality mismatches, hasty decisions, and lone or small group takeovers of decision-making.

How might MHE be aided or enabled? MHE might be helped by sensitization, training, and skill development. MHE participants and those interested must be sensitized to the idea of MHE and understand how it works. Although most DAP take action on their own, not waiting for outside assistance from the government, NGOs or others, without knowledge or connections they may still have difficulty implementing their ideas and may resort to experimenting. Organizational skills and having or forming an organization with individuals willing to accept leadership responsibility can be useful (e.g. Kupietz). Political skills and connections can aid when governmental help is essential. Transportation may be needed for many DAPs to go shopping for groceries, food and supplies or to go to government offices. Employment and economic needs may be paramount for some, whereas for others (such as the elderly) socializing might be crucial, and some might need education, hobbies or time-passing activities (e.g. TV, radio, movies, news, etc). Physical possibility-making may be needed by those with mobility restrictions.

Although studies and evaluations of resources (e.g. Biswas & Puriya 2019; Chang, Wilkinson, Patangaroa & Seville 2010) and comparative studies are appearing, these do not provide much information on MHE. Even though an important part of disaster recovery, MHE have largely been neglected by scholars, policy makers, and practitioners. It is not enough to incorporate MHE, in the early stages it will be useful to evaluate its effects, what could be done to implement it more effectively, efficiently, and to the satisfaction of affected DAP. We expect that adjustments will be required not only in the next application but each time it is applied in a different cultural, geographical, and contextual situation. Nevertheless, transferability can reasonably be expected because of the nature, starting point, and focus underlying this effort.

In conclusion, a few points and speculations can be made. A conjecture earlier in this chapter dealt with the absence of MHE. Now let us assume a situation in which MHE was enabled and supported. In this scenario, much could be achieved if DAP and, more generally citizens or residents could know what particular resources would be provided (along with any qualifiers and restrictions). With this information, people would know about resource limitations, what kind of work was clearly disallowed, and when to stop their efforts.

11.4.8   MHE's Importance

If the idea of MHE is taken seriously, this book can form a consequential contribution to post-disaster recovery, one that could benefit from and be supported by governmental and administrative policies, appropriate financing, and timely aid.

This work thus becomes a clarion call for more attention to MHE. There is a need for more studies and in-depth and detailed analysis of MHE. Each of the chapters provides a lead for the next research or scholarly activity on MHE. More work on preparation, organization, and attention to cautions regarding missing or underrepresented viewpoints is needed. Importantly, with an emphatic call for people-centredness, attention to MHE will very likely focus on the needs, understandings, and viewpoints of DAP in a way that is inherently conscious, conscientious, and sensitive to the persons producing the MHE and other DAP. The book itself is an MHE on the part of the authors.

The need for considering MHE is clear because it is the humane and responsible way to honour those who are affected by one or more disasters, not just because we are asking for it. Those who send or provide aid, or show up to offer help have the intention to act appropriately but may lack the knowledge on how to do so. If seen as a clarion call, a major intention will be fulfilled. If it results in action by planners, administrators, and government officers, it might lead to more thoughtful actions that are likely to have both near- and long-term effects. The authors and editors hope that some of this will happen.

A final note. The editors and most of the authors have witnessed disasters or later observed some of the destruction, loss, and disorientation in the aftermath of disasters. What makes people return to continue to live in known disaster-ridden zones? The argument has been made that place attachment (Mishra, Mazumdar & Suar 2010; Mazumdar & Mazumdar 1993; Mazumdar 2005, 2016) and a deep sense of love and devotion to the place lead people to stay in such places, though from a distance this might seem strange or illogical behaviour. Some, such as fishermen, need to live near the coast even though it might be known to be a tsunami-prone area. Natural disasters, however, are not predictable, and may occur relatively frequently or only sporadically. A compassionate, understanding and warm-hearted approach that pays attention to and supports their micro human efforts can go a long way in helping DAP adjust and reconstitute their lives by rebuilding and in helping partners in their effort to be more reflective about their cultural and contextual transactions.

Notes

1 https://mainichi.jp/english/articles/20240402/p2a/00m/0na/016000c
2 https://www.ntv.co.jp/englishnews/articles/2021jxwx8yolfumg7xfa.html
3 The Japan News 03 February 2024: https://japannews.yomiuri.co.jp/society/noto-peninsula-earthquake/20240203-166584/
4 e.g. Lyle Lovett in an interview talked about people helping each other after disasters https://www.youtube.com/watch?v=lUrq-foUf4o, checked 02/04/25
5 e.g.: Dalton 2017; https://palletshelter.com/blog/understanding-the-post-disaster-housing-continuum/
6 Facts & Details 2014 https://factsanddetails.com/japan/cat26/sub161/item1744.html

References

Biswas, Arindam & Puriya, Anshul (2019) Comparative assessment of Indian post-disaster temporary housing strategies, *Journal of Architectural Engineering*, 26(1) (December). https://doi.org/10.1061/(ASCE)AE.1943-5568.0000386.

Caminos, Horacio & Goethert, Reinhard (1978) *Urbanization primer*, Cambridge: MIT Press.

Chang, Yan, Wilkinson, Suzanne, Potangaroa, Regan, & Seville, Erica (2010) Resourcing challenges for post-disaster housing reconstruction: A comparative analysis. *Building Research & Information*, 38(3), 247–264. https://doi.org/10.1080/09613211003693945.

Criss, Doug (2017) This Texas man has a boat — and a mission: 'Go save some lives', *CNN*, August 27, 2017. https://www.cnn.com/2017/08/28/us/harvey-citizens-helping-moments-trnd/index.html.

Dalton, Melissa (2017) 7 Inspiring solutions for disaster relief housing, *Dwell*, November 3. Retrieved October 12, 2020 https://www.dwell.com/article/7-inspiring-solutions-for-disaster-relief-housing-c2ec6783.

Facts & Details (2014) *Rebuilding after 2011 tsunami in Japan*. https://factsanddetails.com/japan/cat26/sub161/item1744.html

Goethert, Reinhard, Hamdi, Nabeel, & Gray, Sebastian (1988) *Making microplans: A community based process in programing and development*, London: Intermediate Technology Publications.

Isagawa, Teriyuki & Ohno, Ryuzo (2018) Influence of residents' cognition of their local environment on evacuation behavior from tsunamis: A case study of Onjuku, Chiba prefecture, *Japan Architecture; Review*, 1(4), 486–503. https://doi.org/10.1002/2475 8876.12045.

Iwasa, Akihiko (2011) 仮設のトリセツ－仮設住宅を*120%*住みこなす方法－ (Hacking Manual for Temporary Housing – How to Live 120%). Iwasa Lab., Department of Architecture, Niigata University Faculty of Engineering, Niigata, JPN. Retrieved September 1, 2015 https://kasetsukaizou.jimdofree.com/一覧/ダウンロード/.

Iwasa, Akihiko (2012) 仮設のトリセツ－もし、仮設住宅で暮らすことになったら (*A* Guidebook for Temporary Housing – When You Have to Reside in a Temporary Housing). Tokyo, JPN: Shufunotomosha.

Iwasa, Akihiko, Hasegawa, Takashi, Shinkai, Shunichi, Shinozaki, Masahiko, Yasutake, Atsuko, & Kobayashi, Kenichi (2012) A practical approach to temporary housing for disaster victims, *Journal of Asian Architecture and Building Engineering*, 11(1), 33–38. https://doi.org/10.3130/jaabe.11.33.

Maly, Elizabeth (2018) Building back better with people centered housing recovery, *International Journal of Disaster Risk Reduction*, 29(August), 84–93. https://doi.org/10.1016/j.ijdrr.2017.09.005.

Mazumdar, Sanjoy (2005) Religious place attachment, squatting, and "qualitative" research: A commentary. *Journal of Environmental Psychology*, 25(1) (March), 87–95.

Mazumdar, Sanjoy (2012) A cultural ecological approach to disaster planning. *Joint Conference Proceedings, 9th International Conference on Urban Earthquake Engineering/ 4th Asia Conference on Earthquake Engineering March 6–8, 2012*, Tokyo Institute of Technology, Tokyo, Japan, 1901–1906.

Mazumdar, Sanjoy (2016) Place attachment research – Extending boundaries: Considerations related to approach, culture, process, terms, and meanings, *Man-Environment Research Association Journal* (*MERAJ*), 18(2)(March), 43–44.

Mazumdar, Sanjoy (2024a) How does culture influence design? In Silva, Kapila D. & Fernando, Nisha Ashanthi (eds), *Theorizing built from and culture: The legacy of Amos Rapoport*, New York: Routledge, ch 20, pp. 265–279. https://doi.org/10.4324/9781003372110-25

Mazumdar, Sanjoy (2024b) How does design affect culture? In Silva, Kapila D. & Fernando, Nisha Ashanthi (eds), *Theorizing built from and culture: The legacy of Amos Rapoport*, New York: Routledge, ch 21, pp. 280–289. https://doi.org/10.4324/9781003372110-26.

Mazumdar, Sanjoy, Itoh, Shunsuke, & Iwasa, Akihiko (2021) Post-disaster temporary housing: An *emic* study of lived experiences of victims of the Great East Japan earthquake and tsunami, *International Journal of Mass Emergencies and Disasters*, 39(1) (March), 87–119.

Mazumdar, Shampa & Mazumdar, Sanjoy (1993) Sacred space and place attachment, *Journal of Environmental Psychology*, 13(3) (September), 231–242.

Mishra, Sasmita & Mazumdar, Sanjoy (2015) Psychology of disaster preparedness, *Ecopsychology,* 7(4) (December), 211–223. https://doi.org/10.1089/eco.2015.0006.

Mishra, Sasmita, Mazumdar, Sanjoy, & Suar, Damodar (2010) Place attachment and flood preparedness, *Journal of Environmental Psychology*, 30(2) (June), 187–197. http://dx.doi.org/10.1016/j.jenvp.2009.11.005.

National Centers for Environmental Information (NCEI) (2011/2025) On this day: 2011 Tohoku Earthquake and Tsunami, National Oceanic and Atmospheric Administration. https://www.ncei.noaa.gov/news/day-2011-japan-earthquake-and-tsunami.   visited 05April25.

Oliver, Paul (1987) *Dwellings: The house across the world*, Texas: University of Texas Press.

Popper, Karl Raimund (1966) *Of clouds and clocks: An approach to the problem of rationality and the freedom of man*, Issue 2, Washington University, 38 pp.

Schauwecker, Stefan (May 25, 2016) Five years after the tsunami. https://www.japan-guide.com/blog/recovery/160525.html (photos).

Spencer, Molly (2025) How tall was the 2011 Japan tsunami? *Geographic FAQ*, NCESC.com.   https://www.ncesc.com/geographic-faq/how-tall-was-the-2011-japan-tsunami/ visited 04/03/25.

Subasinghe, Chamila (2013) Spatial confrontations: Abandonment of self-labor in transitional sheltering after a natural disaster, *International Journal of Disaster Risk Reduction*, 6, 78–86.

Subasinghe, Chamila, Sutrisna, Monty, & Olatunji, O. (2021). Multidisciplinary perspectives of micro human efforts in post-disaster recovery, *International Journal of Mass Emergencies & Disasters*, 39(1), 1–10. https://doi.org/10.1177/028072702103900101.

Turner, John F.C. (1976) *Housing by people: Towards autonomy in building environments,* London: Marion Boyars.

Index

Note: Page numbers in *Italics* refer to figures; page numbers in **bold** refer to tables

For Product Safety Concerns and Information please contact our EU
representative GPSR@taylorandfrancis.com
Taylor & Francis Verlag GmbH, Kaufingerstraße 24, 80331 München, Germany